T0154238

# READ & BURN
A Book About **WIRE**

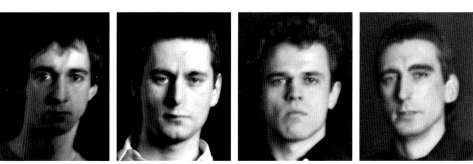

# READ & BURN
## A Book About **WIRE**
### Wilson Neate

# READ & BURN
## A Book About **WIRE**
Wilson Neate

A Jawbone Book
First Edition 2013
Published in the UK and the USA by Jawbone Press
2a Union Court,
20–22 Union Road,
London SW4 6JP,
England
www.jawbonepress.com

ISBN 978-1-908279-33-0

Volume copyright © 2013 Outline Press Ltd. Text copyright © Wilson Neate. All rights reserved. No part of this book covered by the copyrights hereon may be reproduced or copied in any manner whatsoever without written permission, except in the case of brief quotations embodied in articles or reviews where the source should be made clear. For more information contact the publishers.

**EDITOR** Tom Seabrook
**DESIGN** Paul Cooper Design

Printed by Regent Publishing Services Limited, China

1 2 3 4 5 17 16 15 14 13

# CONTENTS

# Foreword
## by Mike Watt

truth be told: the first ten years of my experience w/wire were solely through their first three albums and the singles up to 'our swimmer', including the b-sides. I had never seen them play a gig 'til 1987. maybe they'd like it that way. I'd never even read an interview w/them then – I knew them solely through those recorded works of theirs. I will tell you they were way deep on me and d. boon and changed our lives forever. maybe they were more intense on us than ccr ... there is us before hearing pink flag and there is us after hearing this music from england that made an abstract connect a concrete dream. we became minutemen from whatever we were before.

I love those cats so much and I know for sure d. boon also – we just want the best for them cuz we owe them a butt-load, a fucking ton-worth, I swear. they gave us the courage to try and look and find ourselves, they were the righteous friends you met from the middle of nowhere – just there cuz they are ... we owe them cats SO FUCKING MUCH – we were from working people and they helped us by just them being them.

what I'm trying to say is let's say you got a penknife and the art ain't in the penknife but what is to be carved w/it. of course this ain't my idea but it's a way I can try to relate to something like this. you get your mind blown by something you weren't ready for and all of a sudden you find a launch pad for what you might call an inner speak, a resonance of that dna manifested by stuff like your thumbprint but w/a face, w/a kind of intent but also that of a flail (even dervish-like). and in our case, a launch pad for our minutemen way: boiling down stuff into what we called 'econo', which also happened to fit our lives, coming from working people. yeah, we got the idea of 'jamming econo' from these wire works. making something big out of lots of little things.

yeah, this thing about econo, about making bigger things out of simple stuff, making one big part out of a lot of little parts, econo drama from tension through repetition via sensibilities like the subtle morphing of a brickwall, brick by brick, econo hihat click by click – it's the world of possibility that wire opened up to us, the no coercion part of emma goldman made alive to us in a music sense that had a human face and a spirit ... fucking righteous, a dance in the head – free for all!

the way the words were put on the pink flag inner sleeve made me think of being at a place that was showing art on a wall and next to it was a description of each painting. it was as if the more I try to look at each work w/its description at the same time, the more the words would absorb the piece and not be like a cue sheet for a vocalist to follow at a recording session. and in a parallel universe, I got the same sensation in their sound, more and more as they moved onto the chairs missing and 154 albums – I guess part of their journey was about gigs but damn if I wasn't connected that way. anyhow it wasn't just that first experience and all that about little songs and boiling them down to the bare nada which was righteous and berlin-wall-busting-important but wire was further profound on me in making me feel things freed from the need for associations. it all got very emotional for me and still is … they always win the fight to be subjugated w/in me, they are living beings – even pink flag got reignited in this context though now looking back, of course it was the original springboard... I can hear popeye learning me 'I am what I am' and it's ok cuz the kafka funny is one righteous backhand upside the head.

I'm talking about my own head cuz I feel any other way would be jive. I can't speak for others though I get curious about hearing others – that book by wilson neate on the making of pink flag was wild for me cuz of course I had my own mind being sculpted by it first-hand (via the ear hole) in my san pedro, california town and to read these men talk about their work was a trip but at the same time it never "reduced the painting by its description" – more like footnote stuff.

here I am, on tour again like I have been for thirty plus years and part of my encore this time around is doing a cover of '106 beats that' and having my guitarman tom watson sing it so I can watch and hear him do it. yeah, I'm working my bass to it and though neither me or tom or drummerman raul morales could or more important WOULD WANT to tell you what it means, I do know we all feel way down in our bones, feeling it most authentic to us. now that's a trip but that's the trip about wire.

on bass, **watt**

7

# What This Book Isn't

*Read & Burn* seeks to do justice to Wire's highly influential and restlessly inventive body of work – of which I have been a fan since 1978 – by developing a sustained critical account of their shifting modus operandi.

Although Wire granted me considerable access during the research and writing processes (via interviews and correspondence), this isn't a book that will always please each of the band-members. Rather, it takes their oeuvre seriously by creating a framework for understanding and critically evaluating it. To my mind, this approach pays a far higher compliment to Wire than would an exercise in gushing fandom or a simple transcription of interviews.

*Read & Burn* combines my analysis and interpretation with the band-members' own words and perspective – drawing on approximately 100 hours of exclusive interviews with them, plus email exchanges. The interviews were conducted between 2007 and 2012, the bulk of them in 2011 and 2012. While the focus is very much on Bruce Gilbert, Robert Grey, Graham Lewis, and Colin Newman, I also interviewed various associates of the group, including touring members, producers, managers, and sleeve designers, as well as journalists and other musicians. Unless otherwise stated in the text, all quotations in this book derive from my own interviews.

Discussing the way in which Wire developed their aesthetic in 1977, Bruce Gilbert told me: "The only things we could agree on were the things we didn't like. That's what held it together and made life much simpler." Graham Lewis made the same point, explaining how Wire constructed their early identity in terms of rejection and refusal; he even listed a set of unofficial, almost entirely prohibitive, rules that the band followed: "No solos; no decoration; when the words run out, it stops; we don't chorus out; no rocking out; keep it to the point; no Americanisms." This contrarian, negative self-definition was a foundational Wire characteristic. In much the same spirit, here's a list of what this book is not and what it does not do:

☐ This book was not read, vetted, or approved by Wire before publication

☐ This book is not a biography of Wire collectively or individually

☐ This book is not about the band-members' solo projects

☐ This book does not forensically dissect each of Wire's albums

☐ This book does not mention every Wire song, record sleeve, tour, or gig

☐ This book does not provide a complete discography

☐ This book does not compile or comprehensively analyse press coverage

Some of the above can be found elsewhere.

Some sections of this book draw on my own previously published writings: features and several reviews, my liner notes for *Send Ultimate*, and my book *Pink Flag* (Continuum, 2008).

# 1976 And All That

Wire's résumé highlights a diverse body of recorded work dating from 1977 to the present. And yet, wherever you look, you'll find Wire categorised as one, two, or all three of the following: a *punk* band, a post-*punk* band, or an art-*punk* band. Notwithstanding its occasional modifiers, the p-word has endured, as critics and commentators cling onto it in an attempt to capture the essence of Wire's innovative uniqueness. As a result, Wire remain chained to a narrow and reductive musical identity – even though their long-term trajectory, which has always centred on a constant remaking and remodelling, stubbornly resists the notion of any fixed identity.

To continue to define Wire in relation to punk is like labelling David Bowie a mod or Brian Eno a glam rocker. 'Punk' carries with it a specific historical coding – in spite of its continuing half-life and its new iterations – so any ongoing linking of Wire with punk also implies that all their important work was executed before they went on hiatus in 1980, an idea disputed by the evidence of the band's releases since then.

Of course, nothing happens in a vacuum. Like any band, Wire were born in a particular historical context and, in their case, that was the summer of punk. Therefore, it's impossible to discuss their origins without talking about punk rock: Wire formed in 1976, and their earliest history was enacted on the new musical and cultural landscape opened up by the Sex Pistols. That much is incontrovertible. In fact, looking at Wire in relation to this moment in British cultural history is productive, to show how they constructed an identity on the basis of their difference from what became orthodox punk, and how they initiated their career-long deferral of any defining essence.

To get an accurate sense of Wire's relationship to punk in Britain, it's important to recognise that even during its brief lifespan, punk underwent a transformation: in 1976, it was very different from what it had become by mid 1977. Live performances in 1976 by bands such as the Sex Pistols, Buzzcocks, and Siouxsie & The Banshees, as well as punk's earliest vinyl manifestations ('Anarchy In The UK', 'New Rose', and the January 1977 *Spiral Scratch* EP), made an impression on various members of Wire – a pattern that repeated itself throughout the UK as a generation of similarly inspired individuals formed groups. This was what Jon Savage has called punk's "second wave". Insofar as Wire's genesis was inextricably linked to what the band-members had seen and heard during punk's beginnings – and to the extent that Wire initially played a variant of generic, roughed-up rock, sharing venues, bills, and pages in the music papers with those who had followed the same trajectory – they were part of that next wave. Despite these early intersections, however, Wire did not share the homogeneous character that the class of 1977 swiftly forged.

Undoubtedly, punk's second generation made the singles chart a marginally more interesting place (not entirely difficult) and opened up a space that new-wave artists would expand, setting British pop on a refreshing course. Nevertheless, British punk rock in 1977 was already stagnating. The potential unleashed by the likes of the Sex Pistols was squandered as bands failed to grasp the significance of what had happened: punk was at first radical and liberating in its challenge to received ideas about who could make music, what it could sound like, as well as how that music could be made and performed. Rather than increase that autonomous creative space, run with the newly released energy, and exercise their imaginations, the majority of the second-wave bands reconstituted uniformity and narrowness by taking punk as a musical and visual *style* to be cloned and aped. As the original spirit of newness was lost and as creative energy dissipated into imitation, punk's resistant cultural value quickly waned.

That process perhaps began with the appearance of the Sex Pistols on Thames Television's *Today* show on December 1 1976, an event that provided punk's point of entry into the national consciousness. Filtered and simplified by mass-media representations in terms of mere shock value, punk lost its subcultural invisibility as the phenomenon was named and framed by various mainstream discourses: it became tabloid fodder; the subject of the political rhetoric of outraged officials; a fashion style; a topic of comedy; and a commodified part of the broader economic nexus, as record labels raced to sign their very own punk band. Punk therefore became visible, represented, and normalised in inevitably one-dimensional terms, famously being reduced to a caricature. It's in that sense that punk was spent as a vital cultural force by mid 1977 – as most second-wave bands settled for that popular image, failing to explore new options.

By contrast, Wire remained true to the original moment, emphasising consistent innovation and adventurousness. Crucially, though, they did so not in the name of punk, or any other movement, but simply for themselves and their work. And from punk forward, they would occasionally intersect with other cultural moments, if only to hold up a distorting mirror to the zeitgeist.

11

## CHAPTER 1

# Four People In A Book

Before tracing Wire's emergence, it's useful to consider where Bruce Gilbert, Robert Grey, Graham Lewis, and Colin Newman came from, and what they brought to the group. This is by now very well trodden ground, but it's necessary to revisit it in order to understand how the band-members' backgrounds might have shaped aspects of Wire's creative interaction. This offers insight into what enabled them to accomplish so much and yet, by the same token, periodically impeded their ability to work together effectively.

**BRUCE GILBERT** left Wire in 2004, some 28 years after founding the band with Colin Newman and George Gill. That's a long time for someone who claims he never much wanted to be in a band. What kept Gilbert at it for so long was a conviction that Wire were not simply a rock group but a larger artistic endeavour. "I've always been slightly uncomfortable with the notion of 'the group'", he says. "I liked the idea of it being a 'non-group'. It's not a band. It's four people who make this noise, which for all intents and purposes sounds like songs. It's a sort of project. I always thought it was a project, really: a living, breathing, noisy sculpture."

Well before Wire existed, the concept of the 'living sculpture' had been explored by performance artists such as Bruce McLean (working with Gary Chitty, Robin Fletcher, Ron Carr, and Paul Richards as Nice Style, "The World's First Pose Band") and, of course, by Gilbert & George. Meanwhile, the merging of rock group and art project had precedents in the likes of The Velvet Underground and Roxy Music. Nevertheless, Gilbert's broader, more sustained and rigorous approach with Wire is striking. When talking about music, rather than engage with the customary vernacular of pop and rock, Gilbert draws on the lexicon of the plastic arts. Sounds and instruments are 'materials' and 'tools'; songs and records are 'pieces' and 'objects'; singles and albums are described as 'works' that are 'made'. To Gilbert, a band offered rich possibilities for creative expression both within and beyond the confines of song-based entertainment: the songs themselves could be objects of experimentation, musically and textually; cover art, advertisements, and promotional materials furnished another canvas on which to work; gigs provided a space to experiment with visual presentation, as well as an opportunity to interrogate the nature and potential of performance itself.

Gilbert was the most consistent and articulate advocate for Wire as a wider aesthetic enterprise, and this more expansive conceptualisation of 'the rock band' produced some extraordinary work; but the wilfulness and perversity that often accompanied the enterprise also undermined Wire's chances of commercial success.

Effectively a generation older than Newman and Lewis, Gilbert was born in 1946 in Watford, on the northern edge of London. His father served in North Africa in World War II and worked as a plasterer after demob; his mother was a part-time cleaner. Gilbert has lasting memories of his childhood during the age of austerity. ("Everything was brown.") Although the War had ended before his birth, it lingered on in the popular consciousness well into the 50s, its residual presence making itself felt among Gilbert and his friends when they periodically discovered bits of old army kit in each other's houses, artefacts that were incorporated into their games. "We used to put on old gas masks," he recalls, "and swim around the street, pretending to be frogmen."

If the War's hold on daily life persisted, it was eventually replaced in Gilbert's young imagination by the more immediate nuclear threat of the Cold War, an obsession that stayed with him. "I remember seeing a huge photograph of a mushroom cloud on the front page of the *Daily Sketch* at my grandparents' house, and I thought: That's it. It's over – any minute, obliterated. After that, the bombs got bigger and the photographs more frightening. I was terrified. It's never left me."

Gilbert developed a precocious interest in films, thanks to his mother. She was a keen moviegoer ("obsessed" is the word he uses), and from the age of four he accompanied her to films aimed at mature audiences. "I was constantly being taken to 'A' films, as they were called – strong subjects." This attraction to cinema went hand in hand with a passion for books, as Gilbert, with his mother's collection at his disposal, became a "manic reader" of fiction intended for adults. In both media, his childhood experience of narrative was unorthodox and inevitably unsettling, as he was exposed to material that would have been hard to understand, the plots seemingly arbitrary and characters' psychology difficult to grasp.

It's tempting to see all this as creatively formative. Books and films were Gilbert's introduction to worlds that, to a child, were uncanny – never entirely explicable or recognisable, subject to random disruption by unfamiliar, disorienting elements or containing dimensions that remained opaque. This primal encounter with *otherness*, stemming from a sense of there being more going on than he was equipped to fathom, might account for some enduring preoccupations and strategies in Gilbert's work. His preference for noise, drones, and discordant menace over the familiarity and comfort of melody, for example, translates into sound something of the nagging, indefinable strangeness that he would have felt. Moreover, his work has always embraced the notion that things do not have to make logical, conscious sense or achieve resolution.

If Gilbert's mother opened the door to an awareness of otherness through film and fiction, his father's influence was less tangible, as his only real interest was gardening. ("After the War, he became an obsessive chrysanthemum and aster grower.") While Gilbert did not share his father's horticultural obsession, in the 90s he did start performing inside a garden shed.

Gilbert's mother loved music. She was "a very, very good jazz singer" who had performed with a band, and Gilbert remembers her listening to Sinatra, Ella Fitzgerald, and Lena Horne. But although he heard music from a young age, as with film, his relationship with it was unconventional. This came across in the way he listened to songs. He tended to focus on one detail that drew his attention, compartmentalising it and separating it from the arrangement. Such elements were often those he found unusual and uncanny, sounds seeming to transcend their context to function independently of the compositions of which they were a part.

Just as Gilbert calls himself a "manic" reader, when recalling early aural experiences he talks about "obsession" – an obsession frequently attached to one of those sonic components conveying otherness. Stan Kenton's instrumental version of the Cuban *son-pregón* 'El Manisero' ('The Peanut Vendor') became an unlikely first object of fascination. Gilbert was fixated on it not because of its exotic flavour but because it embodied something deeper and portentous – a quality apparent to him, although not immediately comprehensible. Only later would its mystery and significance be revealed. "As a child I was obsessed with 'The Peanut Vendor', and I made my mother buy it. There was something about it that intrigued me, and it wasn't until some years later that I heard my first blues thing and I thought: there's something here, there's something fundamental. It was *the riff*."

All the aspects of music that excited him coalesced in the blues, especially the work of Howlin' Wolf: something *other* in the singers' voices ("as if they'd come from another planet"); an emphasis on repetition; and a layer of noise or imperfection, deriving from the dissonant, out-of-tune quality of the records he heard. While the formulaic nature of the lyrics, as well as the repetitive musical structure, might seem to undercut the alien charge of the blues and render the listening experience banal, Gilbert found the opposite was true. "I accepted that most of the structures were very similar, as were most of the subjects. That didn't worry me: I think it released one in a strange way to actually listen to the textures and the rhythm." Although he took a passing pleasure in pop, it was only in terms of individual elements within songs that evoked the raw textures and immediacy of the blues. He bought the first Beatles album in 1963, purely because of the harmonica on 'Love Me Do', but quickly went off the band ("too musical for me"). The same year, he saw The Rolling Stones play at St John's Hall in Watford. "I liked the Stones when they played the blues. It had a fantastic visceral quality."

Gilbert's first forays into making music were characteristically unorthodox. His parents owned an upright piano, but "it was just a piece of furniture", and he wasn't given lessons. That didn't stop him from approaching the instrument in a way that resonated with his listening strategies, as he used it to generate individual sounds that appealed to him. It became another object of obsession. Left alone, he'd spend hours underneath it with his ear to the soundboard, playing the same low keys over and over. "That was 20 times better than any music." (Decades later, history would repeat itself when Wire spent the first day of the *Chairs Missing* sessions under a grand piano in Advision Studios.)

While the 50s witnessed the rise of teenagers as an entertainment-focused consumer bloc, Gilbert – despite his brief flirtation with The Beatles and the Stones – doesn't appear to have been a typical teenager. Unlike many of his peers, he didn't tend to buy pop records or indulge in fandom. He wasn't content to listen, play, or consume according to established models, and preferred a more creative, participatory involvement. Access to a tape recorder gave him his first real chance to undertake experiments that, in a modest way, subverted and redefined the roles of the listener, the producer, and the consumer. Gilbert's explorations used Duane Eddy's 'Peter Gunn', which he loved because of its big guitar riff and repetitive structure. Feeling it wasn't long enough, he waited for it to be played on the radio and taped it on multiple occasions, thereby creating a longer 'remix' out of recordings that ran back-to-back. The tape recorder was also an important tool, as it allowed him to intervene in pieces of music, to isolate parts that intrigued him and then to manipulate and change them in primitive ways. "I always seemed to have a tape recorder," he says. "I was always interested in the notion of slowing things down and things going backward – playing with it."

Bearing in mind his early musical experimentation and his formative exposure to film and fiction, it's unsurprising that Gilbert came to identify closely with Dada, facets of which have always informed his creative practices: a predilection for the absurd, the nonsensical, and the irrational; an openness to contingencies and happy accidents; a prioritisation of process over product; an interest in collage, montage, and found objects; a delight in upturning conventional structures and received ideas; an attraction to the uncanny amid the everyday; and a willingness to explore multiple media. These traits would all manifest themselves throughout his work. Asked to name his main artistic influences, he replies: "There's only one, really, isn't there? Marcel [Duchamp]. He fits the bill."

Gilbert is hesitant to single out an overarching feature or concern of his diverse projects. "If there is one, I couldn't define it," he says. "Maybe an element of absurdity? That's the closest I can get." Even so, when he discusses his work there is a recurring theme, namely the search for an encounter with otherness through experimentation, which has been at the heart of his endeavours across different art forms, from childhood play to Wire and beyond. He sees this process as a journey, the focus not on the destination but on the points along the way where, by pushing and manipulating his materials (sonic or plastic), he arrives at a moment of what he calls "strange recognition" – a paradoxical awareness that you've come to a place you *don't* know, at which new structures and textures emerge.

In addition to his fledgling explorations with sound, Gilbert began investigating other media at a young age – particularly drawing and painting. As a pupil at one of Britain's secondary moderns ("Oh, there was so much hope – the headmaster even wore a gown," he says with wistful irony), Gilbert gravitated toward the art department. On leaving school, he passed through several unfulfilling jobs that made him acutely aware of the persistence of the class system, which he wasn't thrilled about, refusing to address supposed superiors as 'Sir'. "We won't be having any of that, *mate* – those days are over," he recalls telling a co-worker.

The employment experience bolstered Gilbert's sense that his path lay elsewhere: "In my heart of hearts, I knew I had to go to art school." Having gained additional 'O' Levels, he enrolled at St Albans School of Art for a two-year foundation and pre-diploma course. Gilbert found art school in the 60s a stimulating, enriching environment and made the most of it,

16

developing his interest in painting. (There he became friends with another painter, Mick Collins, who would later be Wire's manager.) He was also drawn to the burgeoning counterculture, albeit superficially. "I wasn't very convinced by the hippies. I quite liked the idea of a flowery tie, though. If I was anything, I was a beatnik – something from the early 60s."

By the end of his time at St Albans, Gilbert had a wife and child, but he was eager to pursue his studies. As he was doing mostly illustrative paintings at this point, he eventually applied for a graphic design course at Leicester Polytechnic, assuming that he would be able to use it as a pretext for developing what he really wanted to do. At Leicester, though, he quickly lost interest because the course didn't accommodate his fine-art orientation, and he spent most of his time with the painting students or using the photography dark room. Having attempted to switch to fine art, he dropped out before the end of his first year in 1971.

With a family to support, Gilbert took various random jobs before ending up at Dacorum College of Further Education in Hemel Hempstead as an audio-visual technician. He subsequently held a similar position at Watford College of Technology's School of Art, where he also started playing the guitar with a friend who had a regular gig at a local hotel. "He asked me to make some noise with him," Gilbert recalls, "so I bought an electric guitar from Woolworth's and learned to play with an open tuning. It was the same thing every time: when we did a blues song, I'd do a stupid slide solo."

Although he'd shelved his plans to study fine art, Gilbert continued to make paintings in his council flat. His canvases displayed the same experimental affinity that had marked his earliest musical investigations, rendering the familiar unfamiliar and moving deeper into abstraction. Painting, however, led Gilbert back to the medium of sound. He had begun to produce larger and larger, more abstract works, but he soon felt he had run out of dimensions. "Things needed to get off the canvas," he says. "They needed to have sound involved and be 3-D."

Using the basic facilities and equipment at Watford, Gilbert began "to paint and sculpt with noise", inspired partly by Brian Eno, who was a guest lecturer at the college. A student named Ron West became curious about what Gilbert describes as his "quite violent sonic landscapes", and the two collaborated on further abstract pieces using sound generators, oscillators, and reel-to-reel tape recorders. (This work was released in 1998 as *Frequency Variation*.)

Gilbert's tendency not to consume music (especially since the late 70s) is something he considers vital to his experimentation with sound. He links this with a desire to maintain a blank slate, since listening to work in a similar territory has at times impeded his creativity. He remembers the troubling experience of seeing This Heat perform: "I went with Graham [Lewis] when we were starting Dome, and I said to him: We just have to give up. We can't top that – that's the best live thing I've ever heard. Ever. It was brutal, clever, not really music. It was quite depressing. It felt like we might be wasting our time and might not be able to get even close to what they were doing."

Another band presented similar problems: "I was very keen on Cluster, but I became uneasy about how much I liked them. I was nervous about getting too influenced. I wanted a clean sheet, as far as I possibly could. I just wanted to react to the sounds around me and sounds I could manufacture by accident. Except for technical purposes, or the occasional treat, I stopped listening to music entirely around 1980. The last record I ever bought was a Cluster record. That was the end of my consuming of music."

In mid 1976, Gilbert got involved in a traditional rock venture. Although no longer working at Watford, he had been roped in as a guitarist with a student band called Overload that had formed to play an end-of-term party. The group featured George Gill, also on guitar, and vocalist Colin Newman, with West on bass plus a couple of backing singers (including Gilbert's girlfriend, Angela Conway). After their one forgettable gig, Gilbert, Gill, and Newman persisted as a trio, thrashing away on guitars in Newman's bedroom. This was Wire in embryonic form.

Although punk's DIY message appealed to Gilbert, he had already taken his own DIY cues from the likes of Eno. "I have a lot to thank Brian Eno for in terms of the idea that you could operate in music without a great deal of musical skill. I thought this was an ideal opportunity to experiment and see what happens, albeit with song-based material, word-based material." Gilbert had enjoyed early Roxy Music, but his interest lay primarily in what he saw as Eno's singular role as an artist working in his own avant-garde space with materials provided by his bandmates. "They were the most interesting band at the time. And in Brian Eno, they had a non-musician doing squiggly noises and processing other musicians' stuff. It seemed almost perfect."

Gilbert was cautiously excited by punk's potential as an environment sympathetic to the sort of project he had in mind, one that combined art and music, and he acknowledges both The Velvet Underground and Roxy Music as models in that regard. "The Velvet Underground seemed much more to do with art than with music. Obviously, Lou Reed was a musician and songwriter, but my general sense of The Velvet Underground was that it was a piece of art. I think there was definitely an element of that with Roxy Music too. The pop-art angle."

To Gilbert, Wire too would be a work of art, with a specifically experimental inclination. "My objective, if I was going to be involved with other people in a group project, was to make it as interesting as possible for myself, to create something of not necessarily lasting value, but something that felt valuable: an exploration of what was possible, what the possibilities were, and how far you could stretch something before it becomes invisible."

Gilbert's fine-art sensibility, coupled with his rejection of the role of consumer, raises larger questions about art's place in the economic landscape – an issue central to Wire's story as a band operating in the business of music. While Gilbert is a staunch modernist in his tastes and approaches, he has a Romantic view of artistic purity, according to which he has striven to keep art and commerce apart – remuneration apparently being important only insofar as it enables him to keep working. His ambivalence about commercial success was a challenge for Wire. What seemed, to others, to be pragmatic moves sometimes struck Gilbert as compromises of the artistic vision. Lewis sees Gilbert's motivation in deeper psychological terms: "I think Bruce has a fear of success, and that's when he tends to come up with radical solutions." Those "radical solutions", in Newman's view, have been to "sabotage" Wire's chances of success at key points, to "drive the bus off the cliff". Or in Gilbert's terms, perhaps, to make it "invisible".

If Bruce Gilbert introduces a note of paradox at the start of the Wire story with his belief that Wire, while functioning as a rock band, weren't necessarily a rock band, then **ROBERT GREY** continues that contrary trend. Grey is a unique musician who doesn't consider himself a musician, but merely a drummer. And as a drummer, he undoubtedly bucks the stereotype, an obvious anomaly in a long and ignoble lineage of voluble, room-trashing, defenestrating, over-indulging, and largely deceased showmen.

'Showy' and 'indulgent' are two words you'd never associate with Grey: while the size of a drummer's kit tends to increase in direct proportion to a band's success or longevity, at times during Wire's career Grey very deliberately reduced his – famously playing live through much of the 80s with only a bass drum, snare, and hi-hat. That striking image encapsulates his core values and accentuates his reputation as Wire's arch-minimalist: with drumming, as with farming (Grey's occupation outside of Wire since the mid 90s), his fulfilment derives from physical engagement, working with his hands, focusing on how much he can do with less, and then taking satisfaction in a job well done. This intimate, almost unmediated engagement with his role in Wire stands in stark contrast to the highly mediated, distanced aesthetic that characterised much of the band's work until the mid 2000s. Grey's total immersion in, and identification with, the physicality of drumming has put him at odds with Wire's direction over the years, as the band has explored areas that he felt didn't accommodate his role and contribution.

Often reticent to discuss Wire's music and the band's creative processes – because, as he self-effacingly observes, "that's not my department, I'm just the drummer" – Grey is the quietest member of the group. But when he does speak, his words are carefully chosen and considered. Historically, he's been the silent presence in band interviews, or simply absent from such situations, but one-to-one he has much to say about Wire – particularly about the band's nature and identity. It makes sense to use Grey's attitude toward percussion as a metaphor for his customary silence: he dislikes percussion, considering it an unnecessary adornment to the art of drumming; similarly, in group interviews, one can imagine him feeling that there's no need to add to what his loquacious bandmates have already said.

Inevitably, Grey's quiet absent-presence does create a degree of enigma, and that notion of his elusive character can be connected even to his surname itself, which has changed twice. In his case, the signifier that gives us a first strong sense of identity and attachment was always somewhat fluid and ambiguous. Born Robert Grey in 1951 in Leicester, he changed his surname to Gotobed in 1972. Four years later – during a time of Johnny Rotten, Rat Scabies, Captain Sensible, and Klive Nice (of whom more later) – this was assumed to be just another punk handle. In fact, it had been his family name until his grandfather began using 'Grey' because he felt that Gotobed, an Anglo-Saxon name, could be distracting and would make people less likely to take its bearer seriously. Grey, however, re-embraced his original family name, an act that he explains as a youthful assertion of his own identity, a way of defining himself on his own terms. (By the mid 90s, he'd come around to his grandfather's point of view, and reverted to Grey.)

Grey's introduction to pop music came via Radio Luxembourg, where shows presented by DJs like Alan Freed and Keith Fordyce had begun catering to the nascent audience of teenage music fans in the mid 50s. If he would later be punk *avant la lettre* in his choice of name, his first record purchase also displayed some modest, age-appropriate rebelliousness: Mike

Sarne's 1963 rocker anthem, 'Just For Kicks', which extolled the virtues of biking with one's bird and doing a ton down the M1. This contrasted sharply with the sounds of Frank Sinatra – one of the few concessions to popular music made by Grey's father.

The family's tastes didn't extend to more serious or sophisticated forms of music. Grey recalls that his father (a hosier by trade) didn't like classical music, and there was a sense that such things were not for them – that the world of 'culture' was something that "happened elsewhere and didn't really touch us". Unsurprisingly, Grey was not encouraged to play an instrument as a child, although his father and sister played the ukulele, something he now remembers with bemusement: "That just didn't connect with me."

Grey had an ambivalent early relationship with music. He was attracted to the idea of playing an instrument but felt it to be an essential talent that he lacked and his schoolmates possessed, by virtue of coming from musical families. One example was his friend Nick Garvey (later of Ducks Deluxe and The Motors), who was a chorister and multi-instrumentalist. It was Garvey who opened Grey's ears to classical music, playing him a recording of Holst's *Planets* suite one day at school. Ukuleles notwithstanding, Grey certainly didn't consider his own family a musical one. "At that age, everything you draw on comes from your family, and I didn't have any family influence of anybody who played, so I didn't have any way of connecting with it. I didn't know it was a matter of application, that if you wanted to do it, you could learn. I had no idea that that was a way into it."

Despite being mystified by the process of acquiring the skills to make music, Grey enjoyed listening to it. By his mid teens, he had discovered rock and was regularly tuning in to *Top Gear* on Radio 1. Cream were one of his first loves – not exclusively because of drummer Ginger Baker, but he concedes that Baker was a hero in those days. Although he felt he had no aptitude for music, Grey noted specific aspects of Baker's playing that stood out, such as the different arrangements and patterns he brought to each song. Led Zeppelin were another band Grey first heard at school, and he developed a strong appreciation for John Bonham's playing, recognising similarities between Bonham and Baker in terms of their inventiveness and the way they added to the songs, "putting in lots of wonderful colourful touches but always playing in the meaningful sense. It came across as very natural".

Grey was also a fan of The Who but wasn't as taken with Keith Moon's drumming. "I loved The Who. I saw them in Leicester in 1967," he remembers, "but when I saw Keith Moon, I didn't think that was something

I could do. I didn't listen to him in the same way as I did to Ginger Baker. It all seemed to be so wild that you couldn't easily pick out what he was doing. And there was also something about people who thought they could play like him – they weren't taken very seriously; they were just sort of loony." In 1969, Grey attended the Isle of Wight festival, which he recalls as a gruelling 14 hours of standing up, culminating in a Bob Dylan set; he didn't return the following year to see Jimi Hendrix.

As his secondary education drew to a close, Grey tried to secure a place at university to study English but only managed to get on a general degree course at Dundee. This held little appeal: "I certainly didn't want to go and live in Dundee." After a summer in London working as a porter at St Mary's Hospital, Grey returned to Leicester to re-take his 'A' Levels and make another attempt to get into university, with a view to becoming a teacher. He ended up back in London at Thames Polytechnic, having been accepted onto a humanities course, but dropped out before the end of his first year. ("I wasn't really interested in what I was being taught, and I'd had enough of exams and education.")

Grey remained in London, living with friends in Highgate. He signed on for a while and held a succession of jobs through the early 70s, attending gigs on a regular basis. "There were so many things on offer," he remembers. "It was difficult to see bands in other parts of the country, but in London you could see live music just in a pub." The emerging pub-rock scene excited Grey, who enjoyed the performers' proximity to the audiences and the chance to observe the relationship of the players with their instruments. Most of all, Grey liked the way pub-rock demystified his concept of the musician. In this more intimate setting, musicians were no longer distant individuals practising an art to which he could not relate. "There was something about the home-grown roots feel that made it more real," he says. "It was a different experience, seeing people close-up. Pub-rock only seems to carry negative connotations now – a bit like trad jazz – but at the time it offered something unique. There's a special experience of a small, packed venue where the performers aren't on a pedestal." Grey frequented storied venues – such as the Nashville Rooms (later the site of Wire's first gig), the Greyhound, the White Horse, and the Kensington – where he saw, among others, Dr Feelgood, Kilburn & The High Roads, and The 101ers.

Around this time, Grey also recalls attending larger gigs by established artists. Like the other members of Wire, he was a Roxy Music fan and saw them in their post-Eno incarnation at the Rainbow in 1974. He did see Eno in concert that year – not in a rock context but as a clarinettist with The Portsmouth Sinfonia at the Royal Albert Hall. Grey appreciated the way that the Sinfonia's disciplined-yet-shambolic amateurism playfully undermined the serious, sanctified aura he had always attached to classical music. (Playing cello for the Portsmouth Sinfonia that night was Gavin Bryars, with whom Grey would be invited to participate in a John Cage piece almost 25 years later at the Barbican Centre.)

By 1975, Grey was performing in a band for the first time, having joined Nick Garvey (who had quit Ducks Deluxe) in a pub-rock group named The Snakes. Although he was the vocalist, Grey says: "I'm not sure where the idea came from that I could sing." Garvey explains: "Rob Smith and Robert tossed up to see who would play the bass and who would be the singer. Robert turned out to be a rather remarkable singer. He had fantastic attitude. He sounded fantastic. He stood up there, and he looked like: don't fuck with me! We were just a Chuck Berry group, but he was fantastic – looking menacing in leather jacket and boots, spitting out rock'n'roll classics." The Snakes lasted a year or so, playing on the pub circuit around London and putting out one single, a cover of The Flamin' Groovies' 'Teenage Head'. In view of Wire's *anti*-rock'n'roll orientation and the quiet role that Grey would assume, this is an ironic item: adopting an unlikely Americanised accent, he drawls lines about being "California born and bred" and boasts that his woman's "a teenage love machine".

When The Snakes disbanded, Grey took up amateur dramatics – almost making it to the Edinburgh Fringe Festival in a Eugène Ionesco play – but the arrival of punk pulled him back to music. He played one gig in 1976, subbing for ex-Snakes drummer Richard Wernham (aka Ricky Slaughter) in an early version of The Art Attacks, a band also featuring Steve Spear, Edwin Pouncey (aka Savage Pencil), and Marion Fudger (aka M.S.). "When The Snakes split up, I borrowed Richard's drums. That was when I started practising on my own. I played with The Art Attacks because Richard had drunk rather too much, and he wasn't able to play. So I was asked to do it, having never played drums on a stage before, and I didn't know any of their material, either. It happened so quickly that I didn't have time to think about whether I should do it or not. I don't know what the results sounded like, but I don't remember anything being thrown at us." Another obscure set of circumstances led to Grey drumming on The Art Attacks' 'Rat City', the B-side of their single 'Punk Rock Stars'.

In the summer of 1976, Grey met Colin Newman at a party in Stockwell. The latter urged him to try out as a drummer with the band he'd just started in Watford, but Grey, believing he wasn't good enough, told Newman he'd be better off with Wernham. "I didn't think I could rehearse with a group, with people I hadn't met before, but Colin talked me into coming to a rehearsal." Newman recalls Grey's reluctance: "Rob merely claimed to have 'access' to a drum kit. He thought we should be using Richard Wernham, but frankly, he looked wrong."

Although he was excited by the opportunity, Grey had misgivings about his lack of skill. Nevertheless, the amateur spirit of punk and its democratic ethos gave him heart. "I suppose if they thought I looked alright, or if I was the sort of person they could get on with, that was probably more important than what I could play on the drums." His overriding memory of the rehearsal is one of complete panic – and trying not to make too many mistakes. "I kept my eyes closed. I didn't think I had any ability, as I'd tried to explain to Colin. Having been in a group before probably did give me a little bit of confidence, thinking I could get away with it, that it sounded like somebody playing the drums, but it was pretty uncomfortable."

In spite of this unpromising start, Grey's drumming would become the spine of Wire's sound, his idiosyncratic style praised by critics for its motorik and metronomic character. For Grey, however, the idea that his work lacks affect is anathema to the way he approaches his instrument. "I wouldn't want to only be metronomic and mechanical. If the feel of what you do is metronomic, maybe you've gone too far in the mechanical sense. A degree of looseness is a good thing. I prefer to do something that is both responsive and mechanical when required. I don't apply 'mechanical' to everything, but that is how I'm generally described."

Grey's reaction to technology during his time with Wire has been notoriously vexed. It suggests an artistic and emotional investment that differs from that of his bandmates – an investment that was at the heart of his decision to leave the group in 1990, as they fully embraced sequencing and programming in the music-making process. (He rejoined them in 1999.) For an understanding of Wire's meaning for Grey, as well as for some insight into that decision to withdraw from the band, it's useful to consider his philosophy as a farmer, since it appears inextricably linked with his approach to playing music. Grey follows the methods proposed by the Austrian philosopher Rudolf Steiner for organic growing and humane ways of rearing stock – maintaining his farm, as much as possible, as its own self-contained system, growing his own cattle feed and producing fertiliser. Grey is at his happiest and most satisfied when playing his part in this largely autonomous, self-perpetuating environment. In much the same way, Wire for him exists in its most fulfilling, core form as four people interacting with each other in the live setting – their work immediately apparent in real time, the product of hands-on, mutually supporting labour, without the extended technological mediation of the studio. "One of Wire's attitudes is to work from ideas rather than from a logic of music," he emphasises, and he certainly subscribes to the conceptual underpinnings of the band. But crucially, it's the live execution of the concept that he sees as the essence of Wire, and which underlies his commitment to the group and their work: "Wire in its purest form is four people playing."

In Grey's opinion, Wire as a self-contained, organic system was breached when the band brought in synthetic elements from the outside, especially computer-oriented options for the rhythm component. To him, this disrupted and unbalanced the basic ecology that gave Wire its uniqueness, and the essential experience that he found in the physicality of the group's live collaboration was lost. Some band-members refer, dismissively, to Grey's insistence on simply "wanting to play drums" as a limited, almost Luddite mind-set, bringing about his own obsolescence by closing himself off to new possibilities and by rejecting any engagement with their evolving vision of Wire. Such an interpretation may have some validity, but Grey's departure in 1990 was not the product of pure stubbornness – it was an issue with which he wrestled for years, rooted in a far deeper view of Wire than he is often given credit for.

After nearly 40 years working in music, give or take the odd hiatus, Grey has a relationship with what he does and how he sees his creative identity that remains complicated. On one level, he bypasses the issue completely: "If you say you're a drummer, that's going to arouse curiosity, and it's harder to explain than if you say you're a farmer – usually, I don't even tell people I'm in a group." But when pressed on the musician versus drummer question, he still settles on the latter to describe himself. "If you tell someone you're a musician," he says, "it creates the image of so many things that I don't feel associated with: guitar solos and that sort of thing. I'm not sure why it's such a difficult question, but I definitely feel more comfortable describing myself as a drummer."

One of Wire's salient characteristics is the band's self-identification as *European* as much as *English*, an affinity that's strong in the case of **GRAHAM LEWIS**, a resident of Uppsala, Sweden, since the late 80s. Born Edward Graham Lewis in the Lincolnshire town of Grantham in 1953, he spent his first few years in Germany and Holland, where his father was stationed with the Royal Air Force. Postings eventually brought the family back to Britain, and during the height of the Cold War, Lewis grew up around air bases along the east coast. At RAF Wattisham in Suffolk, his father worked with ground crews servicing English Electric Lightning jet fighters, two of which stood armed at 10-minutes' readiness, 24-hours a day, on Quick Reaction Alert duty. This was the first line of defence against any potential Soviet attack, and the threat from Eastern Europe made Lewis's day-to-day surroundings unusual, instilling in him an early sense of dread and menace – emotions that, in his view, resurfaced in some of his writing. And that's hardly surprising when you consider that he was often awoken in the small hours to participate in drills simulating the outbreak of World War III, episodes that led him to explain his tiredness at school the next day with a casual, "Oh, we had a nuclear attack last night".

Despite that moderately traumatic awareness hanging over his childhood of an unstable and fragmented Europe, it was Lewis above all who later embraced European culture when Wire began to play on the Continent in the late 70s. "When we went to Europe, and Germany especially," he recalls, "that was our release. It was like: This is it. Now we're home. This is what our heritage is. This is *our* Europe."

It's become common to characterise Wire in terms of a tension between two axes committed to competing philosophies and methodologies: experimentalism versus song-based music; noise versus melody; art project versus band. That narrative is reductive and misleading, but it is true that Lewis forged, with Bruce Gilbert, a creative and political alliance that exercised a marked experimental influence over Wire's direction. Although Lewis was of the same generation as Newman, and shared a similar educational background, from the outset he always had more in common with Gilbert, to whom he gravitated as an artistic collaborator. Indeed, his earliest memories of interaction with the sonic world hint at a sensibility like Gilbert's, boding well for their future partnership in Wire and other endeavours.

Lewis's initial exposure to pop music came not in the traditional way, via easily recognisable songs heard on the radio, but in a unique context, in which songs formed part of a dynamic landscape. This took place in the seaside town of Mablethorpe, where Lewis encountered music played at high volume through the bass-heavy sound systems in amusement arcades and at funfairs, around dodgem cars, carousels, waltzers, and assorted attractions – teeming hives of social activity that bombarded the senses. It wouldn't be a stretch to imagine this as a primal scene: dark, noisy industrial atmospheres, found sounds, relentlessness and chaos, aural contingencies and the blurred boundaries of audio identities – all of this would bubble up in Lewis's later work. His reaction at the time to this cacophonous playground even anticipates some of his subsequent creative tactics: like Gilbert, he rejected the role of passive listener, preferring to engage in the possibilities offered by the environment, experimenting with simple ways to enhance and to alter the experience in much the same manner as he would approach the recording studio. One method was to explore how the perception of sound could be transformed as he moved among various funfair rides with their own sound systems: by shifting his position between and within these competing sonic fields, Lewis was able to engineer what he calls his own "peculiar mixes of sound".

Notwithstanding this inventive, active listening strategy, like the rest of his generation Lewis also enjoyed the more conventional access to music provided by the radio in the early 60s. The first band to register with him via this medium was Cliff Richard & The Shadows, whom he remembers as "a very acceptable face of rock'n'roll" (evidenced by his mother's approval of them). A pivotal moment in his growing musical consciousness was the receipt of his own transistor radio for Christmas, at age 11; through the 60s, he consumed a random diet of rock and pop, emanating chiefly from pirate stations like Radio Caroline and Radio London. "This was extraordinary," he enthuses. "Suddenly things appeared from the sky which were inexplicable. The very best in terms of American music: Motown, Hendrix, The Electric Prunes. It seemed unmediated, just coming out of a transistor radio."

Lewis's first contact with live rock music came at his youth club in Wattisham in 1967, where he witnessed a local band called The Nite Sect, notable for their lead singer. "One was told in no uncertain terms that he was to be stayed away from," he recalls. "He had long hair, a long leather coat, and a suitcase adorned with various press-cuttings of gruesome murders. He went to art college in Ipswich with Eno, it turned out." Thanks to the youth club, Lewis also got his first taste of a large-scale rock event: an outing to the 1968 *NME* Readers' Poll Winners Concert at the Empire Pool, Wembley, featuring The Move, The Rolling Stones, and Scott Walker, among others.

Around this time, having moved back to the Northeast with his family, he started attending concerts in Newcastle, seeing the likes of Pink Floyd, Free, The Faces, and The Groundhogs and discovering the music of Captain Beefheart. He also began to pay more attention to the bass, as played by

Cream's Jack Bruce and Free's Andy Fraser. Jack Bruce intrigued Lewis because he was the first singing bassist he'd seen, whereas Fraser's appeal was bound up with his Motown influence and his melodic style. Lewis received his first bass aged 15 – a gift from an ex-Teddy Boy named Jimmy Moore, who worked as a coffin maker. "He was the kind of person who became interested in something and then built it," says Lewis. "So he built a bass. It was never very good, but it was a beautiful-looking thing." Further experiments ensued as Lewis plugged it into a valve radio and achieved stimulating, albeit non-musical sounds. This exploratory impulse also manifested itself in such rudimentary attempts at sonic manipulation as taking a pin to a flexi-disc on his Dansette portable, an activity that revealed to him "the realm of noise and repetition".

In addition to giving Lewis his first instrument, Moore set him thinking about art college as the next step after grammar school. Lewis's final years at school were also a period during which he had begun to learn about Dada and surrealism. Dada resonated with his love of the absurd but also, more significantly, introduced him to the value of concept and process in art and to the notion that the ideas surrounding an art object could be as important as the object itself. Surrealism, with its poetic juxtaposition of the quotidian and the exotic, alerted Lewis to novel ways of stretching language. This would all be central to his artistic identity, both in the context of Wire and beyond – especially in collaboration with Gilbert.

Although he was considering a place at Birmingham University to study architecture, Lewis opted for a foundation course at Lanchester Polytechnic in Coventry, starting in 1971. There he immediately began to absorb new cultural experiences (such as hearing Stockhausen for the first time) and met teachers whose combination of energy, curiosity, and discipline inspired him – among them John Mockett, the motorcycle designer, who was his tutor. The extra-curricular side of Lewis's foundation year proved equally rewarding, as he worked on the entertainments committee and immersed himself in early-70s art-rock – attending gigs by Roxy Music, Van der Graaf Generator, Kevin Ayers, and others.

Eno reappeared at 'The Lanch' as a guest lecturer, impressing the students with his assertions that it was possible to blend interests in the avant-garde and doo-wop in one's work. This enthusiastic talk of blurring artistic boundaries and collapsing cultural hierarchies excited Lewis. Ultimately, the most valuable lesson he took from his foundation year was that the art-school milieu, with the interactions and connections it facilitated, was devised most of all to encourage independent thought.

From Lanchester Polytechnic, Lewis moved on to Hornsey College of Art in autumn 1972, to study for a degree in textiles. While it was no longer the charged institution it had been in spring 1968, when it was the site of Britain's most intense and protracted student action, that episode did add to the allure. After a year at Hornsey, however, Lewis began to find his textiles course constraining, and he switched to the fashion department. There he thrived, pursuing a growing interest in process and mass reproduction in relation to design, as well as an interest in mixing media and disrupting the conventional distinctions between high and low sensibilities.

As he had done at Lanchester Polytechnic, Lewis encountered inspirational teachers. One of them was Brian Harris, who would design the typography on the inner sleeve of *154*, but visiting lecturers were again vitally important. Art-school graduates now established in the fashion world gave insight into career options and showed Lewis that there was a community of like-minded creative individuals out there doing exciting work. Among these visitors were Jim O'Connor and Pamla Motown, who had designed clothes for Roxy Music and for the hip London boutique Mr Freedom. In 1974, they gave a memorable slide-show lecture at Hornsey, titled 'Fashion Lib'. Lewis felt instant kinship with them. "These people knew what was going on. They'd travelled, made their break out of the Royal College earlier, and so I felt less lonely. It was that thing of finding one's peers."

Lewis was drawn to O'Connor and Motown particularly because of their links with Roxy Music. Like Gilbert, he was fascinated by the way that Roxy Music, more than anyone else at the time, embodied the rich possibilities of the rock group as 'project', combining music with a wide range of aesthetic experimentation – in presentation, choreography, costume, and record artwork. Lewis would develop a more personal connection with Roxy: his girlfriend from the late 70s until 1986 was fashion designer Juliet Mann, muse and associate of Antony Price, who with Motown, O'Connor, and Keith Wainwright had played a key role in Roxy Music's styling. (Mann later joined Bryan Ferry's management team.)

At Hornsey, Lewis became social secretary. Among other things, this entailed spending time at venues like the Lord Nelson on the Holloway Road, checking out pub-rock bands with a view to booking them for college gigs. There he saw Kilburn & The High Roads and Dr Feelgood, doing a deal with the latter for "£60 plus the petrol back and forth from Canvey Island". Eventually, he took his first steps toward playing bass in a group. Hornsey was full of budding musicians with whom Lewis would have been well matched, and many of them cropped up in punk and post-punk bands

– Stuart Goddard (Adam Ant), Viv Albertine (Slits), and Lester Square (Monochrome Set), for instance – but he fell in with a rather different crowd. "I got asked to a rehearsal by these guys called The Medium Wave Band. They were very impressed by the whole Canterbury scene, which I wasn't terribly interested in anymore." His tenure with them was brief.

Having finished his degree in 1975, Lewis launched a career as a fashion designer in London. His big break came thanks to Lynne Franks (the inspiration for Edina in *Absolutely Fabulous*), who saw his work and hooked him up with Jeffrey Rogers, for whom he developed a T-shirt collection that received wide editorial coverage and went on sale in high-street stores.

Although his fashion career was taking off, Lewis was still eager to play in a band. "College had been a disappointment in that regard and, after college, I was beginning to think it wasn't going to happen." However, through art-school friend Angela Conway, he met Bruce Gilbert. "We talked music," recalls Lewis. "We disliked many of the same things and shared a few crucial tastes: Free, Beefheart, and two tracks by The Groundhogs." On the basis of this narrow common ground, Gilbert invited him to rehearse with the band he had formed with Watford students.

His first meeting with the group was far from promising, thanks to Gill and Newman's attitude. "'Hostile' might be a good way of putting it," Lewis says. As he sees it, this had to do with jealousy on their part: he was based in London, had attended Hornsey, and had a decent job. Things didn't improve when the rehearsal started and they discovered he couldn't play. He went home thinking the entire episode was best forgotten, but a few days later Gilbert called him and asked if he'd be interested in coming to another rehearsal.

Traditionally, there have been two variants of the British art-school narrative as it pertains to musicians. In one, the educational and cultural environment plays a part in shaping creative thinking and practices; far more commonly, the educational aspect is irrelevant, as the aspiring musician uses the time and space that come with being a full-time student as a context in which to launch a band. Long before **COLIN NEWMAN** arrived at art school, he knew what he wanted to accomplish: he was in art school to form a band.

Although he did a foundation year at Winchester School of Art and a diploma course (incomplete) at Watford School of Art, that time is not central to Newman's narrative of his artistic growth. Art school was a place that gave him little intellectual nourishment and instead simply allowed him to meet his bandmates and establish Wire. Newman's strong sense of purpose and the relatively incidental value he therefore places on the art-school experience contrast with the histories and outlooks of the other former art students in Wire. That difference explains some of the creative tension that has, on the one hand, led to great work by Wire, and has also, at times, compromised the band's ability to function.

It's possible to tie Newman's life story to his single-minded focus on a career in music from the start. He was born in the cathedral city of Salisbury in 1954. Salisbury is rich in history, with Neolithic origins and mentions in *The Domesday Book*, but as a child Newman would have doubtless been more excited by the fact that the successful 60s band Dave Dee, Dozy, Beaky, Mick & Tich hailed from the city. His uncle, who worked in a music shop, had even met them. Newman spent his early childhood in the village of Durrington, moving in 1962 to the nearby Berkshire town of Newbury. By then, he was precociously obsessed with pop music (above all The Beatles) to the exclusion of everything else. Books, films, television, sport; none of them elicited much interest.

Newman's lifelong love of The Beatles began early. "I was only seven when I first heard them, but I remember my friend saying: we have to be into this, because this is *our* music. We were younger than the intended audience, but it worked its magic." Newman now identifies in The Beatles' classic work two features that informed his own songwriting: an affinity for melody and a rejection of rock'n'roll cliché. For him, they initiated "a melodic arc" in British pop, and their music offered something different from the straight-ahead, American-style rock'n'roll that had dominated the British consciousness until the early 60s – a form to which he seems to have been congenitally allergic. "I didn't get turned on by Elvis. I just thought it was 'old stuff', whereas The Beatles' music had much more depth to it. I consider it incredible luck to have been there at the beginning."

If we're looking for a single Damascene moment in Newman's musical life, however, then it came when he first heard The Tornados' 'Telstar' on the radio in 1962, having been dramatically described by the DJ as "the music of the future". That characterisation of the music – as much as the actual sound – captured Newman's imagination. His reaction to the track and its framing foreshadowed what would emerge as two core motifs in Wire's collective sensibility: a relentless quest for the new and a keen attention to the discourse they would use to frame their music.

As the British pop scene of the 60s took shape, radio became the centre of Newman's life, a direct connection to the music that obsessed him. "I

31

used to be in the dining room doing my homework and listening to the radio, and the rest of the family would be watching telly in the front room. I listened to whatever I could. Before Radio 1 started in 1967, I would listen to every pop programme on the BBC's Light Service, and I used to listen to Radio Luxembourg and all the pirates: Kenny Everett, Stuart Henry, and all those people playing pop music in the 60s." Thanks to his uncle, Newman also learned about music beyond The Beatles. "He told me about this group called The Yardbirds, who you couldn't hear on the radio at all – they were what you were *really* into if you were into music. He also showed me a copy of *Melody Maker*, and I became aware that there was a whole other culture as well – and I wanted it all." Indeed, the music press grew to be another focus of Newman's attention. He reports that, by the age of ten, he was reading the *NME* from cover to cover. ("I even used to do the crossword.")

Throughout this period, Newman was quietly preparing for what he felt certain would be his future life. This took the form of fantasising about being in a band with famous musicians, composing songs in his head and improving existing songs – even those that he conceded were already near perfect. He took a first step toward rock stardom in his mid teens at St Bartholomew's Grammar School in Newbury, linking up with classmate Desmond Simmons to start writing and playing. Theirs is a classic story of teenage rock ambition, fuelled as much by an obsession with music as by social ineptitude (and dismal failure with the opposite sex).

Newman's father (an electrical engineer) and mother (a bookkeeper) divorced around this time, initiating a difficult period and presumably making rock music an attractive refuge. "Desmond was the one with the obvious talent," says Newman. "He could already play guitar, and he could already compose songs. I was the bloke who could sing and hit the box." The pair formed several bands but played no gigs. Nevertheless, they dedicated themselves to their craft in preparation for inevitable success. "We didn't want to perform in public, because we considered that too demeaning. What we were doing was songwriting and rehearsing, and we would record everything so we'd know how to perform in the studio when we got our record deal – it was obvious to us that it was going to happen."

When they weren't honing their tunes in anticipation of the call from EMI, Newman and Simmons also attended concerts. Newbury was a regular stop on the gig circuit for prog and art-rock bands in the early 70s, and they saw King Crimson, Genesis, Van der Graaf Generator, and Hawkwind, plus less celebrated acts such as Andwella and Black Widow.

After grammar school, in autumn 1973, Newman began a yearlong foundation course at Winchester. "I can see now that, in terms of art education, I was entirely clueless," he admits, "because I'd gone for the wrong reason. I'd gone because I thought it was going to be full of people who wanted to be in bands." The popular myth of art school as a factory for rock musicians was already well established, and Newman "subscribed to that myth 100 per cent". Most of the musicians whose records excited him had been to art school, so he felt it was the logical place to be.

His introduction to the course at Winchester will be familiar to anyone who went through British art education in the late 60s and early 70s, as the tutors exposed their charges to new aesthetic possibilities, challenged their preconceptions, and encouraged them to discover, for themselves, which discipline best suited them for their subsequent diploma or degree courses. On the first day, *Piano Phase* by Steve Reich was played to the students, making an impression on Newman. "I thought it was a fantastically exciting piece of music," he remembers. It was the first of many musical revelations at Winchester. "That year was a year of discovery, and I found new things that I was into. It might not sound quite as highbrow as Steve Reich, but I discovered Todd Rundgren and Steely Dan, both of whom were huge influences at the time."

Despite the auspicious start, Winchester was something of a let down. Eno had studied fine art there in the late 60s, and Newman assumed that there would be an awareness at the college of his accomplishments with Roxy Music. But whereas Steve Reich's work was deemed important enough to present to the students, Eno was ignored. This puzzled Newman, since he felt the latter was as serious an artist as the former – in his own way. Even more disappointing was the fact that, by the end of the course, Newman hadn't found a band. He would have another chance, though, as he planned to continue his art-school education. Stringing things out for three more years also made sense because he was "petrified of having to get a job".

Although he'd had some interest in fine art, Newman decided to study illustration. Overlooking the minor detail that he couldn't actually draw, he figured he would acquire skills that could be useful in his rock career: namely, the ability to design record covers for the band that would materialise during his course. He eventually secured a place at Watford to do a diploma in graphic arts; he describes this as a "lowly" vocational programme without the "pretension or intellectual rigour" of the school's foundation course, whose faculty included the sculptor Michael Werner and the painter Peter Schmidt. Newman still wonders how he was accepted and suspects the worst: "There was a theory that went round that the guy who interviewed the applicants for my year was leaving and decided to let in a bunch of ne'er-do-wells and general rabble to screw over the guy who succeeded him."

During his first year, Newman lived in Hendon with a girlfriend and Simmons, who was now at Middlesex Polytechnic. The pair continued to play music together, but the anticipated band still didn't appear. When Newman's girlfriend dumped him, he moved to Watford, where he shared a house in Leavesden Road with fellow students Slim Smith and George Gill.

Watford offered a potentially catalysing environment: regardless of whether the students were studying foundation or more vocational diploma courses, they had access to all the college's facilities (including film and recording equipment), as well as to an array of artists who came as visiting speakers. The guest lecturers during Newman's time at Watford included Mark Boyle, Eduardo Paolozzi, Abram Games, Tom Phillips, Dieter Roth, Mayo Thompson, and, of course, Brian Eno. The last was a regular fixture, working with the students on projects such as Scratch Orchestra-style experiments. (Newman's housemate Smith fondly remembers performing part of Cornelius Cardew's *The Great Learning* under Eno's direction.) Eno even involved them in his own work: at least one edition of the *Oblique Strategies* cards – designed with Peter Schmidt, whose portraits of Eno adorn *Taking Tiger Mountain (By Strategy)* – was printed and assembled by students at the college. Newman, however, doesn't recall being particularly inspired by any of the cultural opportunities on offer at Watford.

Within the context of his coursework, Newman does remember some interaction with Charles Harrison, one of Watford's senior academic figures. Harrison was a founding member of the Art & Language group, whose work had a far-reaching impact in the realm of conceptual art, emphasising the importance of discussion and text as much as paintings and conventional art objects. Newman took a required course with him but thinks that Harrison's erudition was lost on most of the students. "I was really the only person in the class who understood half of the stuff he was talking about. It was shocking to be in art school with a bunch of people who didn't know anything about art." This lack of knowledge apparently extended even to some of the faculty. Newman recalls a college excursion to a museum in Holland, during which his art classes at St Bartholomew's came in handy as he was able to help the faculty member leading the trip. "I actually took the person who was my year tutor around and explained to him what Mondrian was doing, because I had learned art history at school."

By the end of his first year at Watford, Newman had lost interest. He stopped going to classes and was saved from expulsion only by his second-year tutor, Hansjörg Mayer, the renowned experimental typographer and publisher. As Newman tells it, Mayer enabled him to pursue Variant Two of the musician-at-art-school existence, keeping the college authorities at bay and making it possible for him to skip most of his final year, thereby giving him the opportunity to devote all his energy to Wire. "I got away with murder," he says. "Hansjörg was pretty special: he was prepared to put up with my arrant nonsense and allowed me to actually do what I wanted to do. Had I knuckled down to doing the set work, there is no way I would have ended up in Wire."

Ironically, then, Mayer played a significant role in Newman's art-school experience, not as an influential or inspiring creative figure, but because he facilitated the realisation of Newman's goals. Newman explains: "I think it is the highest form of any interpersonal relationship to be a person who helps and enables another to realise their own ambitions. Inspirational figures are usually ones people try to emulate; Hansjörg offered nothing to emulate, but without him there would have been no Wire."

One thing Newman did gain from the artists he encountered at Watford was the strengthening of a key element of the narrative that has driven his work with Wire: just being in contact with such figures solidified his sense of himself as an artist – even though he was still a student with no real creative accomplishments to show. For Newman, interactions with Mayer, Schmidt, and Eno tacitly confirmed that he really was an artist, without needing further training or apprenticeship from art school. "Hansjörg used to give me a lift back to Hendon," Newman remembers. "He'd always give Brian and Peter a lift, too, and often I'd be in the car with them and we'd just chat. More than anything, Watford gave me the sense that I could be with those people who were artists and had their own level of importance – not just Brian but the others as well – and they didn't treat me like some stupid student. I could talk about what I wanted to talk about. There's a process by which individuals go from being just a general person to being someone who can inhabit the kind of life you need to if you're an artist. I went through that process there."

Newman remains ambivalent when he looks back at his experiences at Winchester and Watford, acknowledging their place in his development but feeling that they simply confirmed the path he had already determined to follow, rather than introducing him to anything that truly impacted him or ignited his curiosity. "Watford gave me three years in which to grow enough to find my feet in something that I wanted to do, and for that I shall be eternally grateful. Even at its least exciting, British art education can offer that. I think the main thing you learn in art school is to smoke a cigarette in a meaningful way: number one skill. And learning how to bullshit."

Newman's principal achievement at Watford was to form Wire. "I did get something out of art school, but I don't have a piece of paper that shows anything that I passed. In the end, I refused to take the exam. It was one of those exams where you could have got some kind of pass with very little effort, but I just thought: no, I don't want to do that. I felt: I know what I've done, and I have got something out of this – because by the end of three years, we'd already done our first demos for EMI."

Although Wire would not have existed had Newman not gone to Watford and met Gill and Gilbert, he also stresses that much of the preparation for Wire had been completed *before* arriving there. "There are a lot of myths about what's good about art school and how it's encouraged generations of young British musicians, and it so happens that my story could support that myth; but I could see how some very valuable stuff had been done before art school. I was already writing songs; even if they were rubbish, it didn't matter. I already had some kind of idea."

What's most striking about Newman's account of his identity as an artist is the conviction that it was not directly shaped or influenced by anything exterior to him (except, perhaps, The Beatles). Inevitably, such belief in the fully formed autonomy of one's work and ideas can present difficulties for the creative, collaborative partnership of a band – where others may come with their own, equally strong ideas, which might involve alternative working methods or objectives. Newman's single-mindedness – coupled with his singular focus on pushing forward with his concept of the band and with his plans for how it should develop – has been both a driving force enabling Wire's work and, at times, a source of tension when his bandmates have wanted to approach the work differently or explore other directions.

While the shortlived Overload probably weren't quite what Newman had been hoping to find at art school, things began to look more promising once the band had been scaled down to a trio and rebuilt. A few Watford students were considered for the bass and drum positions, including one who Newman recalls "had been in a band that had been favourably compared to The Sweet and had a haircut like Dave Hill". To Newman, though, Grey and Lewis were ideal as they had no links to the college: that they were making a commitment and travelling to rehearsals in Watford ("which Graham regarded as being at the ends of the earth with a bunch of oiks") forced Newman, Gilbert, and Gill to treat the project with equal seriousness.

Once the five-piece line-up was in place – with Newman as lead singer and occasional guitarist, and with lead guitarist Gill writing the bulk of the songs – a band name had to be found. Options were jotted on pieces of paper, pinned up on the walls of Newman's digs and mulled over. Everyone agreed that items of clothing and parts of the body did not work well, and one possibility, fleetingly, was The Geezers. The two final candidates were A Case, rejected for sounding too pretentious, and Gilbert's suggestion: Wire.

## CHAPTER 2
# 1976–77

### *Pink Flag*, again

*Pink Flag* is an impressive record but not a *great* record; it's Wire's best-known record but not their best. *Pink Flag* is the favourite Wire album of people who aren't Wire completists, people who don't approach it from a position of obsessive familiarity with the band's oeuvre. That statement isn't intended as an indictment of their taste or as a critique of their credentials for enjoying the record. It's simply an acknowledgement that, at the level of more casual music fandom, *Pink Flag* is perceived quite differently from the way it's viewed by Wire aficionados.

My objective – wearing the hat of rigorous Wire aficionado for the purposes of this book – is to place Wire's work in context: in the context of its genesis as well as in the context of the band's broader achievements. And when *Pink Flag* is considered in those terms, it's obvious that this is not Wire's strongest or most compelling album. (This chapter necessarily draws on the material used in my *Pink Flag* book. However, in keeping with Wire's own contrariness, here I'm contradicting some of the ideas I've previously articulated and making a different argument about the album's significance.)

*Pink Flag* is Wire's most straightforward record. It doesn't encapsulate the multifaceted nature of the band's creative identity as it would develop on subsequent albums: it's a record of small gestures, not a fully realised statement, and it only hints at Wire's mature personality. Although some of the trademark characteristics traditionally associated with Wire do feature in prototype, they're not yet fleshed out.

The theory and ideas behind *Pink Flag* were in place before the execution had been perfected. One on level, *Pink Flag* was a reaction to its cultural moment. According to Colin Newman, one of the album's aims was "to give punk rock a good kicking with the tools of punk rock". Similarly, Graham Lewis adds: "A lot of *Pink Flag's* stance is *against*. *Pink Flag* sets itself up against what exists, and it exists because of what went before. A lot of it comes out of a 'NO' attitude – although there are a few 'maybes'." But the band's precocious ambitions also went beyond a rejection of the immediate status quo. "I sat in my room in Leavesden Road in Watford," Newman reminisces, "and thought music needed reinventing, and that was where all the stuff that came to be *Pink Flag* came from."

Beneath the mythmaking and the grandiose sense of mission, there is an important, more interesting point: a commitment to the new would be central to Wire's identity. From the time that founding member George Gill departed in early 1977 and the band was reborn as a four-piece, Wire attempted to enforce this commitment stringently: material and ideas were quickly shelved if they had even a whiff of familiarity about them. "If something started to sound familiar, then that would be stamped out," Robert Grey explains. "There was always a feeling to try to avoid rock clichés, something you'd heard before. That was a working method we had." And as he attests, the process could be detail-oriented and ruthless. "I once worked out a tom pattern of some description, and I remember Bruce saying: that sounds too much like Bo Diddley – you can't do that."

Nevertheless, Wire don't give punk much of a "kicking" on *Pink Flag*. For the most part, they reconstitute an orthodox punk language, only occasionally using it against itself or creating something truly innovative. Despite the intention to subvert and move beyond punk, the record is clearly identifiable as a work made in 1977: Wire push at punk's boundaries, showing flashes of going elsewhere, but aside from several memorable tracks and some unique lyrical content, the record doesn't consistently set itself apart. As Newman admits: "Bits of *Pink Flag* seem forward-looking, but much of it is of its time – and even slightly behind its time."

Wire's early development has to be framed in terms of their relationship with and resistance to second-wave punk orthodoxy. What's striking about the picture that emerges is how much the early Wire project was guided by very specific ideas that comprised an almost systematic negation of punk ideology in all its manifestations. But while this negation was apparent from the outset in Wire's record artwork, their sartorial style, the choreography of their performances, and their self-presentation in interviews, it didn't carry over fully to the sound of the first album.

### Our friends were people who were artists

Each of the members of Wire – except Gill – had watched punk's birth in the summer of 1976 with interest, and like other fledgling musicians at the time, they were eager to explore the artistic space and opportunities that this cultural revolution promised to open up. They subscribed to punk's contention that contemporary British music was largely moribund, an entertainment business accessible only to artists who satisfied safe, conservative expectations of commercial potential or demonstrated an acceptable level of musicianship. In the face of that sterile, narrow culture, punk's demand for newness and its democratic, anyone-can-do-it ethos appealed to Wire.

Gilbert, Grey, Lewis, and Newman (as well as their eventual producer Mike Thorne) had all witnessed the Sex Pistols, Subway Sect, Siouxsie & The Banshees, and The Clash on September 20 1976, at the first night of the 100 Club Punk Special. This made a strong impression. Newman was excited by the Banshees' challenging, improvised performance. Grey – a man not given to hyperbole – felt this was a "unique" event, a clear sign that "something was happening" in a wider sense. He was struck by the media attention that night and by the fact that the audience members were being photographed and filmed – a source of amusement for Lewis three decades later, when he spotted his youthful likeness walking across the frame of some archival footage. Gilbert, meanwhile, was intrigued by the way that the club – like other early punk venues he'd observed – became "a laboratory", a vibrant environment to which the audiences, with their clothing and behaviour, brought as much as the artists onstage.

Wire themselves entered the fray on December 2 and 3 1976 (with Gill still on board), performing live for the first time – at the Nashville Rooms and Saint Martins School of Art in London. By the end of 1977, they'd played 38 of their first 54 gigs in and around the capital. They appeared to tick all the right punk boxes: short hair, no flares; attitude and an unsettling stage presence; fast, brief, loud songs. They played the same venues (the Vortex, the Roxy) and on the same bills as punk bands like The Boys, The Sods, The Lurkers, and Adam & The Ants; they used the same musical tools with the same lack of skill; and they'd attended some of punk's ur-events. And although it seems unlikely now, they even had *noms de punk*. For a short while, Newman answered to Klive Nice ("instead of being 'Rotten', I'd pretend to be *nice*") and Lewis was Hornsey Transfer, an alias bringing together his interest in football, his art-school credentials, and his peripatetic background.

Despite these apparent similarities, however, there was a feeling that Wire didn't fit in. Responses at their first gigs suggested that they weren't embraced as part of the scene: as Grey recalls, their set at the Nashville Rooms was condemned as the "death throes of cock rock" – and that comment was made from the stage by Susan Gogan, the singer with the

40

headline act, The Derelicts (an R&B band, ironically). The audience itself was unresponsive. At Saint Martins the following night, the students were underwhelmed and pulled the plug on Wire in mid-set. Their relationship to punk was also something that preoccupied the music press almost from the moment they began gigging, the issue often coming up in some guise in coverage of the band. Their first *NME* cover in December 1977 ran with the caption "No Pun(k)s Please, We're Wire", which was essentially the thesis of Phil McNeill's feature: "They aren't a punk rock band ... Wire stand alone in the class of 77."

Wire's separateness from their contemporaries was evident in social terms, too. "One of The Clash may have once said hello to me," jokes Newman, but the point is an important one, as Jon Savage explains: "They were always outside of everybody. They weren't an inner-circle punk-rock group. They weren't matey with the main players. They weren't keyed into the groups around The Clash and the Sex Pistols, the punk inner circle. They were always quite separate."

Newman does report some slightly more substantive interaction with The Jam, whose front man predicted a bright future for Wire. "The last conversation I had with Paul Weller in 1977, he said: You mark my words – in, like, ten years' time, both of us are going to be really famous. He was half-right." But overall, Wire tended not to associate with other musicians. As *Mojo*'s 2006 retrospective on the band put it: "No guitar solos, no clichés, no mates" – a perfect epitaph for Wire's gravestone. It's important to note, however, that they weren't inherently anti-social, and there was no conscious decision to remain aloof and detached. In large part, it was just a reflection of the internal dynamics of Wire at the time. In 1977, apart from Newman and Grey, they didn't live near each other, and rarely socialised as a group: they weren't close friends, and they didn't spend much time together beyond rehearsing and performing. Consequently, they didn't mix as a band with other bands.

Wire's age is another factor to consider when looking at them in the context of punk's second wave. In 1977, Gilbert was 31, Grey 26, Lewis 24, and Newman 23. They were marginally older (much older in Gilbert's case) than most of the other groups, and it's not hard to imagine a lack of enthusiasm on their part when faced with the prospect of spending quality time with a bunch of adolescents. By the same token, in a youth subculture that emphasised image, pose, street cred, and rebelliousness, just a few years' age difference could be an issue, and hanging out with Wire (average age: 26) might not have been a wholly attractive proposition. It wasn't only other musicians who judged Wire in these terms – some audience members at the band's gigs made no secret of their animus toward these elderly interlopers. "When we played the Roxy once in early 1977," says Grey, "there was somebody barracking Bruce, shouting out: You're an old man! Get off! – and Bruce must have only been about 30 then."

There was also something about Wire's artiness that contributed to perceptions of the band as outsiders. Countless people involved in punk shared the group's art-school background, but it didn't make for a tight bond between Wire and their contemporaries. Somehow, it actually seemed to compound their isolation. If they didn't mix with other bands, detractors would inevitably find ways to interpret that as a superior attitude. "We probably had a reputation for being arrogant, because we kept ourselves to ourselves," speculates Lewis. "Our friends were people who were artists." Not surprisingly, a narrative developed according to which Wire hadn't simply been to art school like everyone else – they were arty and pretentious. And this of course encouraged the penchant we English have for knocking down anyone who stands out and who, in our view, believes they're better than everyone else.

This dynamic was acute during punk's second wave, which took on a populist, philistine character – not without a lot of bad faith with regard to class. Lewis's refreshingly unconcealed 'posh' accent would have only compounded the sense of Wire being unlike everyone else. (This is best documented on a live recording from the Roxy, during which the bassist exhorts a heckler to "fuck off" in a nicely modulated BBC voice.) In this context, Wire, who never hid their interest in art and made it a prominent aspect of their image, were ripe for opprobrium: details such as the mention of Duchamp in early interviews played into the hands of those looking for evidence that Wire gave themselves arty airs and graces.

### The same old rock

Most depressingly, Wire's ostracism because of their arty disposition showed how quickly punk was becoming an unimaginative, homogeneous milieu in which anyone trying to fulfil its original mandate (that is, do something different and new) was treated with suspicion. Early on, Gilbert began to get the disturbing feeling that the punk scene was all about rock-as-usual and that Wire were viewed as inauthentic and unwilling to get their hands dirty with everybody else. "I got the impression that some of the musicians we came into contact with thought we had no right to be there," he says. "We weren't 'rock' – we were stuck-up artists, or something."

(Interestingly, Wire *were* appreciated by punk's first wave: Glen Matlock, Rat Scabies, and Captain Sensible are among those who have praised Wire precisely for attempting to do something different, against the grain of 1977's rapid homogenisation.)

Gilbert's sense that Wire were considered to be lacking the necessary rock credentials gets to the heart of the band's musical argument with punk orthodoxy. Wire had rejected the ideological purification of the Year Zero diktat – which, in any case, punk itself barely followed. Wire didn't even bother to pay lip service. "I never sold any records when you were supposed to murder all your heroes," stresses Newman. Yet there were particular forms that Wire were keen to consign to the historical dustbin: namely pub-rock, a genre they felt should have been an obvious candidate for punk's purge. At first, Gilbert saw punk as an antidote. "Music seemed to be in a rut in this country – we're talking about pub-rock – so the idea that there was going to be a new way of making music seemed a very attractive idea," he says. Grey agrees, explaining that he was attracted to punk in part because "it was taking the place of pub-rock and R&B".

But in early 1977, it appeared to Wire that punk was showing scant signs of breaking new ground, notwithstanding its voluble scorn for the rock and pop that preceded and surrounded it. Worse still, punk had hardly moved beyond pub-rock. Although the latter had reinvigorated the live music scene in the mid 70s, laying some of the groundwork for punk, its brand of R&B offered little cause for genuine excitement. To Wire, it had come to embody another strand of musical orthodoxy, with its stereotypical gestures, its paradoxical insistence on authenticity, its conventions, its formulae, its looseness, its guitar solos, and its Americanisms.

Despite playing up its Britishness, punk resurrected and consolidated, via pub-rock, a clichéd, antiquated American form, rehashing Chuck Berry-style rock'n'roll. At best, it borrowed from the edgier outgrowths of 60s US garage rock, such as the MC5 and The Stooges, but overall it reconstituted a very traditional sound. "What was wrong with a lot of punk rock was the rock gesture," says Newman. "It was like rock songs from the 50s speeded up a bit. It's really obvious: there wasn't such a great difference between your Dr Feelgood and your Eddie & The Hot Rods and your Clash and your Pistols." In conceptualising their own music, Wire knew what they wanted to avoid – and it wasn't just the 'rock' component. They had no time for rock'n'roll's cheerfulness and looseness either, which they located in the 'roll' part of the equation. So that had to go as well.

It was the persistence of this rock'n'roll traditionalism that, to Wire, signalled punk's squandering of an opportunity in 1977. Its rhetoric aside, punk remained by and large a guitar-oriented, R&B-based form that traded on rock's past glories instead of charting a fresh course. "The whole idea around punk was that it was supposed to be new," Newman maintains. "In 1977, it was failing in its promise. Elements of punk were starting to look awfully like rock'n'roll, and that was the one thing I was totally convinced about: it didn't matter what I was doing, it shouldn't be rock'n'roll."

When British punk turned to more recent American music for inspiration, it found it in the likes of the New York Dolls and the Ramones, neither of them exactly innovative in musical terms: get beyond the Dolls' make-up, flamboyance, and attitude and slow the Ramones down a little, and the conventional rock'n'roll framework is unmistakable. As far as home-grown inspirations went, although UK punk in 1977 preserved the energy, playfulness, and colour of glam, it drew most heavily on that genre's least stimulating representatives: it's not Bowie or Roxy Music, for instance, whom you hear in most second-wave punk but the oikish populism of Noddy Holder and Dave Hill. To Wire, therefore, UK punk was musically reactionary insofar as it looked mainly to an American past for ideas, as well as to cartoonishly unadventurous British chart fodder.

Wire, it should be emphasised, also drew some inspiration from American music, but their primary interests lay in contemporary artists such as Patti Smith, Television, and Talking Heads, whose relationship with rock was disinterested or ambivalent. "It was very stimulating," comments Gilbert. "It sounded like art rather than pub-rock." And while Wire shared punk's love of The Ramones, they took the band's stripped-down version of rock'n'roll not as a model but as a challenge to see how much further they could go: early Wire draws on the Ramonic template, if only to render it in a more pared-down form, often faster and with an abstract lyrical vision. As for older American influences, the austere, repetitive minimalist side of The Velvet Underground had certainly resonated with Wire, particularly with Gilbert. In a similar vein, The Modern Lovers' long-delayed first album found favour with the band.

### How could you possibly imagine that was any good?

It took some time, however, for Wire to reach a point in their evolution where they could transcend punk. The band's original sound – when they began, as a five-piece distilled from the Watford group, Overload – was still arguably pre-punk and quite deeply mired in rock'n'roll. The first step for the four members who would continue was to embrace the anti-rockist commitment that punk at least professed and to expunge the rock'n'roll proclivities of their bandmate, George Gill.

Born in 1949, and closer to Gilbert in age, the group's lead guitarist was a no-nonsense Yorkshireman with little patience for what Newman calls "soft Southern bastards" – among whose number he counted himself. "He was a fantastic character," remembers Gilbert, "a sort of troubadour figure, a heavy rock drinker"; others, like housemate Slim Smith, recall his more aggressive, rabble-rousing tendencies. Most importantly for the development of Wire, his guitar-centric excess and cliché became a foil, a paradigm to subvert. "A lot of early Wire was about reacting to the George version of the band," explains Newman, "because George was much more rockist, much more chaotic; it was a lot of noise, shouting, and attitude around a very traditional rock core." Even in Wire's formative stages, then, Gill unwittingly initiated a valuable process as Wire started to resist the contributions of their most able musician and songwriter: his writing and playing confronted them with the kind of unoriginal rock elements they were eager to avoid and sparked their creativity, forcing them to find and define their own sound.

Apart from some cover versions, such as The Modern Lovers' 'Roadrunner', and a few early efforts by the other band-members ('TV' and 'Feeling Called Love'), Gill's work dominated Wire's late-1976 repertoire. The only extant document of this five-man line-up is an August 1976 rehearsal tape made by Grey's school friend and Snakes bandmate Nick Garvey (then on the verge of pop success with The Motors). Garvey recorded Wire on a four-track machine at his house in Stockwell, but their efforts didn't make a profound impression. "What I remember most," he says, "is that none of them seemed to know what they were doing."

The song titles alone give a good idea of the lyrical and musical territory they cover: 'Outside The Law', 'Gimme Your Love', 'Midnight Train', and 'Bitch', for example. At its best, the material has a sub-Velvet Underground relentlessness, raw garage-rock energy, and even some heavy-rock heft (the riffs of 'Prove Myself' and 'Bitch' coming perilously close to 'Paranoid'). A couple of tracks require further elaboration, if only for their comedy value. 'Mary Is A Dyke' was a pre-political-correctness meditation on a lesbian aunt (Newman cops to some involvement in the music but insists: "I'm in no rush to claim it"); 'Bad Night At The Lion' was inspired by a pub-rock singer to whom Gill took a dislike; 'Bitch' is best described by Newman: "It was entirely formless and chugged around on two chords. It was mainly George shouting 'it's a bitch' and then losing it." Gilbert's appraisal of Gill's

45

songwriting is more generous. "He was ahead of his time in terms of lyrical content: challenging, though at times misogynist – but in an ironic way, rather than truly misogynistic. From time to time, he had a way with words."

If Gill wrote most of the songs, he also made his presence felt in their performance, above all with his ubiquitous noodly guitar licks. "He played a Telecaster," remarks Lewis, as if remembering something unsavoury, "and there were what one would call 'solos', which ran through everything." For his part, Gilbert enjoyed the repetition and the sheer absurdity of Wire's earliest incarnation, especially on the occasions when it was supplemented with Newman's guitar. "It was a wall of noise. Three rhythm guitars churning away, with exactly the same solo for every song."

Besides 'Roadrunner', they also covered J.J. Cale's 'After Midnight'. This accelerated version was no homage to its creator but a symptom of subversive urges and a sign that Gill's days were numbered. "George actually did like J.J. Cale," recalls Newman. "In 1976, to say you liked J.J. Cale was close to admitting you were responsible for Auschwitz. It was the most heinous crime possible. A horrible, polite funkiness was what we wanted to do away with, in whatever way we could – and actually doing 'After Midnight' was a way of taking the piss out of George, a way of saying: how could you *possibly* imagine that was any good?"

Unsurprisingly, Gill didn't share the musical tastes of the other members of Wire. 'Roadrunner' aside, Newman recalls him declaring that The Modern Lovers were "too weird", and he was unmoved by the artier strain of New York punk – although he told Newman that Patti Smith was "OK – for a girl". And while his bandmates were initially enthusiastic about British punk, Gill was indifferent: Slim Smith even remembers the guitarist assuring him in late 1976 that punk was a trend that would "be over by Christmas".

Wire's live outings as a five-piece were messy and unpredictable. The Nashville Rooms performance set the tone for gigs during Gill's tenure since it was marked (and marred) by his histrionics and his fraught interaction with the small crowd. "George became very animated," Grey recalls. "He shouted at someone sitting near the stage: What are you looking at? Go back to your beer. George had this aggressive approach. At one point, he threw his guitar back into the dressing room, off the stage." Lewis was entertained by this. "I remember some guy going: you're fucking crap! And George said: you get back in your beer, *cunt*. That was one of the things George was superb at. And then he proceeded to thrash all the strings off his guitar."

As Gill's position in Wire became more insecure, so his live participation became more erratic, and he spent progressively more time offstage. The band's February 1977 gig at Carey Place in Watford was a watershed moment. Gill lost his temper, threw his guitar across the stage, and stomped off, but the others continued, adjusting to his absence, as Slim Smith recalls: "They played on, the sound becoming more stripped-down and spare without George's guitar – and they sounded good."

Things became even clearer when Gill was briefly out of commission and unable to rehearse after being hospitalised with a broken leg, suffered whilst allegedly trying to filch some musical equipment. At this point, Wire began to discover their sound in earnest. If Gill had at first given them something to reject, his absence was now equally important: without his unremitting guitar solos, the others could suddenly hear what they were doing and started to be aware of the potential in it. No longer corralled in what Gilbert describes as the bustling "safari park for rhythm guitarists", the band ventured into a cleaner, less cluttered musical landscape, where the songs grew shorter and sharper, the arrangements scaled back and more accurate.

If Wire were now to move definitively in the direction that Gill's temporary absence had revealed, they would have to dump him. However, for all of his loathed musical traits, he had written most of the songs, so firing him meant they would have to come up with a set of new material. They didn't waste time: Lewis presented some lyrics to Newman, who wrote a tune – 'Lowdown' was born. As Newman explains, this would be the mode of composition for most of *Pink Flag*. "I'd get a bunch of words, usually Graham's, and an acoustic guitar and bash out tunes. I'd play them over and over and over again until I'd memorised them – because I had no means of recording them. Then I'd turn up at rehearsal and say: right, here are the new tunes – and then I'd demonstrate them."

Each song would nonetheless be credited to all four members. "We carved *Pink Flag* out from months of rehearsing," says Gilbert. "We made the songs, and it seemed the fairest way of doing it." This arrangement would stand until the 2006 reissue of the album.

During Gill's layoff, 'Three Girl Rhumba', '12XU', and several others also emerged and were rehearsed alongside the retooled Gill material. On his return, Gill struggled through rehearsals, finding little space for his guitar in the precise, disciplined reconfigurations of his songs or in the new tracks. With his leg still in plaster, he made a final appearance with Wire at the Roxy on February 24 1977. He was sacked days later – or as Newman puts it: "We left George."

I asked Gill if he would like to offer his perspective on Wire's early days

47

– something he's never done. He declined. His written response, which I don't have permission to quote, is intriguing and curiously ambivalent. On the one hand, he told me, in no uncertain terms, that he had nothing to say and wanted to be left in peace; yet, at the same time, he very definitely wanted to articulate his feelings about his experience with Wire, even taking the trouble to craft his message in a poetic form. The sense I got from his words was that, even after all these years, Gill was wounded and embittered by his dismissal. While he doesn't mention Newman or Grey, he makes a point of recounting that Gilbert brought Lewis into the band and that he and the bassist did not like each other. He recalls then starting to feel that he was being pushed out of Wire – whose name he wrote in inverted commas. Most tellingly, perhaps, he goes on to state that for him, Wire and Gilbert were synonymous. He remembers expecting to be dropped from the band and knowing that it was just a matter of waiting for Gilbert to break the news – he makes it clear that he would accept this decision only from Gilbert. Eventually, he says, Gilbert gave him the news he'd been expecting. In spite of the rather anguished tone of all this, he concluded by wishing the band well.

## A hatred of gratuitous fat and unnecessary decorative gestures

Wire's elimination of Gill's writing and playing laid the foundations for *Pink Flag*'s aesthetic of negation. If, as Lewis says, the album was "about refusal, about rejecting what we didn't want", then Gill's removal was a concrete example of Wire's minimalist impetus. This would now be central to their approach, as they concentrated on culling the inessential from all areas of their work. In the run-up to *Pink Flag*, Wire pursued that method, defining themselves on the basis of what they were *not*, rather than what they were. Their decision-making processes and creative strategies were motivated not by a desire for familiarity – an identity based on similarities with other artists – but by a desire for otherness and difference. This process was assisted by the band's naturally contrary disposition. "The only things we could agree on were the things we didn't like," notes Gilbert. "That's what held it together and made life much simpler."

Although Newman, Gilbert, Lewis, and Grey had initially defined their difference from Gill partly through their common sympathy with punk, his departure gave them the space to imagine a more radically original musical identity. Henceforth, they would strive to avoid reproducing characteristics that would identify them with punk. "We challenged the orthodoxies of the time," says Gilbert. "We were all reading from the same page in terms of rejecting things that were clichéd and knowing we were right." Lewis elaborates on this negative self-definition with some unofficial early Wire rules regarding the basics of the songs and their performance. "No solos; no decoration; when the words run out, it stops; we don't chorus out; no rocking out; keep it to the point; no Americanisms."

With Gill's material mostly excised, Wire were transformed. A handful of songs were granted a stay of execution: 'Mary Is A Dyke' and the cover of 'After Midnight', along with 'TV' and 'Feeling Called Love'. An unreleased recording from March 1977 (known by the band as *The Orange Rehearsal Tape*) featured these older tracks (except 'TV') along with a batch of new numbers. Together, these formed the bulk of Wire's 17-song Roxy set for April 1 and 2, which – in addition to another ironic cover, The Dave Clark Five's 'Glad All Over' – included ten tracks that would appear on *Pink Flag*: 'The Commercial', 'Strange', 'Brazil', 'It's So Obvious', 'Three Girl Rhumba', 'Straight Line', 'Lowdown', 'Feeling Called Love', '12XU', and 'Mr Suit'. Five months away from the making of *Pink Flag*, almost half of its 21 tracks were in place, and the band's sound was rapidly taking shape – as the Roxy recordings (released in full in 2006) demonstrate.

This foundational burst of creativity was very much down to the tunes Newman was now writing on guitar, but in performance he focused on his duties as lead singer and front man: only when the band began the *Chairs Missing* cycle of work would he resume playing guitar onstage. The April dates at the Roxy were auspicious. On Wire's previous outing, the club's co-manager and booker, Barry Jones, had deemed them "terrible" and told them to come back only when they'd improved. What he heard on April 1 was a different band, and he was impressed. That night Wire also met Mike Thorne, who was taping performances for a live compilation he was making for EMI: the infamous *The Roxy London WC2 (Jan–Apr 77)*, which would feature 'Lowdown' and '12XU'.

Thorne was an Oxford physics graduate with a diverse résumé. He'd been a tape operator on Fleetwood Mac and Deep Purple sessions at De Lane Lea studios, dabbled in journalism, and studied piano composition at the Guildhall School of Music and Drama. He'd eventually become a house producer at EMI, bringing the Sex Pistols to the label and recording demos with them in December 1976. Excited by what he saw and heard, Thorne immediately understood the paradigm-shifting potential of punk's first wave, its insubordinate philosophy speaking directly to his own dissatisfaction with the contemporary culture of record production and its institutional context.

Thorne was eager to subvert the received wisdom around the recording process and to explore working methods that avoided imposing a standardised production mould on artists. "I've always thought the production environment and the sensibility should defer to the music, rather than the other way around," he says. "I had a certain amount of musical and technical knowledge, but I was always careful not to hand that down like stone tablets – as many contemporary production priests in their white robes seemed to be doing."

In Wire, not only did Thorne recognise the best qualities of the first wave of punk that he'd previously seen in the Sex Pistols, but he was also attracted to their minimalist bent. This was an affinity he shared. "I hate listening to music with gratuitous fat on it, with unnecessary decorative gestures. That, of course, fell right in line with the sensibilities of these four people." So impressed was Thorne that he began to think about getting them signed to EMI and producing them himself. With the backing of his boss, Nick Mobbs, he brought Wire into the label's Manchester Square studios on May 4 1977 to make demos of 'The Commercial', 'Mr Suit', and a newer track, 'Pink Flag'.

Wire's evolution can be traced through two additional sessions, from May 25 and August 12, both recorded at Riverside Studio in Chiswick. The August 12 performances are tighter, the band plainly benefitting from several months of intensive practice. These two sets of recordings document ten more new tracks: 'Reuters', 'Different To Me', 'Ex-Lion Tamer', 'Mannequin', 'Champs', 'Start To Move', '106 Beats That', 'Fragile', 'Surgeon's Girl', and 'Field Day For The Sundays'. By early August, the last of Gill's numbers and some of the others' earliest efforts had been retired, and the 21-track line-up for Wire's projected first album was complete.

In the meantime, Mick Collins had become Wire's manager. Andy Czezowski, who ran the Roxy, had briefly held the position, but his plan to put the band in pink leather trousers led to a parting of the ways. Gilbert expands on their aesthetic differences: "He was very interested in the 60s approach to everything: he saw us as a pop-art project, which was not a good idea."

On Friday September 9, Wire signed a multi-album deal with EMI, joining its Harvest imprint. The following Monday, they started work at Advision Studios in London, with producer Thorne backed up by engineer Paul Hardiman and assistant engineer Ken Thomas. Hardiman had worked with Slade, The Groundhogs, Mott The Hoople, and Rick Wakeman, among others, and he'd been a mixing engineer on Eno's *Here Come The Warm Jets*.

Thomas had started out on Bowie and Queen sessions at Trident Studios, graduated to Rush and Gentle Giant recordings, and then embraced punk – engineering Snatch's 'All I Want' and working with Martin Rushent.

## Getting the best performance

If Wire weren't able to move beyond punk completely on *Pink Flag*, there is a banal yet significant reason: it was a question of musical competence. Although there was an intellectual distance between Wire and their second-wave punk contemporaries – in terms of how Wire saw themselves and how they theorised and presented their work – in 1977 they were still constrained by their skill level. Notwithstanding the innovative structural elements on several tracks, the gap between Wire's ideas and their abilities left them equipped only to make what was, for the most part, an exceptional punk-rock album.

As *The Orange Rehearsal Tape*, the Roxy recordings, and the demos show, the writing of *Pink Flag* had been finished well before the band entered Advision. The songs were in an advanced state, and the studio process involved little development of the material, which was, effectively, the band's live set. The emphasis was on doing one thing exceedingly well: performing that material.

On *Pink Flag*, Wire used their own instruments (some purchased with EMI's advance) as well as gear made available by Thorne. Lewis played his own Fender Jazz bass through an Ampeg combo, occasionally with an MXR flanger. He tried Thorne's Fender Precision but found his hands weren't big enough to manage it comfortably. Gilbert mostly used a Gibson Les Paul Pro, sundry MXR pedals, and a MusicMan 212 amp, all provided by Thorne. Newman performed his few guitar parts on a brand new, white Ovation Breadwinner. Grey had bought a second-hand Ludwig Classic kit (he selected Ludwig because it was Ginger Baker's brand of choice).

Rather than put Grey in a separate booth, Thorne had him play in the room, in order to use the studio's ambience: in addition to close-mic'ing the kit, Thorne had hung a mic to add depth and to capture the sound of the room. Looking back on Wire's work at Advision between 1977 and 1979, Newman still marvels at the acoustics. "When I listen to those albums, the loudest thing I hear is the room at Advision. It's unique." As the singer, Newman was confined to a vocal booth while the rest of the band worked together out in the open space of the studio. At the suggestion of engineer Paul Hardiman, Thorne had them wear open-ear headphones so they could hear one another and interact more naturally.

There had been some apprehension on entering Advision, a prestigious studio at the time. The Yardbirds, The Who, T.Rex, The Move, and David Bowie had worked there, and by the mid 70s it had become a second home for prog-rock artists like Gentle Giant, Yes, and ELP. "Anybody is anxious when they first go to a studio," says Lewis, "and this was definitely one of London's top-line studios. We were very nervous about it all." Gilbert agrees: "I was certainly a bit in awe when I walked into the studio. It was incredibly large and full of strange things. In one corner – with a barrier around it – there were about 100 guitars from the band working in there previously. Every type of electric guitar known to man – owned by one person."

Grey believed Wire shouldn't even have been at Advision, but that wasn't because of the studio's status: he was simply anxious about recording at all, because he thought Wire couldn't yet play well enough to make a record. The rhythm section felt the most pressure: without their foundation, nothing could be built, and this led to strained relations, with Grey and Lewis blaming each other for things not holding together. Lewis claims a drumstick was once thrown at him with such force that it lodged in the wall next to his head; Grey dismisses this story as apocryphal. Newman, by contrast, was not fazed by the studio or the recording process, taking it all in his stride. "It just seemed that it was part of what you do. I thought some of it was tedious. I started to become more interested in what was going on on the other side of the glass than what was going on where I was."

At the start of the sessions, Thorne had the band run through the album material several times, to get them accustomed to the surroundings and the equipment. "We just played and played nonstop," recalls Gilbert. "It felt like two days, and I was totally convinced that we'd finished the album. I said: you must have got it by now – but no … because obviously I was unfamiliar with studio protocols and techniques. It seemed like we'd done it. We were never going to play that well again!"

Gilbert, Grey, and Lewis feel they first began to attain musical proficiency via the extensive drilling of the sessions, which found them working at the edge of their ability. "*Pink Flag* is where I really started to learn to play the guitar," says Gilbert. "It was just repetition, over and over again until we got a good take." This is critical for understanding *Pink Flag*: although it's a studio recording, it's also essentially a live record. "*Pink Flag* is still pretty much the sound of the songs as we played them live, with some textural beefing-up," says Newman. Therefore, while there was a traditional process of addition and subtraction, as parts were redone and replaced, multi-tracked and overdubbed (up to 12 guitars on 'Strange'), it remains that *Pink Flag* was the product of an effort to document Wire's live sound in its optimum form. "With *Pink Flag*, we were desperate and really happy to basically get the best performances we'd ever done," Lewis says. "That's what we were trying to do: just get the best performance."

Having Wire's material written and rehearsed before recording began chimed with Thorne's working philosophy. "In the studio, without an audience and with little feedback, it's important to generate performance excitement: much harder if you're simultaneously having to put together basic mechanics. I thought that getting songs rehearsed and coherent before recording time was very important. Also: if you go into the studio and write, generally getting it together, it dilutes the excitement of being in that intense environment. Recording should be a big event. You only do it once for the Preservation Society, and the adrenalin should be flowing." Insofar as Thorne's methodology on *Pink Flag* centred on the unmediated simplicity of live playing, it actually resonates with the older notions of rock authenticity and essentialism at the heart of second-wave punk. Ironically, for all of punk's suspicions about Wire's inauthenticity, the album was made in a conventional manner, in that the recording was geared toward achieving an authentic sound: the sound of their live presence.

But while the emphasis was on performance, it wasn't for ideological reasons. It was a case of 'needs must'. Exploration of the studio as an instrument wasn't yet on Wire's agenda; being able to play their instruments well enough to record the songs was the priority. With experience, increased confidence, and greater competence, this would change radically on their second album, which makes problematic the very notion of authenticity: on *Chairs Missing*, Wire began treating the studio as a playground in which to expand the sonic horizons of the material and to translate their ideas into more adventurous musical constructions. (There were some minor instances of studio experimentation on *Pink Flag*, but these were conceived and initiated by the producer alone.)

## A body of work to be heard in full context

Some other, more specific production choices also bound *Pink Flag* to its time. Thorne singles out the way the vocals were mixed, which was less innovative than some of the work he and the band had been doing on the actual vocal arrangements. Although it's rarely recognised, *Pink Flag*'s approach to vocals was slightly atypical of punk, and even with Newman's Mockney shoutiness, Wire were more inventive with regard to this aspect of their sound than they're often given credit for. They use vocals as texture (the criss-crossed radio chatter on 'Reuters'), they incorporate harmonies ('Mannequin', 'Fragile'), and they explore the interplay of backing and lead voices ('Ex-Lion Tamer'). "Wire always thought vocally," says Thorne, "which wasn't at all true of other groups around this time." However, the movement away from punk in some of those arrangements was not matched by a similar direction in the vocal production and recording. Thorne is well aware of this, but he does think that *Pink Flag* fares better than *Never Mind The Bollocks* in this respect. "I think Chris [Thomas, producer of *Never Mind The Bollocks*] had a very clear idea in his mind about what a punk record should sound like, and I'm afraid the Sex Pistols record sounds like a punk record: you can't hear the words, it's just an assault of guitars, and it sounds very dated because of that. On *Pink Flag*, I was certainly guilty of under-mixing the vocals, which was very much of the time, although you can hear the words."

He feels, too, that some of the album's guitar sound is a little dated. "I think the chainsaw guitars on that particular record also sound very much of their time – unlike the similar instruments on *Chairs Missing*. But they sound distinctive, and that's because, in fact, I got most of the guitar sounds at the amp, and there was very little processing or equalising in the control room. Everything you hear probably sounded like that just coming out of the amp. I got less dogmatic by the time we got to *Chairs Missing*, but it felt like the appropriate approach at the time."

Although Wire's playing skills were still quite basic when they came to record *Pink Flag*, this hadn't stopped them from generating a great deal of material. They had around 30 songs from which to choose, and they were most excited by newer tracks that were starting to take them in a fresh direction, away from the mainly one-dimensional, accelerated pieces that would characterise a lot of *Pink Flag*. They had already written 'I Feel Mysterious Today' (which would appear on *Chairs Missing*) – obviously a different sonic proposition from the work they had done thus far – and there was a feeling on Newman's part that Wire were already beyond *Pink Flag* by the time they made it.

Thorne was alert to this. Before embarking at Advision, he had started to see how their tracks could be assembled into a unified statement, and his ears told him the newest songs did not belong on *Pink Flag*, as he envisaged it. He realised he had to move quickly to map out the album's contents with the band, locking in the material before they ditched it in favour of songs that shifted the focus. While Thorne's decision to hold back the newest songs had to do with preserving *Pink Flag*'s integrity as an organic whole, it also emphasised the punk side of the record's identity, as it meant retaining tracks that the band felt they had outgrown and were ready to jettison.

EMI had wanted Wire to concentrate on singles. Newman wasn't so sure. "We wanted to make an album. We didn't see ourselves as a singles band." Gilbert concurs, stressing that, in contrast with punk's ostensibly nihilist no-futurism, Wire had an eye on longevity. "I said: well, what happens after that? We'd seen what happened to other people – being stuck forever with their single, and that was it, the blueprint for the rest of their lives. It's like a coffin of your own making. We were keen to make the relationship work with EMI without actually engaging too much with the corporate rock'n'roll aspect." Above all, Gilbert saw Wire's work not as individual songs but as a collection of pieces belonging together, framed as an album: "We knew we had a body of work which ought to be heard in full context."

With 21 tracks in mind, Thorne devised the running order before starting work. The sequence was designed to balance the sometimes divergent sounds and structures with an overall cohesiveness – creating a narrative that accommodated continuity and discontinuity, similarity and difference, ultimately presenting the songs as a single piece of work. Lewis is still impressed by the results. "Although there are 21 tracks, it's remarkable how unhurried the whole thing feels. It feels so inevitable and so well paced. Mike's sequencing is extremely good. Now, one can't imagine the songs being put together in any other way."

While the selection of tracks to be included on *Pink Flag* may have emphasised the more standard punk-rock fare, the running order underscores the record's unique elements. 'Reuters', for instance, isn't your usual punk-rock opener. It's a slower, building number that draws in the listener and announces, unequivocally, how Wire at their most innovative differ from their contemporaries. Meanwhile, 'The Commercial' may be an unremarkable instrumental, but its function, derived from its placement, is key: as an intermission, it links the two original vinyl sides, reinforcing the album's construction as a musical suite, as a complete, linear experience – not something to be dipped into at random.

### The same but different, different but the same
Compared to the largely monolithic punk albums of 1977, *Pink Flag* boasts a relative diversity of styles: mid-tempo, melodic pop ('Mannequin', 'Fragile'); super-fast Ramonic thrashes ('Brazil'); tracks that finish before they've started ('Field Day For The Sundays'); slower numbers accentuating

menace as opposed to all-out assault ('Lowdown', 'Reuters', 'Strange'); and even an instrumental.

Much has been made of the extremely compressed numbers. Five tracks under 50 seconds ('Field Day For The Sundays' is a mere 28-seconds long) test how much abbreviation a song can bear and still be recognisable as a song. However, the conceit is shallow: beyond brevity, there's little in the music to distinguish these numbers from the mass of short-and-fast tracks churned out in 1977. Newman is clear on this: "It's only because they're so short that they're remarkable. If those songs had gone on longer, they'd have just sounded like standard punk songs. You'd have seen them for what they were." Ironically, such tracks are one of the record's biggest legacies, influencing myriad bands who would self-identify as punk, from Minutemen and Minor Threat onward – with ever-diminishing returns.

A conventional drums-bass-guitar-shouty-vocals configuration dominates *Pink Flag*, apart from a few idiosyncratic touches – all but inaudible güiro on 'Three Girl Rhumba', which still offends Grey's anti-percussion sensibilities; flute (played by Kate Lukas) on 'Strange', plus an elaborate tape loop and Thorne's improvised percussion (a fire-escape door frame); and some Fender Rhodes smuggled into 'Reuters' by Thorne. What we mostly hear is straightforward, albeit excellent, punk rock: 'It's So Obvious', 'Brazil', 'Mr Suit', 'Different To Me', 'Field Day For The Sundays', 'Start To Move', and 'Champs' all reflect the spirit of their day more than distort or subvert it. In turn, some tracks that do depart from the punk template fail to break much new ground, in spite of Wire's best efforts not to recycle or repeat. Two of the better pop songs, 'Mannequin' and 'Fragile', sound slightly retro; 'Feeling Called Love', while no less memorable, is 'Wild Thing' meets 'Louie Louie'; and 'Strange' owes something to The Velvet Underground's 'Sister Ray'.

By their own account, Wire did pursue some experimentation in aspects of the writing and execution of the music on *Pink Flag*. The chord structure of '106 Beats That' was based on the first letters of the names of train stations Newman passed through on a journey into London from Watford; 'Pink Flag' imagines the sound of 'Johnny B. Goode' reduced to two chords; and '12XU' was an attempt to write a song with no real music in it – as well as an experiment with speed. "It was almost sport to try and play as fast as possible," Gilbert comments. "What's the fastest one can play, and what would happen to something, what would it be like, if it was insanely fast? It becomes an almost abstract thing."

These experimental frameworks and conceptual springboards aside,

*Pink Flag*'s most enduring tracks are those that eschew punk's one-dimensional, one-speed, one-mood uniformity and instead display variations in structure and tempo and pay closer attention to space, texture, and atmosphere. 'Reuters' and 'Pink Flag' are two standouts in that respect, discarding punk's smash-and-grab sound and achieving an epic quality, despite running to less than four minutes each. Their more expansive, varied sensibility underlines Wire's eagerness to deviate from the claustrophobic punk norm: rather than cram songs from start to finish with all their constitutive parts firing simultaneously, they probe different spatial possibilities.

Although Newman feels that "a lot of *Pink Flag* has the same rolling smoothness that a lot of punk rock had", some of the album's musical innovation is located in its modest incorporation of non-rock, dance-oriented rhythms. It does so in a way that anticipates post-punk's break with the hegemony of the straight-ahead rock beat that dominated punk. The droning 'Lowdown' is, in essence, a funk number, rendered at iceberg speed. 'Three Girl Rhumba' is more immediately striking. It's not 'angular', but it does have something of the stop-start jerkiness that became a post-punk leitmotif. Newman might have preferred a more dignified legacy for his work, but Elastica's eventual recycling of the song's signature riff and its use in advertisements nevertheless attest to its brilliance as a piece of pop music with timeless appeal.

While *Pink Flag*'s originality is writ large on numbers such as 'Reuters', 'Lowdown', 'Three Girl Rhumba', and the title track, its inventiveness is also found in some of the more subtle details of song construction. Wire's experimentation with verse-chorus structures and with framing offers two fascinating instances of this. The beginning and the end of a track, with their familiar, traditional musical and structural motifs, can be seen as a song's basic framing devices. Wire's attentiveness to these components grew out of an early concern simply to execute the material accurately: being able to start and stop cleanly and effectively – something at which they excelled, against the grain of punk's ragged, sloppier attitude. An emphasis on beginning and ending might seem obvious, a necessity for a band learning to play, but Wire's approach to these elements occasionally manipulated the frame in ways that asked intriguing questions about the nature and identity of the song.

One example is the way Wire use the count-in in 'Surgeon's Girl' ("*un-deux-trois-quatre*") to play with the song's boundaries. Studio recordings sometimes include the count-in as a signifier of 'live' authenticity, as if giving the listener a glimpse into the moment when the song was performed for the recording. Normally, a count-in also foregrounds the performing artist's authoritative presence, showing his or her control over the instant at which the song will actually begin. Instead, the count-in is included here in a way that disturbs the arbitrary construction of an inside and an outside to the song – what is and what isn't part of the performance. This disruption results from the fact that the track doesn't even start with the count, which comes seven seconds into the number, after the guitar intro. Its inclusion after the song has begun also demonstrates that this customary signifier of rock authenticity is just another artificial facet of the performance, something that's further highlighted by having the count in French.

'Pink Flag' also undermines the clarity of where the song begins, as well as where it ends, unsettling the conventions of starting and finishing. 'Pink Flag' opens with 25 seconds of drum rolls and false starts before the guitar crashes in. It builds to the repeated "how many dead or alive" line after 1:30, and by 2:00 it begins to give the impression of winding down. However, that closing sensation is sustained for a minute and a half with a sequence of false endings – climaxing at 2:48, then continuing for another minute and mirroring the way the track began, with more false endings over the last 45 seconds. Consequently, more than half of the song is in fact the frame.

Wire's playful subversiveness is also evident in the treatment of verses and chorus. This is the case with 'Ex-Lion Tamer', whose formal innovation compensates for its unoriginal lyrical content. There appears to be a typical verse-chorus demarcation, but the distinction is unstable. The choruses are longer and more complex than the verses; in turn, the verses display the properties generally associated with choruses. This inverts the verse-chorus hierarchy: verses are usually where the song's meaning is constructed; choruses tend only to reinforce the content of the verses – punctuating the space between verses, they repeat and reiterate but contain little that expands the song's meaning or moves the song forward. But 'Ex-Lion Tamer' collapses that hierarchical relationship and disrupts the chorus's function as a framing device within the song.

'Straight Line' offers a different take on the verse-chorus relationship. The song answers the question: can a song with only one verse still have a chorus? The repeated line, "oh it's unlust and the one-dimensional boy" sounds unmistakably like a chorus. The music takes a distinctive turn: chord changes make the line instantly catchy, and the song swells, stressing the importance of this moment. Key to this effect is the *all-together-now*, sing-along feel, imparted by the layering of Newman's vocals and Lewis joining on backing vocals. But this line certainly doesn't fulfil the normal function of a chorus, which is to serve essentially as icing between the layers of the cake (the verses): once it has kicked in at the end of the first and only verse, it is simply repeated for the entire remainder of the song. Whereas 'Ex-Lion Tamer' inverts the verse-chorus structure, so that one becomes the other, 'Straight Line' all but abandons the verse component.

## Mending the fridge

Although the more innovative song structures on the band's first album reflected a unique, experimental artistic vision, the overall sound hovered between that vision and the less interesting vestiges of punk rock. Wire's *presentation* of their music was arguably more consistently original and more fully developed than the music itself. The anti-rock, minimalist aesthetic that had impressed Thorne was emphasised in Wire's post-Gill gigs in 1977, as they spurned the physical, behavioural, and musical gestures typical of rock's live rituals. Their performances were out of place in the context of punk's riotous assemblies, which regardless of some unprecedented attitude, a new dance, and new audience etiquette such as spitting, did little to challenge rock-concert protocol. (Wire encountered spitting at its most virulent among Stranglers fans – as if opening for The Stranglers weren't unpleasant enough. "It was rather silly," says Gilbert, "not to mention unhygienic.") Onstage, Wire weren't chaotic or shambolic, they were generally uncommunicative (abstaining from banter and clichéd band-speak), and they didn't encourage any form of audience participation. Most of all, they thought about the visual impression they were creating and maintained a clean, clear stage: there was no mess or clutter, they avoided drinking and smoking during sets, and they kept lighting simple and sparse – harsh white light was preferred, enhancing the austere, distanced feel.

An attention to choreography and presentation gave Wire's performances the air of modernist theatre spectacles: affect was eradicated; movement abrupt and limited (Newman occasionally holding mannered poses or moving his head like an automaton); and the band-members didn't brandish or play their instruments in a showy, rock'n'roll way. Instead, they seemed slightly removed from them – as well as from the noise they made – in contrast with the hackneyed rockist tendency to make guitars and mics a part of the body. Gilbert, for example, remained immobile, absolutely focused on his instrument, as far from a guitar hero as you could get. The detached, almost severe character of Wire's physical presence became a motif as reviewers likened them to robots or mannequins and played up their mechanical, dispassionate demeanour. As Newman confirms, this was not coincidental but devised with the aim of differentiating Wire from other acts. "When Wire started, we had this thing of not moving at all onstage, because the whole idea was to be as un-rock as possible. We didn't want to look like a bunch of rockers." Gilbert echoes this: "We didn't want our things to look like anybody else's."

Because of Wire's singular approach to performance and visual style, early audiences anticipating punk rock were disappointed and confused. Gilbert was aware that Wire didn't give the punters what they wanted. "It's their Friday night. They go out to see a punk band, jump about, scream and spit – that was the orthodoxy of the time. People coming on as if they'd come to mend the fridge wasn't what audiences were looking for."

In addition to Wire's physical bearing and their inexpressive stage presence, clothing choices played a part in crafting a spectacle that was un-punk and, indeed, un-rock. Lewis remembers that restricting the colour and style of their stage clothes was crucial to the "whole conceptual angle of what [the performance] should look like". Wire were mostly a sober, smart, monochromatic affair, their clothes contrasting with punk's multi-coloured, messy accoutrements. "Sing If You're Glad To Be Grey" ran the Tom Robinson pun in the headline accompanying the *NME*'s November 1977 review of *Pink Flag*. Gilbert stresses the role of colour in the general scheme of the project: "Plain, dark clothing evolved because we didn't want any distractions. We didn't want people looking at us and thinking we were a rock band." Wire's efforts to divorce themselves from punk at the level of visual coding were successful: live photos from 1977 reveal practically nothing in their clothing or appearance tying them to that moment. Even Newman's father noticed this. "My dad always said that what he liked about Wire was the way we looked: very smart. We didn't look scruffy – like punks."

While Wire never emulated what had become, by mid 1977, a de rigueur punk style, their stage attire did extend to a few theatrical elements that stood out amid the homogeneity. Newman, for instance, sometimes performed barefoot, wearing a surgical gown provided by Angela Conway – "an escaped mental patient look," according to Gilbert, who concedes that his own stylistic experiments may not have been wholly sound. "I had this ridiculous affectation of wearing ballet shoes onstage … with pink bed-socks. Also, Graham's girlfriend had this really weird jacket, which looked like a Friesian cow kind of effect. I was rather taken with that and borrowed it."

The role of women around Wire in the late 70s shouldn't be underestimated, particularly as they contributed to the shaping of the band's image. "My girlfriend at the time [Conway] was instrumental in dressing Colin up," says Gilbert. Newman confirms this: "In the early days, Angela used to dress me – I had outfits!" Also important was Newman's first wife, the photographer Annette Green, who taught at Watford and had studied at the Royal College of Art as a contemporary of Zandra Rhodes and David Hockney. In the 60s, she had photographed John Lennon, her work appearing in *Vogue* and elsewhere. She was responsible for the images used on Wire's first two albums, as well as for numerous early, iconic band photographs.

The composition of Wire's live sets was another factor that subverted expectations, as they often gave preference to new, unrecorded tracks. Notwithstanding punk's ostensible rejection of the music industry and its ideology, most of Wire's early audiences wanted to hear the records they'd bought. They didn't question the convention of gigs as a showcase for 'the record' and were unhappy when presented with new songs instead of familiar numbers. Gilbert also recalls the band starting to experiment with running orders, disrupting the audience's relationship with the flow of the music and frustrating its sustained enjoyment. "Sometimes we'd do anti-sequences where it would be a total bloody disappointment at the end: no payoff of any description." A more extreme example of this distancing technique, and the denial of identification and pleasure, was the performance of the shortest, fastest songs, which made it hard to do punk's 'dance', the pogo. Ending almost as soon as they'd begun, such songs weren't conducive to any kind of dance. Wire enjoyed this. "It was very amusing," says Gilbert. "It was a good dynamic. I don't think it was deliberate, but it was delicious to observe."

Despite the construction of a sense of remove from their own musical material, Wire took their performances very seriously. And although they were working with meagre abilities in 1977, they always endeavoured to play with discipline and accuracy. This earned them some suspicion. When *The Roxy London WC2 (Jan–Apr 77)* came out, the quality of their contributions prompted claims that the tracks had been redone in the studio. That suspicion of Wire's more disciplined style came through in early reviews and features that, in their references to automata or showroom dummies, conflated the band's tight performances with their affectless stage persona.

In an *NME* review, Phil McNeill reports an audience member at a late-1977 gig heckling Wire as "smooth twats" and "posers". McNeill agrees with that sentiment, but only insofar as the comment actually gets to the heart of a fundamental, positive difference between Wire and others. "The band *is* smooth compared to, say, the Pistols or The Clash ... there was none of the raggedness which seems almost a vital ingredient of the punk vision. Wire respect their compositions above all else, and adhere strictly to structure." Newman elaborates: "Just because you have limited means, you don't have to be shambling. I never got that as an aesthetic. Why would you make records that sounded like bumbling? For me, it doesn't matter how basic it is – it's that it's cleanly executed. So it was just logical to do it like that. *To do our best*." Gilbert makes the same point, stressing the importance of hard work in the creative process: "We always wanted to be absolutely perfect, like a machine. I think we had a good work ethic: the only way you can create new things is to work at it."

Audiences tended not to appreciate this, however, and often took against Wire. "The abiding memory is of bewilderment or outright hostility," says Gilbert. "We didn't look like other punk bands so we couldn't be a punk band, which was fine by us. Yet we were playing very fast, noisy, loud stuff. I think the audiences often got very, very confused – confused to the point where they started throwing bottles of beer, glasses of beer. The waste! Up North, it seemed to be something of a sport."

Much of that hostility to the detachment Wire projected goes back to punk's paradoxical demand for authenticity. On one level, punk was all about style, surface and image: constructions, in other words, not essential characteristics. Identity was something you could assemble and change; it was fluid and open to multiple possibilities. This is what Gilbert liked about punk's early laboratory, but during the more populist second wave, experimentation solidified into a single style; musically, it remained aligned with R&B and with that form's values as pure, honest, unmediated musical expression. Wire were deemed phony and inauthentic because they built distance into their performance and shunned the usual rock signifiers.

## As modern as it could be

Wire's rejection of rock, and of punk rock in particular, is present in their artwork and even their choice of name. Record sleeves and band names have always offered the most explicit displays of rock ideology as they're inextricably linked with the construction of image. Wire foregrounded their shift away from punk with the reductionist, minimalist aesthetic of their record sleeves – and with the name itself.

By the time of punk, there was an established lineage of band names reflecting white rock music's traditionally Romantic, male ideology, emphasising authenticity, creativity, self-expression, individuality, and the notion of the artist pitted against society. This comes across in the preponderance of names connoting an outsider or outlaw sensibility. Many punk band's names embodied that same Romantic narrative: The Damned, Subway Sect, Generation X, and The Unwanted all suggest (largely) urban alienation and nihilism. Some, however, tapped into the surface-oriented postmodern moment. The Adverts, The Cortinas, and X-Ray Spex were recycled from consumer culture, while other found-names were lifted straight from the institutional and journalistic language of the UK's economic and political crises (Social Security, 999, Dole Q, The Clash).

What these variants have in common is that they refer to vivid, specific phenomena. 'Wire' was different. The name was unusual for the period in that it was chosen for its relative lack of connotations and for its lack of association with a concrete image. 'Wire' is generic, its metallic referent evoking, if anything, the absence of a discrete identity. If there is any connotation, it underscores Wire's self-contained nature, directing the focus inward, toward their music, and encapsulating their pared-down, hard-edged, industrious ethos. All this was communicated by the band's plain, generic logo, as Gilbert explains: "I thought the word itself was powerful enough. So the logo should have no real personality at all. It should be as basic and simple as possible – and as modern as it could be."

Record sleeves offer a more elaborate canvas than band names for the expression of rock ideology. British punk's artwork was rich in unsubtle signifiers of youth, attitude, rebellion, alienation, and anti-authoritarianism. Some of this might have been shocking, but it was still, in effect, a cultural narrative that had existed since the 50s. Wire resisted this rock imagery: their early artwork established no connection with the contexts of popular music or youth culture. In fact, they discarded realism entirely. The sleeve of 'Mannequin', their first single, is a perfect example: it's a harshly lit Polaroid of a naked dummy, its chest adorned with a heart-shaped appliqué, standing in a dingy room (in Lewis's West Kensington flat) by a bed containing a silhouetted form. "We wanted something inexplicable in the picture, possibly slightly sinister," remembers Gilbert, "so Angela got under the covers of the bed."

And if punk artwork emphasised cheapness and disposability in theme or design, Wire's first three abstract album covers were timeless objects in themselves. Clean, austere, spacious, and mysterious, they gave scant indication that they were the sleeves of rock records, especially compared to most punk-era covers. They have more kinship with fine art than with standard album art. *Pink Flag* and *Chairs Missing* feature stylised, framed

63

images, while *154* recalls modernist canvases by Kandinsky, Mondrian, and Malevich. These covers were objects to be contemplated and appreciated – almost revered, although this becomes playful and ironic on the sleeves of some of the band's singles, given the kind of objects represented: a caged leopard ('Outdoor Miner'), for example, and, most memorably, a topiary swimmer ('Our Swimmer').

The idea for *Pink Flag*'s cover had existed for a while, although it didn't arise in any conscious planning: Gilbert and Lewis had each stumbled on the same image, having independently doodled similar flags and poles in their notebooks. On discovering this synchronicity, they knew they had the image for the album jacket. They came upon the real counterpart to their sketches, by chance, on Plymouth Hoe: a flagless flagpole matching their drawings, which was later photographed by Annette Green. David Dragon at EMI prepared the sleeve, using Green's image; Gilbert and Lewis explained the effect they wanted. The key idea was that the final image should make no pretence of photo-realism and should instead convey artificiality, so the sky was airbrushed pale blue, the flag was painted in as flat colour, and a negative frame was painted around the image. The decision was also made to omit the album title: the signifier was unnecessary as the object was depicted there in all its (artificial) glory.

The front cover of *Pink Flag* is emblematic of the way Wire would approach much of their artwork over the years, favouring constructed images and deconstructing realist representation. Not surprisingly, the band-members are absent from the front of their studio albums, featuring on sleeves only in a typically limited, idiosyncratic fashion. On the back of *Pink Flag*, individual black-and-white photos were a compromise with EMI, who insisted Wire appear somewhere. Even so, they introduced a subversive touch, reducing all biographical information to names, role in the band and a single, generic physical characteristic to identify each individual: weight (Lewis), eye colour (Gilbert), hair colour (Newman), height (Grey). That these features couldn't necessarily be discerned from the monochrome images further deconstructed rock's cult of personality. They removed all personality; the record wasn't about them.

### Keeping it unreal

*Pink Flag*'s original artwork also incorporated the song lyrics, reproduced on the inner sleeve. Few punk albums included lyric sheets, and this indicated the weight Wire gave their words. "The lyrics were important," asserts Newman. "They weren't just *I-love-you-baby* rock'n'roll. And we didn't see ourselves as being another punk band. We were important. We were up there with the greats. They had lyrics on their records, so we thought we should too." Printing them on the sleeve stressed that they were part of the artistic whole, not a throwaway supplementary component. But while the words could be read and considered, Lewis differentiated between rock lyrics and literary verse. Knowing that the two should never be confused, and feeling his work belonged to neither category, he identified his words in detached, functional (and vaguely theoretical) terms, as "texts". The format of their reproduction – in non-verse blocks without line breaks – graphically distinguished them from poetry and song lyrics.

There's an aesthetic link between *Pink Flag*'s artwork and its lyrical content, in that the strongest lyrics – like the front cover – reject the basic tenets of conventional representation dominating punk in 1977. Punk lyrics generally focused on unmediated energy and unfiltered expression. They rarely strayed far from one-dimensional realism and psychological verisimilitude, heavy on the first-person pronoun (singular or plural) or addressed to a generic 'you'. As Jon Savage notes, the effect was frequently akin to "a rather bad teenage diary". That mode is largely absent from *Pink Flag*, as it avoids literal renderings of the everyday and the direct, unambiguous articulation of emotion or opinion.

This difference is rooted in Wire's questioning of the terms of realist representation. Whereas second-wave punk lyrics were mainly predicated on a belief in the transparency of meaning and the unmediated presence of an authentic voice, Wire's words were grounded in a contrary set of assumptions: that meaning is never automatic and transparent and that songs are representations and constructions – not naturally occurring expressions of the self. If punk's raison d'être by 1977 was to keep it real and authentic, Wire's lyrics show a conviction that – because of the complex nature of the relationship between words and reality – the only option is to keep it unreal. In this sense, Lewis's preference for the term 'texts' is apposite, as a designation that foregrounds an awareness of their identity as constructed, open-ended linguistic and semiotic patterns.

Wire's lyrics (especially Newman's and Lewis's) regularly emphasise their own artificiality: they don't look outward at the world but turn in on themselves. Often fragmented, impressionistic, and elliptical, they appear less concerned with the representation of reality than with the ambiguity of language itself. The lyrics play with the notion that reality is not an unproblematic, objectively comprehensible matter and that language is unpredictable and unstable. The slipperiness of language is illustrated by *Pink*

*Flag*'s '106 Beats That': this was an experiment in writing a song with exactly one hundred syllables, or beats, but Lewis ended up with 106 – hence the title. (Or so he thought: the lyrics as printed on the record sleeve have 107 syllables.) In certain cases, the song titles alone on *Pink Flag* play a part in eluding meaning: ranging from single adjectives adrift from nouns ('Strange', 'Fragile') to phrases that double as cryptic crossword clues ('106 Beats That', 'Ex-Lion Tamer'), they reveal little of what the track might be 'about'.

Many critics in 1977 failed to grasp the pleasure Wire took in the open-ended processes of language. As a result, few engaged with the way the lyrics functioned; most instead concentrated, as rock critics have customarily done, on the least interesting question: what do the lyrics mean? They were hung up on this dry interpretative methodology, failing to see that the words were often about the process of producing meaning, not a specific, straightforward meaning. Since the words didn't offer access to an easily identifiable message, they were seen simply as obtuse, difficult, bewildering, and 'weird'. Symptomatic of this was Greil Marcus's observation, in his *Rolling Stone* review of *Pink Flag*, that "the lyrics seem less revelatory than teasing or maybe just pointless". By failing to consider more interesting questions – how the lyrics were constructed, how they worked – critics overlooked a pivotal aspect of Wire's aesthetic, an ingredient contributing to their songs' sense of otherness, and moreover, an element highlighting their process-oriented approach.

In rejecting "*I-love-you-baby* rock'n'roll" cliché, Wire also expanded rock (and particularly punk)'s narrow vocabulary. There are stirrings of this on *Pink Flag*: "uneasy", "climate", "unhealthy", "to project", "relegation", "correspondent", "wrench", "slivers", "fleeting", "to seed" – these aren't the sort of words you'd routinely hear on records by the likes of Sham 69, The Lurkers, The Vibrators, or Generation X. This tendency would become more pronounced after *Pink Flag*, as *Chairs Missing* and *154* continued both to raise the level of discourse and to show that the most un-rock words or phrases could feature in a rock song ("becalmed", "Plimsoll Line", "captionless", "prehensile", "servile", "gentile", "inference", "anaesthetised", "denuded", "silverfish", "serpentine", "divergent", "filament", "amphibious", "contrition", "calibrate", "anatomical", "*Nouvel Observateur*", "precipitous", "symphonic", "*noblesse oblige*", "cartologist", and "graph").

However, while the lyrical content is one of *Pink Flag*'s more inventive dimensions, it does keep one foot firmly in 1977. Newman's ode to Mick Collins – 'Mr Suit', an accusatory rant notable only for its spirited use of the f-word – could be a page torn from one of Savage's "teenage diaries". Two other songs run into difficulties when they tackle a prominent punk theme: the media. All punk bands had an anti-TV song. 'Ex-Lion Tamer' is Wire's, its simplistic critique of the link between mass media, consumerism, and alienation accentuated by its "stay glued to your TV set" refrain. Similarly, 'Field Day For The Sundays' is a run-of-the-mill indictment of tabloid journalism. And 'It's So Obvious' might have been unique for the time, as a meta-punk song about getting beyond punk, but its theme also anchors it permanently in 1977.

## The other side of the glass

*Pink Flag* remains one of the most striking and memorable albums of 1977, despite being a mixed bag that mingled the punk rock of its day with much more innovative music. In retrospect, its position has been comparatively weakened by the arrival over the next two years of *Chairs Missing* and *154*, with their incredible strength and diversity. Ultimately, though, it's difficult to see how, at the time, *Pink Flag* could have been a more fully realised statement of Wire's originality – given the band-members' limited technical sophistication, both musically and in recording and production.

Mike Thorne's role in helping bring Wire to the point of *Pink Flag* was significant. Certainly, some of his decisions were instrumental in aligning the record with the sound of 1977: his pre-studio exclusion of Wire's new, forward-looking tracks and his decision to record the band in a very traditional manner undoubtedly contributed to *Pink Flag*'s period feel. But these may have been absolutely the right choices for Wire at that point. Thorne was the most able musician and arranger present, as well as the most experienced studio technician, and he made choices that were pragmatic and logical in light of the band's limitations and lack of experience. The object of the exercise was to record a debut album making the best use of the available material and talent, and Thorne knew that *Pink Flag* was the best album Wire were capable of at the time – and he was well aware that some of it was clearly *of its time*. But he also knew there would be a second album, a chance to develop the new material and explore the ideas and territory that he and the band had already started to glimpse.

The producer created the conditions for Wire to deliver to the best of their ability, as Lewis notes: "He gave us the discipline to follow good habits, and he was good at getting us to realise more potential than we thought we had." That Thorne was also able to help with arrangements, tightening and strengthening them, was something that Grey valued. "Mike's knowledge of music meant he could interpret what we were doing into something that was musical enough to record. He knew a lot about music that we didn't, and we benefited from that and also from [his knowledge of] the way that songs are put together in a studio. That was new to me. I'm sure it was new to everybody – just the possibilities that a 24-track studio offered. We couldn't have done it without him." Gilbert agrees, praising both Thorne's studio expertise and his "musical imagination", acknowledging him "as an incredibly creative force" in constructing the band's "sonic landscape".

Although Newman, like his bandmates, has also spoken in past interviews about the vital role played by Thorne, more recently he's revised his opinion. He now feels that the producer's importance has been exaggerated by fans and critics, especially those who, he believes, perceive Thorne as the genius who turned Wire's rudimentary, amateur efforts into an iconic record. "He got a reputation of being a George Martin figure, but my gut feeling is that Mike was over-credited. People thought: oh, they can't have done it, Mike must have done it. That idea needs to be taken away. That it was all down to him is not true."

Newman's urge to set the record straight about Thorne's part in creating *Pink Flag* reflects a general impulse of his to revise the narrative of Wire's development, particularly with regard to re-evaluating the contribution made by their producers. His comments aren't a criticism of Thorne's work per se, but when it comes to Wire's other producers, Newman does consistently express reservations about their work. That tendency – along with the evidence of his own early ambitions (that interest in "what was going on on the other side of the glass") – points to a persistent undercurrent in Wire's story: Newman's desire for the producer's chair, which was finally realised during the *Send* era.

If the producer directs and guides a project according to his vision and has considerable say in its final identity, it's little wonder that this role should be so coveted – especially in bands composed of individuals with strong artistic personalities. But whereas Newman aspired to this position, Gilbert and Lewis always favoured having an independent, objective producer in order to avoid the problems that would ensue if one of the band were to assume that responsibility. As it happened, even with external producers, Wire would experience extensive fragmentation. The fault lines would start to show on the third album, as the group settled into factions with conflicting views of Wire's goals and how to achieve them. This loss of a shared vision and the resulting tension would challenge Gilbert, Grey, Lewis, and Newman in the 80s above all, leading to a succession of albums about whose merits they are still divided.

Both Newman's desire to produce Wire and his retrospective unhappiness with others' production work are also symptomatic of a larger struggle over creative control within the group that now colours his feelings about its past. In interviews for this book, Newman offered a frequently negative perspective on most phases of the band's activity, primarily its output from 1985 to 1991. He chronicled his frustration with the ways he felt that he – as the principal songwriter – was prevented from setting Wire's direction and from realising his conception of Wire's creative identity. Bearing in mind his deep dissatisfaction (which actually prompted him to leave the band during the making of *The Ideal Copy*), it's hardly a surprise that he should now be critical of some of Wire's past endeavours. His at times brutal reassessment – questioning others' contributions as well as disavowing songs and even the odd album – indicates that there is more at stake here than the familiar perfectionism that leads artists to value current projects over previous work.

It's possible to see the central story of Wire as a long, uneasy, fertile balancing act between the competing forces of Newman and Gilbert – until Newman eventually prevailed. Thus Newman's narrative, with its negative appraisal of so many aspects of their career, seems motivated in large part by an anxiety to underline his sense of Wire's greater strength and health post-2004 – ie, after Gilbert's departure. For Newman, that was the moment when he could finally assume his rightful position in the band. With the emergence then of another version of Wire, he took the reins at almost every level: as producer, as creative director, as main songwriter, as label boss, as overseer of the group's business affairs, and as chief Wire spokesperson in interviews. It's not an overstatement to say that without his ambition and resolve, Wire would not have continued to exist and thrive.

With Newman's position consolidated, the tenor and thrust of his responses during our interviews suggested that the focus of his efforts now is a retroactive attempt to shape the way in which Wire's entire story is told. In contrast with his bandmates, who appeared less interested in establishing such narratives, Newman seemed to approach the context of this book – a project that looks back and seeks to evaluate Wire's work over time – as an opportunity to frame the group's past in terms of his perspective as the prime creative force, one that was for too long unappreciated and marginalised.

## CHAPTER 3
# 1977–78

### Two drummers *and* a percussionist

In November 1977, EMI sent Wire out on the road as the support act for American pantomime rockers The Tubes, who were touring the UK on the back of their *Now* album, having had a minor hit with 'White Punks On Dope'.

While both Wire and The Tubes were, to different degrees, concept-oriented, with a theatrical sensibility in their live presentation, the two bands could never be confused: if Wire's pared-down approach to performance evoked the sparseness and simplicity of Beckett, The Tubes' shows were like Billy Smart's Circus meets burlesque. At the opposite end of the spectrum from Wire's minimalist, monochromatic performances and their oblique lyrics, The Tubes staged elaborate, colourful spectacles satirising consumerism, mass media, and show business. Their 1977 concerts featured partially clothed female dancers, choreographed routines, costume changes, simulated sex and violence, bondage, whips, large inflatable phallic cigarettes, banks of TV monitors, motorcycles, and chainsaws. Most importantly, for Grey, "they even had two drummers, *and* a percussionist".

In late 1977, punk was still provoking moral outrage and frothing indignation among the usual suspects (the tabloids, council officials), and The Tubes, while not a punk band, offered another perfect opportunity to those looking to be outraged and offended. Preceded by their reputation for 'scandalous' performances, the group had arrived in the UK, with some media fanfare, declaring that they would be more shocking than the Sex Pistols. Concerned local government officers pored over lurid reports of Tubes concerts in the US and, unsurprisingly, threatened to block gigs. Talking to the Newcastle *Evening Chronicle*, the chairman of the city council's recreation subcommittee warned his American visitors: "No hanky-panky or the plug will come out."

Given the prurient interest generated, the concerts received coverage beyond the music press, with predictably disapproving notices running in venues such as the *Daily Mail*. ("Would you want your daughter spending her pocket money going to see this? I don't think so.") Amid all of this, Wire went unnoticed and were barely mentioned in any of the reviews, but that didn't bother them. "It was an unbelievable experience, a massive change of circumstances," says Grey. "It was so extreme to go from playing to about 30 people in a pub to 3,000 at the Hammersmith Odeon." Lewis remembers the tour as "exciting, mad, and daunting". They were also struck by the treatment they received from The Tubes and their crew, who were supportive and genuinely interested in what Wire were doing. (A stint on the road with Roxy Music 15 months later would be a very different story.)

The Tubes tour ran from November 6 to December 7, coinciding with the release of *Pink Flag*. Wire also played some gigs separately; of these, two nights at Hammersmith's Red Cow, between concerts with The Tubes at the nearby Odeon, represented a watershed moment for the band. "We were slightly taken aback by the amount of people who showed up," comments Gilbert. It wasn't just that the size of the audience was changing: the demographic was also diversifying, and for the first time, Wire began to feel a connection with the people who came to see them. "That was the turning point," Lewis emphasises. "They were people who looked more like us, really – people from the margins who'd been around the whole punk thing, from the colleges, people who were looking for something a bit different."

### The deformed finger of Sarah Bernhardt

With the Tubes tour complete, Wire returned to Riverside Studio on December 14 to demo new material. The session yielded 13 numbers, seven of which would feature on *Chairs Missing*: 'Practice Makes Perfect', 'French Film Blurred', 'Sand In My Joints', 'Too Late', 'I Am The Fly', 'Heartbeat', and 'I Feel Mysterious Today'.

It's no coincidence that 'Practice Makes Perfect' was the first track on the demo and subsequently the opening track on *Chairs Missing* itself. Just as 'Reuters' had been Wire's statement of intent, an assertion of their difference and originality at the start of *Pink Flag*, 'Practice Makes Perfect' would have the same function on the band's second album. 'I Feel Mysterious Today' was the first *Chairs Missing* track to arrive, but 'Practice Makes Perfect', which came shortly afterwards, held the key to the album. It had no precedent in Wire's work thus far and signalled to the band that they had found another creative gear.

"A lot of *Pink Flag* is just cheerful rock'n'roll," says Newman, "although put through the grinder a little bit"; but the demo version of 'Practice Makes Perfect' (as well as the strikingly odd 'I Am The Fly') already announces a greater diversity of style, mood, and tone than the band had achieved on their debut. 'Practice Makes Perfect' doesn't simply deconstruct rock cliché, redeploying its components in playful ways, or subvert it through extreme reductionism, as *Pink Flag*'s strongest numbers had done; rather, on this track Wire are starting to bypass rock'n'roll entirely and to explore the avenues of form and sound that led to their first truly innovative work.

'Practice Makes Perfect' came together with remarkable speed and ease when Newman initially presented it to the group, its significance immediately evident. "By the end of playing the song in the rehearsal room," he remembers, "the arrangement was completely worked out by the band. There was no question that it was the most exciting thing we'd done. 'Practice Makes Perfect' was the track that changed everything. It was the future." There was indeed a shared sense of discovery and an awareness of a new direction. "It was obvious. It worked straight away," agrees Gilbert. "We found ourselves in a stimulating landscape where lots of things seemed to be possible. If we could execute something like 'Practice Makes Perfect' and be confident about it, it meant that the doors were opening for us creatively." Grey, too, saw the track as a turn away from the familiar: "I remember appreciating that it was us making a different sound, rather than a rock sound or a punk-rock sound, and I enjoyed the strangeness of it."

To Newman, 'Practice Makes Perfect' showed some continuity with 'Lowdown' in terms of what he describes as its "de-funked" or "tortured funk" feel, but overall it's a new rhythmic proposition for the band, "completely regimented and rigid and Germanic" – an eradication of any final traces of that "rolling smoothness" he loathed in punk. And if it was different for Wire, it also stood in contrast with what other guitar-based bands were doing in 1978. "That wasn't like anybody else's music," Newman insists. "There was nothing out there like it at the time. That was new."

Although it would be foolhardy to claim that 'Practice Makes Perfect' invented a genre, it can be seen as a track that at least anticipated a characteristic aspect of post-punk: namely, its angular, nervy strain. There had been stirrings of this on *Pink Flag*, but with 'Practice Makes Perfect' it comes together as a fully formed sound, rendered as a song, not just one component of the song. The jerky guitar riff ("doubled with a heavily distorted RMI Electra-Piano," notes Thorne) is the brilliantly deformed spine of the track, defining the rhythm, with everything neatly folding around it. Lewis recognises this and stresses that Newman's guitar parts on *Chairs Missing* are central to the revised sonic picture. "Colin's guitar is directly in the mix, and that's a really important part of the record. The interaction and the space that's created suddenly gave the bass another place to be, to jump between the guitar and the voice."

There is an off-kilter quirkiness to 'Practice Makes Perfect'. Much of this comes from the rhythm's football-clapping choppiness, the use of echo, and the manic vocal touches, especially the backing vocals – all resonating with Gilbert's bewildering, macabre lyrics. While these elements establish an unsettling atmosphere, the effect is one of camp-horror theatricality; it's not laugh-out-loud humour, but it's undeniably funny. Gilbert's words epitomise a particular variant of Wire's lyrical humour. One type, mostly the province of Lewis and Newman, is seen in surface-level linguistic playfulness; another, often the work of Gilbert, is found in heavily ironic visions of a fundamentally doomed human condition; a third, also largely from Gilbert and typified by 'Practice Makes Perfect', goes for disquieting absurdism. (Newman still recalls his immense amusement on reading the words when Gilbert gave them to him.)

Of this set of lyrics, Gilbert says: "It might have been a half-remembered dream, some ghoulish notion of someone having a secret." However, he is able to identify the source of the song's most startling, sinister image – the presence of the hand of Sarah Bernhardt in the narrator's bedroom. "I've got this very old bound collection of the *Strand Magazine* from 1886 or something, and it's full of very odd things, very stimulating things – one was handprints in negative, one of which was Sarah Bernhardt's hand. She had a deformed, distorted finger, and she had to wear big rings to hide it. It all seemed to gel into an idea that it was a special hand, and that some freak would be hiding it in his bedroom."

For Wire, the arrival of 'Practice Makes Perfect' early in the preparations for *Chairs Missing* raised the bar extremely high. "Once we'd come up with 'Practice Makes Perfect', it was a different game," Lewis says. "Certain other things didn't stand up to scrutiny anymore." That point is emphasised by several numbers from the December demo. "Some of them weren't the most educated pieces," Newman laughs, referring to 'Oh No Not So', 'Stalemate', 'It's The Motive', and 'Love Ain't Polite', tracks in the *Pink Flag* mould, bordering on his dreaded "cheerful rock'n'roll". The last of these, in particular, is a throwback to the Gill era – if nothing else, just the idea of a Wire song title containing the word 'ain't' is plain wrong. In a similar vein, the working version of 'French Film Blurred' sounds like fast-and-shouty juvenilia at this point in its development, almost unrecognisable when compared to its austere, atmospheric *Chairs Missing* incarnation. Of the other December demo tracks, 'Underwater Experiences' didn't make the album, and 'Culture Vultures' would crop up on Wire's first John Peel session in January 1978.

The importance of Peel's weeknight show on BBC Radio 1 at this time can't be overstated. It was the only nationally broadcast UK programme featuring new, non-mainstream music. For sessions, bands played 15 minutes' worth of material: usually four songs from their most recent album. The tracks were recorded live and mixed by in-house engineers for transmission later. Although *Pink Flag* was ostensibly the album Wire were promoting, they began as they would continue on their Peel sessions, in this case performing just one track with which listeners would be familiar ('106 Beats That'). Along with 'Culture Vultures' (next heard nine years later, on the band's *Peel Sessions* EP), they played the two key numbers from the Riverside demo, 'Practice Makes Perfect' and 'I Am The Fly'.

'I Am The Fly' was released as a single in February 1978, with 'Ex-Lion Tamer' on the B-side. It came in a curious snakes-and-ladders style picture sleeve. "I had this idea about a board game," recalls Gilbert. "All those bits and pieces on the cover – the 21, the enigmatic elements and images [including a pink flag, the dummy's head from the 'Mannequin' sleeve, and the heart-shaped appliqué] – were to suggest there was a way of playing it, if you knew the secret. But of course, there wasn't one. It incorporates one of my favourite images from an old 1930s 'tips and hints' book – how to practise swimming while wearing a black suit. Well, it didn't actually say you had to practise *wearing* the suit, but this was the way they chose to illustrate it. It was one of those kinds of books." (A version of that image would also grace the back of the sleeve for the 'Outdoor Miner' single the following year.)

Wire made a final set of demos at Riverside on April 14, a month or so before starting work on *Chairs Missing*. They played 'Mercy' (titled 'Finistaire'), a revised 'French Film Blurred', 'Marooned', 'From The Nursery', 'Outdoor Miner', 'Used To' (titled 'Chairs Missing'), 'Being Sucked In Again', 'Men 2nd', and 'Another The Letter'. Also recorded were 'No Romans', a track that wouldn't make the cut on *Chairs Missing*; an early rendering of 'Indirect Enquiries', which appeared in a totally different format a year and a half later on *154*; plus both sides of the next single, 'Dot Dash' and 'Options R'. (Fourteen tracks from the December and April Riverside demos were later collected on the 1995 EMI compilation, *Behind The Curtain: Early Versions 1977 & 78*.)

### Underwhelming experiences

While 'Practice Makes Perfect' had been the centrepiece of the December recordings, Wire were also very excited by 'Underwater Experiences', feeling it was one of the strongest demos from that set. This was the first track they focused on when sessions for *Chairs Missing* began at Advision Studios (with Thorne again joined by Paul Hardiman and Ken Thomas), and it played a foundational role in the recording process – even though it didn't appear on the album.

Wire didn't exclude 'Underwater Experiences' from *Chairs Missing* because they felt it was passé by the time they came to record – if anything, the track was still beyond them, and would remain so for some time. Although they had rehearsed and demoed it, they found themselves unable to produce a satisfying version at Advision. "It was actually one of the best songs, one everybody liked," says Newman, "but we just couldn't make it work. The original version was a bit like [Fleetwood Mac's] 'Albatross', in that there was nothing in it to keep the rhythm, and we had no real ability to know how to do that." Grey explains: "It was to do with the timing. It was very spare and open, and coordinating it was too difficult. There wasn't anything really to hold it all together." (The Riverside demo of the song can be found on *Behind The Curtain*.)

To overcome the problem and to develop a recordable version, they set out in an unusual experimental direction, working with the studio's grand piano. "I don't know why anyone thought that preparing a grand piano in Advision for two days would enable us to play 'Underwater Experiences' in time," says Newman. "It might have had something to do with what we were smoking, to be honest. We couldn't get anything like a steady take, but we spent two days under the piano and didn't use the song. Then we just got on with making the record."

Thorne recounts some details of the experiment: "We tried scrubbing the piano strings with drumsticks, with the loud pedal held down. We didn't get a satisfactory rhythm track, but we persevered with it, and the track didn't achieve lift-off, although it's a good song." As far as Lewis was concerned, this false start was, paradoxically, a perfect starting point for the album: "We spent two days interfering with the grand piano, trying to reignite our imagination, and after two days we realised, no, this isn't going to work out. But it actually set the sessions up in a good way: going in with really high expectations, we got grounded really quickly."

'Underwater Experiences' never quite went away. Rearranged for playability, it appeared in live sets in 1979 and 1980 and was resurrected, in that format, for gigs in 1990, and then again 18 years later. In 2010, Wire also recorded a studio version for the *Strays* EP, which was given away with

*Red Barked Tree.* A version closer in format to the song that had proved resistant at Advision would be corralled for performance in 2011 and then recorded for the band's 2013 studio album.

Although 'Underwater Experiences' was stubborn and elusive in 1978, Gilbert enjoyed "chasing it". In addition to the obvious absurdity value of the endeavour, he appreciated it as an example of the band's growing engagement with the possibilities offered by the recording environment. "We loved the idea of it, but it was impossible to do it. We all realised at the same time that it was a ridiculous thing to attempt – ludicrous, crawling around under a bloody piano! But it was one of those situations where it was an opportunity to really experiment with the studio and to find unusual noises to go with pieces, to enhance them. It excited me, at least. There was quite a bit of that on *Chairs Missing.*"

Despite the failure of 'Underwater Experiences', this episode emphasises how, from the beginning, the making of *Chairs Missing* would differ from the making of *Pink Flag.* Wire were no longer novices, working under Thorne's guidance and dependent on his expertise. "On *Pink Flag,*" says Newman, "Mike was introducing us to the studio. He didn't have that role any more, and it was a bit more of a collaboration. By *Chairs Missing,* we'd already been introduced to the studio. We knew what it was like. We were familiar with it; we were happy there. It was a great, creative place to be." Rather than arrive with completely finished songs, a more confident Wire came with ideas to explore and with songs that were open to further development – and they embraced the studio as a tool in that process. "*Chairs Missing*'s more produced and more arranged," Newman says. "There's more going on. There's a lot of overdubs and parts that we weren't able to do live. It's more of a studio record."

Like Newman and Gilbert, Lewis felt at home at Advision. "We were now in a place that was far more natural: it was *our* place." It became a different environment from the one they encountered for the first time on *Pink Flag.* Instead of delivering performances on demand, in search of the best take, they became active participants. "We were starting to understand that the studio was a place where you could think a bit more," says Lewis, "whereas what we did for *Pink Flag* was very reactive. We were thinking *and* doing now – not just desperately trying to get the best performance out of ourselves. Now we were in a situation where we were trying to make something new. The template wasn't as precise: we were trying to find out what it might be. If *Pink Flag* is mostly about 'no', *Chairs Missing* is very much about 'yes': let's do this, let's see what happens. We had some songs that remained pretty true to how we'd been playing, but it became more expansive and more melodic. It was a more relaxed, freer atmosphere, and that inevitably led to a degree of improvised creativity in which pieces developed. That was something we'd never experienced in the studio before."

Grey agrees that the first-album anxiety had dissipated, and that the shift away from performance-based recording was liberating. "We weren't just recreating a live performance, and that took some of the pressure off. Already having experience in the studio meant we knew more about the possibilities of what you could do: if you made a mistake, it wasn't the end of the world, and things could be rearranged. We could enjoy the process more, rather than feeling anxious about whether we could do it or not." Grey's enjoyment, like that of his bandmates, came mainly from an "involvement with the studio – using anything that was there to make things more interesting, exploring more possibilities". He feels that the piano interlude with 'Underwater Experiences' – mystifying as it may have been – was emblematic of the increased confidence and creativity that would push Wire to experiment and to engage with their surroundings on *Chairs Missing*, making the record a very special one. "If you could convince somebody else that an idea like that was a good one – that it had potential and could be used, even if that idea turned out not to be of any direct use – then it says a lot about the recording session. We were approaching things with the mind-set of 'anything could happen' and trying to see if we could expand things, rather than just go in and use what we'd worked out beforehand."

While the opening-up of the studio process was liberating for the band, Lewis got the impression that it sometimes caused unease for the producer, who, despite being sympathetic to (and a willing participant in) the band's experimentation, ultimately had a record to make for his bosses at EMI. When a new sound or a new idea presented itself during the construction of a song, exciting the band and suggesting another new direction to pursue, Lewis felt that Thorne became uncomfortable. "We'd go: wow, that could be a whole new track!" he recalls. "And we'd sense Mike thinking: oh no! And he'd respond saying: but it's like *this* – and we'd say: But it isn't any more. That feels wrong now. It's like *this*. Obviously, one of the reasons he was there was to be a gatekeeper, but in the end I think it was something that always terrified him. He gave the appearance of being OK with it, but I'm sure there were less tranquil waters underneath. You could just see him thinking: *oh no …*"

From Lewis's point of view, this kind of creative tension would become more pronounced on the next album. Contrary to Lewis's comments, Thorne believes he took Wire's unpredictable energy and wilfulness in his stride – even if it meant discarding work that had previously been considered more-or-less finished. Instead of recreating the material as it had been played live, the band now often overhauled it in the studio – a modus operandi that, according to Thorne, aimed "to strip out the stylistically familiar in favour of something new". During *Chairs Missing*, some of that extreme revision took place when the construction process was at an advanced stage. "We were well into corrective overdubs," Thorne recalls, when the band decided to jettison significant parts of songs. To him, this didn't undercut what had already been achieved; rather, he felt it was a vitally important step toward the creation of some unique work. "Dropping out whole layers was an inspired move," he says, in that it made way for "creative replacement overdubs" that gave the tracks their definitive identities. 'Used To', for example, was subjected to the most invasive surgery, the results prefiguring the sonic climate of *154* more than any other track on the album.

There was an air of excitement at Advision during the making of *Chairs Missing*, and the collective mood was positive: it was a glorious spring, the band were firing on all cylinders, and everybody was getting along well. Although comic relief was not required, it was supplied (unwittingly) by the group working in the studio upstairs. "We kept seeing Slade coming in," remembers Lewis. "And Mike came down one day, and he gets the giggles and he was doubled over – and it took a while to get out of him what was going on. It turned out that when they'd recorded *Slade Alive Vol Two*, the recording engineer had forgotten to turn on the ambient mics, so they were coming in for weeks to record themselves as the audience in a drum booth at Advision, to make up the sound of several thousand people."

### Genius and complete rubbish

The attempt to manufacture a sound for 'Underwater Experiences', in order to facilitate the track's execution, is one facet of Wire's creative approach to the studio on *Chairs Missing*. There was another variant of that process, as individual sounds that hadn't been manufactured – but that came up *by chance* during the exploration of the environment and the technology – became catalysts or foundational components for a song. Such sounds began to appear when the band-members started tinkering with guitar effects and pedals. "For *Chairs Missing*, I think the new effects boxes Mike was bringing back from America – that weren't really readily available in this country – were a big influence on the material," asserts Gilbert, "because a song could be built around one sound: that gave an atmosphere immediately, and we could follow that up. One became very interested in staring at the windows in music shops, looking at the new effects boxes."

Although Thorne had introduced Wire to basic effects on *Pink Flag*, by the time of *Chairs Missing* he was picking up the latest gear in New York (where he was spending more time) and then making it available to the band in London. "I'd charge one per cent of a machine's value if it was used on an EMI session," Thorne recalls. "It beat having to hire at 15 per cent and then find you didn't like it anyway." As Gilbert mentions, these boxes and pedals played a decisive part in guiding Wire's move away from *Pink Flag*, enabling them to enrich the soundscape of the second album. "We'd become more confident and relaxed. We knew we couldn't carry on with the fast, simple, thrashy things – although they were always enjoyable – and there was a definite shift of emphasis to slightly stranger areas. We'd built up our collection of effects boxes, and we were experimenting with those. We were still very new to guitar effects, so it was an interesting exploration, a more creative situation. We were seeing the possibilities of creating different atmospheres: using effects rather than thrashing away just trying to get good versions." Even on the band's demos, the impact of the effects is already apparent on the most forward-looking material. "Listening to the demos, it's the effects that you hear," Gilbert stresses, "pointing everybody in very different directions, giving time and space to explore certain subject matter in a more interesting way. The effects were very important. Messing with them, it was very inspiring."

In Gilbert's view, 'I Am The Fly' – described by Newman as "a combination of genius and complete rubbish" – is "a classic example" of a track developing from a sound that had arrived by accident, from "messing" with equipment. The song, which is Lewis's response to journalists of the *NME* variety ("It seemed to be such a reactionary paper"), was constructed around a noise found in Newman's MXR flanger. For the recording of the final version, a new pedal was purchased by Thorne "for north of £120 in Denmark Street on the morning of the session". Gilbert explains how the song had first come together in rehearsal: "Colin had this flanger, and we were just messing around with it, and we did this rhythm, and everyone just joined in. You started playing what everybody else was doing, and it was just there. Rob started drumming. Then it just needed lyrics." Grey remembers the moment well. "It's another good example of finding new things. When we were rehearsing, I recall Colin saying: I've got this – what do you think? And I thought: wow, what a great sound! The sound itself made the song, really."

79

'I Am The Fly' provides another key to *Chairs Missing* – particularly since it was the first track to be recorded, for its release as a single, months before the rest of the album. It gave listeners a clear indication that the band were mapping new creative dimensions, beyond the territory of *Pink Flag*. Not only does it offer an example of the way that random, individual sounds could become the basis of a song, it also foregrounds the eccentricity and humour that would manifest themselves in the *Chairs Missing* material.

There was some levity and some surreal lyrical content on *Pink Flag*, but apart from the minor touches on 'Strange', Wire's debut has none of the oddball sonic qualities of *Chairs Missing* – epitomised by 'I Am The Fly' and 'Practice Makes Perfect'. The theatricality of the latter is shared by the skewed pop songs 'I Feel Mysterious Today', 'Another The Letter', and the Eno-esque 'From The Nursery'. For these numbers, enigmatic narratives are paired with instrumental and vocal tics that supply cartoon soundtrack-like resonances: bells, temple blocks, güiro, and shaker on 'I Feel Mysterious Today', along with somewhat literal punctuation like the humming, droning guitar ("everything's humming loudly"); agitated Oberheim synth on 'Another The Letter'; and uncanny buried voices on 'From The Nursery' ("as you might imagine dolls to speak or pets to whimper," says Thorne).

For Lewis, the accentuation of this weirder tone had to do with the self-assurance that Wire had acquired. "It's a lightness of touch and a wit that comes from confidence," he says. "It really captured where we were at the time: we were jettisoning anything familiar from *Pink Flag*, and the quirkiness and battiness has to do with that new confidence." With specific regard to the lyrics, Lewis felt his work had also benefitted from that increased self-belief, the subject matter and its execution becoming more imaginative and ambitious. Describing the change in his writing, he uses the term 'swerve' – an important entry in Wire's lexicon, employed by the band to characterise the process by which the unexpected happens to a piece of work, the process by which it becomes *other*. "It's now less linear," he says of his work on *Chairs Missing*. "There's less reportage. It's more wiggly, the angles are a little stranger. Things *swerve*."

The songwriting process for Wire's second album remained mostly unchanged from *Pink Flag*, with Newman again responsible for the majority of the music. This time, though, there would be no four-way composition credit. Newman had been unhappy with that arrangement, as he felt it unfair that his greater contribution wasn't reflected. This, coupled with Lewis and Gilbert's emergence as writers, led to individualised credits for each track on *Chairs Missing*. (All four members, plus Thorne, receive a credit for arrangement.) This revised format also appears to have proven unsatisfactory, however, as the 2006 reissues of the first three albums – what Newman calls the "definitive" versions – feature adjusted composer credits. These specify the writers of the melody (as opposed to 'music') and the words. 'Men 2nd', originally credited to Lewis alone, now lists the bassist as the writer of the words and Newman as the writer of the melody; 'Used To', first attributed to Gilbert and Lewis, now credits them as lyricists and Gilbert and Newman as writers of the melody; and 'Too Late', initially assigned just to Gilbert, lists Gilbert and Newman as writers of the melody.

## We're prog-rock, mate: deal with it!

As tracks like 'Another The Letter', 'Used To', and 'Marooned' reveal, a large measure of *Chairs Missing*'s distinctiveness derives from the incorporation of keyboards and synthesizers. There's a certain amount of typical Wire contrariness in this new dimension, something that comes across in Lewis's succinct explanation: "It seemed like a natural development; it was still an anti-synth period." But although it may have been in Wire's DNA to go against the grain, this was also a "natural development" in that it responded to the changes taking place in the band's work itself.

"The material dictated it," says Lewis. "There was space that had to be made. We were looking to produce atmospheres so that the more simple elements could hang, and so you needed washes of sound." Newman concurs: "We wanted a broader sound, and we felt keyboards could do that."

Growing confidence was therefore leading Wire away from *Pink Flag*'s one- or, at best, two-dimensional tendencies as the new compositions explored a greater range of mood and atmosphere. Rather than anxiously fill up all the open space in a track – "thrashing away", as Gilbert put it – or try to get in and out of songs in under 90 seconds, they were stepping back and allowing spaces to expand and breathe. A cursory look at the track list of Wire's second album is instructive: in comparison to *Pink Flag*'s 21 mainly fast, stripped-down songs, *Chairs Missing*, a longer record, had 15 numbers. They were also generally slower and more developed, only one of them clocking in at under a minute and a half. "It was all opening up in terms of what was possible, what could be in the song and the sonic landscape – and the songs could be enhanced by having guest noises and voices," says Gilbert, referring to keyboards and effects.

According to Grey, there was also a very practical aspect to this evolution. "Keyboards were used to create atmosphere, but also to get beyond the limitations of guitars." This appealed to Gilbert, who was starting to feel that his instrument was slightly inadequate and too confining for the more expansive soundscapes he had in mind. "I quite often found myself trying to imitate a keyboard or a synth with a guitar, using a long sustained drone. I felt uncomfortable thrashing away very quickly on guitar and having it blur in a load of effects or delays, so using keyboards was really good. It made the whole thing sound a bit more sophisticated."

While there is a strong conviction that the use of new instrumentation was demanded by the nature of the material itself, Lewis also reports that the band drew inspiration from a handful of artists whose work showed how keyboards and synths could be used in innovative ways. "Roxy had used keyboards really well on their first album. And we were aware of Kraftwerk, obviously, and definitely what Bowie was doing with Eno: they were the only people we thought we were in sync with, because of the nature of what they were doing and their subject matter. Everything else seemed rather prosaic, really." Newman also mentions Bowie and Eno. "The songs on *Low* were anthems of a bleak, dark time. It was brutal and dark, it was the end of the Cold War. That dark European vibe was really fashionable, and it certainly informed what we did, although you saw that with a tongue-in-cheek perspective from our point of view, in our songs."

But while Newman says that Bowie and Eno "informed" Wire's work, like Lewis, he stops short of calling their records an influence. He also stresses the band's contrary spirit: "It wasn't a case of wanting to have synths because Brian and Bowie had synths; it was more like engaging with all the things you're not supposed to have, because synths are prog-rock – Yeah, OK, we're prog-rock, mate: deal with it! We'd had punk orthodoxy, and that was so boring, so let's say we're into Genesis. What more direct way was there of saying you didn't give a fuck than to say you were into Genesis?"

Thorne was the first choice to play keyboards on *Chairs Missing*, given his musical expertise, plus his familiarity and sympathy with Wire's work. It made no sense to Gilbert to bring in an outsider. "Mike was a musician – and he had the gear." It was obvious to Newman, too: "We didn't want a keyboard player. It was part of Mike's function in working with us. He brought keyboards and guitar effects, and we could fiddle with them. He was classically trained, and we couldn't play, so there was no point in us doing it. And he could work out the parts quickly." Thorne was at first reluctant, using the excuse that he couldn't move his fingers fast enough. Resorting to threats, the others said they would enlist Eno if Thorne didn't sign on. "If you don't play keyboards, we'll get that Brian Eno in," he recalls Gilbert warning him. This had the desired effect – "I was horrified," Thorne says – and he accepted the job, contributing piano, RMI Electra-Piano, Oberheim synth, and EMS Synthi AKS (the portable version of the VCS3).

Wire took the creative lead on *Chairs Missing*, but Thorne's role also expanded. Not only did he play the keyboard parts (even performing live on several UK dates in 1978, again under duress), he became more involved in the arrangements, as his sleeve credit indicates. "We'd had chats," says Gilbert. "He'd come down to the demo studios, and I remember him writing copious notes. He could see it was all opening up, and he had lots of ideas for the songs before we got into the studio – ideas about arrangements, augmentation, and what sounds and extra instruments could be added. He had a bigger role. It wasn't excessive – just ideas." According to Newman, "Mike played under heavy instruction. It was always a battle of wits to try and squeeze something in. Bruce would always joke: I don't want your fucking organ all over this."

Although he helped shape the unique sound of *Chairs Missing*, Thorne is modest about his contributions. "I treated them as colouring rather than as anything which would step forward, and it wasn't until *154* that I thought it was appropriate for me to propose a keyboard gesture on something which was pure support."

Most importantly, for Thorne, the incorporation of additional musical tools, effects, and manipulation led to a blurring of the boundaries between discrete instruments. Wire began to achieve a radically different, more integrated sound. "The beauty of what happened on *Chairs Missing*," explains Thorne, "is that instead of it being keyboards on one side and guitars on the other, every sound is a genuinely electric sound, and most people won't know whether it's a guitar or a keyboard. On *Chairs Missing*, I got my keyboard, and the first thing I did was to put it through a distortion pedal, which has honourable antecedents – Mike Ratledge of Soft Machine used to play through distortion."

One of the more arresting examples of keyboards on *Chairs Missing* can be heard on the glacial miniature epic 'Marooned'. "It was a highlight and really adventurous," says Lewis. It's also one of Grey's favourites, perhaps because of the minimalist nature of his participation: he plays only hi-hat and ride cymbal for the duration. Newman had envisaged it as a sparse piece and was determined that its simple, stark power not be diluted by any extraneous parts as it was assembled in the studio. "It just drops away to one held Oberheim chord. I fought and fought to keep it that naked and slight. I really wanted that drama in it. One thing you can do with keyboards is just hold a chord – that's not something you can do with a guitar; you've got to keep strumming."

The track also features tubular bells in the middle eight. "A bell tolling seemed appropriate," recalls Thorne, "but Bruce very properly thought the sound corny, so I stuck it through a ring modulator on the AKS with another signal." Grey, who remembers "hitting the bell under Mike's instruction", thought this an unnecessary instance of percussion, but he still recognises its value as another example of the newfound creativity that defined *Chairs Missing*. "That's pure Mike, and it wouldn't have happened if we hadn't explored the studio."

The song's lyrical vision is devastatingly bleak, fitting seamlessly – as on 'Practice Makes Perfect' – with the music. It's another grim Gilbert visualisation (with some input from Lewis) of the human condition – again drawn partly from antique reading matter. "It was from a very old book by this curious millionaire couple who wrote about their travels around the world," Gilbert recalls. "They'd seen this polar bear on a small ice floe, and the woman was saying – and I can hear her voice in a very clipped English accent – 'Oh the poor thing, I wonder what his future will be?' That set it off. The song has a nice double meaning. Loneliness and isolation. We're all doomed." Doomed indeed. The track includes some of Gilbert's most harrowing lyrics – a fleeting glimpse of self-immolation, amid the song's otherwise frigid landscape: "As he pours more petrol on, he feels no fear / As the flames get nearer, his thoughts get clearer."

## An idea is a painting ... until it's a song

In addition to keyboard and synth textures and guitar pedal-based exploration, other creative approaches to sound helped move Wire's music into its own, increasingly hard-to-define category.

On the surface, 'Sand In My Joints' – Lewis's first lead vocal with Wire – is the *Chairs Missing* track that's musically still most closely aligned with 1977's second-wave punk. "The style draws from punk frantic," agrees Thorne, "but the sounds are better than that." Specifically, he's talking about the idiosyncratic guitar break, created with some very un-punk technology and an experimental, collaborative approach to performance and recording, as Gilbert and Newman played simultaneously via the ring modulator on the AKS. They had to play at the same time since the ring modulator needed a signal present at both inputs before the modulated result was output – that result being one guitar modulated by the other. Although the sound was highly mediated and artificial, dependent on planning, organisation, and some moderately sophisticated physics, once the mechanism was set up the subsequent noise is still characterised by what Thorne calls "wild unpredictability": this exciting, unstable sound is one of the track's most memorable features.

Not all the innovative gestures on *Chairs Missing* are of the loud-and-raucous variety. On the 'Heroin'-tinged 'Heartbeat' (originally called 'Preview' – Newman's pastiche of the image of him constructed by the music press), the atmosphere is enhanced by a subtle flute part – again performed by Kate Lukas – a breathy pulsing, produced by a simple alternation of major and minor chords.

Although 'Another The Letter' is, at 1:06, the shortest track, it contains what was, for its time, the album's most novel element. The song had been played live by the band but was developed further in the studio using sequencing, which gave it a completely new feel. "The whole track was performed to a backbone of a sequence in my Oberheim, very frantic," remembers Thorne. "I could never play the part live." This is a classic piece of Wire, combining music and lyrics that pull in different directions: in this instance, the light, breezy tune and jaunty vocal delivery accompany a fraught, elliptical narrative that concludes with the report of a suicide. The lyrics are a paradigmatic example of Gilbert's tendency to think across disciplines in that they began life in another medium, hence the unusual title. "It was going to be a painting called 'The Letter'," Gilbert recalls. "It was going to be a hand holding a letter on one side of the canvas and another hand reaching for it. But I didn't do the painting, I did the song instead."

Underscoring *Chairs Missing*'s diversity, conventional melodic tunes rub shoulders with its warped pop songs, as well as with more experimental numbers: in the mould of 'Mannequin' and 'Fragile', a case in point is 'Outdoor Miner', which reminded some reviewers of Steve Harley. Just as Gilbert wasn't a fan of *Pink Flag*'s poppier moments and involved himself only minimally in them ("I always felt like it was another band"), he kept a distance from 'Outdoor Miner'. The obvious explanation for his non-participation in the recording appears to be that the track was too mainstream for him – musically speaking, at least, since Lewis's entomological fantasy text (a glimpse into the world of the *Liriomyza brassicae*) is another matter. Nevertheless, Gilbert attributes his absence from the recording to purely practical considerations: "I attempted to play on it, but there were too many minor chords, so Colin had to do that one."

This overview of production details and inventive approaches to sound emphasises the leap forward from *Pink Flag*, as keyboards, synthesizers, and effects – along with more expansive, ambitious arrangements and a new rhythmic sensibility – all contributed to the incredible originality of Wire's second album. However, these creative components also caused problems for reviewers, once again in relation to the question of authenticity.

## Punk flawed

Reviews were for the most part favourable, although not quite as enthusiastic as they had been for *Pink Flag*. Even those who received *Chairs Missing* positively didn't seem to engage with it to any significant extent and appeared reserved in their praise, as if they weren't entirely sure what to make of it. This didn't go unnoticed. "We couldn't understand how they didn't get it," says Newman. "We were exasperated by that." Some reviewers seemed unable to accept the extent of the difference between *Pink Flag* and *Chairs Missing*; still stranded in 1977, they were apparently stymied by the idea that a group and their sound might evolve. As Thorne notes: "There were several very stuffy reviews from unreconstructed punk purists." Lewis echoes this, homing in on a specific reason for that critical ambivalence. "I think they were less able or prepared to listen to something which had keyboards; they were still stuck on promoting punk or whatever it was supposed to be."

Monty Smith's *NME* write-up was one example. Underlying his dissatisfaction was a feeling that, on *Chairs Missing*, "artifice has replaced art" – that Wire had sacrificed their unmediated, essential personality and sound (as heard on *Pink Flag*) for something impure and inferior. As a result, the "immense promise" of the debut album remained "unfulfilled". Smith's piece is, ironically, useful. The record's 'artificial' ingredients that he singles out as weaknesses – those aspects rendering it substandard in comparison with *Pink Flag* – are in fact the things that make *Chairs Missing* such a striking record and account for its enduring appeal.

Still deeply invested in the Year Zero mind-set, Smith's review above all attempted to dismiss *Chairs Missing* for displaying tendencies attributed to one of punk's bêtes noires: progressive rock, at its stereotypical, straw-man worst.

At the heart of his critique is a haut-rockist rejection of synthesizers and keyboards, as used by a band that has "succumbed to an unhappy attack of the Pink Floyds". To Smith, synths are "unnecessary" ("Wire require synthesizers," he quips, "like Liverpool need a replacement for Kevin Keegan"), but worse still, they're "arty" – an adjective he uses to denote a negative quality having more to do with *artifice* than *art*: 'Being Sucked In

Again' is "tainted" by "arty-spacecrafty" synthesizers, he writes, and he complains that, elsewhere, synths prevent him from hearing Wire. "I didn't hear them," he claims, "I heard Ray Manzarek on frenzied Sooty organ," presumably referring to 'Another The Letter'. ("That's an inspired line," laughs Thorne, 34 years later.)

It is true that Wire, wittingly or unwittingly, break their own rule on *Chairs Missing* by allowing in various elements that evoke Pink Floyd's early sound: the echoey backing vocals on 'Practice Makes Perfect', for instance ("Graham's excellent idea," says Thorne); the foregrounding of bass, most memorably on 'Being Sucked In Again', 'French Film Blurred', and 'Marooned' ("That was because Mike had confidence in the way it sounded," recalls Lewis); the various bizarro sound effects ('From The Nursery'); as well as some nursery-rhyme whimsy or stream-of-consciousness fluidity in certain lyrics. "I don't think I'd ever heard a Pink Floyd record," says Gilbert, although Lewis fesses up: "It's there. It's undeniable. I won't deny it. I loved *The Piper At The Gates Of Dawn* and *Ummagumma*. The early Floyd records are incredibly good, very inventive. They made a strong impression on me. Nobody else was doing that with that sort of power and that manipulation of sound. The early things are extraordinary, quite inexplicable, and so extremely English – and that was something that one valued a lot."

It is instructive and worthwhile to link Pink Floyd and Wire, but not through a simple identification of musical quotations. Beyond Smith's synthesizer hang-up and beyond the handful of Floydian details and motifs on *Chairs Missing*, a comparison is only meaningful in terms of the bigger picture, one that grasps the wider, shared cultural importance of the two bands. What Wire and early Pink Floyd have in common is that they were – up until that point at least – among the only groups in British music to record songs that had blended pop and experimental sensibilities so successfully. This is a key achievement of *Chairs Missing*, and it's also something that would become a hallmark of Wire's identity.

From the perspective of the Romantic rockist values held by punk purists such as Smith, *Chairs Missing* (like most of Pink Floyd's music) is inauthentic: rather than embrace an ideal of art as unmediated, pure expression, the album prioritises surface and formal components over deeper emotional substance. Ironically, this is in part what gives it its identity as an innovative album, not just in Wire's catalogue but alongside other new music of the period. Newman is adamant about the record's significance in defining the band's character, especially in relation to its predecessor:

87

"*Chairs Missing* is Wire discovering their next phase, and it's Wire discovering their identity. It's much more a band-defining record than *Pink Flag*; *Pink Flag* is still very much coloured by punk, and although it's full of Wire weirdness, it's not as representative a Wire record as *Chairs Missing*. There's nothing on *Pink Flag* that has a lasting quality in terms of what Wire are and how Wire likes to see itself. Wire didn't stay as what *Pink Flag* defines; *Chairs Missing* defines what Wire became, and what they have remained. *Chairs Missing*'s much more harmonically rich and more beautiful. It's a much harder record to place in time than *Pink Flag*. And although it doesn't have the grandeur of *154*, it's a special record. It's appealing but a little bit unhinged. It has a certain kind of energy to it, and a certain oddness – it's not quite as definable as it might be, and you don't know what to call it. I think it was a real touchstone for Wire. It's where Wire came into their own. It's where you really see the personality of the band developing."

Ultimately, there is a useful truth to noting the progressive inclinations of *Chairs Missing*: Wire, like contemporaries This Heat, *were* a progressive band – in the best possible sense. Although their emergence had coincided with punk, they were part of a British art-rock tradition dating back to the early 70s, a tradition that (as Simon Reynolds has noted) incorporated everything from progressive rock's edgier extremes to glam's smarter manifestations, engaging in varying degrees of musical experimentation in territories ranging from jazz to the avant-garde, rejecting clichéd American rock expectations and occasionally displaying a conceptual orientation.

When punk's least imaginative voices sweepingly dismissed 70s British music, they overlooked a fertile, diverse seam of home-grown art-rock – artists such as Roxy Music, Bowie, Eno, Fripp and King Crimson, Henry Cow, Van der Graaf Generator and Peter Hammill, Peter Gabriel, Bill Nelson, John Cale, and Robert Wyatt. Wire might not have sounded like any of these (who, in turn, might have had little in common, stylistically, with each other), but because of their willingness to experiment and explore and their refusal to settle for the familiar, Wire are part of the same lineage. Connecting Wire to the art-rock tradition and thereby expanding the context of their music beyond punk's limited frame of reference makes possible a more accurate appreciation of the band and the significance of their work.

That Wire were on Harvest reinforces their place in this tradition. Established for EMI's artier, more progressive acts, the imprint had been home to, among others, Pink Floyd, Soft Machine, Syd Barrett, Kevin Ayers,

Be-Bop Deluxe, and The Pretty Things. Harvest boss Nick Mobbs thought it logical to have Wire on the label. "Rather arbitrarily, some 'punk' acts ended up on Harvest," he recalls, "but Wire had more reason than any to be on what had been founded originally as a 'progressive' music label. I doubt the marketing people saw this subtlety, and I expect Wire were perceived as just another punk band. Wire's attraction, to me, was that they could outrace and outshout any punk band but had many other tricks up their sleeves involving atmosphere, humour, intelligence, menace, and, yes, *art*. They were original; the only comparisons I could think of at the time were with The Velvet Underground and early Pink Floyd."

## Mr Sooty

As it happened, Monty Smith's reference to Sooty and his organ was apposite: Harry Corbett's puppet protégé played an unlikely part in the creation of *Chairs Missing*'s artwork.

Gilbert conceived the front cover image and the album title. The latter was borrowed from an expression his father-in-law liked to use, to suggest that someone wasn't all there ("she's got a few chairs missing in her front room"). The cover was inspired by a scene Gilbert had witnessed, by chance, in the Duveen Gallery at the British Museum, home to the Parthenon (or Elgin) marbles. He had been there alone at closing time one afternoon when, in a flurry of activity, members of the custodial staff arrived carrying a long table, which they set down and draped with a cloth, before promptly disappearing. Another employee then materialised, placing a vase of flowers on the table. "It was a wonderful vision, and it stuck in my mind," recalls Gilbert.

The location chosen to shoot the cover photographs was a theatre in Rickmansworth, which was hosting a live version of *The Sooty Show* at the time. "Yes, we shared the bill with Sooty," admits Grey. The band and photographer Annette Green were allowed to use the stage space for a few hours, under the suspicious eye of an individual identified by Lewis as "Sooty's roadie", who made no secret of the fact that he didn't think Wire were in the same league as his ursine employer. "He looked like he could have walked straight out of the theatre and worked for Motörhead," Lewis remembers. "He had the big bunch of keys and the torch and the seedy truck. He said our time was up and sent us on our way. He took his job very seriously. After all, Sooty was playing bigger places than we were."

The front cover recreates Gilbert's vision in the Duveen Gallery in stylised fashion. As with the *Pink Flag* artwork, Gilbert wanted the photograph treated and retouched, "to make it look unrealistic". To that end, white paper was used as a cloth, on a table that the band had positioned on the stage. Plastic flowers also enhanced the artificiality, although according to Gilbert, that had not been planned. "We'd gone to a florist looking for a biggish, colourful flower to put in the vase, and we just couldn't get one that was suitable, and so we ended up with these big, ridiculous plastic flowers. The leaves might have been real, but the flowers certainly weren't." Lewis's recollection of the scene and its constitutive elements differs slightly. "The flowers were artificial: we constructed them out of paper or fabric and lashed them to some poles. The flowers were totally unreal – like the title, they were actually 'missing' or absent. So the photo, which was also tinted afterwards, was totally artificially created."

The photo shoot was also noteworthy for an incident that cemented the term 'dream sequence' in the Wire lexicon. The moment preceding that occurrence is preserved on the inner-sleeve photo, which captures Grey yawning. Seconds later, he leaned back and stared up into the lighting gantry. "If you looked up," he remembers, "there were giant black toy spiders, which were for the frightening bit of Sooty's performance: they were lowered down on him during what Sooty's roadie told us was the 'dream sequence' of his show." Lewis adds: "It was the heaviest part of the show, the ultra-violent Sooty dream sequence." This caused great amusement, which didn't go down well. "That was when we were ushered out of the theatre by Sooty's roadie." Grey recalls that the expression was stored for future reference. "That's where the phrase 'dream sequence' in Wire-speak came from. It was adopted to indicate when something strange happens in a song – that would be the *dream sequence*." Or, in Gilbert's definition, it was "a gap in a song where something unresolved could happen".

The encounter with Sooty wasn't the only unusual shared bill for Wire in the early days. Uncharacteristically, in late 1977, they had aligned themselves with a topical cause by playing a Rock Against Racism benefit in Stoke Newington, alongside Steel Pulse. Wire were the least 'topical' of bands: there was little that directly connected their work to the here and now, as they rooted out sonic traits linking them to their contemporaries, and their songs weren't 'about' things in a conventional sense – least of all, identifiable current events or issues. Even more atypically, they took part in a closing 'Do They Know It's Christmas?'-style ensemble number with the other band.

"It was a jam. It was terrible. It was really embarrassing," is all that Newman will say. Lewis is more forthcoming. "I think someone offered me a tambourine, but I declined. I didn't actually share the stage with them; I shared the chalice and had a bit of a skank at the back." Grey is still bemused by this event. "I don't know how it happened, but I seem to remember doing some kind of 'singing' with Steel Pulse. That can't be right, can it?" (Unfortunately, the evening ended on a sour note as Wire were taken to task by a right-on, and rather literal-minded, interviewer for the use of the word 'rape' in the lyrics for 'Reuters'.)

Throughout 1977, Wire had gigged mostly in the South of England. They'd gone to Newcastle, Manchester, and Birmingham with The Tubes, and played a few of their own dates in the Midlands and Liverpool, but they'd rarely strayed north of the Watford Gap. This changed in early 1978, as they began looking more to the provinces. Although they still played chiefly in and around London, the North became a focus for live activity. "We seemed to spend an awful lot of time crossing the Pennines," Lewis recalls. "For me, it felt natural to be up there." To Lewis, this wasn't about getting back to his roots but about the discovery of kinship with people who were at a similar remove from punk. "By the nature of what we were doing, and the fact that we weren't part of the whole Pistols-Clash-Damned-Stranglers axis, the people felt a sort of outsider sympathy for us. We weren't seen as part of what had become a fashionable, starry kind of elite thing. In Manchester, we had genuine support, and we had a strong connection with Liverpool, with Eric's. The people were interested in music in a wider sense than just punk. It was people who talked about Beefheart, who knew about German music, and who knew about dance music. I enjoyed that. And I think what we were doing perhaps suited the weather better. It was grim and fun."

Newman also remembers a more diverse audience, albeit a distinctly odd one, in places like Doncaster, Hull, Huddersfield, and Harrogate. "There were a lot of people displaying their weirdness – like people with coat hangers on their heads – but not necessarily a punk audience. We used to get the weirdoes, and of course it was mainly blokes in those days." And while they'd received little media coverage beyond the music press in London and radio airplay on John Peel, they were embraced by Tony Wilson in Manchester; he put Wire on *What's On*, recording them during a soundcheck at the exotic Keighley venue, Knickers. This was the occasion when Wilson requested that they play 'Fragile' "for an old hippie" and, for his trouble, was told to "fuck off". (They played 'Reuters' instead.)

Wire released their third single, 'Dot Dash', in June. Although it had been recorded in closer proximity to the *Chairs Missing* material than 'I Am The Fly', the latter earned a spot on the album – a surprising choice, in view of the speed with which Wire turned material over. The consensus was that 'I

Am The Fly' fitted with the album's overall character, whereas 'Dot Dash' was heading off in another direction. Gilbert's automotive cover art for the single was a readymade. "It was a non-design design," he explains. "I'm very keen on things that design themselves, using mirror images, putting two images together. The basic thing was found in a car manual of some description. It was a very obvious choice of imagery, given the subject matter."

## Him from Talking Heads

In July 1978, although Wire still hadn't played in continental Europe (or Scotland and Ireland, for that matter), they visited the United States for the first time. More accurately, they visited New York City, where they were booked to play a residency at CBGB on July 13, 14, and 15 (two gigs per night). Work-permit issues caused them to arrive two days later than planned, and they missed half of the scheduled shows; a couple were rearranged for the following weekend, and the group also performed a set in a nearby vacant theatre for broadcast on WPIX-FM.

The band-members had obviously heard of CBGB but had no real idea what it was like, and they were shocked by what they found. "By comparison, it made the Marquee seem grand," says Lewis. The reception was positive, and the gigs were sold out, with various luminaries in attendance – but the alleged behaviour of one individual still annoys Newman to the extent that he can't bring himself to speak the person's name. "Brian Eno came backstage. He came to see us with 'Him' from Talking Heads, who didn't come backstage. And, from that point, I decided I didn't like Talking Heads, because He wouldn't come and see us. It wasn't very good manners. Brian came to say hi because that's what you do."

Gilbert, Grey, Newman, and Lewis recall this trip fondly, but while the time spent in New York was memorable and eye-opening, it wasn't important for Wire in creative terms: its significance lay in the impact it had on them on a personal, experiential level, as travellers and tourists. At this point, none of them had been far afield, certainly not to America.

These were less complicated times, when America wasn't viewed with quite as much ambivalence by the rest of the world, its mythology exercising a more positive hold over the popular imagination. Indeed, it was surprising to hear the members of Wire – dour, affectless robots according to the UK music press in 1977 and 1978 – *still* talking excitedly about this trip in 2012. "It was a fucking amazing experience," raves Newman, "a bizarre, fantastic experience." Lewis explains what it meant to him: "It was like a dream come true, one of those things you had on a list of ambitions, but it came around a lot quicker than you expected." The US jaunt made its mark on Grey, too. "It was definitely a big moment – going to America to play in a band, it was exciting. And the whole place smelled of pizzas! It doesn't now."

Newman recalls the band feeling welcome, in part because of their novelty value. "New York wasn't crawling with Brits like it is now, so people would engage you in conversation because of your accent." Grey had a similar perception. "I remember finding New York friendly in a way that London isn't, and it was partly to do with an English accent. People would ask why you were there, and if you said you were in a rock group, they'd be really enthusiastic about it. Even cab drivers – thrilled that you were in a band." Grey also enjoyed the unprecedented experience of being recognised. "Someone even walked up to me on the street and said: hi, are you Robert Gotobed? Which was quite exciting." Accent issues were a source of amusement, too. "We'd never heard anyone speaking like that for real," says Newman. "We didn't know people really spoke like Marlon Brando in *On The Waterfront.*" Broader language differences also made for moments of comic awkwardness. Newman remembers grappling – in the pre-political correctness era – with the finer points of cultural translation, wanting to order a *black* coffee in a diner but deciding not to risk it in case such terminology was deemed offensive in the USA.

The band stayed in Midtown but spent much of the time in Lower Manhattan, around CBGB. The downtown scene was famously vibrant at this stage, the East Village a magnet for artists, performers and musicians, drawn by cheap rent in what was something of a wasteland inhabited by a predominantly black and Latino urban underclass and a sizeable junkie constituency. This environment had fostered the growth of alternative art spaces and clubs. Gilbert identified the stirrings of something culturally significant amid the grim surroundings. "I was aware there was something quite bad going on: people were sinking, there were a lot of empty lots, and there was clearly a lot of poverty, but as with most cities, where there's poverty, there's openings for artists to have cheap spaces. There was very much an element of bohemia."

Lewis was shown around by Judy Nylon, who briefed him on the do's and don'ts, advising him, for instance, to carry an extra $20 bill – for use in the event of street hassle that might require the payment of local taxes. He found it all exhilarating. "It was a wild town, one of the few 24-hour cities in the world." While Gilbert also appreciated New York, he was a little unsettled. "It was a bit disturbing. Just off the main drags, there seemed to be a lot of people just hanging around. It wasn't just in particular areas. It was everywhere. People looking very sinister, lurking, looking for something … looking for victims. That's what it felt like." Grey found the natives friendly, but he also remembers feeling intimidated. "The place was fairly scary, especially the subway, although it wasn't quite as threatening as I'd heard. They had Guardian Angels on the trains, which was slightly reassuring."

During their stay in New York, they made the most of the opportunity to explore what was happening musically. Grey went to the Village Vanguard to hear some jazz and attended a Television gig at the Bottom Line. Gilbert was most impressed with James Chance & The Contortions and Teenage Jesus & The Jerks, whom he saw at Max's Kansas City with Lewis. "It was very stimulating. A very arty crowd. I loved the dynamics. Very choppy. Very abstract." Lewis is more effusive: "Bruce and I thought it was the best thing we'd ever seen."

Newman didn't share that view. He was unmoved by Teenage Jesus, who he felt were trying too hard. "Teenage Jesus were rubbish. It seemed very hollow. There wasn't a lot of content: it was all out-there and didn't seem to come from anywhere, except *we wanna shock, we wanna get some attention for our super-weirdness.* They seemed so self-consciously weird, but in a way, I thought they weren't weird enough. We had bands in Britain, like The Prefects, who were darker and weirder and more believable." Not that Newman was entirely unaffected by their pose: "A proposal came through Lydia Lunch's manager that we make an alien love child. I was a bit frightened of Americans, especially the arty ones."

The No Wave bands aside, Gilbert and Lewis were disappointed to find a more general lack of musical imagination. Although Wire's shows went well, the crowds, while enthusiastic, didn't seem to be on the same wavelength. "The gigs were sold out," says Grey, "but I think the audiences were a bit mystified. I had the sense that they wanted us to be punk, and I don't think they knew that we were actually trying to get away from punk." By the time Wire arrived in New York in the summer of 1978, CBGB was no longer the epicentre of new music: even though "Him from Talking Heads" had shown up, few of the first-wave artists to have emerged from CBGB were as active on the scene now. Having signed to major labels, the likes of the Ramones, Blondie, Patti Smith, and Talking Heads were now spending much of their time on the road, and no one had taken their place. Wire had been inspired by some of the New York bands, and when they got there, they encountered a tendency to mimic what was being done in London. "By this time, you had all these wannabes," laments Lewis. "It was bizarre to us because we'd really enjoyed and fed off music that had come out of New York. Then we'd arrived back there, carrying the ball so to speak, and there were these people trying to play catch-up or basically playing limp R&B and claiming to be part of the new wave or whatever it was."

There also seemed to be a larger element of narrow-mindedness that was anathema to Wire. "The whole anti-disco thing was going on, too," Lewis recalls. "I thought aspects of disco were fantastic, but people didn't seem to realise how you could live in all of these areas and appreciate all things." While not an habitué of discotheques, Gilbert did visit one such establishment during his time in New York. He suspects it was the storied Studio 54, but time has erased the details. "I was so not happy, but Angela insisted," he explains, describing a miserable wait outside the club with crowds of people hoping to be deemed cool enough to enter. Just when it looked like they'd never make the cut, and Gilbert felt he could make his escape, the pair were singled out by the doorman; he'd noticed how differently they were dressed, compared to everyone else, and ushered them past the velvet rope. The subsequent experience wasn't a pleasant one. "It was horrendous," remarks Gilbert, "and there were an awful lot of people in the toilets."

If Wire's arrival in the USA hadn't gone to plan, they met with further problems once their CBGB stint was over. On attempting to check out of their hotel, they learned that the bill hadn't been settled – and manager Mick Collins was nowhere to be seen. "He flew back to London without telling us and didn't pay the hotel," Grey recalls, "and we had to get the money from the record company." This oversight was a sign of problems to come with Collins's handling of the band.

## Songs for Europe

Back home, following a month off, Wire returned to the BBC's Maida Vale studios on September 20 to tape another Peel session. Although *Chairs Missing* had only just been released, the band elected to play four new tracks that would appear on *154* a year later ('A Mutual Friend', 'Indirect Enquiries', and more preliminary drafts of 'On Returning' and 'The Other Window'). "EMI were pissed off," Lewis says. "Surprise, surprise." But while the band didn't compromise for Radio 1, they did make some concessions for their live performances throughout this period: when they went on the road in the UK at the end of September in support of *Chairs Missing*, their set focused on that album – although quite a few newer numbers were also included, most of which would show up on their next album.

95

After their UK dates, in November Wire travelled to continental Europe for the first time, playing in Holland, Belgium, and Germany. Exciting as the US trip had been as a tourist experience, it wasn't especially meaningful for Wire as a band; they had exhausted what America had to offer in terms of influence during the phase of work that led to *Pink Flag*. "Playing in Europe was where we really expanded," explains Lewis. "That was where our real confidence came from. We really felt we'd come home. This wasn't America. We'd already used up the American part of our heritage; the European part from the early 70s, there it was." Newman, too, emphasises the group's European experience. "It was monster. It was absolutely huge. Even though we only played a handful of gigs there in 1978, the influence was enormous – more enormous than you could possibly imagine."

This gravitation toward the Continent is another characteristic that situates Wire within the British art-rock tradition, which looked beyond US rock'n'roll and displayed a marked European sensibility. The latter had been absent from second-wave punk, with its Little England mentality and its rock'n'roll core: just as most mainstream punk overlooked innovative musical history at home, it was also apparently unaware of revolutionary sounds made across the Channel in, say, Germany in the early and mid 70s. Neu!, Faust, Kraftwerk, and Can, among others, had produced inventive, adventurous work, but few punks immediately acknowledged them.

Europe was important to Wire mainly because it seemed a world away from the by-now meaningless punk scene in Britain. In addition to being artistically irrelevant, that scene was insular and inward-looking, with an ideologically suspect whiff about it, as latter-day punks clung onto the Sex Pistols' subverted-nationalist iconography well past its sell-by date and embraced their identity as an unofficial tourist spectacle for foreign visitors to London. For Wire, the New York visit hadn't been a complete antidote to all of that, but on the Continent in November 1978 they found a culture that was moving beyond punk and, crucially, people to whom it had never been central in the first place. Wire felt an instant connection. "People didn't buy into punk the way they did in Britain," observes Newman. "They were into something that was a bit more arty – and we were very much that kind of thing." Gilbert has a similar recollection. "There were some punks, but people seemed to be thinking about it the way we thought about it: the simplicity and the violence of punk got turned into something more experimental. It wasn't 'fast pop' there: they took a much more avant-garde view than the pop scene in Britain. That a punk-type thing could be avant-garde just wasn't in the brochure here – not in the imagination of anybody."

The difference from Britain was dramatic and energising. "There was a sense that we'd suddenly come home," says Newman, echoing Lewis's sentiments. "We got strong receptions, and people were excited we were there," Grey recalls, "more excited than at gigs in England." Newman stresses how differently Wire were perceived and how they fitted into the cultural landscape, in contrast with their experience in the UK. "When we were touring Britain, there was an element of us being 'the Friday night entertainment'. We always had an audience, but they didn't treat you very well. When we got to continental Europe, suddenly the way the people treated us was so different: you played gigs, and the place was still open afterwards, and everyone wanted to meet you. They were interested and engaged and wanted to know what you thought about stuff. In Britain, you'd play the gig, get back to the hotel and nothing's open and no one talked to you – apart from telling you to fuck off. But in Europe we felt part of it. We felt welcomed."

This sense of recognition and belonging was strongest in Germany, where there was even some mainstream media interest: the band appeared on the ARD music programme *Szene 78* in Munich, miming to 'Practice Makes Perfect'. (Also on the show were Magazine and Elkie Brooks.) Above all, what Wire discovered in Germany was a cultural sensibility that resonated with them. This was immediately apparent when they arrived at the Ratinger Hof in Düsseldorf during their short run of November dates. At the Ratinger Hof, with its spartan décor, bands and audience rubbed shoulders with students and faculty from the nearby Düsseldorf Art Academy, creating a unique setting where interests in new music and experimental art co-existed, spanning generations. "The people who'd go there were aged between 16 and 78," comments Lewis. "It was a bar Joseph Beuys used to drink in. And I met Gabi Delgado of D.A.F. for the first time there. He must have been about 16. It was very diverse. It was the art scene that didn't really exist in London. It was something that we hoped existed but never quite found there."

If Wire felt most at home in Germany, for Gilbert, paradoxically, feeling at home had to do with unfamiliarity. Gilbert experienced a new, acute sense of otherness in Germany that intrigued him. "It was the typography on buildings and shops, it was so foreign. And, for me, the main thing was that the people were so different. The intensity was interesting. It was very stimulating." To Lewis, that intensity derived from the spectre of terrorism hanging over the country since the previous year's spasm of violence linked to the Red Army Faction. Memories of the *Deutscher Herbst* (German autumn) were still raw, the threat of violence part of the fabric of everyday life. "This was the time of the Baader-Meinhof gang," says Lewis. "There was a definite sense of heading toward civil war." The atmosphere of heightened tension and alertness was something he found creatively inspiring.

Grey also experienced that unsettled attraction. For him, it was more explicitly about the Cold War context framing Wire's first visit to Berlin. "It felt very different. It was about Berlin being an exotic place, because it was in the East, and so you had to drive through the corridor to get there and go past East German checkpoints, with armed guards who didn't smile. I felt slightly uneasy. So the whole build-up to the idea and the event of playing in Berlin made it atmospheric and exotic. You were on an island in the middle of East Germany. It did feel quite alien."

Berlin impacted Wire perhaps more than Düsseldorf. This was because of its peculiar geopolitical and cultural situation. The music the band-members listened to together on this trip reveals a vivid awareness of their surroundings and a psychological investment in the mythology of that environment: both Grey and Wire's road manager, Bryan Grant, recall that Bowie's 'Berlin albums' *Low* and *"Heroes"* were regularly played in the bus on this tour. "I remember the interminable drives," laughs Grant, "with Bowie and Eno blaring out through the cassette player at distorted volumes." Newman, too, has a clear recollection of this. "I remember in late 1978 when we were in Berlin, we had a trip down to the Wall playing *Low*, getting the Cold War vibe. It was exciting. I remember having shivers up my spine. It was so perfect. It was so bleak."

Gilbert saw parallels between New York's downtown scene and Berlin, insofar as the German city also nurtured artistic experimentation, the inhabitants creating their own culture in this singular, liminal milieu. "It was similar to New York, in a way. There were very few new buildings. It hadn't quite got on its feet. There was a decadence, I suppose. Lots of young people, very few of them from Berlin. It was a magnet. It was glamorous because it was an island, and it had been heavily subsidised: businesses could get a loan and open a bar. All you needed to do was find a space, get it decorated, get some stock. Very, very exciting. Lots of vintage shops, too. Young people were all dressed in vintage clothes from these shops. It was all very experimental." According to Lewis, this was where Gilbert first saw 'The Mac', one of the outerwear choices that would become de rigueur for the post-punk generation. "That's what Bruce came back with. I remember him praying for it to rain so he could wear it."

Much of the uniqueness of Berlin that made such an impression on Wire was encapsulated in the club they played there, SO36 in Kreuzberg. This was another venue with deep cultural roots: originally a 19th-century beer garden, after World War I it was the site of one of Berlin's first cinemas; by the early 1970s it had become an artists' squat and studio space, eventually transforming into a music venue that was managed for a time by Martin Kippenberger. Like the Ratinger Hof, it gave Wire a feeling of aesthetic community, embodying a cultural ethos with which they felt an affinity; in this case, however, there was also a greater sense of newness, a forward-looking spirit reflected in the club's industrial design and layout. "In addition to the whole Cold War thing, Berlin was super-hip," says Newman. "We did three nights at SO36. It was so cool. Cool and metallic – everything in Britain was grubby at that point, but this was already anticipating the 80s. It was clean and cool." Grey agrees: "It was more sophisticated than upstairs in a pub." Lewis describes in a little more detail what made SO36 stand out: "It was designed by guys who were avant-garde theatre designers. It was a clean aesthetic: glass fridges, no drinks on the bar. It was extraordinary. I'd never seen anything like it. It was the whole European style. It was a very different scene. It wasn't rock'n'roll."

Newman's identification of and connection with a sensibility that was "anticipating the 80s" is important for understanding what happened next to Wire. The following year would see the release of the magisterial *154*, an album that was already very much an 80s record in terms of both the ambition that drove its creation and the sonic terrain it charted. It would be an ambivalent achievement, though: while the greatness of this hard-fought album stemmed in large part from the emergence of three strong songwriters, each with his own vision, the same fragmentation and tension that made *154* possible would become a factor leading to Wire's seeming dissolution.

## CHAPTER 4
# 1979

### Don't believe the hype

The year 1979 began with an incident that augured badly for Wire's relationship with EMI. 'Mannequin', 'I Am The Fly', and 'Dot Dash' had all failed to make an impact on the charts, but the label was still pushing for a Wire hit. *Chairs Missing*'s 'Outdoor Miner' was the obvious choice. No single had been released in conjunction with *Chairs Missing*, and the 'Outdoor Miner' seven-inch came nearly four months after the album (with 'Practice Makes Perfect' on the B-side). At 1:45, it had initially been deemed too short for a single, so it was extended by a minute with a Mike Thorne piano solo, plus an expanded chorus. As chart material, it seemed to be a shoo-in: like 'I Am The Fly', it was an infectious sing-along; unlike 'I Am The Fly', it was a gorgeous, melodic pop song; it came in an unusual picture sleeve (designed by Mick Collins and his wife); and a limited edition release on white vinyl made it a collectable item, albeit one with dubious fidelity.

If Bruce Gilbert thought the album version had gone too far in the pop direction, then the musical enhancements carried out with a view to chart success didn't make him feel more enthusiastic about the song. The others accepted the changes as a means to an end. "It was all right," Graham Lewis says. "It was a bit of pragmatism. But what wasn't all right was that it was on white vinyl and sounded like shit. The cover was great; the record sounded crap. And then EMI got caught doing something we'd explicitly asked them not to do."

Lewis is alluding to the fact that the band were sucked into a controversy over sales. Two weeks after its release in January – as it sat at Number 51, en route for the Top 30 – 'Outdoor Miner' was removed from the charts by the British Market Research Bureau. According to *Melody Maker*, the BMRB's action may have come after "one of its officials became aware of the possibility that inducements had been offered for sales of the single to be exaggerated in chart-return shops". A routine performance check on new entries and fast-rising singles then indicated that 'Outdoor Miner' should not have been placed in the chart. Speaking to *Melody Maker*, the BMRB's

Chris Baker maintained that it was "not particularly a check for hyping or malpractice", and EMI publicity officer Brian Southall dismissed suggestions of payola, but the damage was done. In the end, it wasn't the label that would suffer. "EMI didn't take any flak for it," remarks Lewis, still justifiably aggrieved. "It had been our name that had taken that." This was the nearest Wire would come to a hit, their closest call with commercial success.

Undeterred, Wire went about their business, visiting Belgium in February for a handful of gigs and an appearance in Brussels on the RTBF television programme *Follies*, alongside Siouxsie & The Banshees. On Valentine's Day, they travelled to Cologne to perform live on WDR's *Rockpalast*, the music show hosted by ex-pat Briton Alan Bangs. Refreshments at the Ratinger Hof in Düsseldorf the night before had left the band-members the worse for wear, and their spirits weren't lifted by the (seated) audience in Studio-L, which seemed to have been bussed in from a librarians' convention. Lewis wasn't impressed. "We looked at them and thought: this isn't terribly inspiring, really." Even so, the hour-long performance – the only substantive visual document of Wire playing live in the 70s – catches them at a highpoint. Like most gigs from the period, the set drew fairly evenly on *Chairs Missing* and *154*, the latter still several months away from recording.

*154* had in fact been demoed in its entirety at Riverside Studio a fortnight before Christmas, along with 'A Question Of Degree' and 'Former Airline', which would see release as the A- and B-sides of Wire's fifth single in June, and 'Stepping Off Too Quick', a mediocre song that could easily have been a refugee from the *Pink Flag* era. The demo versions of the *154* tracks make for fascinating listening. At Advision, the band and their producer would construct a spacious, textured sonic landscape, but even in these simpler, slightly raw run-throughs, the basic arrangements are in place, and the strength and distinctiveness of the songs is already incontestable – notwithstanding 'I Should Have Known Better' and 'The Other Window', which would be totally revised. Two months on from the Riverside session, the *Rockpalast* performance showed that the *154* material was in a more advanced, road-hardened state. "We were bulletproof by that point," says Lewis. "We understood the opportunity. You can really see how we managed to develop the material in such a short period of time: we were doing it live on the road, editing it and arranging it."

## For your displeasure

The year had begun badly with the 'Outdoor Miner' fiasco, but it got worse.

On February 27, Wire embarked on their second major outing as a support band, spending the next three weeks opening for Roxy Music, who were on the continental leg of their *Manifesto* tour. As with The Tubes, EMI shelled out a respectable sum for this privilege, although Wire were of course paying, since the label would recoup the money from the band's royalties. The expectation was that Roxy's reflected glory, plus exposure to their considerable audience, would foster wider popularity and more substantial sales for Wire; in turn, it was hoped that this music-business rite of passage would enable Wire to headline bigger venues themselves and to continue the process with their own support act in tow. None of this transpired, and the tour was unexpectedly taxing.

It was a learning experience. Wire were accustomed to hostile audiences, but the scale of things made this a unique challenge. Whereas Roxy Music fans in 1972 might have appreciated some aspects of Wire, Roxy Music fans in 1979 did not. "Wire were the last thing they wanted to experience," notes Gilbert, a fact that was made clear by the negative reaction – so extreme that it shocked even road manager Bryan Grant, a seasoned veteran who'd toured in various capacities with Miles Davis, Led Zeppelin, and Pink Floyd, among others. "Roxy by that time had become very MOR," he recalls. "Audiences were attuned to Bryan Ferry and nice suits – the fashion-oriented side of it – and the music had become very mainstream. When these little herberts got onstage, the audience just *hated* it. Usually, the reaction to a support band is one of boredom or people just go to the bar. What I found interesting was this violent, visceral reaction. I thought: Fuck! Why is it so violent? What is this about? I even remember the German promoter coming backstage to apologise. It was very brave of them to keep going out there and get booed and yelled at."

The unfriendly reception prompted a strategy on Wire's part. "The audience didn't want to see you, so you developed an antagonistic edge that I think improves your playing," says Robert Grey. "You have to be assertive and quick, do what you're supposed to do. I think that was a good thing for us – it was testing." Lewis lays out that strategy in more detail: "The Roxy thing could have been a disaster – it was monstrous, really – but we turned it to our advantage. We went into a creative-survival mode. It was 'character building', as they say. We thought: We're going to have fun with this. If they fuck with us, we're not going to lie down. At the beginning of the tour, the set took 45 minutes; by the end, we were playing it in about 30 – without any gaps. It started intense and just got more intense and more and more exciting. Then, for the last song, we just dropped it, pushed it off the cliff:

we played a really, really slow version of 'Heartbeat' and destroyed all the energy." And it didn't end there. Wire contrived a final touch for their ungrateful audiences, as Lewis explains: "Then we left the stage, one at a time, walking slowly, very deliberately, off this huge stage – with 8,000 people whistling and chanting for Roxy – until Rob hit the last drum beat and the lights went out. What we did was to suck the oxygen out of the room, taking all the adrenalin with us."

But it wasn't just a matter of dealing with hostile crowds. Wire also had to contend with Roxy Music's road crew. "We were very small, and they were like an army," says Lewis. "It was eight of us and 50 of them – and that's not very good odds, really." One problem was that the crew seemed to delight in progressively reducing Wire's stage space. Gilbert describes this peculiar process: "They kept making our playing area smaller and smaller, so eventually we were practically teetering on the edge. There was a very narrow ribbon of activity at the front." What's more, Gilbert is convinced that Wire were expected to give the lighting technician a backhander. "It was made clear that some 'inducement' would be required for him to give us any light – to make it worth his while."

Wire pressed on regardless. According to Gilbert, "Our answer to the shrinking stage and dimming lights was: Carry on, do what you like. We'll still play, even if that means in the dark. The more the Roxy Music crew inched us out of inhabiting the stage, the better we liked it, because it was a limitation: we can use limitation because we'd played at the Roxy Club with a two-inch stage. We could deal with that. But we certainly weren't prepared for people who wanted bribes for more light. So it became almost an obsession – what are they going to do next? Are we going to have to play behind the curtain at some point? We could do that."

Bryan Grant, however, doesn't believe anything underhanded was going on. "I remember Graham and Bruce saying they thought there was some sort of conspiracy in the Roxy camp. It's true that the crew won't give support acts the whizz-bang-wallop that the main act gets – they're being paid to look after them. It's just the way of it." Nevertheless, he did make it clear that his band weren't to be messed around. "On the first day, the head of Roxy's crew, Fat Bastard – as he was affectionately known – said to our engineer: you're only getting three mics. And I walked up to him and said: Fuck off. We get what we need, or I'll knock you out. It was quite easy – he'd actually worked for me before. That's the way you had to be. You had to fight your corner in those days."

Grant is sure that the band's perception of an ongoing campaign of subterfuge was coloured by the generally stressful nature of the tour. "I think the guys maybe built it up in their minds as something other than what it was, because it was probably incredibly traumatic. They didn't have that much gig experience at that point, and this was their first experience of arenas. And this violent reaction was, I would imagine, incredibly scary. So I told them it was bullshit. Roxy didn't feel threatened. I said: You have to understand something – I doubt Roxy even know you exist. That's the way it is. It isn't a conspiracy."

While the challenges – perceived or real – motivated Wire to raise their creative game, their mood was negatively affected by seeing, close-up, what had happened to a band they had greatly admired. Roxy Music had been a major early inspiration for Wire, but it was a grim spectacle to witness that group now past its prime, performing slick, rigidly organised sets in vast auditoriums night after night. "The first night when we saw them playing," recalls Lewis, "I was almost in tears, thinking: what have we done? It was a pale shadow of what had been so incredibly inspiring in 1972. It was sad and so lame compared to that. The noise wasn't there. What I liked was the interaction between them all, and that was gone." Gilbert was similarly disillusioned. "Without the Brian Eno element, it was now all rather depressing, and they were being interviewed all the time, so there was no spare time for any interaction with us. There was no going down the pub with *them*."

Grey did enjoy some fleeting bonhomie with the headliners. "Paul Thompson talked to me about my drum kit – he was the only one who behaved like an ordinary person." A passing "You're looking fabulous" from Bryan Ferry was the extent of Colin Newman's interaction with Roxy's front man but, as he notes: "To have a style icon tell me I was looking good was gratifying."

Most worryingly of all, the Roxy Music dates revealed to Wire the full horror of how they might end up if they were to take the same career path. It wasn't an attractive proposition. "Here we saw a band who had been like us," says Newman. "They'd been at the top of their generation, and what were they doing now? They were playing stadiums as Bryan Ferry's backing band. We thought: Fuck! Is that what we've got coming?"

It wasn't all negative, however. The fate of their art-rock idols might have given Wire pause, but the tour also provided them with a useful context to further shape and sharpen their new work. As Lewis observes: "We'd decided to take about 60 per cent new material on the road – *154* essentially. So, basically, we were rehearsing to make what was *154*."

## Just say (E)no

As the time drew close to return to Advision to make *154*, ideas were bounced around regarding the album's producer. While Eno had been invoked as a way of persuading Thorne to play keyboards on *Chairs Missing*, Lewis remembers Wire now considering him again – this time, to produce *154*. "It was more of a bar conversation – it never really went further than that – but we thought: wouldn't it be a good idea if Mike did one side and Eno did the other? That was quite a radical concept. But it was mentioned to Mike, and Mike wasn't very enthusiastic."

Newman wasn't enthusiastic, either, mainly because he felt that Eno's artistic philosophy and working methods, which were more sympathetic to the Gilbert–Lewis axis in Wire, would unsettle the band's creative balance. "Brian was interested in us; whether that meant he wanted to get involved, I don't know. I think it was Bruce's idea. If we were getting Eno in, it would be to strengthen Bruce's hand, with his focus on process. I was against it. We needed someone who had some idea of how it worked technically. We didn't want it to be random. I tend to like form. I had a fear of having 24 tracks of random crap and it just getting mixed into something."

Besides, Newman insists that the band-members were more than happy with Thorne and that there was no need to change a setup that had been proven to work well. "We were still in a period where there's no way we could have produced our own records, and we were all very excited about Mike. It was a period where Mike was a very good foil for us, setting a framework for us to work within – quite an expanded framework – and giving us some of the tools. And he came to the sessions armed with guitar pedals." Consequently, the team of Thorne, Paul Hardiman, and Ken Thomas was left unchanged.

## Your band's shit

While *154* and *Chairs Missing* are very different records in mood and scope, *154* has a lot in common with its predecessor with regard to the process of its creation – that is, the questing impulse at the heart of the material's development and recording. "*154* is a step further in using the studio to your advantage, making more use of it," says Grey. Lewis agrees: "It was a natural extension of the direction that had started on *Chairs Missing*." For Gilbert, Thorne's role in that process remained key. "Mike obviously saw that this area we'd started with *Chairs Missing* could be expanded and that it could be much more interesting. He was getting more daring with production ideas, and there were more opportunities for him to broaden the spectrum in terms of the way tracks could be constructed or created, which suited us very well because we were working at home now too – and lots of ideas which weren't necessarily to do with straightforward music were being developed."

Also crucial to the making of *154* was the burgeoning technology, which inspired the band and revealed new sonic vistas. "It was a natural progression," Gilbert comments. "It's not just to do with guitar pedals but also studio equipment going forward in leaps and bounds. There were all sorts of things that Mike was au fait with, as an inveterate gadget buyer – remarkable reverb machines, for example. They weren't just steel tubes with a spring in them; they were very sophisticated, tuneable."

Lewis, too, underscores the band's intensified focus on the possibilities opened up by the recording environment and its tools. "It was about more and more noises. We were buying more effects pedals, hoping to find another noise we could explore. The way the guitar sounds had developed, it was perfectly natural to extend. Bruce was really out there." Thorne remembers Gilbert's interest in pedals, not just as the starting point for a track – as the source of an interesting random noise – but also as tools with which to engage in the continuing development of pieces. "One post-session, Bruce borrowed some of my effects, saying, 'I have some homework to do.' He came in the following day and laid out some simple and elegant parts which changed the target tracks, including the opening lick for 'On Returning'."

Above all, Wire's renewed engagement with technology expanded that "genuinely electric sound" discovered during *Chairs Missing*. *154* capitalised on the shift in emphasis away from discrete instruments to an effects-based blurring of boundaries between keyboards and guitars, as Thorne explains: "We were all delighted with the keyboard additions, with the emergent philosophy that we were just making an integrated electric sound which didn't have an obvious source. No guitar heroes or keyboard flash here – I couldn't have done that anyway. We all got better at 'electric' and defining a style out of nowhere."

To Newman, the significance of this "integrated electric sound" lay in its newness and in its potential as a larger, state-of-the-art canvas for Wire's rapidly proliferating ideas. "We just wanted to increase the sound palette. Everything was *better*. We considered ourselves at the top of our game. We were the best, and everything had to be the best, had to be new. *Modern* is what we were after. We had new and better synths, and we had more pedals: more of everything. We really wanted that expansive sound." One of the keys to achieving that overall effect was the use of multi-tracking. Although this was nothing new, on *154* that technique became more pervasive as a means of augmenting the "sound palette". "We'd done guitar tracked to death, as far back as *Pink Flag*," Newman notes, "but by *154* everything was tracked. We recorded at least three of every part and bounced them down to one track, and they sounded bigger. And also with vocals: I was doing masses of vocals so, often, a lead vocal will be two vocals."

Size certainly mattered on *154*. For Lewis, it was an essential element in the sensibility of the material itself, which had evolved and come together, most of all, in the large performance spaces encountered on the Roxy Music tour. "The scale of things had changed. When you work in a big space, you start to make work that's appropriate to that space, and it resonates with that space. It's more symphonic. It was about size. These things were big: they'd been big live, and we'd been learning to play them in very big places. We weren't scared of the dimensions. Those epic qualities had developed naturally, because that's where we'd been singing these songs of love and alienation."

The live experience played an important role in the evolution of the *154* tracks. The Roxy Music tour had posed challenges to which Wire had risen, and they were arriving at *154* in a position of strength. "We'd survived what was thrown at us, and we were writing huge amounts," Lewis stresses. "It was a highly productive period, with material again being turned over rapidly." Newman also remembers this as a fertile, adventurous phase. "We'd hit *Chairs Missing* with the confidence of having played quite a few gigs and people knowing we were pretty good; we hit *154* with the confidence of knowing that, basically, we were the best band in the world, that we were going places, and that we were going to show them."

Newman and Lewis's observations convey the notion that Wire came to *154* with a sense of the moment, poised to make their best work thus far, an album of widescreen, expansive material: this was going to be a *big* record. It's in these terms that the album can be seen to anticipate the zeitgeist of the 80s. Looking back, Newman is convinced of this. If there was a concept for *154*, it was, he says, "to be the best. I think the whole point it comes down to is the *ambition* of it. In many ways, *154* is an 80s record. It prefigures the 80s by its ambition. It was a status symbol. The statement we were making was: Sorry mate, we're the best. We're better than you. Your band's shit. Why don't you give up? We were saying that to everybody: Here we are – fist on the table – this is Wire. Deal with that. Our heads were big. We were full of ourselves. We were in receipt of so much praise. People from all the really cool bands regarded Wire as being THE band. So *154*'s a little bit oversized and less playful than *Chairs Missing*, but that isn't to say that some of it isn't really great."

Interestingly, Gilbert suggests that *154*'s grand scale and its weighty, serious tone may also have derived from an awareness on Wire's part that they were about to make their final album, as the dynamic changed within and around the band. "I couldn't say for sure, but it could be that it comes from a sense that this might be the last record – that it's got to have some gravitas, something substantial about it, because it might be the last chance to make the Wire statement."

## Storming the charts

On the face of it, Wire's self-regard and drive at this point, coupled with their productivity, might imply that the band and EMI were on the same page. As far as EMI was concerned, after two albums, this was Wire's moment, and *154* was the record that would break them. (*Pink Flag* had failed to chart and *Chairs Missing* had stalled at Number 48.) However, it soon became obvious that band and label had different ideas about what success meant, as well as how it should be achieved. According to Newman, "the atmosphere for *154* was set by Mike coming in at the start, fresh from the A&R department, and saying we had to make a series of singles that would be compiled into an album, and we'd storm the pop charts; Bruce arrived with the idea that it was time to make the Big Statement of Western Art."

There was definitely a growing tension between Wire and their label, which seemed to be in transition and heading in a direction that worried the band. The bigger corporate picture in mid 1979 was grim, as EMI itself was in the midst of financial difficulties that would result in its merger with Thorn Electrical Industries by the end of the year. This contributed to the general climate of instability. "Everybody was becoming edgy about our relationship with the label, especially after the attempted hyping of 'Outdoor Miner'," says Gilbert. "It was really starting to get a bit funny: there was a smell of fear in the air at the label about the need for commerciality." In his view, Wire's estrangement was compounded by a turnover in staff, which meant that many of the people in place when the band had come to EMI were no longer around. These were people with a better understanding of Wire, who backed their work. "The personnel had changed," Gilbert recalls, "and they didn't have the same philosophy as the people originally working on Harvest, like Nick Mobbs" (who had left the previous year).

Predictably, EMI's plan for *154* to be driven by singles found little favour with Wire. Lewis remembers: "The band's reaction was: Fuck that! We're doing an album, and there'll be some singles amongst it. That didn't go down particularly well." But if the tension between label and band over the methodology was a worrying sign, the apparent differences of opinion within the band were also raising a red flag.

Gilbert certainly felt that *154* could and should be an impressive statement – although the notion of the album as the "Big Statement of Western Art", attributed to him by Newman, is a traditionalist concept to which Gilbert himself wouldn't subscribe. Putting it another way, Newman provides a less exaggerated account of how he saw the competing philosophies going into *154*, with "me at one end of the spectrum and Bruce at the other, wanting to make something very experimental". While the album does suggest a division along those lines, it's not a black-and-white issue: some tracks undermine that idea of an experimentation-versus-pop, Gilbert-versus-Newman dynamic. According to the original composition credits, Gilbert supplied two of the album's memorable pop songs ('40 Versions' and 'Blessed State'), while Newman's music for 'Indirect Enquiries' and 'A Mutual Friend' is hardly evidence of a superficial pop sensibility.

Whether the creative conflict was as straightforward as the one Newman outlines, divisions were surfacing nonetheless. The prospect of Wire at a highly motivated artistic peak might have boded well for the album they were about to make, but that same ambition, confidence, and wealth of ideas were also a liability. Ultimately, creative differences would threaten dissolution as Lewis, Newman, and Gilbert focused, to a greater extent than before, on their own respective ideas and designs for the record. The songwriting credits on the original British release of *154* illustrate the separation that was taking place: five of *Chairs Missing*'s 15 tracks were originally assigned to one writer, while on *154* the proportion is higher, with eight out of 13 numbers penned by one band-member alone. (As with *Pink Flag* and *Chairs Missing*, however, there were changes to the 2006 reissue, which saw Newman receive credits for melody on '40 Versions', initially attributed to Gilbert alone, and 'Single K.O.', at first assigned only to Lewis. Gilbert's credit for 'Map Ref. 41°N 93°W' has been cut completely.)

## A bit of a war

In Newman's opinion, for *154*, individuals were bringing work to Wire that didn't belong on a Wire album, putting personal ambition before the band. "Before *Chairs Missing*, when I came with 'Practice Makes Perfect' and said, 'this is the new direction', the others were there immediately, but it all became more complicated on *154* because suddenly Graham and Bruce had pieces they wanted to do, and there wasn't the space for everything. Not for the first or last time, Wire became a vehicle for the ambitions of several of its members, and it's not a vehicle that can contain every single version of what everybody wants in everything; sometimes people have to realise things outside the band. You've got to give to Wire what is Wire's. That was always my idea. There are times when Wire has seemed to be about people being after what they want, more than the band. And I wasn't less guilty than anyone else in that, but for me it was always about the material – whether it was right for Wire." Newman leaves no doubt as to his feelings concerning some of the material his bandmates brought to the record. "There were some genuinely amazing and exciting bits of *154*, and there were some bits I absolutely hated. *Pink Flag* was just the sound of the band playing, *Chairs Missing* was a fantastic leap into the unknown, and *154* was between brilliant and rubbish."

Gilbert has a different take on how the ideas that the band-members were independently developing affected Wire. "I think the working method, in terms of creating material or playing, was changing. Everybody by that time had home-recording facilities of varying qualities: Graham and I were having ideas about outside projects, and there were ideas already for Colin about making a solo album." He accepts that the band-members had ambitions with respect to their own ventures but doesn't agree that they tried to distort Wire into a vehicle for achieving those ambitions. To him, everyone understood the line of demarcation between Wire's work and solo endeavours, and he feels that their individual work was in fact starting to lead them away from Wire, rather than being forcibly channelled into it:

"There was a definite air of fragmentation. Listening to *154* now, you can hear that it's flying in all kinds of directions, that the approaches were becoming separate. In many ways, some of the tension was more to do with what was going to happen next. Obviously, we were all still committed to the idea of the Wire project, but through Wire the home-recording thing had grown, and confidence was building. Ideas and material which normally would have been steered toward the Wire project were now being steered toward potential solo material: Colin was storing away things for his album and Graham was thinking in those terms too, and there were things of mine that were maybe a little too weird for the Wire project."

Indeed, Gilbert was acutely aware of holding back and not bringing all his experimental impulses to bear on the group's work. "I always liked thinking: What qualifies as music? How far can you go and still have it sort of fit into a musical framework? I think there was a bit of that on *154*, although there were times I thought it could have gone further, that it could have been odder." In the end, the feeling of separation and an increasing focus on his own work almost led Gilbert to take a radical step before embarking on *154*. "I would have been very happy to have stopped Wire then. In may ways, I thought it would have been more stimulating to have stopped and to have just carried on recording at home and hopefully just develop a project."

Although Newman talks of others' ambitions becoming a problem, Gilbert believes that Newman's own ambitions manifested themselves quite clearly during the making of *154*. "It was a different atmosphere from before. Sometimes it seemed to be more about what Colin could learn about the studio than it was about making the actual work. He was obviously thinking in terms of producing, and Mike was very happy to show him the ropes." While Gilbert didn't think Newman's interest was, in itself, problematic, he did feel that it started to weaken the band as a unit when Thorne and Newman began to work without the others. "Mike was happy to have the so-called main songwriter in on it. The 'junior producer' was spending so much time with Mike that it felt as if Colin was actually working with Mike, as if they were making *154* together – and the rest of us were onlookers."

Gilbert is reluctant to apportion blame or to infer any negative intentions. "'Hijacked' is too strong a word. I think it was more that Colin took advantage of the situation. He was determined to make the most of the recording experience to learn the trade. And I suppose it was one of those situations where things drift. We weren't actively excluded. There were occasions where Mike would say something like: we're going to multi-track this voice or do some processing, so you might as well go to the pub. And I might say: play it over the headphones, and I'll muck around along to it and maybe come up with something else. But they'd say: No ... we're concentrating on this particular part, and the last thing we need is another part. *From you*. Well, it wasn't actually said like that ... that's a bit wicked, really."

The gap between the creative camps widened, and Gilbert and Lewis, feeling marginalised, didn't see much point in waiting around at Advision. "In the end, Graham and I allowed them to do that," Gilbert concedes, "but it had this feeling that it wasn't really firing on all cylinders like it had been, and if there's nothing going on in the studio that's interesting to you, you can't just sit there. We were very restless, so we started to spend more and more time away from the studio while they were doing overdubs or new vocals. We went to the pub and plotted and planned."

However, Gilbert can also see the Thorne–Newman axis as a logical development, in the broader context of the band's relationship with EMI. Thorne would have been under some pressure from the label. "I'm sure there'd been conversations with EMI," Gilbert speculates, "and they said: this is the third album, and you're not contracted to do any more, so it'd better be good. So Mike was trying to do a professional job, determined that it would be efficiently made and the highest quality he could do, in the time frame – and that probably meant keeping Colin close to him, with Colin's musical abilities. That's probably why he gravitated to working with Colin, who was a much more straightforward musician in most ways – much more about the music rather than the atmosphere, the soundscape. Although there are quite a lot of odd things on *154*, there's also quite a lot of music."

From Newman's standpoint, Gilbert and Lewis's attitude during *154*, which he sometimes portrays as destructive, contributed to the divide. As he tells it, they actually caused him to align himself with Thorne. "One afternoon, Graham and Bruce came back from the pub with a series of ultimatums about how it was going to be. It was like: we're going to do this and this and this – and there was no arguing about what we were going to do. And I got forced into the situation of being allied with Mike, who was very supportive of me as the songwriter, the person who needed things to be formalised in a certain way. I think at that point, the idea that there was a common process going on just disappeared, and it became a bit of a war. There was now a huge factionalisation. Mike had always encouraged me, so that became a divide between me and Mike and Graham and Bruce." Gilbert admits, in a roundabout way, that he and Lewis may have made things worse with the occasional ill-considered comment. "It might have come close to arguments at times. If we came back from the pub and listened to what they'd done and said: What's that? That's a bit boring, or unnecessary – a throwaway remark – it would have been a bit disheartening to the people who'd been working on it, grafting away for hours."

If it was "a bit of a war" as far as the band-members' recollections go, it seems to have been a cold one. "It didn't develop into arguments," says Grey. "It was just a feeling that everybody wasn't happy with the direction being taken or with the choices being made. Or people thought somebody had too much influence. I suppose it was a power struggle, but it was hard to define. There were disagreements going on as an undercurrent. I wasn't really involved, but having an undercurrent of disagreement didn't help and recording anything at that time was fairly stressful." To Lewis, "it was all very mysterious and extremely English, because nobody talked about it, really. People just got pissed off, and eventually Bruce and I just said: OK, we'll be down the pub if you need us, because obviously you feel you don't."

Newman confirms that, despite the generally strained atmosphere, there was little open hostility. "There was no shouting, just a lot of tension. It wasn't as bad as *The Ideal Copy*, but it was pretty awful. I can't separate *154* from how miserable it was to make it. *Chairs Missing* defined us; *154* damn near killed us. That's why it's not my favourite Wire album: it's not flawed only because of the music, but more because of the fact that it was hard work to make and that it wasn't done in the spirit of *Chairs Missing*."

For his part, Grey offers a stoic final assessment of the *154* sessions: "It seemed that the end result was so good that it was worth the pain involved."

## This is our fucking record

When Lewis revisits *154*, there's an edge to his comments on the way the sessions unfolded. His anger seems rooted in what he considers the producer's failure to grasp and to engage with the intense energy and creative confidence of the band at that time: in his view, a degree of misjudgement on Thorne's part compromised the working process at Advision.

Lewis emphasises the position of strength in which Wire found themselves prior to *154*, sure of the material and eager to get into the studio. "We'd just been fired out of a fucking gun, and we knew what we were doing, and everybody understood how good it was. We'd already made two of these things, and we were playing shit-hot. The first album, we learned to play in the studio: that captures the best performances. The second record: Hello! We've got imagination, we want to use it! The third record: We can fucking play, and we've gone somewhere else on this material. It's got imagination. This was a group that was transformed in terms of its musical craft. You had a band firing on every cylinder. We were getting harder, more decisive about what we were doing, so there were more voices in the room and more opinions. With *154*, we now understood how you make a record, so everyone had ideas, and inevitably, the conversation increased."

Like Newman, though, Lewis also saw that the band-members' growth as songwriters led inexorably to competition: "You've got the extraordinary amount of individual ambition in the group and an incredible amount of pressure about what would actually be selected for the record and who's going to support whose tracks. You've got three writers working in different combinations. Our ambition, individually, in terms of the amount of material we were producing, was a big problem." He identifies similar rifts within the production team. "Also, Mike's coming under pressure from Paul [Hardiman], because Paul is going: we've made two albums, and I certainly think my contribution is rather important. So there was an awful lot going on."

Lewis believes the producer failed to recognise the significance of these factors and, as a result, mishandled the band and their work from the outset. "We did those [December] demos with him, and if I'd been him, I'd have thought: fucking hell, these guys certainly know what they're up to. It would have been an idea to stand back a bit. As it was, Mike came in immediately with this idea of a two-week period of doing vocals, only with Colin, and it was a very poor idea, I think." Like Gilbert, Lewis was frustrated, but he is more explicit about his dissatisfaction with the direction in which Thorne and Newman seemed to be taking the material. "After a week or so of Mike doing these vocal sessions with Colin, we were invited in to have a listen – and it has nothing to do with the quality of Colin's singing – but it was just fucking wrong. Mike just got it wrong. I just think he didn't understand what the material was about, somehow. We'd always had a very open studio, but suddenly to start having demarcation lines of things that are allowed and not allowed, I think that was really bad politics. I think it was a mistake to put Bruce and I outside the studio – that was a bad idea."

After all this time, Lewis remains passionate and insistent in his belief that Thorne's approach was flawed and that the creation of *154* was made unnecessarily difficult – although he considers the album a great accomplishment. "I think Mike got his psychology very badly wrong. What you must understand is who you're working with, and Mike just didn't understand what we'd been through. We'd changed and everybody's lives had changed. I remember saying to him at some point: 'You're getting this wrong – this is *our* fucking record. We exist. You are here to make and serve this fucking record. This is our record. It's not your record.' But I'm not blaming him. I don't want to shift the blame onto him. It's just that we were all in a situation we'd never been in before. I don't think any of us had been in anything so bloody intense. I don't think any of us handled it particularly well."

## Side One

*154* increases the focus on the individual voice, thematically (in terms of songs foregrounding the subjective perspective of a narrative 'I') and also in technical terms, because of different production choices from Thorne. Both tendencies are encapsulated in 'I Should Have Known Better'.

Thorne's Yamaha CS-80 synth contributes an appropriately glacial opening tone to Lewis's rather chilly relationship autopsy, the track itself a fitting preface to an album that dramatises a breakdown in the band's creative unity. The accent on the subjective, via a prominent first-person viewpoint, symbolically highlights the sense that collaboration is yielding to individual sensibilities and ambitions. The physical prominence of Lewis's vocal performance further underscores the idea, from the start, that this is almost an album of solo pieces played – for the most part – by the band.

The air of gravitas and angst – teetering here on the edge of melodramatic bombast – sets the general tenor for *154*. "It's not quirky, jolly-dolly stuff," offers Lewis, drawing a contrast with the playfulness of *Chairs Missing*. For Newman, that gravitas and the grander, more expansive feel, typified by 'I Should Have Known Better', comes in part from the revised approach to vocals. "Vocals were definitely part of it. Again, it's all multi-tracking on *154*. You can't really achieve that sound with one voice. It was all very 'in' in the 80s. It was definitely the coming thing, the huge vocal sound. It was all part of the aesthetic. In the 80s, everything was huge: big hair, big voices, big shoulders, big everything."

As Thorne has observed, the vocals on Wire's first two albums had been under-mixed, "in the style of the time", and *154*'s difference in that regard is striking, the voices often seeming larger, playing a more significant role in the songs. Part of the story of *154*, as Thorne sees it, was "Colin and Graham developing as vocalists, and all of us developing as arrangers. We got better. As did the recordings. On *154*, I managed to set up overdubs to parallel vocal lines, which could then sit comfortably and be heard." Although the treatment of vocals on *154* is adventurous and inventive, with the tracks emphasising the voice in different ways and exploring its varied possibilities as an instrument within the arrangements, it's an aspect of the record that's often overlooked amid the many arresting sonic dimensions.

Above all, Lewis saw the compositions on *154* as a means of framing the vocal performance. "A lot of the time, I wasn't thinking about a group playing, really – of course, it *is* a group playing, and it's very much a group playing that it's based on – but you become more focused on the voice and what the voice is saying. It just sounds more modern."

In specifically musical terms, Lewis traces the origins of 'I Should Have Known Better' to his time in America the previous year. "It's proto-dance. It was one of the things I'd brought back from the New York experience. Rather than going to the American line of 'disco sucks', I felt the opposite." Newman claims a pivotal role in the song's construction, making changes to Lewis's original ideas. "It was a horrible heavy-rock song to start with. I wanted to make it into something good. That was a coup on my part, actually. It was done very early on. Bruce and Rob and I started playing it together, and then Graham asked: can we play my song now? And I said: we are playing it. He kept playing the bass part he'd been playing all along and realised it made him sound better."

The demo recording of 'I Should Have Known Better' – titled 'Ignorance No Plea' – bears little resemblance to its finished version. Lyrically, it would undergo an extensive makeover, losing some intriguing material, such as the rhyming of "Berettas" with "the upsetters" – or possibly "The Upsetters". Musically, while no longer what Newman describes as "heavy rock", the demo is still definitely a straight-ahead rock song with none of the drama or atmosphere of the album version. Lewis's "proto-dance" beat, inspired by New York, is nowhere to be heard; in its place, Grey's drumming adds driving heft.

There's no evidence of Newman's desired "expansive sound palette" on the second track, 'Two People In A Room'. Minimal, menacing, and brutal, it recalls some of Wire's hard-edged earlier work, channelling the claustrophobic explosiveness of '12XU'. It's also the perfect musical setting for another Gilbert psychodrama, but the weirdness of 'Practice Makes Perfect' is gone. This is dark stuff, a punk rock *Huis Clos* with half as many characters. "It was another one that could have easily been a poem or a short film," Gilbert says. "It's a bit like 'Another The Letter'. It came from the same area as a lot of my other ones: real or imagined scenarios 'in the yellow-bulb light' – a sickly yellow-bulb-lit room where appalling things happen. Psychological warfare."

Like several of Gilbert's most memorable pieces, 'Two People In A Room' deals with relationships. From that perspective, it's his grimmest assessment yet. "A lot of relationships are basically war that can flair into a more physical thing – or more interestingly, psychological conflict. Equally, it could describe intense relationships. Living in a small space with somebody else, it's got to be love, or else it doesn't work. As we know, especially in a small space, it can just flip very easily. Or it can erode. I was quite frightened of it happening, to be honest. Frightened that a love relationship could erode and have all sorts of frightening psychological consequences."

On a lighter note, the track also includes some minor experimentation from Grey. "I overdubbed the snare. That was something new – trying to get a special quality to the backing sound."

One of the album's strongest pop songs, 'The 15th' was a logical selection for release as a single. That this didn't happen is, for Newman, something that still rankles. He sees it as a casualty of band politics. "Bruce didn't play on it, and that was a tactic," he claims. "'Outdoor Miner' had been a single, and Bruce hadn't played on it, but because it was Graham's lyric and my tune, EMI could get away with releasing it as a single. Then, 'The 15th' was the one that EMI wanted from *154* as a single, but it's my tune, my lyrics, and Bruce didn't play on it, so it's not a 'band' song. Therefore, it couldn't be a single. Groups are brutal. Wire aren't alone in that."

Thorne isn't so sure about Newman's analysis. "If [Bruce] refused, it was only for musical reasons. Nothing political, unless I missed something – I often did. I was just an observer on a few tracks that I saw no need for synthesizers on and refused, so to speak." ('The 15th' *was* released as a single, 24 years later, in the form of a cover version by Fischerspooner, who registered a minor US dance-chart hit with it.)

'The 15th' features a technique employed widely on *154*: the fadeout. While this might not seem noteworthy, it was entirely absent from *Pink Flag* and barely used on *Chairs Missing*. On *154*, seven of the 13 songs fade, enhancing the continuity from track to track and contributing to the album's unity and cohesion. Thorne views this as a deliberate shift away from the punk norm. "It was just adopting a device which punk and early new wave overlooked, since they grew very directly out of live performance." For Newman, the difference between the hard stop and the fade had to do with the speed and duration of tracks, which had changed markedly from *Pink Flag* to *154*. "It's to do with pace. You're coming from *Pink Flag*, where you've got a 30-second song – that would mean ten seconds of music and 20 seconds of fadeout. The hard stop was a Wire gimmick, and when we go really fast it's quite easy to crash 'em into a wall; when they're going medium-pace or stretching out, it's more difficult."

The other band-members feel there was also something intrinsic to the material on *154* that made fadeouts desirable and sometimes necessary – in particular, a sense of open-endedness. "It felt natural for the tracks to fade," says Lewis. "They had that soundtrack quality to them: the movie fades. It wasn't conclusive, like *Pink Flag*, where it was *nonononononomistersuit*. It didn't feel like that. It was: come back next week, this movie is still running." Gilbert agrees that the nature of the material suggested continuity rather than closure, and so fadeouts were more faithful to that notion. "It seemed perfectly natural for a track to fade if it was cyclical or if there didn't seem to be any natural way for it to end without it being pretentious or self-conscious."

In general, Gilbert also believes that fades potentially added another interesting dimension to the material: "I've always been a bit of a fan of fadeouts, especially if something new starts during the fadeout, and it sounds quite interesting." This technique of footnoting or supplementing tracks expands on the experimentation with framing that was pushed seemingly to the limits on *Pink Flag*, offering a new twist on the false-ending approach. Although the fadeout on 'The 15th' doesn't introduce a new, closing-seconds element, it is part of an idiosyncratic conclusion – what Thorne calls a "double ending": Grey appears to down sticks only to resume the beat five seconds later, continuing to play for another ten seconds to the bottom of the fade. The producer describes how this came about: "We were trying for another master-take and going over a previous slightly slower take. When we got the master, we stopped recording, leaving the tail of the previous take still intact. When overdubbing, we all just picked up and played along with the fragment until the very end. It was a very nice accident."

Invited to comment on the lyrical content, Newman keeps his counsel: "It's about what it's about. I don't talk about the lyrics."

The making of 'The Other Window' was, in Lewis's recollection, particularly contentious. He was already frustrated by what he saw as Thorne's creation of a divided studio and felt the recording of this song foregrounded more serious creative differences between the producer and Wire. Here, the issue related to the problem Lewis had already noted during *Chairs Missing* – a perceived discomfort on Thorne's part when the band began to make changes to a work-in-progress.

It would be an understatement to say that 'The Other Window' experienced a transformation between the Peel session and its final version (via the December demo): the jaunty, bouncy December rendition, sung by Newman, sounds (in a certain light) curiously reminiscent of Squeeze's 'Cool For Cats'; the album incarnation is a very different matter. "When we recorded it," recalls Lewis, "Bruce was saying: it's not right, it sounds a bit ordinary. That's what happens when you get in the studio: things that sounded great live can sound weaker when you put them under the microscope. And a big fault line opened up when Bruce said: I think this sounds stupid – keep the choruses, all that kind of crap. I'm going to do it again. Take the drums out, take this and that out. I'll do the vocals. That was the point where Mike walked out into the live room, saying something like: oh, you've taken over the session."

According to Lewis, the drum track was the straw that broke the camel's back. 'The Other Window' involves some proto-sampling with a two-track drum loop, which Newman identifies as "a mix of the drum track from 'Single K.O.', slowed down a bit." He explains: "It was chosen because it was the best-sounding drum track on the album. It's also one of the best drum events on any Wire record, in my opinion. There isn't actually any sync between the drums and the track – but the ear finds an accommodation." As Lewis sees it, Thorne's reaction to this creative move highlighted his unwillingness to accept changes in direction proposed by the band as the process developed. "Introducing the drum loop was a rogue element that came in at the end. We had ideas about how to use the studio. We said: sorry, this is the way it's got to happen, because we don't like the way it is. And Mike would say: but you turned up with this material, and that's the way we're approaching it. And we said: yes, but you change your mind. Perhaps that's why the idea of Eno as producer was an easy one for us to have – because where we come from, it's not against the rules to have another idea. It was always a problem for everybody we worked with subsequently, because we weren't short of ideas. Getting a consensus as to what the idea is, is something else."

For Lewis, this is all germane to an understanding of *154*, as well as to a broader understanding of Wire. "Up until *154*, we hadn't disputed what the working method was. This is what *154* is about: people discovering or having ideas about things. In terms of creativity and working as an artist in a collaborative way, what you hope is going to happen is that you're going to have a change of philosophy somewhere along the line during the process. This is the whole idea of trying to make something. Otherwise, you've got something that's dead. I think what freaked Mike out was that he felt cheated that we'd been totally willing to be humble before, when we didn't know anything. But when we did, we were like: Fuck that! We know something, and what we want to do is *this*. And I think he found that a betrayal."

For all of the friction that the track apparently caused, Newman didn't feel deeply invested in it. "I can't say I loved it very much," he reports. "I think it has a gimmicky quality to it, although everyone was excited about it at the time – including me."

Disagreements aside, this track is notable as the first of only three Wire songs to feature a Gilbert lead vocal. "There were various attempts at it. Graham and Colin tried it, and I knew it wasn't right," Gilbert remembers.

"And I was pressurised into it. I am grateful for that, really. I hate the sound of my own voice, but I knew I could deliver it in a way that wasn't singing – more hovering between almost singing and intoning." Thorne recalls that Gilbert took "big-time" persuading. "For once, he was shy, as Graham had been when encouraged very supportively to sing his 'Sand In My Joints'. We all need our prod – as did I when press-ganged into keyboard duty – but the whole band was on his side and supportive. I think that his consequent delivery has an appropriate reticence, which complements the train-traveller's avoidance of nasty sights in favour of 'the other window', with 'a nicer view'."

Gilbert talks about the source of the song's unsettling lyric, tracing it to an acquaintance's experience of a holiday-gone-wrong. "I had a friend who worked for the railway in the late 60s and early 70s. He got a cheap ticket to the South of France once. It was a story that stuck in my mind. He'd stayed in a youth hostel in the South of France, and the way he described the whole thing had a touch of *Death In Venice* about it – a really horrible, insect-infested youth hostel. On the first day, he ventured out onto the beach and fell asleep, and he got horribly, horribly sunburned and spent the rest of the holiday inside, in this horrible youth hostel, covered in unguents of various descriptions. That always stuck in my mind as a classic thing."

Taking his friend's unfortunate trip as the framework for his narrative, Gilbert then inserted an uncanny detail from a train journey of his own. "So this idea popped in my head as I was going to bed one night: I imagined his journey down there and the thing with the horse, which is something I saw – or it was something I *thought* I'd once seen on a train journey. It was a horse tangled up in something. It was that thing of fleeting images: *Did I see that? Is that real?* All the train-journey stuff and imagining his thoughts, it wrote itself in about ten minutes, and I jotted it down in a book, switched the light off, and woke up in the morning – and it was there."

Lewis characterises 'Single K.O.' as "a text describing love and conflict", couched in the lexicon of professional wrestling. Although at 2:22 it's one of the shortest pieces, within that compact frame it boasts unlikely depth and texture – thanks largely to Thorne's spectral piano at the song's core and the intricate, building vocal harmonies. The rapid advances of technology notwithstanding, one of the track's unique sounds derives from some basic equipment dating back to Wire's earliest days, as Newman recalls: "The pizzicato part is my old Woolworth's guitar – the Woolies red 'string-breaker', as it was called – put through some fairly luxurious effects. It's the only occasion when that guitar, which is what I used to play in the early 'three guitars' version of the band, proved useful in recording." That detail aside, Newman's not a big fan of this number. "It's got a great drum track," he says, "but it's a bit of a rubbish song."

Like 'I Should Have Known Better', 'A Touching Display' is an epic, portentous affair wavering between genius and bombast, with Lewis at the centre, holding forth on romantic disquiet. It appears to cover similar psychological ground to 'Two People In A Room', but on a wall-sized canvas. Part song, part soundscape, this is a larger-than-life piece – at close to seven minutes, Wire's longest thus far. It hinges on two inspired components: Lewis's highly improbable bass solo and an electric viola part by Tim Souster.

Recruited by Thorne, Souster had read music at Oxford in the 60s and studied with Stockhausen at Darmstadt, later serving as the German composer's teaching assistant in Cologne. Souster's work spanned the classical, the experimental and the popular. During his time as composer-in-residence at Kings College, Cambridge, he formed the improvisational electronic group Intermodulation. He would go on to arrange and perform the theme music for the *Hitchhiker's Guide To The Galaxy* television series and to win a BAFTA award in the Best Original Television Music category for *The Green Man*. Lewis has good memories of the session. "Tim Souster was from that lonely place which is English electronic music. He even did the music for the Birds Eye peas advert. His own music was often very dry, very academic. He had a ball, though. He went crazy. It was so loud: at the time it was the loudest thing I'd ever heard. It had the excitement of some of the early Velvets records."

Thorne configured the studio so that Souster's viola fed through three separate time delays into three MusicMan combos, recording the results with four microphones. Souster's sonic maelstrom lays the foundation for Lewis's vocals; then, with Grey's tom-tom and crashing cymbals in support, it accompanies Lewis's gargantuan bass solo, enhanced by the wonders of an MXR Blue Box octave fuzz distortion pedal. If Andy Fraser was an early favourite of Lewis's, then this is Wire's very own 'Mr Big'. Thorne was especially fond of this number. "'A Touching Display' is one of my favourites: Graham doing so well."

Although Newman had performed on early live renditions of the track, he excused himself from the album version. "I didn't play on 'A Touching Display'. My live part was a guitar freak-out. It was purely visual. On record, someone freaking out with a guitar in the middle just didn't seem to go with it." Newman's vaguely dismissive tone seems to suggest that he didn't much care for the track. "They were having meetings and planning this fantastic thing that was going to go on. I felt I didn't want to rain on Graham's parade. If he wanted all that going on on the track, let him have it."

More taut, multi-layered, and intense than its demo and Peel-session versions, 'On Returning' highlights the growing importance of travel to Wire, something Lewis and Newman feel informs the overall sensibility of *154*. "It's about 1978, about summer in Europe and spending time in the South of France," Newman says. "Travelling changed our lives so much. You forget how much it changes you. By 1977, I'd only been out of Britain once, and that was on a school trip; by 1979, I was almost commuting. I'd become an international person. It's about the casualness of it, coming home with your second language. It's about the trappings of being cosmopolitan. I was trying to capture that in a more poetic way than maybe was necessary – but I had to keep my end up!" Musically, the track underwent some revision, at the behest of Gilbert and Lewis. "They said it sounded too boring, so I added guitar parts," remembers Newman. "I was annoyed at the time but pleased with how it turned out."

## Side Two

The Eno-esque 'A Mutual Friend' is an unusual song, starting from almost nothing and building to a symphonic wall of sound. This is one of the tracks that disprove the notion that Newman was simply Wire's pop person. "I sang the *cor anglais* line to Mike, and he played it on piano and wrote the score for the person who played it [Joan Whiting; Kate Lukas also contributes again on flute]. I wanted it to be orchestral. The song itself is slight. It's tension, tension, tension and then massive release. You get hit with everything in an orchestral sense, not a heavy-metal sense: layers of harmony and, suddenly, there's a big tune there that you haven't heard throughout the song. That's the structure."

A significant part of the harmonic impact has to do with the beautifully wrought vocal arrangement that lifts the song into another dimension. Lewis and Gilbert may have been frustrated by the time and effort Thorne and Newman devoted to arranging and recording vocals, but the results of that labour here – and throughout *154* – are undeniably special. In this case, Thorne also enlisted the huge bass voice of CBGB founder Hilly Kristal (recorded at Media Sound in New York and mixed in), which complements Thorne's deep-droning synth.

'Blessed State' is an ornate, melodic number by someone supposedly averse to such things. Gilbert is characteristically understated, almost offhand, about the writing of the tune itself. "I was just messing about on a guitar, and I found this cyclic thing that didn't really change but had parts that made you feel like the structure was changing." The bright, light electronic sheen, courtesy mostly of Gilbert's chorus-pedal-effected guitar, contrasts with the lyrical content, which drips with dark irony. We're back on familiar ground. "Again, it's about the horror of existence," Gilbert laughs. "I started looking at an old thesaurus, and it was a technical exercise in getting as many phrases meaning the same thing" – that is, *the world* or *life in general*. "It's about the horror," he continues. "That's why we're in the pub, to get away from it for a few hours and forget what it's like to be alive in a dysfunctional world. I think it's the threat of the A-bomb, again."

The track also features Lewis's best lead vocal on *154*, perfectly tailored in tone and size to the song. "It's a lovely vocal from Graham, who was well confident by then," remarks Thorne.

Although the studio played a prominent role in expanding the sonic scope of 'Once Is Enough', that wasn't achieved with the latest technology or gadgetry; rather, the band and their producer took advantage of the studio as a place for simpler, more primal play. The song rings with the sound of improvised percussion – various bits and pieces of metal, struck by a hammer-wielding Lewis. "It's all Graham's inspiration, all his credit," Thorne says. "We hired all sorts of stuff and pulled in a few found objects. It was terrific watching him rush around. I sympathised immediately – it reminded me of the mind-set (which came from nowhere I can ever rationalise) when I proposed hitting the fire escape with drumsticks at the end of 'Strange'." With idiosyncratic accelerating and decelerating tempos, there's an off-kilter, manic energy coursing through this track, magnified by the rollercoaster vocal ride, as swooping, multi-tracked voices are momentarily halted by sung-spoken punctuation before careening off again.

If there was, at least, a clear reason why 'Outdoor Miner' did not succeed as a single, the failure to chart of 'Map Ref. 41°N 93°W' – "a stonking pop song", in Newman's words – remains one of life's mysteries. Like 'On Returning', it's a track that draws on Wire's broadening horizons, as they began gigging outside the UK in 1978. "It's a piece about the joy of travelling," says Lewis, who composed half of the words on a flight from Los Angeles to New York and the rest while on the road in Holland. It's a lyrical highpoint, a fine piece of writing.

Just as 'Outdoor Miner' showed how subject matter that was apparently impenetrable and obscure could be rendered in an effortless sing-along,

'Map Ref.' displays similar transformative properties, conjuring seemingly prosaic thematic and linguistic materials into timeless pop. Its clever, linguistically self-referential quality never gets in the way or turns the lyric into a mere exhibition of clever wordiness – a crime of which Wire are guilty on occasion. This is perhaps the closest Lewis's lyrics have come to conventionally poetic language. 'Map Ref.' employs a vocabulary of rigid structure, complexity, and precision in a sweeping travelogue, which resonates in the tune's irresistible propulsiveness. It's a snapshot of something greater and more expansive, not ending but fading, in a way that implies continuity beyond its 3:37 frame. As Lewis says: "It's about travel. It continues to travel. It doesn't hit a brick wall. It's concise, but there was no conclusion."

Although *154* was a studio album in the purest sense, privileging construction over performance, 'Map Ref.' is one of Grey's favourite songs, largely because he feels it catches something of the original performance. "It comes across that we could play it well. That was live playing captured in the studio, so that's very satisfying. Obviously, it had overdubs, but it still sounds mainly live." Having listened to the album in its entirety for the first time in over two decades, in preparation for an interview for this book, Grey remarked on his relief at finally reaching track 11. For him, it's an antidote to the record's generally serious, heavy mood. "I did have to make myself get through it. I found myself thinking: Where's 'Map Ref.'? When's that coming up? – because that did give you a bit of light relief against some of the other stuff that was, well, a bit unrelenting in its effect. It makes it fairly demanding to listen to. How much seriousness can you take? I was thinking: how many more tracks before I can have a bit of a rest from this? It's the third song from the end. It's not an ordeal, but I did think I could quite easily stop. 'Map Ref.' has a more uplifting feeling to it. It's certainly more of a contrast to the other tracks."

Completely unrecognisable from its April 1978 punk-lite demo version, 'Indirect Enquiries' was another piece that caused tension as it required intensive work involving Newman and Thorne alone. "I spent a couple of days doing voices with Mike," remembers Newman. "I did it in spite of certain people thinking I was indulging."

'Indirect Enquiries' is among the tracks that problematise the idea of a simple division in the band between pop-melodic and experimental-noise sensibilities. As Thorne points out: "It's too easy just to say that Colin was heading in the pop direction and Bruce and Graham were heading in a more explorative direction – Colin was too: the poles of exploration weren't mutually exclusive." The track's closing section centres on a progressively more disturbing concoction of manipulated voices – not the sort of thing you'd find on a chart single. "We had the most fun doing the vocals," Newman says, "vari-speeding the tape and doing lots of performances of me saying: *you've been defaced*. It was supposed to be spooky and scary. It sounds like mad munchkins." Thorne still enthuses about this: "Colin really delivered on the lead, [especially] his delivery of 'lying prone'. He came back to the applause in the control room and said: it just popped out. The last *you've been defaced*s were disturbing. Magic. Typically, our partners would arrive at the studio for the ride home, to relax with us as we wound down. I remember mine and others' arriving as Colin was delivering that brutal line repeatedly, as we recorded it at different speeds. They kept very quiet on the back sofa."

Lewis sometimes used his texts to execute structural or linguistic experiments. He had previously tried, with *Pink Flag*'s '106 Beats That', to write a song with a predetermined number of beats; 'A Mutual Friend' was conceived, in part, to mention all 12 months of the year. Similarly ludic is the incorporation of "prune" as an unlikely rhyming word, mocking the unimaginative variant of moon-June lyricism in pop – although Frank Zappa got there first with 'The Duke Of Prunes' in 1967.

While it sounds like another potential single, '40 Versions' is unorthodox for its time. According to Newman, "Part of the idea was: Why do we have to have drums on everything? Why does everything have to be bass drum and snare drum – why can't we put something different on it? [The December demo collected on *Behind The Curtain* features Grey's kit-playing.] So we lost the drum track, and regular drums were replaced by gated noise. It was prefiguring sampling. We wanted to be more modern. It was in the latter part of the album when we knew the die was cast and we weren't going to work with Mike again. We could feel that things weren't as they might be." (Despite his minimal involvement, Grey considers this song a favourite. "I think it's very special; it has such a good feel about it.")

Gilbert's topic is decidedly postmodern, approaching identity as a construction or a performance. "The guy who 'The Other Window' was about descended into schizophrenia," he explains. "He wasn't a classic schizophrenic in terms of a split personality, but I became interested in the notion of split personalities and also the notion of being different people to different friends. It was an expansion of that idea. I suppose it's a tension that a lot of people have in their lives in order to function successfully in a job or a social situation: you become a different person to fit in, so you end up, in a mild way, with multiple personalities. So it was an expansion of that idea and, of course, 'we're all doomed, is it really worth it?' – back to that again."

The track ends with some extended, intricate Newman–Lewis interplay, highlighting – in *154*'s closing moments, aptly enough – the degree of vocal inventiveness that was one of the album's memorable, albeit subtle, accomplishments. As far back as *Pink Flag*, Thorne had recognised how well their vocals worked in unison. "They had nicely contrasting voices, so when they sang together, Graham's deep, warm voice complemented Colin's fairly reedy, harder sound." This arrangement offers a superb example of their combined effect.

## Funky drummer

Initial pressings of *154* included a seven-inch EP. Gilbert remembers that this came about as a result of the "big push" by EMI. "The promotion department were thinking: this is the difficult third album, we're going to throw some money at it, is there something extra we can do? So we said: let's have an EP as a part of the package." With a track by each member, diverging considerably from the album material, this gave a clear indication of the different directions their individual work was taking at this point. "Because everybody had been experimenting at home, apart from Rob, it was a good wheeze to have this very odd object," says Gilbert. "It's symptomatic of what was occurring, and we all thought it should be reflected in some sort of external non-Wire format. For me, it was a statement of intent, saying: it's not just *this* – there's other things going on. I thought of it as the other side of the coin."

The physics-lab thrum of Gilbert's 'Small Electric Piece' more than hints at the electronic minimalism to which he would dedicate much of his solo work. Meanwhile, the haunted ambience of Newman's 'Get Down (Parts I & II)' is a revelation, emphasising that the difference between the two camps in Wire was perhaps less about a clash of pop and experimental approaches and more about varying levels of experimentation.

Lewis is proud of his contribution, 'Let's Panic Later'. "It's about Berlin, based on simple sequencing and field recordings. It's an emotional, charged piece. It's a bio of the times: you can hear Bryan and everyone in the van and the fun we were having. It was exploring where we could go, but I didn't bring it to the table for *154*."

For his 'Song 1', Grey wrote a guitar part but didn't perform it himself. "It's a good thing for drummers to try playing a melodic instrument," he says, adding with a laugh, "but it's not for me." His description of the desired sound is illuminating, since there's little obvious connection between his piece and the artist he names as an inspiration. "I've always liked James Brown sort of songs – that was an element of what I was trying to do, something with a hypnotic feel to it."

## Art on sleeve

As with *Chairs Missing*, the sleeve concept and design were primarily Gilbert's. The previous covers had been un-rock and atypical for album art, but the abstract image on the sleeve of *154* was radically distinctive, setting a similar tone to the work Peter Saville produced for Factory artists. "I felt there had to be a change of visual dynamics," says Gilbert. "I did two or three small, carefully made roughs, quite carefully painted. I just did it and turned up with them while people were still thinking about the idea, so it was a kind of fait accompli." If he conceived of *154* as Wire's definitive statement, this sleeve was worthy of it. It had its origins in some of his earlier work. "It was improved and developed from stuff I did when I was still painting. I'd gone into an abstract area, an obsessive geometric area, and I made very carefully painted geometric things. I was making endless, abstract variations on them. The last ones I did in that period became the basis of the *154* cover – taken a little bit further. A little odder."

Gilbert's preliminary work was rendered in-house at EMI, again by David Dragon. "I gave him the dummy that we'd all decided on, and he formalised it. I had a long talk with him about it, about the colours. The colours were terribly, terribly important. He matched them as close as he could, using Pantone slides, because I'd just done them with normal watercolour-type paint. I'm eternally grateful to Dave. It was so nice to meet somebody at EMI who actually cared about it and had nothing to do with the corporate culture and daft notions. He was very sensitive about it." Problems arose when EMI insisted that the band name and the album title (the number of gigs played up until that point, according to Grey's diary) appear on the front cover. "There had to be no type on it. I said: that's what it is," Gilbert recalls. "But there were certain execs who said: you've got to have the name on it because people will be looking through the racks. And I said: it doesn't look like any other record – if they want it, they'll find it. Eventually, we even got the marketing people on board, and we did a page ad, too."

Upon release in September 1979, *154* garnered lofty praise. "(This Is) The Modern Art," proclaimed the headline of *Record Mirror*'s review (even if the force of that statement was undercut by its allusion to The Jam). In the *NME*, Nick Kent was so enthusiastic that he unwittingly inflated the title, calling the record *159* throughout a write-up that placed Wire at "the forefront of rock's new music vanguard". For Kent, the album's blend of rock and electronics surpassed even the contemporaneous efforts of the Thin White Duke: it was "the album Bowie really wanted to make when he and Eno worked on what became *Lodger*". Just as Kent marvelled at *154*'s excess of creativity ("there's much too much going on"), in *Melody Maker* Jon Savage highlighted the record's "embarrassment of ideas". Savage's closing words, however, proved disappointingly prescient: "Quite whether it'll reap a commensurate commercial success now depends on EMI's efficiency."

## Fifteen minutes of infamy

By the time of their third John Peel session, which coincided with *154*'s release, Wire were already developing material for a fourth album. If their previous Peel appearances had been unorthodox in their focus on new, unrecorded work, this session was more unconventional still. Instead of playing several numbers from *154*, the band premiered a solitary unreleased track, the 15-minute, largely improvised 'Crazy About Love', a piece that had evolved from rehearsal-room experimentation. "It rather confused the two Johns" – Peel and producer Walters – says Lewis. In his opinion, this piece was a measure of their growing confidence, regardless of their evermore-precarious position at EMI. "We were feeling incredibly strong, even though everything felt dodgy around us. We just thought we'd do what we'd always done, which was be creative and move on to the next thing, and 'Crazy About Love' came out of that." Also, as far as Lewis was concerned, Wire had given Peel a session based on *154* a year earlier. "We'd already played the stuff from the new album for him on the previous session, so we thought: *fair do's!*"

The decision not to play available material also reflects how invested Wire had become in studio work and how much they valued what they were creating. The idea of giving Peel ropey live versions of numbers they had painstakingly crafted in a 24-track studio didn't sit well with the band, as Newman recalls: "None of us really liked the idea that we did crap versions of songs from the records, and then he played them on the show and didn't play them again. We just wanted him to play the tracks from the album. It was a big, big record that fully used the recording process, and you couldn't knock it off in an afternoon." Grey saw it the same way. "It was a bit of a waste of time, trying to recreate something you'd spent a month on in the studio – trying, in an afternoon, to get four tracks of the same songs but not recorded in such good conditions. It's never going to be as good as the original, sound-wise. And it's not even a live broadcast, so it seems rather a pointless exercise."

The track they played for Peel was an example of Wire's restless, exploratory character at its most imaginative. For Lewis, its development had been part of a refreshing experience after the challenges of *154* and the stress that had built up in and around the band. "We were looking for depressurisation," he says, "an antidote to *154* and what had gone before. We were looking to expand all the time." According to Newman, 'Crazy About Love' was also intended to send a message to John Peel himself: "Peel was never a Wire fan. He was more a fan of the uncouth and the unmediated – that's why he liked The Fall. We weren't his darlings. We were highly rated by the press, but we weren't getting the radio support we felt we deserved. So it was two fingers to John Peel, in a way, because he didn't really support us to the extent that we felt he should have. It was a ruse."

Gilbert didn't see this as a snub ("Not at all!"). To him, it was only a "ruse" in that Wire would earn some money because of the length of 'Crazy About Love'. "We realised before we recorded it that there were PRS [Performing Right Society] rates for anything over five minutes, so they'd have to pay more – as if it was a proper piece of music, not a pop song. That seemed quite amusing." Gilbert believes the session was an ideal "artistic opportunity", another context in which to pursue the improvisational methodology in which they'd been engaged. "We'd experimented in the rehearsal studio, but not to the point of knowing what we were going to do. Everyone kind of knew their parts, but it wasn't formalised. Everyone had their sounds or options for sound: they knew what their bits were; they had their noises. We were used to rehearsing a lot, and we were used to listening to each other and picking up on things – the natural organic understanding of each other's moods, giving each other space. It's apparently structureless, but the structure made itself. I think it's fairly symphonic."

Lewis recounts some details of the preparation leading up to the Peel session: "We went into rehearsals and jammed. I brought a beat-box and stuck it through an amp so we could groove along. Rob came with this broken sax, and I picked it up and started playing it through my pedals. I became a sax player for three weeks, mercifully for the others, because it was broken. It was like a prepared piano, and I worked out what its repertoire of noises was. Then Colin picked up the bass. And I wrote a text based on the best clues from the *Evening Standard* crossword, but fucked up. There was a bit of a siege mentality. We'd circled the wagons. We just blew for a couple of weeks, and things started to appear. We didn't write loads of things and go in and go *bang*! We just jammed and recorded, then edited. I guess this was how Can made what they do."

Gilbert's enthusiasm for 'Crazy About Love' hasn't waned, and he's eager to emphasise the importance of the track as it was documented on the Peel session. "This wasn't idle noodling. This wasn't a jam. It's a *piece*. This was making a piece as it went: we were all in that time and place, thinking and listening, stone cold sober. No one thought it was rubbish. It was worthy. It was solid and very stimulating from my point of view. It had all sorts of elements, and it was quite emotional in some ways. I think it's one of Wire's proudest moments."

Grey, too, was convinced of the track's artistic worth. He considers it an example of Wire at their most creative. "For Wire, there's always a temptation to do something new and a necessity to do something new. That carried it along." Gilbert was impressed by Grey's contribution, something he makes a point of stressing. "It was a huge revelation to me that he was so sensitive to it. By the end, there's a rhythm, a beat – which I think was a great relief to him. I think it's one of his finest performances, because it's just little touches, no drums, just cymbals. I don't think Rob thought he'd ever be doing something like that."

Newman wasn't as happy with 'Crazy About Love' as the others. "It's one of those infuriating pieces: there's the core of a fantastic piece of music, but it was very meandering, and some of it's a bit rubbish. It's typical of extemporised music. The only bit that was worked out beforehand was my bassline. Graham just made a lot of noise with his Willy The Wasp synth and played the sax, which he couldn't do. That was very 'in' – playing sax badly in mock-jazz mode was all the rage. You had to have someone in the band do it. And you can always guarantee that if someone in the band is going to do it, it'll be Graham."

While EMI felt the Peel session was simply another promotional opportunity squandered, Newman thinks that Wire's approach to it was indicative of their ambivalent relationship with the business side of music. "It didn't make EMI very happy, but we didn't understand promotion or marketing. We didn't make any money out of our records, so why would we understand any of that process? If everything was – in Bruce's words – an 'artistic opportunity', why not do something special? We didn't tie the notion of money to art, because we weren't making any money from art."

## You can't sell music on television

After the release of *154*, Wire's days at EMI were numbered. "At this point, EMI was in a really confused state," says Gilbert, "and it was becoming clear that these weren't really the sort of people we should be working with." Lewis agrees: "They didn't seem to know what they were doing, and they didn't know what to do with us." As Bryan Grant succinctly puts it: "EMI just didn't get Wire." And it wasn't only the band-members who were uncomfortable with goings on at 20 Manchester Square. Over the previous year, Thorne too had grown frustrated with the direction in which EMI was heading and had decided to move on. "It changed for the worse, which is why I left. I was signed as a house producer to A&R: find and produce interesting new acts. It worked nicely for a while. Then the company retreated, and I found they wouldn't sign the sort of people I'd care to work with."

Various factors were now converging to seal the band's fate: their own wilfulness and creative intransigence, their tenuous grasp of the business side of their career, the changing of the guard and the culture at EMI (against the backdrop of the looming merger), and shifts in pop-music trends at the end of the 70s.

Wire had initially been indulged by EMI, in that they had been allowed to devote themselves to making albums. This approach was part of a traditional, 70s rock mind-set and wholly appropriate to an imprint like Harvest, but economics got in the way of what had at first seemed a good idea. "EMI had heard people say we were like Pink Floyd," says Newman, "and even though they didn't understand it, they thought: we'll give them some money to make an album. People said: they're great, and they'll sell a lot of records eventually. But, of course, we didn't sell any records." Wire were finally caught between two stools as the end of the decade saw EMI intensifying its focus on the pop market, which Wire's singles had failed to crack. "After *154*," Newman notes, "you're on the cusp of the 70s and the 80s where there's a big attitudinal shift: pop was what EMI wanted. At the start, it was prog and Kevin Ayers; by the end of the 70s it had all changed, and it was all about singles. They wanted Wire to be a pop group. They weren't interested in anything long-term now. They realised they didn't want Wire. They wanted Duran Duran: pretty boys with slightly obscure pop songs."

As the original idea for *154* as a set of singles showed, EMI was still angling for a Wire hit, and this was the last throw of the dice. While the band didn't object to releasing 45s, they wanted to avoid a crossover of album and single material, as Newman explains: "Wire weren't averse to making singles, but we wanted things to be separate: singles were separate recording events, and we wanted to release them separately." EMI weren't convinced, as it was standard practice for albums to include singles. Wire's efforts to maintain a degree of separation were also linked to their feeling of disconnection from the business of music. "It was all oddly disengaged from money," says Newman. "Money was involved only at the beginning: we got advances, which related to the records, but at the start of the recording process, not at the end, and they weren't related to sales. You heard about sales, but only in the sense of 'if you sold a lot then you must be popular'. But it bore no relationship to money at all. So we decided singles in a very purist way, in terms of 'what's gonna be a seven-inch?' and not 'what's gonna sell?'"

Despite being understandably irked at the position they'd been put in by EMI over 'Outdoor Miner', Wire strove to preserve a workable association with the label. This was evident in their approach to *154*, as they had sought to balance EMI's demand for singles with their own artistic designs. "We felt it should have some commercial aspect," Gilbert stresses, "even if we were going to explore things that weren't particularly commercial." Indeed, *154* boasted several possible singles, but Lewis remembers EMI still being unhappy. "When we delivered *154*, they couldn't decide what the single was, because there were so many – and they acted like that was a problem. It had four tracks you could pick as a single. We were trying to service the machine, and they didn't know what they were doing. And people were saying the record was two years ahead of its time. Great! What do you want, if not something that's ahead of what other people are doing?" When the band proposed a new, non-*154* number, 'Our Swimmer', as a single, the label selected 'Map Ref. 41°N 93°W' instead. This was released a month or so after *154*, with the non-album B-side, 'Go Ahead'.

'Go Ahead' had been recorded after *154*, without Thorne, at Magritte Studio, at the same time as 'Our Swimmer' and 'Midnight Bahnhof Cafe' – neither of which would surface on vinyl for another two years. (Newman recalls the Magritte experience as a comedown after Advision: "It was a bit like seeing how the other half lived. They had no line of sight between the control room and the playing room.") If 'Map Ref.' provided EMI with the sort of pop-friendly 45 they coveted, its menacing, syncopated B-side presented a more experimentally oriented facet of Wire. 'Go Ahead' could have been the work of a completely different band, one with no interest in hit singles. The lyrics were also a flick of the 'V's in EMI's direction –

**ABOVE**: An early portrait of Wire, taken at the band's first photo session with Annette Green in Rotherhithe, South East London, early 1977. *LEFT TO RIGHT*: Bruce Gilbert, Colin Newman, Graham Lewis, Robert Grey.
**LEFT**: Another shot from the Rotherhithe session.

**RIGHT:** A page from Robert Grey's diary, showing the band's first run of gigs (and what they were paid for each one).
**BELOW:** Around the corner from the Commonwealth Institute in Kensington, West London, with manager Mick Collins.
**FACING PAGE ABOVE:** Signing to EMI, September 1977. *LEFT TO RIGHT:* Grey, Harvest boss Nick Mobbs, EMI staff Fred Cannon and Jo Allen, Newman, Gilbert, producer Mike Thorne, Collins, and Lewis.
**FACING PAGE BELOW:** An outtake from the *Pink Flag* cover shoot, taken on Plymouth Hoe in late summer 1977.

**CLOCKWISE FROM TOP RIGHT:** Four shots of Wire onstage in London in late 1977. Newman and Gilbert at the Hope & Anchor; Grey and Gilbert at a Rock Against Racism gig in Stoke Newington; Grey and Newman at the Red Cow; Gilbert at the same venue.

**ABOVE:** Another Annette Green portrait of the band, taken just prior to the release of *Chairs Missing*. *LEFT TO RIGHT*: Gilbert, Lewis, Grey, Newman.
**FACING PAGE ABOVE:** Gilbert and Grey at Newman's flat in West Norwood, South London, late 1978.
**FACING PAGE BELOW:** Grey and Newman at Newman's West Norwood home.

**ABOVE**: Grey, Lewis, Newman, and Gilbert onstage at the SO36 club in Berlin, Germany, November 1978.
**LEFT**: The provisional setlist (from Lewis's notebook) for the final show of Wire's first phase, at the Electric Ballroom, London, February 1980.
**BELOW**: A shot from Wire's November 1979 residency at the Jeannetta Cochrane Theatre in Holborn, London, with Lewis on saxophone.

5/10

REQUEST : 12XU
UNDERWATER EXP.
EVERYTHINGS GOING TO BE NICE
PIANO TUNER (MAN + INFLATEABLE)
20 WE MEET UNDER TABLES (VEIL)
ALL I COULD DO WAS WHISTLE (B. HAT)
30 HITTING THINGS –
EASTERN STANDARD (GLOBE)
44 SWOPPING BIT
UNDER THE VEIL (RUNNING)
PART OF OUR HISTORY
EELS SANG LINO
REVEALING TRADE SECRETS
INVENTORY
AND THEN . . . . (SANDWICHES)

a none-too-subtle jab at the commercial imperatives that had apparently driven the label to hype 'Outdoor Miner'. Newman sneers an ironic meditation on marketing and promotion ("Critical acclaim cannot explain / The extent of the sales / Or why this one pales / In comparison") and Lewis follows up with a spoken section satirising sales-meeting speak. Tracks like 'Go Ahead' – as well as the previous B-side, the noisy, manic, loop-based 'Former Airline' – were further symptoms of Wire's creative restlessness. They underscored the point Gilbert had wanted to make with the *154* EP ("It's not just *this* – there's other things going on").

The cover of the 'Map Ref.' single was unlike any of the band's other artwork thus far, which had been by turns detached, cryptic, unsettling, or simply peculiar. It contrasted dramatically with Gilbert's sleeve for the previous 45, 'A Question Of Degree': a black-and-white demonstration photo he'd found in "an ancient Swedish massage book", featuring a formally attired masseur-cum-torturer (the reverse was given over to what looks like a spinal x-ray). The aeroplane-window image for 'Map Ref.', drawn and painted by Lewis, has the old-fashioned warmth of a 1930s *Boys' Own* illustration to it, departing from Wire's anti-representational tendencies – and even bearing a direct relationship with the song's lyrical content. Still, there was a playful meta-narrative aspect to the cover since the image was in fact based on a photo taken by Lewis during his 1978 transcontinental flight – as he was writing the first section of the lyrics.

Another factor that exacerbated the deteriorating Wire–EMI relations was the band's refusal to promote *154* via the standard touring route. "There was a budget to promote *154*," Gilbert remembers, "and it felt like there was a clichéd panic going on at EMI. It was as if they felt: we've really got to break this now, we've got to spend lots of money buying our way onto a tour – and it just didn't seem right to us." Still riding the creative momentum of the album, the band-members believed that, rather than play dates in support of *154*, their time (and money) would be better spent pursuing the new ideas that were developing rapidly. (During their UK summer tour, two months ahead of the record's release, about half of their set had already been devoted to post-*154* tracks.)

For Newman, the decision not to tour *154* was related to the band's miserable Roxy Music experience earlier in the year. "It was partly about the culture of Wire and partly about the Roxy tour, which was just horrible; it was so destructive. Up to that point, with Wire, we thought that it was all about this great artistic venture and that we were following in the line of fantastic artists like Roxy – and then you see one of those artists turned into mush. And we were paying money to be on a tour, supporting them and being hated by their audience. It wasn't just about what happened to us; it was about them and what they'd become."

Instead of going out on the road, Wire had started to think of alternative ways to promote their work. Gilbert remembers some specific ideas. "It seemed to me that all this money they were prepared to invest in an all-out push could be put to more creative uses – like making a video. Not just miming to a song, but making a film and using some of the funds that would have been for tour support." The band even had a song in mind. "We had a video idea for 'Map Ref.'," says Newman. "We thought it was a pop song, that it should be heard, and it would be great if we could have it on TV." Gilbert also recalls pitching the idea of television advertising. "I said: What about TV? It would be great – a 15-second ad with just the abstract cover, no music, just that image. Fifteen seconds on TV and silence. And they were saying: People will go, *what the fuck is that*? That's not selling it! And I said: *yes, but it is*."

Wire's ideas were rejected by EMI's marketing experts, who assured them that the advertisements wouldn't work and that there was no potential in music videos. MTV launched just two years later. "We were told that you can't sell music on television," chuckles Gilbert. "I wonder where those people are now."

Although no longer involved with Wire or EMI, Thorne stayed on friendly terms with former colleagues at the label and was aware of the difficulties Wire were facing. "At one point, after a meeting to discuss budgets, my boss Brian Shepherd informed them that EMI wasn't the Arts Council. I think I shielded them from that trouble, partly by delivering accessible – I thought – but innovative records. After I fled, there was no sympathetic intermediary. I knew that things wouldn't go so well for them after I quit their production brief, but I couldn't stand the gig any longer. Brian gave them some leeway, but they were lost."

## A different mess every night

Since there was still money to be used for promoting *154*, Wire proposed a compromise of sorts: a series of gigs to be played at one venue, rather than as a tour. "We thought we'd have a show which would run for three or four days," says Lewis. "We felt it would be more meaningful for us to approach it like that. So we used the budget for *People In A Room*."

*People In A Room*, a November residency at London's Jeannetta Cochrane Theatre, would effectively bring the curtain down on Wire's tenure with EMI. The theatre was affiliated with the Central School of Art and Design (later merging with Saint Martins School of Art to become Central Saint Martins College of Arts and Design) and had hosted an array of significant productions, ranging from contemporary drama and dance to conceptual performance art. Joe Orton's *Loot* had its first revival at the Cochrane in 1966, the same year that Yoko Ono staged *Music Of The Mind* there, and the theatre had also accommodated the work of rock groups: in 1968, Ballet Rambert's *Pawn To King 5* featured music by Pink Floyd.

EMI's budget enabled Wire to undertake a high-quality collaboration with students from Central's theatre department, who offered expertise in set and lighting design. Also involved were individuals working in the then-new area of video art. All of this was exciting for Wire, but EMI didn't share their enthusiasm. "EMI were initially extremely sceptical and disappointed," says Gilbert, "and then they got extremely worried: *were we going to play the actual album?* That became a bit of a concern for them." Lewis also detected some anxiety. "When we were rehearsing, EMI sent down a couple of chaps to scout out what we might be doing. They were there basically to ask how many things from the album we were going to play since we'd played none of it on Peel. It was starting to look like commercial suicide to them. These were the same people who'd said that you can't sell records on TV when we wanted to do video. We were starting to have a very jaundiced view of the world's biggest record company – and its future."

Each night at the Cochrane, a video camera relayed – to an onstage screen – time-lapsed scenes from the theatre foyer, so that the audience members taking their seats were greeted by footage of themselves arriving a little earlier. Thus they were incorporated into the show – a detail that was emphasised by the programme, which listed "Audience" as the first part of the evening's entertainment. This was followed by separate artistic interventions – in diverse media – by each band-member. Gilbert executed a performance titled 'Tableau', which consisted of him pushing a trolley with a glass on it around the stage; a stagehand would periodically fill the glass, with Gilbert pausing to drink from it. The programme notes gave some insight (although not much) into the concept underlying the piece: "Change cannot exist without non-change. Non-change does not exist. Therefore change does not exist. What is repetition?" Lewis devised the more elaborate 'A Panamanian Craze?': for this, Grey and Wire associate Angela Conway danced around the stage with tights on their heads (and oranges in the feet of the tights), while Lewis made a couple of trips out to the foyer to tell the waiting Mick Collins what was happening onstage – their conversations appearing onscreen in the auditorium via the video link.

For 'An Unlikely Occurrence', Newman led a proto-Glenn Branca/Rhys Chatham ensemble of massed guitarists: five playing $E$, five playing $A$, and five playing $D$. Last but not least, Grey did an action painting ('The Decorator'). "I don't know how I had the nerve to do it," he says. "It was a horrible mess. A different mess every night! But I met people afterwards who were in the audience, and they were telling me what they thought it meant. Thank goodness there's no footage of it on YouTube."

After all of this, the group played a set featuring just three tracks from *154*. Predictably, 'Map Ref. 41°N 93°W' was not among them, despite EMI's deliberate release of the single in proximity to the Jeannetta Cochrane residency. The other eight numbers were as yet unreleased: 'Crazy About Love' (slightly shorter than its Peel session version), 'Remove For Improvement', 'The Spare One', 'Lorries', 'Underwater Experiences', 'Ally In Exile', 'Over My Head', and 'Our Swimmer'. (Newman would record his own, solo versions of 'Remove For Improvement' and 'Lorries' in the 80s.)

The audiences at the Cochrane were mostly receptive. Lewis remembers Eno's positive response after one show: "It was the best one, when the power failed during Colin's 15-guitar-player piece. In the pub afterwards, Brian told me he thought the power failure had been intentional." Not everyone was persuaded. Whereas the music press (and even the *New Statesman*) had praised *154* specifically for combining the medium of pop music with a strong artistic sensibility, reviewers were less kind to this ambitious, multi-dimensional staging of Wire, which they felt enforced an awkward division between the art (the individual performances) and the songs.

The write-ups tended to characterise the prefatory component as pretentious and unconvincing. "Wire's *People In A Room*," wrote *Melody Maker*'s Paul Tickell, "tells the usual sorry experimental tale of arty types overestimating the flexibility of rock as a good medium." As Newman puts it: "They just thought it was self-indulgent art-wank." Dave McCullough's assessment in *Sounds* ventured a slightly more sophisticated critique, dismissing Wire's avant-garde tactics – boldly experimental to some – as dated, tame and, worse still, thoroughly bourgeois. For McCullough, this was "a warm, predictable, terribly comfortable experience ... Wire are Tom Stoppard, Ian McKellen, Melvyn Bragg, they're paid up members of late-20th-century artistic mediocrity". Overall, he was bored. "I'd missed *Coronation Street* to see the show, but the effect was much the same, because nothing very special happened."

Despite the poor critical reception, the Jeannetta Cochrane gigs were in fact a logical extension of Wire's modus operandi since their emergence as a four-piece in spring 1977. Although Wire accepted that they were operating in the realm of music as commercial entertainment, they had always striven to subvert that context, seeking new possibilities within it. And their scant interest in the conventions of rock was always foregrounded onstage. In that environment, their work was especially inventive and considered. Shorn of the gestures, rituals, and clichés traditionally associated with rock performance, it aimed to provoke not just a gut reaction but also an intellectual response. In the case of the Cochrane concerts, though, McCullough may have had a point, since it could be argued that they were hardly radical. Even if a rock band's use of non-musical artistic elements to complement live performance was still a relatively novel idea in 1979, by then some of those artistic elements were, in themselves, a little stale. Action painting, for example, had its heyday in the 40s and 50s, and it had been appropriated by a rock group more than a decade earlier: The Creation's Kenny Pickett regularly spray-painted a canvas onstage during gigs, and when he'd finished, he even used to set it alight.

Moreover, the broader setting of the performance reproduced the ideology and structures of mainstream theatre, with its restricted role for the spectator: each night, the doors closed at 8pm, and the audience, in its plush seats, was very much a captive one. That formal theatrical structure even extended to inserting an intermission between the two parts. In Gilbert's view, this dynamic, which subjugated the audience, was desirable. "I think a lot of people were uncomfortable about sitting down, but that was how it was going to be. They were confronted with the four performances before the music. I think they were wondering what was going to happen next and whether there was actually going to be any music. I think we had them in the right psychological state." Lewis takes a similar position: "It was theatre; we were in control."

Wire's avant-garde strategies, the traditional theatrical context, and the audience's passive function in that context could all be construed as conservative in terms of high art: the individual pieces may have shared modernism's rejection of bourgeois artistry, but they were now somewhat outdated and bourgeois themselves, and a conventional hierarchical relationship between performer and audience remained more or less intact. Still, Gilbert is indifferent to such analysis. "We were just thinking about it in terms of what a group normally does, and that we should do something different. I didn't realise rock critics were aficionados of experimental performance. But one never took any rock critics' write-ups seriously: we chortled around the pub table at that sort of thing."

145

Whether the Cochrane engagement was authentically radical or not, EMI didn't warm to it. "It went down like a lead balloon," says Lewis. "They didn't care for it at all." Gilbert has a vivid memory of the label contingent: "They sat through all this weird shit, and then we played some music at the end – and there were grey faces: *Oh God, this is not what we thought it was going to be. At all*." Grey didn't pick up any encouraging signs either. "I don't think it reviewed particularly well, so I don't suppose EMI were all that pleased. I don't remember us meeting people who oversaw things – communication was all rather vague, and this was close to the end of it, which suggests it went down a bit badly. Maybe EMI thought it was going a bit far."

To make matters worse, the label had also recently dismissed further initiatives proposed by the band: Wire had pitched the idea of establishing a new EMI imprint that would release an annual album by the group, as well as work by Gilbert and Lewis and a Newman solo album. EMI had expressed enough interest in Newman's record for him to go ahead and book a studio, but after *People In A Room* they shelved that project, at the same time declining to give Wire an advance for their fourth album – contrary to previous verbal assurances.

## Try again. Fail again. Fail better.

Newman's appraisal of Wire in late 1979 highlights the disconnect between critical acclaim and commercial success (*154* only reached Number 39 in the UK album charts). "We were a band that could be on the cover of the *NME*," he says, "but we weren't a successful band." Lewis makes a similar point, underlining the absurdity of Wire's predicament. "It was a very odd situation. Critically, you had people saying you were ahead of your time, and then you had the label saying you owed them money. We needed protecting at that point. It was an intense time, personally and professionally. People at EMI were going: do you know how much money you owe us? And I wondered: Does that include the chart-fixing money you gave to people? Was that on the budget? Did we pay for that as well?"

Eventually, the lines of communication between Wire and their label fell silent and, in early February 1980, the band issued a statement asserting that they were "no longer under any contractual obligation to EMI".

The situation that Wire found themselves in following *154* was ironic. They'd made an extremely strong, highly praised album, and yet, just months after its release, they were without a recording contract and had no real prospects in that respect. Although they were in a place more common to bands that are creatively spent, Wire hadn't exhausted their ideas. On the contrary, they were in creative overdrive: by the end of 1979, they already had enough tracks in gestation for their fourth album. The problem, however, was that the band no longer had a collective vision for that material: the dilemma facing them wasn't a lack of direction but, more accurately, the absence of a *shared* direction – as well as, it would seem, a lack of interest in finding one.

The differences that had emerged during *154* had set in, and the band-members were now concentrating on their own work: from summer 1979 onward, Newman had been rehearsing material with Grey and Thorne, and Gilbert and Lewis's Dome project was taking shape. (At Advision, during *154* downtime, they'd already made the track 'Drop' with Angela Conway, which would become one side of the first A.C. Marias single – released on their Dome label in late 1980.) Crucially, the band-members were unable to reach a consensus regarding how Wire should move forward. "We had no agenda about what kind of record we wanted to follow up *154*," says Newman, "and there was a huge bust-up between two different ways of looking at the work. You could see it as being about power, ambition, lots of different things. Bruce and Graham didn't want to make another album like we'd made *154*, but I did. Bruce in particular wanted to make a different kind of record – and I didn't really understand what kind of record he wanted to make."

When Gilbert describes what he had in mind, you can see why Newman might not have had a clear sense of his bandmate's plans for Wire's future. "One of the ideas I had just before we left EMI was that we should have two months off without doing anything, and that everyone should go home and make an instrument: electrified, acoustic – anything at all – but everybody should make an instrument that they could operate fairly effectively, so they'd know what they were doing, rather than it just being random. And then I thought we should make a group – who were Wire – but playing instruments that we'd made ourselves. And, without knowing what everybody else was doing, we'd go into a rehearsal room and make a noise – because we'd got quite good at that – and make it into something cohesive, something you could have for arrangements, but using very odd, non-standard instruments."

This radical concept was a response to what Gilbert saw as a major problem facing Wire: the fact that "we'd become institutionalised". By this, he meant that their thinking had become deeply entwined with the idea of being on a label; they had come to take for granted the corporate ideology and structures within which they were working, viewing them as natural

147

and inevitable. To Gilbert, the extent of this hit home after Wire left EMI. One of their first impulses, as he recalls it, was to find another label and become part of another organisation: "We were thinking: Where can we go? Who can cope with this thing? You see: we were *institutionalised*." His sense was that their only chance of progressing lay in attempting to work outside of that institutional context, finding a way to separate their creativity from a reliance on the music business – idealistic as that might sound. The notion of making their own instruments and reinventing their creative interaction seemed to Gilbert to be a potentially successful way of rebooting Wire and progressing.

Gilbert now looks back at the plan with some amusement. "I'd already made a ridiculously huge finger piano out of steel rulers. It only made one noise, really. Of various pitches, but that was it. Totally impractical." Nevertheless, he still feels that the conceptual underpinnings of the overall idea were valid. "It was totally impractical, but that's why I thought we really needed a lot of time off: to be able to fail, basically, and to learn how to make things again. Of course, what would have happened would have been that Rob would have just made himself some drums."

## May I make an observation?

The factionalisation and the loss of common purpose accentuated by *154* did not stop Wire from carrying on as a band. However, the issues that declared themselves during the making of this record would continue to challenge them until the mid 2000s. Speaking with Lewis and Newman about *154* is sometimes difficult and somewhat depressing. Their feelings about this phase of Wire's creative life are complex and unresolved, although they recognise the achievement of the album. During my interviews with them, there was a measure of recrimination, old battles were revisited, and there was an inclination to focus not so much on what happened during and around the making of *154*, but on what they *wished* had happened. Above all, their reflections on the album often epitomised a tendency that would become more pronounced as we began to discuss Wire in the 80s: their struggle to be objective about the band's work, preferring to talk more about their individual contributions.

Without wishing to imply that one person's view is more valuable or accurate than another's, I feel it's best to let Mike Thorne have the final word on *154*. His comments to me on the topic provide what is, to my mind, the most appropriate and dignified coda to a remarkable record:

"The *154* sessions became really fraught, and it was the personal wear and tear which provoked me into resigning from the production post during the mixing (although I still brought all my energy to bear on completing the job). I can't even begin to analyse the recording politics of the time, and don't really care to. It's now 33 years back, and the interactions were confusing even then. What was apparent was that the five of us had outgrown the vessel of 'the Wire album', as the subsequent band split confirmed. There wasn't enough room. After the break, Graham and Bruce chose a markedly different trajectory from Colin and Robert, and that coming stylistic schism was anticipated in heated control-room arguments. Despite, or likely because of, the tensions, the album is an enduring achievement. We should all just be proud of it, celebrate it, and be thankful that, whatever inchoate, scattershot battles were going on, *154* popped out as a concrete, tangible result that still communicates with an audience even after all this time. We argued because we cared."

## CHAPTER 5

# 1980–83

## A jolly evening out

Having left EMI, Wire announced a gig for February 29 1980 at the Electric Ballroom in Camden. This spectacle, memorialised for posterity on the album *Document And Eyewitness*, would make the Jeannetta Cochrane event seem as edgy and challenging as a stadium-rock concert.

*People In A Room* had whetted the band's appetite for further investigations of the theatrical potential of live performance. At the Electric Ballroom, however, Wire took things to an extreme – something Robert Grey sees as a double-edged sword. "There was such a temptation to do things that were different, but that could be dangerous. You could be doing things differently just for the sake of it. The Electric Ballroom gig had a lot of ideas in it, but commercially it was probably shooting yourself in the foot." That perversity was especially problematic in this case, since the gig was intended, in part, to present label-less Wire to the A&R fraternity.

Wire's budget for the Electric Ballroom was non-existent, and notwithstanding the creativity on display, the gig held up a sullied, cracked mirror to the Cochrane shows. The lighting for the evening was emblematic of the band's meagre finances. Lighting technician Simon Miles had just returned from a Ramones tour, but as Graham Lewis points out, "his magic trunk was gutted": the best gels (the blues, whites, and reds) had been burned out, and all that remained were yellows and greens, limiting him to the colour spectrum of healthy-to-less-healthy urine.

Wire had made loose preparations, drafting a setlist and practising for a week. Various visitors dropped in. "That tall skinny journalist chap, Nick Kent, was there," recalls Bruce Gilbert. "I don't know why he was there. I think he was fairly confused." On the night, they played just one song that had been released ('12XU') and retained only 'Underwater Experiences' from the *People In A Room* performances. As they had done at the Cochrane, Wire devoted the set mostly to work that was still in development. Three numbers would later surface on Colin Newman's solo albums ('Inventory',

'We Meet Under Tables', '5/10'), and one would be recorded by Gilbert and Lewis for their Dome project ('Ritual View').

The band also planned aspects of the staging and concocted a sequence of extra-musical components or, in Lewis's words, "various displays of absurdity". On this occasion, rather than repeat the Cochrane format and preface the music with performance pieces, they planned for friends and associates (equipped with assorted props) to carry out chaotic, incongruous actions that would punctuate and fragment the set as it progressed. "I liked the idea of a sequence of unrelated actions," says Gilbert, "basically non-sequiturs, presented for maximum enjoyment and entertainment. You weren't sure where it was going, what on earth was going to happen next. It was asking questions: Is this music? Is this rock'n'roll? I liked the idea of confusing all sorts of things. I thought it was quite a jolly evening out."

Again, it would be a stretch to describe the onstage activity as genuinely radical, since it paid direct homage, consciously or unconsciously, to numerous modernist and postmodernist precursors: Dada and surrealism; the theory and practice of Artaud and Brecht; absurdist theatre; and some of the more extreme interventions of the 60s, such as the *Mouvement Panique* and Gustav Metzger's "auto-destructive art". In spite of the event's high-art precedents, though, Gilbert doesn't make grand claims for the Electric Ballroom show as a theatrical or performance-art spectacle. As with the Jeannetta Cochrane residency, he emphasises that while it incorporated other media, it was still a rock gig by a rock band. But he also feels that the exploration of additional artistic elements at both concerts offered intriguing possibilities for experimenting with rock. "I never thought Wire would make a career out of being performance artists, but I thought it was well worth investigating – seeing how it informed us and whether it could make a difference to our approaches to devising and making music." Gilbert refutes the notion that the performance was *anti*-rock in design or intent. "We had song-based material, so obviously we were indulging in the medium of rock music. As a rock band, you can't really be 'anti' rock music, but you can be against the way rock music is presented – or at least you can question rock music. That's always been a fascinating area to me: how far can you go? If we were completely anti-rock, we'd have been doing something quite different."

For the duration of Wire's set, a six-by-twelve foot white sheet was paraded around and through the performing area. It was held vertically, on poles, by two bearers (one of whom was Tom Johnston, the political cartoonist, who played bass with The The). The sheet's purpose was twofold.

On one level, it served as a crude, vaguely Brechtian means of announcing artificiality, visually disrupting the relationship between the audience and the performance space, and interrupting the event's narrative flow (such as it was). Gilbert outlines how it worked: "The instructions to the people were to keep coming across the stage at random with the sheet and obscuring everything. They had to be encouraged. I told them to keep doing it: Just choose your moment. It doesn't matter what point the performance is at – think of it as interference on a television set or an empty film frame. They picked their way across the stage and tried to obscure us as much as possible." The sheet was also a more basic functional device: it would arrive onstage and then leave – like "a visual bus", according to Lewis – depositing performers or props and having them (not exactly) mysteriously materialise from behind it as it departed.

It's ironic – and another missed opportunity for Wire – that, despite the performance's strong visual dimension, there's no substantive visual document of it, aside from a handful of still photographs. The band-members regret this. "You need the visual input to make sense of the performance," Grey insists, "because there was as much emphasis on the visuals and the space between the songs as there was on the songs themselves. There was always something else going on apart from the songs."

**Not like that ... like that**

Angela Conway was one participant in the goings-on, appearing during 'Everything's Going To Be Nice'. She traversed the stage pulling two men (one of them the former Snakes bassist Rob Smith), who were tied together and towing a large blow-up passenger jet: the trio suggested an expanded version of Beckett's Lucky and Pozzo, or any one of his "pseudo-couples" bound together in relationships of mutual dependency and torment. "Angela couldn't physically drag them across, but the idea was that the men would be unwilling and resistant," recounts Gilbert. "They had to be big men. We tried to get the biggest people we could find, and there were a lot of volunteers – as usual." The inflatable jet belonged to Grey. "I bought it as a souvenir of New York when we were there in 1978. I had it hanging in my house for a long time."

Most of the props were *objets trouvés*, integrated into the performance to bizarre, humorous effect. Some had been discovered lying around in Grey's garden in Brixton, such as the gas stove that Lewis can be heard assaulting on 'Piano Tuner (Keep Strumming Those Guitars)', as well as the hammer he used for the task. The resulting noise was picked up by a contact mic placed on the stove and run through his bass effects. Lewis plundered his home furnishings for one of the evening's more memorable items – a lamp in the form of a life-sized goose. "We had to get it into the performance somehow, because it was such a wonderful object," says Gilbert. "The goose was something I think Graham had bought on tour, probably in Canada." (Wire hadn't yet been to Canada; it was from Habitat in London.) There was some indirect precedent for this artistic appropriation of the fowl. In 1965, Alejandro Jodorowsky decapitated two live geese onstage in Paris during *Melodrama Sacramental*, a notorious *Mouvement Panique* happening. Lewis's goose had a less traumatic function, its role not so much sacrificial as practical: beyond the effect of visual incongruity, it served a specific purpose, since the switching on and off of its light gave cues to the band-members during the deranged, Beefheartian 'Eels Sang Lino'. "We needed cues for arrangements," explains Lewis, "so when the goose's light came on, I sang; when it was off, I wasn't singing." There was also a rigorous logic underlying that song's seemingly nonsensical lyrics: many of the phrases are anagrams of the name of a city or country, prefaced by 'in'. (The title city is Los Angeles, but readers can work the rest out for themselves on a wet afternoon.)

'Zegk Hoqp' was another of Lewis's linguistic experiments. He describes it as "a simple exercise in which the idea was to make a song using all the letters of the alphabet". The members of D.A.F. (who were also on the bill) took to the stage for this track, participating with Lewis in a pseudo-tribal call-and-response of the letters while banging improvised percussion and sporting headdresses fashioned from copies of February 29's *Evening Standard*. "I think Tommy Cooper did it first," remarks Lewis of the headdresses, "making something out of nothing. It was rather like a Norman helmet with palm-like fronds sticking out at the top."

Unusual clothing and accessories abounded. Gilbert and Lewis wore morris-dancing bells around their ankles, the jingling audible at times on the recording. "We went specially to the Cecil Sharp House in Camden Town, the folk HQ that provides the accoutrements for morris dancing," Gilbert laughs. "We didn't actually do any morris dancing," Lewis is quick to stress. "That would have been a bridge too far. It was bad enough as it was." Above all, it was a night for special headgear: in addition to the newspaper headdresses, Lewis recalls that prototypes of the elongated, cylindrical Dome hats made their first public appearance, and during 'We Meet Under Tables', Newman wore an improvised beekeeper's hat with an exaggeratedly long net veil.

Just as the newspaper headdresses were a playful example of creating something exotic from the fabric of everyday life – literally a daily newspaper – the closing piece, 'And Then …', involved a similar exercise. This time, quintessentially banal symbols of the quotidian (slices of white bread) became part of a jarring dramatic gesture, as Lewis sang while devouring two loaves of Mother's Pride and spitting chunks out into the crowd. (Again, this echoes absurdist theatre: Ionesco's *Victimes du devoir* [*Victims Of Duty*, 1953], for instance, which concludes with the characters chewing and swallowing bread en masse.) This was accompanied by a valedictory ceremonial unrolling of two large scrolls, an act that promised to reveal the performance's meaning, yet simultaneously thwarted narrative closure. Gilbert elaborates: "I got a couple of rolls of lining paper and painted some symbols on the beginning of them, with the idea that these nonsensical symbols would emerge, and members of the audience were encouraged to take one end and pull it. And of course it petered out, and there was no message."

## MC hammered

Mick Collins also featured in the proceedings, assuming an unlikely, and ill-advised, role as Master of Ceremonies. He quickly became the whipping boy, the object onto which the audience members heaped their scorn and bile, since he was the only person directly interacting with them. "He got a lot of abuse," confirms Grey. "He had his 'manager's suit' on. His manager's suit probably provoked a lot of animosity. He definitely had a suit era. I'm not sure if he was still in that phase, or whether he dug it out just for the occasion."

Collins and the crowd were at odds immediately, the heckling colourful and to the point:

MC: "Thank you, thank you! … I don't know what else you can say."
Audience member: "You fat cunt!"
MC: "You can say that as well."

"We set Mick up," admits Lewis. "That was really bad, but it was also quite funny. He became the MC under the delusion that this was going to make him loved, particularly after we told him he was getting the honour of announcing '12XU'. What a thankless job that turned out to be." Indeed, the MC's role was conceived, in part, as a way of enabling Wire to perform '12XU'. Newman remembers the band wanting to play the track primarily because it gave them the opportunity to watch him wrestle violently with a leather coat that he used to wear. This was something he'd done once during '12XU' in rehearsals, to everyone's amusement, and they wanted to see it again. "I had the coat on as if it was a straitjacket that I was trying to get out of, and everybody laughed and laughed and said: you have to do it onstage. So we did '12XU' just so I could do the thing in the leather coat."

The problem with performing '12XU', though, was that it had become an albatross around the band's neck; it was the track that embodied Wire for less imaginative fans, the song that crowds always called out for and that Wire had little desire to play. They realised they could now play it only if they avoided one of live rock music's biggest narrative clichés: appearing to revisit the 'greatest hit' in triumphalist fashion, in response to shouted requests. To get around this, they had to find a way to infuse the performance with a sense of distance and irony, yet still play the song the way the audience more or less expected. While it might seem impossible to do both at the same time, they hit on the idea of incorporating the 'request' itself into the overall artifice – by enlisting Collins as Master of Ceremonies and having him mockingly frame it as his personal "request spot".

To Gilbert, this airing of '12XU' was also intended to make the audience look at their own reaction to the set as a whole. "The idea was to suggest: Well, this isn't that far away from the other stuff we're doing. You all want it, but it's not a million miles away from the other things you're experiencing – so why do you prefer it to the other things?"

As the *Document And Eyewitness* recording underscores, the Electric Ballroom crowd played a leading role. The seated, generally respectful Jeannetta Cochrane audience had been replaced by a volatile, latter-day punk rabble, mostly uninterested in Wire after *Pink Flag*. This was now 1980, well into the *post*-punk era, and on February 29 there were two other significant live-music options in London: Joy Division at the Lyceum (with Killing Joke, A Certain Ratio, and Section 25) and Throbbing Gristle at the Scala. Consequently, Wire had to make do with the dregs of punk's living dead, a crowd consisting of what Lewis characterises as "unsavoury skinheads and *Oi!* creatures, shouting and spitting" – for whom '12XU' would be the highlight.

The atmosphere was ugly from the start, worsening as it became clear that this wouldn't be a conventional gig. The crowd didn't share the band's artistic adventurousness and, for them, the dearth of familiar, recognisable songs, as well as the disjointed, chaotic nature of the evening, was a source of irritation and frustration. As Gilbert recalls: "A lot of people may have

155

come who'd heard what happened at the Jeannetta Cochrane and thought: oh well, they won't do *that* again – and they came along still expecting a punk band. I was aware of a bunch of people who took exception to what was happening: Where were the songs? Where were the records?"

Although there was humour in much of what Wire did at the Electric Ballroom, it fell flat before this audience. And instead of finding it provocative in an intellectually stimulating way, the crowd found it provocative in a taking-the-piss way. They responded with open hostility. "The audience absolutely hated us," Newman stresses. "We were viewed as being very confrontational simply because we didn't give people what they wanted, and there was a sense of violence hanging over the gig." For Gilbert, the percolating aggression and the expressions of disapproval were actually a source of pleasure. "It was the kind of threatening atmosphere that I find quite attractive, so I enjoyed it. I think that because they were standing up, they were much more able to vent their feelings without being self-conscious. I can't recall any bottles being thrown. Abuse was thrown."

Grey valued the audience as participants in what he remembers as an interactive dynamic common to gigs of the period – the crowd's behaviour constituting an integral part of the event. "They'd shout out, as if they wanted to contribute to the performance rather than just listen. They could be immediately critical, and that was part of the gig. At the Electric Ballroom, I think the live-ness of the audience makes it more interesting: people shouting things like *GO AWAY* – in slightly stronger language – because they thought it would be nice to hear some Wire songs, rather than see people being dragged across the stage by a rope or people with newspaper headdresses or Graham throwing slices of bread into the audience. They'd paid to see us and, in terms of what they expected, they obviously felt a bit ripped off."

## Creative but destructive

Audience engagement aside, Newman has less than fond memories. "The Electric Ballroom was just a fucking mess. It wasn't very well executed, and some of the material wasn't particularly resolved. There were certainly some nuggets – I'm sure the missing fourth album is in there somewhere – but they weren't really pieces; it was more like: let's just do this for a bit – and after a while it was tedious. It was supposed to be performance art, but it all felt a bit forlorn, really, and somewhat desperate. I didn't enjoy it at all. I hated it." Lewis, meanwhile, has mixed feelings: "I enjoyed it in a limited way. It wasn't one of those gigs where you thought afterwards: that was fantastic, that's going to open up the future. It felt more like stubbing a cigarette out, really."

Newman's biggest criticism centres on the fact that the performance appeared to go squarely against Wire's fundamental aesthetic values. "Wire isn't 'general'; it's a very specific thing. You go for that specificity – not five things all at once so that you're not really sure what anything is anymore. I felt there was too much of that going on. There was no organisation in it, it was just a big mess."

Gilbert disagrees, preferring to focus on the complete event and not just the music. "I thought it was very organised. There was no real rehearsal for the performances – the various actions – but they did happen in the right order, and they did happen on time. From my point of view, that's highly organised. People had their roles mapped out. They knew exactly what they were supposed to do. The instructions were very clear." And to Gilbert, this organisation was absolutely key to the Electric Ballroom concert's conceptual design, as an exploration of randomness. "We wanted to give the impression of random structure, which is quite a good thing to play with. If you come up with a series of ideas that don't relate to each other – but that happen on time and are executed fairly efficiently – you can get to that point where it looks like everybody's being incredibly inventive in their improvisation. But, really, you're setting up a situation where audience expectations aren't allowed to take over."

In the opinion of the artist Russell Mills, who was in the crowd, it was this aleatory dynamic that presented the most difficulty for some. "The problem was caused by the audience's lack of tolerance for this apparent randomness and by a certain lack of imagination." But despite the adverse reactions, Mills believes that the concert was an artistic success. "It was an enjoyable event: disparate, funny, occasionally shambolic (which added to its genuineness), in some parts disastrous or amateurish and in others wonderfully sure and accomplished – and it was never boring." For Newman, however, the music and its presentation remain the priority. "I'm always interested in the material and how it's put across. I'm less interested in the Grand Statement."

Fittingly, the night ended on a messy, inglorious note, as the PA company seized half of Wire's gear in lieu of a payment that Mick Collins had neglected to make.

Reviews of the gig ran from the lukewarm to the chilly. In *Melody Maker*, Chris Bohn sympathised with Wire's broader artistic intentions and appreciated how their work that evening was relatively innovative in the context of rock, but he was still ambivalent: "Parts made sense if you wanted them to … Wire were either stimulating or wilfully exasperating, depending on your tolerance factor." Writing for *Sounds*, Nick Tester didn't mince his words, criticising Wire for trying too hard to be seen as arty and challenging. In his view, their experimentation was "contrived", creating only "a hollow disturbance … they spent an awful lot of time and energy on an exercise that was ultimately one gaping yawn of pretentious crap". He deemed the music "laboured, morbidly self-infatuated and obscure for the hell of it" and declared the whole performance "absurd, but not for the reasons Wire intended".

While Gilbert accepts that Wire's performance looked and sounded – from a conventional perspective – like career suicide, he felt it was honest, showing record-label suitors what they'd be getting themselves into. "From my point of view, the logic of it was: well, if they can take this, they're the right company for us. Obviously, what we did was exaggerated, but I thought that it had to be exaggerated to get the point across that we weren't a normal rock band. I was thinking, since we'd left EMI, that this could be a swan song, but it could also represent a possible future. I was thinking in terms of what kind of group it would be – if that group continued. It could be the start of a beautiful relationship with a company that had come to see us perform and had got it. So the whole point was to show, this is what Wire does or can do – we still make proper music, but be aware that it could be a bit more creative. Sort of creative but destructive at the same time. There were no offers."

Gilbert was also conscious of a deeper contradiction in using the gig as a showcase. Although it would present Wire at their most unconventional, that strategy was still the product of an institutionalised mind-set: newly sprung from an environment in which they'd grown frustrated, their response was to seek a return to the same kind of environment. Realising how deeply ingrained this kind of institutionalised thinking had become, Gilbert began to entertain other creative possibilities outside of Wire.

### Shock followed by relief

A couple of months after the Electric Ballroom gig, Gilbert, Grey, Lewis, and Newman gathered at a pub in Tulse Hill. The outcome of this meeting was a suspension of operations, and the band-members went on to pursue the creative alliances that had emerged during *154*. "It had become increasingly clear to me that there were other things to do besides Wire," Gilbert remembers. "So I said: let's stop it. I might have said: I'm going – but it's the same thing, really. My thoughts were that everybody needed to do their own things. It seemed the cleanest way to refresh everybody." Gilbert could no longer see Wire functioning as a band signed to a label, making work in an orthodox contractual relationship. "Yes, it's a source of income," he concedes, "but it's institutionalised. A label might have given us options for recording – but it's still a 'group': it seemed heavy as an administrative object. I just felt it was the right thing to do, creatively. It was a more dignified way of completing that particular cycle. There was an atmosphere of shock, quickly followed by relief – I definitely had a feeling that there was an air of relief. I know that Colin was thinking about getting on with his solo project, and Graham and I knew we could do things."

Newman is still unhappy with the way Wire dissolved at this point, feeling that Gilbert had effectively made the decision for the band. "We were all conned into it. Bruce announced that we were stopping. He'd already signed up Graham beforehand. Therefore, they already had the 50 per cent, so Rob and I didn't have any choice. It was a classic decision-already-taken. It was all about the Roxy tour. That was used as the argument for not doing it anymore: Is this how you want to end up? We're not going anywhere. I didn't question it that strongly." Grey, too, saw this as a fait accompli initiated by Gilbert and Lewis. "Bruce and Graham would discuss things between themselves in the pub. That was like a separate area from Colin and myself. Things that happened to Wire were decided in other places, when all of us weren't there. It was always a problem to have much discussion between the four of us."

Looking back, Lewis is adamant that the situation wasn't so cut and dried. In fact, he does not accept that Wire 'stopped' in 1980 and, as far as he is concerned, no decision was ever taken to that effect. Even now, Lewis and Newman disagree vehemently over this matter. "We were very, very close to continuing," says Lewis. "It wasn't that it was impossible. The will was there, but eventually everything disintegrated." He maintains that they had considered options away from a standard commercial framework, including the idea of Wire moving forward with a series of independent, one-off projects, managing themselves and free from long-term contracts.

The fact that the band went into Scorpio Sound in early summer 1980 to record two tracks – 'Second Length (Our Swimmer)' and 'Catapult 30' – is perhaps the best indication that Wire had not necessarily taken a definitive decision to stop working together. Moreover, Lewis recalls that around this time, the band had talks with Charisma and also conferred with various old acquaintances regarding potential involvement in some capacity: ex-EMI ally Nick Mobbs, for instance, who had started his own label (Automatic), and Tony Wilson, who wanted to sign Wire to Factory. According to Newman, Wire declined because Wilson's business model didn't extend to giving them any money.

Gilbert remembers telling the Factory boss about his growing awareness that Wire couldn't operate in a traditional label setting. "It had become obvious that, if we really wanted to do what we all wanted to do, there wasn't an external structure that could cope with it." Wilson made a simple suggestion. "His advice was: do your own label." Although such an option seemed beyond the band at this point, Gilbert and Lewis did follow this course of action with their Dome label over the next few years.

In hindsight, Grey recognises that Wire may have exhausted their possibilities by early 1980. "So many things were done on the verge of being unworkable. It's impossible for that to be sustained. After you've done the Jeannetta Cochrane, after you've done the Electric Ballroom, you run out of places to go." Still, he does recall being taken aback by what he understood to be the band's permanent dissolution. "The finality of it came as a bit of a surprise. Obviously it wasn't final, but at the time I thought it was the end and that we were never going to do anything again. If someone had suggested that we not throw away all the work we'd done since 1976 and the success that we'd had, but that we instead just take a year away from Wire and then reconsider – if it had been proposed in that way – perhaps people might have realised that we should have carried on in some shape or form, rather than call an end to it. It seemed to me rather a waste of the effort that had been put into it, that all the success we'd had over three years was being thrown away. But then, most groups don't last as long as that, do they? So maybe that was an achievement in itself."

### No one is innocent

Newman is sure that Wire's lack of attention to extra-musical matters played a significant part in their 1980 demise. He reiterates what he saw as the band's Achilles' heel: "We had no concept of it as a business, no notion of the industry or anything like that – it just didn't exist in the culture of Wire, and to our great loss. There were points at which, if we'd understood and engaged with those things, then perhaps we could have figured out a way of not getting into some of the terrible situations we got into. One of the reasons it fizzled out in 1980 was that we had no money. Throughout the whole of the 70s, we just didn't have any money."

Newman insists that Wire wanted to succeed commercially but simply didn't know how to go about it. "In spite of the fact that there were different views about what we thought we ought to be, we were united in the idea that we weren't just entertainment: we thought what we were doing was serious, that we should be taken seriously, and we did want to make a living out of it. But nobody understood the industry or where the money was going or any of that stuff. We had no real management, no real allies at EMI, no one who could explain anything to us. We weren't coming from a place of understanding. We did that awful tour with Roxy Music. We didn't tour *154*, and we should have done. All we had was a stack of brilliant reviews. We had three years and nothing to show for it. We were just as poor at the end of it as at the beginning."

Wire's situation at this juncture brings into sharp relief the issue of management. Lewis and Newman believe Mick Collins's handling of the band's relationship with EMI left a lot to be desired and compounded their problems. They feel he was a weak intermediary between Wire and the label and did not guide them as wisely as he might have done. However, it's worth noting that much of their dissatisfaction has been expressed long after the fact; and given that Wire were, by their own account, a wilful entity, it's not certain they would have recognised or taken good advice had it been offered. Bryan Grant would learn that when he took over as the band's manager in 1985. Nonetheless, as Newman tells it now, Collins bore much of the responsibility for Wire's sorry state of affairs in 1980. "Mick was useless. He was good at getting a vibe going around the band, but he didn't get the money side of things. We didn't have anyone around us to advise us. There was no one who said: hey guys, you should really be going for it now, because you're in a great position. We needed someone to say: Look, the Jeannetta Cochrane thing is a great idea, but why don't you do a couple of normal gigs in a club as well, something that the other kind of people are going to get excited about, too? And we can do some American dates, or whatever. It just didn't gel."

Although Gilbert appreciated Collins's work, he allows that Wire would have benefited from the perspective of someone with more business savvy. "Mick was a good chap. He did make things happen for us, and encouraged all the ideas, but you either have one or the other: a real business manager or a creative manager – and Mick was a creative manager." Lewis agrees; what Wire needed most of all, he says, was a manager who could fight their corner and take a much harder line in his dealings and negotiations. "Mickey had to be devious and hard, but he couldn't do it. When you saw someone like [Joy Division/New Order manager] Rob Gretton, you knew whose side he was on. Mickey was on our side, but he didn't know how to do it. He couldn't be tough." To be fair, Lewis does acknowledge that, like the band, Collins had little experience and faced a steep learning curve. "We'd been on a very fast trajectory. We weren't prepared. None of us had ever been there before. Mickey hadn't been there before in these circumstances. You're learning on your feet and trying to do your very best. It was a lot to ask."

One serious oversight on Collins's part encapsulated the band's problems. The Roxy tour notwithstanding, Wire had actually begun to garner strong interest in Europe by spring 1979 – thanks to *Chairs Missing*, their live work, and the television appearances in Germany and Belgium. A tour was arranged to capitalise on this and to build their continental audience. "After *Rockpalast*, the German record company were really behind us," recalls Grant. At the 11th hour, though, the dates had to be cancelled because Collins had apparently neglected to finalise the venue bookings. "Mickey hadn't got the deposits together for the gigs, so we had to blow the tour out. The crew were there, the trucks were there, and we didn't do it. That may have been a decisive moment for the band."

Realising that all was not as it should be, the group began to entertain a solution involving Grant, who had far more experience than Collins and was attuned to the business side of management. "We pointed out that Mickey needed help," remembers Lewis, "and the idea came about that Bryan should co-manage the band with him. Bryan understood what we were doing better than Mickey. Mickey's an artist, and he didn't understand the nuts and bolts of things. There should have been a partnership between Bryan – an enforcer, an enabler – and Mickey, with his crazy, good pop ideas." Grant tried to convince Collins that this was the best thing to do. "I sat down with Mickey and said: we should talk about managing this together. He wasn't into that, so I went off on my own and formed Britannia Row Productions."

Grant's account of Wire's disillusionment with Collins seems the most objective. "At the end of the day, they're all very strong-willed people. Mickey could spot talent, that's for sure. Mickey wasn't a businessman. He had some very creative ideas and real flair, and he was a funny guy to be around, but he hadn't come from a management background. There are a lot of bands where the manager has come along with them from the start – and sometimes they get lucky. Can I put my hand on my heart and blame Mickey? It's too easy for them to say it was Mickey's fault. It's never *all* anyone's fault. It's an holistic experience, all of this. I don't think anyone's innocent in this."

With Wire out of commission, the band-members turned to their own ventures. Anything but a selected list of these falls outside the scope of this book: suffice it to say, the breadth of creativity displayed over the next five years is unsurprising given the symptoms that had presented themselves on *154*. Gilbert and Lewis pursued their Dome project and label, releasing their own experimentally oriented recordings, as well as working with other artists in various capacities and configurations: as Duet Emmo (with Daniel Miller) and P'o (with a full band), producing musicians (including Matt Johnson), and creating audio-visual installations and performance pieces (such as *MZUI* at London's Waterloo Gallery and *MU:ZE:UM TRACES* at the Museum of Modern Art in Oxford, both with Russell Mills). Gilbert also struck up a friendship with the dancer Michael Clark, who commissioned a score from him for his production *Do You Me? I Did*, which appeared on Gilbert's first solo album for Mute, *This Way*, in 1984.

Newman released three solo albums between 1980 and 1982 – *A–Z*, *provisionally entitled the singing fish*, and *Not To* – moving comfortably between pop and more experimental territory, often combining the two sensibilities to great Eno-esque effect. He also found the time to produce The Virgin Prunes' *... If I Die, I Die*, before decamping to India with Annette Green in autumn 1983. Grey wasn't idle either, recording and touring with Newman and Fad Gadget, and then eventually leaving London in 1983 to explore his interest in farming.

### Like a socket to the anus

Wire continued releasing work during their hiatus. In 1981, Rough Trade (who had distributed the first Dome album) put out a seven-inch of 'Our Swimmer' and 'Midnight Bahnhof Cafe', the tracks that had been recorded with 'Go Ahead' in 1979 at Magritte Studio. "'Our Swimmer' was the strongest song from the Jeannetta Cochrane period," says Newman, "but recording-wise, it wasn't our finest moment." As for the B-side, the less said the better, as far as Newman is concerned. "'Midnight Bahnhof Cafe' has a good verse; the chorus is just terrible – it sounds like some awful Eurovision group from the 80s."

If the tracks themselves were slightly sub-par, the topiary image on the sleeve was truly inspired. "I'd done a series of little paintings featuring 'impossible topiary'," Gilbert recalls. "Again, the starting point was a funny old book: there was a picture of Cologne station in it, and the stationmaster had clipped his hedge into the letters *K-Ö-L-N*, and I thought: there's something about that. So I started doing things with impossible topiary. I even made a copy of the Cologne photograph out of papier-mâché. It's still knocking around somewhere – unfinished, of course."

Although the Electric Ballroom gig hadn't been filmed, a (poor) two-track audio recording was made: an eight-track machine had been used but, in another characteristic stroke of Wire misfortune, it didn't work properly. Even so, Rough Trade agreed to put the material out on an album in July 1981. Newman wasn't convinced it was good enough to release. "My approach was always to go for the high-quality item, something that would have some life in the future, something that someone will want to listen to. There was a financial argument for making cheaper records, but I was resistant to it. But I wasn't in the majority."

Rather than issue the Electric Ballroom recording 'as is', Gilbert and Lewis framed it in conceptual terms. As Newman puts it: "The idea of the *Document And Eyewitness* album was to make it an art statement, as opposed to just releasing a rubbishly recorded gig." They made no effort to pass it off as a standard live album: that is, as a record that provides listeners with a seamless illusion of the unmediated experience of a concert. Instead, in keeping with Wire's customary aesthetic, Gilbert and Lewis built in distance and detachment, presenting the recording explicitly as a construct – an object to be contemplated. This effect was achieved by splicing in discursive fragments, undercutting the illusion of the live moment with after-the-fact commentary and observations on the night's occurrences. They incorporated the recollections of 'eyewitnesses': Lewis and two Wire associates who were in the audience, Adrian Garston and Russell Mills. (According to Newman, Garston is the individual officially recognised by the band as "The Second-Ever Wire Fan". David Boyd of pragVEC enjoys the honour of being the first.)

There are other, more subtle factors that increase the album's detachment from the actual event – factors undermining its live-recorded *presence*, as well as problematising the notion that the document and its eyewitnesses offer a 100 per cent reliable representation of the evening. Whereas the title implies that the record has documentary status, it is far from an authentic artefact: in addition to the dubious audio fidelity, the album's account is partial because it lacks about 20 minutes of the 'music' performed, suppressing three tracks ('Inventory', 'Ritual View', and 'Part Of Our History') and editing others drastically (on the night, 'Instrumental', for example, limped on for ten minutes). Furthermore, '12XU' is largely excised, with only Newman's spoken intro and its closing section left intact; the body of the track is replaced by Garston's enigmatic pronouncement "I don't need to go to the Arctic to know it's cold".

Replicating the collage effect of the audio, the sleeve art was Lewis's cut-up version of a poster Gilbert had made for two shows that Wire played at London's Notre Dame Hall in July 1979.

The original release of *Document And Eyewitness* came with a 12-inch EP that included part of a more conventional set from one of the Notre Dame Hall gigs, plus a recording of 'Heartbeat' from the Roxy Music tour. The Notre Dame Hall material was compelling for its versions of unreleased tracks like 'Ally In Exile', 'Relationship', and 'Witness To The Fact'. These numbers were in a more cohesive state than most of the pieces performed at the Electric Ballroom and augured well for what might have been the next Wire album in 1980.

Nevertheless, reviewers focused on the Electric Ballroom component of *Document And Eyewitness*, and the responses were typically divided. Having been offhandedly positive about the gig itself, Chris Bohn (this time writing for the *NME*) warmed to the album, declaring that its evocation of the "vicious tension between audience and performers" made it "one of the most compulsive live records in a long time". In *Sounds*, Johnny Waller was equally enthusiastic. "As your standard live 'rock' album, this is a dismal failure. ... As an insight into the Wire approach to 'entertainment' it is a fascinating, intriguing collection of live performance intercut with related dialogue often in a confusing collage of sound on sound." *The Face*'s Dave Fudger called it "irritating, exciting and comic by turns, but never boring ... a very fitting final chapter to their single-minded and uncompromising adventure".

It was left to *Melody Maker*'s Lynden Barber to piss on everyone's chips. He had no time for Wire's "smug haranguing of the audience, unintelligent stabs at minimalism and constant whining", proclaiming the record "a harrowing experience – and not one easily recommended. Late Wire, stripped down to the metal, connect like a socket to the anus. ... A thoroughly shoddy package."

In March 1983, Rough Trade released another Wire single, a 12-inch featuring the Peel session version of 'Crazy About Love'. On the B-side were the two tracks recorded in 1980 at Scorpio Sound, offering different takes on 'Our Swimmer': the frantic speed with which the band complete 'Second Length (Our Swimmer)' would doubtless arouse the suspicions of the World Anti-Doping Agency, and the loop-based deconstruction, 'Catapult 30', could well be an outtake from an exorcism.

**CHAPTER 6**

# 1983–87

### There must be more where that came from

By summer 1983, Bruce Gilbert and Graham Lewis had started to consider reactivating Wire. "We thought it'd be a bit of a laugh," says Gilbert. "That was how we approached it, just wondering what it would be like." During the hiatus, Lewis occasionally saw Colin Newman, and they had discussed the band's future possibilities. "We did meet and talk about making the next record," Lewis recalls. Producers were also mooted for a potential project, and he remembers a get-together at the Angel pub in Soho at which Mike Thorne was sounded out – *154* now behind them. "We realised we'd got over the worst of things and that we had better cause together," says Lewis. "We met and talked about ways of self-financing – just exploratory talks."

The possibility of enlisting Thorne appealed to Gilbert. "Graham and I discussed it. We thought: We've been away from Mike for a long time; I wonder how he thinks now, where his aesthetics are. He seemed to be involved in weird projects and had made some very successful pop records. It seemed to have gone a bit quiet. It was another pub conversation, really: I wonder what it'll be like. Would it still work? – just on that level. It could be very interesting. Maybe he could, in some strange way, refresh the situation or put it back to the old protocols. It was worth sending him a letter to see if he was up for it. We were thinking in terms of: You won't get paid. It could be an eight-track studio, it might be quite primitive. Conceptually, it would have been a very interesting project with Mike in an eight-track studio. Could he make something of value without the high-end technology? That was the feeling we were having. It could be fun. It could be one track. It could be a single. In those circumstances, saying an LP, it's dangerous territory. For Wire, it's about: Does it work? Is it worth it? Are we having fun? Is it interesting? Stimulating? We were just thinking: what would it be like to have Mike on board? Although I don't think Colin was terribly sure. His relationship with Mike had deteriorated."

As far as Lewis was concerned, it was always a question of if, not when Wire would return to active duty. "We were fairly close to doing something

– we certainly had the material – and then Colin went off to India. So that stopped it." Newman spent 14 months travelling in India and came back to England in November 1984, ill with hepatitis, his marriage over. While staying with friends in Heaton Moor, near Manchester, he contacted Lewis with a view to rekindling their writing partnership. They agreed to meet in London and – unbeknownst to Newman – Lewis arranged for Gilbert to show up at the same time. "Colin came down to see if we could rejuvenate what had been there before. I told Bruce and asked him: do you think that, by accident, you could appear in the pub on Saturday night? He said that there was quite a strong possibility of that happening." The meeting went as well as could be expected. "It was a little bit stiff at first," says Lewis, "but we all felt there was unfinished business."

Newman doesn't remember agonising over whether it was a good idea to restart Wire. The decision seemed intuitive – and collective. "We started again because we had no choice. It's a classic 'good' Wire thing: everyone knows when it's right, and there's no need to talk about it. Nobody had any reservations. There was no discussion." Lewis, however, says there was initial uncertainty about Robert Grey's participation and recalls that they even made contingency plans. "It was actually around that time that the idea came up to call it 'Wir' if Robert hadn't been interested. It was something that was on the shelf from then onward."

After what he had understood to be the end of Wire, Grey had begun to think about organic farming as a career. Having left London, he spent time at a Steiner school in Sussex, learning the basics of organic agriculture, and then volunteered on several farms. By late 1984, he was living alone in a cottage in North Wales and, although he was still practising the drums, he wasn't playing with anyone. When Newman phoned to ask how he felt about rejoining Wire, it was the last thing he expected. He didn't immediately commit, but he found the proposition appealing: "I thought in 1980 that it was final when Wire disbanded, so it was a surprise. I was pleased, because I didn't have any other drumming connections. I thought if Wire was going to restart, that would be a good thing. I didn't have any reservations about doing it – that came later."

The feeling of there being "unfinished business" was intensified by the band's memory of the plaudits garnered by *154*: the critical response in late 1979 had suggested that this was Wire's moment, but instead of capitalising on that recognition and interest, ploughing the rich post-*154* creative furrow, they'd walked away. Newman expresses some of the frustration he felt at Wire's failure to seize the moment and realise their potential: "A band that can make an album like *154* must have more to do. A band that can be that influential must have more that can come from it. That's how we saw it."

There was also a sense that Wire had paved the way for other artists who had gone on to achieve more substantial success, and Newman and Lewis felt they were due some of that. "There was a huge amount of unrealised ambition," asserts Newman. "Look at the reviews we got for *154* – and what had we seen out of it? Fuck all." Lewis makes a similar point, albeit more poetically: "With *154*, it was like we were climbing Everest without oxygen. We hadn't been there before, and the landscape we were trying to create hadn't been created. Our disappointment was that we'd created that landscape, and other people got the credit for it. We'd been eclipsed by other people who'd taken our ideas and run with them. It was about dropping the ball. It had been such a difficult process. We should have made more of the achievement."

Gilbert also believed there was something unresolved with Wire. "I felt, probably wrongly, that there was still work to do. It felt like an unfinished project." However, there was another, more intriguing and surprising aspect to his renewed interest. Notwithstanding his strong investment in Wire's detached aesthetic, when Gilbert explains his motivation for rebooting the band in 1985, he identifies a contradictory impulse, one seemingly rooted in authenticist rock ideology. "There's a visceral element about a guitar group which is terribly attractive to me. It's a physical thing. It's deeply embarrassing in a strange sort of way – especially if you're a fairly shy person like me – because it's like someone's getting inside you. It's quite an odd feeling but quite exciting. It's that moment when the noise starts."

To Gilbert, this has nothing to do with playing the axe hero to adoring fans; it's above all about his experience of Wire, in its fundamental form, as a self-contained, interactive enterprise. In this sense, he comes close to Grey's definition of Wire as "four people playing together"; Gilbert, though, is more explicit about the emotional dimension. "It was never about being onstage and having people pay me. There's just that very visceral, hairs-on-the-back-of-the-neck element of being in a room with three other people and making a lot of noise. Plus it's the only group I've ever been in, and it was a functioning unit. We knew each other, we knew each other's moods, shall we say. I, for one, certainly missed that. It'd always been attractive, since I first discovered it at Watford. I suppose I was missing this interaction and making noise, really. So it was about the idea of doing it again, making a bit of a racket, and the element of there being unfinished business."

Like Grey, Gilbert recognises that four-people-in-a-room situation as his ideal of Wire, but where he missed it specifically while they were apart in the early 80s was in the communal, *artistic* process of developing the material. "The rehearsal scenario was, for me, very, very special because it's a studio – an artist's studio, where things are possible, where you make things. It's where you can create things. It takes a lot of warming up, hacking out a beat, improvising: it's about that lovely experimentation part of the process."

Before proceeding, it's important to qualify the discussion and commentary that follow. The 80s were a time of considerable creative tension between the members of Wire, and this period remains polarising when they reflect on it. The recording of *The Ideal Copy* was difficult for the band. Newman was intensely unhappy and now sees little of value in the record. Lewis, on the other hand, is proud of *The Ideal Copy* but less enthusiastic to talk about its creation, which took place at a stage in his life that he doesn't appear keen to revisit in interviews. He was generally guarded about the making of *The Ideal Copy* (and, indeed, much of Wire's 80s work) – his observations given, it seemed, with reluctance. Grey (who faced the biggest challenges during this period) and Gilbert were more open and even-handed in their assessment of Wire's 80s endeavours.

### Year Zero

Being Wire, the band felt that any renewed activity required an accompanying conceptual frame or narrative. This was a calling card to reintroduce themselves to an unsuspecting public, but it was just as much a statement to themselves of how they saw their aesthetic. "We needed something to hang the new story on," Lewis says. That concept, devised by Gilbert, was 'Wire as Beat Combo'. To him, this ironic tag, evoking a sparsely equipped mid-60s outfit, was perfect visual shorthand for the band's new sensibility. "It was a convenient phrase and very old-fashioned: there's a drummer playing very simple rhythms, and you have guitar. From my point of view, it was about stripping it back – and the idea that whatever you cooked up in the studio would be playable live." Lewis agrees: "That seemed to describe what it was. It came out of the visual absurdity of Rob's kit – the size of him and this bass drum, snare, and hi-hat. It looked kind of 60s but obviously didn't sound like that."

The first item of business was to get together in a practise studio. Newman set this up using a pseudonym. "We were so famous in our own minds that we thought if anyone knew we were rehearsing, they'd be trying to get to us. So we booked in under the name 'Intergalactic'." Lewis remembers that the approach was very simple, without any expectations or broader aims. "We just turned up and went: Well, let's play. Let's see if we can start in as naïve a way as we started in the first place, when we started rehearsing in Watford – it worked before." Gilbert also emphasises the purely speculative nature of these sessions: "Nobody came in with songs. It was very primitive. We just wanted to see if there was anything there."

"I was conceptually attracted to the idea, if we could pull it off," says Newman of the back-to-basics Beat Combo, but his comments also suggest that, from the outset, he had qualms about this direction: "Bruce had decided in his typically high-handed way that new Wire was going to be 'Year Zero'. It's a classic bit of Bruce strategy, which is conceptually brilliant and conceptually stupid – designed in part at least to make sure he was the commander. If we were doing it differently, then I couldn't come with songs. I just had to be the singer. And the singer is always less important than the guitarist." By the time Wire came to record *The Ideal Copy* in November and December 1986 (with mixing in January 1987), Newman would be profoundly frustrated with what he saw as the de-emphasising of songwriting.

Wire's first rehearsals in five years started poorly. "The first two days weren't terribly inspiring," reports Lewis. "It was quite stiff, quite difficult. People were a bit reserved about how it might be – if it *could* be. But on the third day, 'Drill' and 'A Serious Of Snakes' appeared." Gilbert characterises the evolution of those pieces in terms of a series of questions: "It was literally about: Does it still work? Can we actually make a noise? Can we make a convincing noise or sound? Are we losing ourselves in a proper way with what each other is doing and not thinking about music at all? Is it still there, is that 'thing' still there? I think that was what the *Snakedrill* EP was totally about: Strip it down to bare nothing. Just us. Four people in a room. Making a noise."

That 'thing' sought by Gilbert was Wire in its purest form, a shared experience of creative engagement, which Lewis thought the band-members would be most likely to access if their interaction were kept as simple and unmediated as possible. "The whole sound was stripped back to the fundamental again, a different fundamental from what became *Pink Flag*: we were trying to find an essence we could build on." That essence was encapsulated, above all, in 'Drill'. "It's just one note – that's the basis of everything," says Gilbert. "It's the rhythm. You're asking yourself: What is the right note? Are you excited by it? Can you continue? Can you extend it into something? That's what it was about. Is the level of cooperation still there, physically, musically? And it was."

Although the eventual success of these sessions proved that the foundational four-people-in-a-room rapport was intact, Lewis does stress the importance of some of the tools they brought to the experiment. Two pieces of equipment were "crucial in the development of the basslines" at the core of 'Drill' and 'A Serious Of Snakes': his newly acquired curiosity, a Westone Rail bass, and a digital delay unit. "Bruce and I had been playing around with the latest digital delays," Lewis recalls. "They gave a possibility that was like sampling. You could set up rhythms, and what developed was that the cymbals got in the way of delays, so the cymbals gradually disappeared, and Rob's kit got smaller." The exploration of this effect very much connects back to the idea that had evolved on *Chairs Missing*, of building around a particular noise. "It was 'the sound' – we were seduced by the sound again," explains Lewis. "We were very excited having those two pieces that were very rhythmic, based in the delay. The music I was listening to all had this groove and a more sonic approach to things – it wasn't so song-based, or even guitar-based. It just so happened that we were using guitars to produce the noise."

With hindsight, Newman identifies in the band's new direction one of Wire's basic flaws following their reactivation: a gulf between ideas and an ability to execute them. This issue would become more vexed as they struggled to engage collectively with new music-making technology and as the area of production became more contested. "When I moved back to London," remembers Newman, "Graham started playing me things like 'White Lines', and suddenly that was the new aesthetic. We knew that was what we were interested in, but we had to realise that with the Beat Combo. How was that supposed to work? There was a lot of ambition without really knowing how to realise it."

For *Pink Flag* and *Chairs Missing*, there had been a close fit between the ideas around the work and the work itself. That was no longer the case when they came to make *154*, since the lack of shared vision complicated matters, but the record did not suffer as a result (although Newman would disagree). In the 80s, the disconnect intensified, the quality of the work becoming less consistent in direct proportion to the polarisation over methods and aims. That this polarisation became so acute on Wire's return was inevitable, as Gilbert, Lewis, and Newman had been immersed in their own creative processes away from Wire for five years – longer than the group's first run.

The band-members also had different priorities regarding the relative importance of ideas versus their execution. There's a sense in which, for the conceptually oriented Lewis and Gilbert, the exploration of ideas is where the work is chiefly located – more than in the finished item. This is especially true of Gilbert's process-centred ethos. His discussion of Wire tends to concentrate mainly on his enthusiasm for the ideas informing the work and on his recollection of the creative enactment of those ideas. It's not surprising, then, that his favourite Wire pieces are a track that exists in multiple iterations and not a definitive version ('Drill') and one that was created in the moment and geared toward improvised experimentation ('Crazy About Love').

This clashes with Newman's outlook. While Newman is no less adventurous, he is, by his own account, more interested in the final, formalised product than the idea or the theoretical statement. Given the difficulty of reconciling these creative attitudes and the working methods they entail, it's little wonder that the band's output should have become inconsistent.

## Rubbish!

Cunning pseudonyms notwithstanding, word got out that Wire had reconvened, and they were invited by David Elliott and Marco Livingstone to perform at the Museum of Modern Art in Oxford on June 7 1985. (This came about via Gilbert and Lewis's connections with the museum, which had hosted their *MU:ZE:UM TRACES* installation with Russell Mills a couple of years earlier.) The band's acceptance triggered a more focused phase. "It was deadline time," says Lewis. "Now it all became more real. Now we needed 30 minutes of material." Playing at floor-level with sparse lighting, Wire looked and sounded more minimal at MoMA than they had done during the *Pink Flag* era. "Oxford was about the Beat Combo idea," says Gilbert. "A few amps, a drum kit, in a gallery space. Not a big PA. It was about: Can we still do it? Is it possible? Do we still have the ability to play together? And what better context."

Wire's set of entirely new songs was well received – "the audience applauded for longer than we'd played," Lewis laughs – although Newman is somewhat scornful about the band's attitude: "We felt like homecoming heroes. We were smug. We were doing 'art'. It was like: we're Wire, and we're really important, and we're going to play a bunch of stuff you've never heard before, and you're going to lap it up. And I think it worked." Grey has good memories of the gig. "It seemed like we picked up where we left off. It wasn't a huge adjustment. I was pleased. We thought that maybe the time we had off had been a useful break."

The following month, Wire played at the Bloomsbury Theatre, a 500-seat London venue owned by University College. In the spirit of the

Jeannetta Cochrane and Electric Ballroom gigs, the music was prefaced by a performance piece: *The Shivering Man*, with Michael Clark, choreographed by Angela Conway and soundtracked by what Gilbert calls "my noise". After this, Wire played a set consisting largely of the material from Oxford. But this clearly wasn't Oxford – after the first couple of songs, a lone malcontent took advantage of the brief respite to denounce the proceedings as "RUBBISH! FUCKING BORING!" before churlishly storming out. "Some of it was awful," admits Newman, "but there are moments in 'Drill' that were really special." (Gilbert's "noise" for Clark would appear a year later on his second Mute solo album, *The Shivering Man*. Also included was the music for Clark's *Angel Food*, a 1985 piece commissioned by Rudolf Nureyev at the Paris Opera Ballet.)

Performed in non-rock, more broadly artistic contexts, the Oxford and Bloomsbury shows were atypical gigs. I saw both, and my impression was that Wire were granted a free pass (Bloomsbury heckler aside): these were the band's first appearances after five years away, and the audiences, aware of the occasion, excused the short, tentative sets composed of unfamiliar material. When Wire stepped up their live activity with a handful of gigs in October and December, things didn't go quite so well. By the time they played at the Paradiso in Amsterdam, the honeymoon was over. "At Oxford it was an arty crowd, and people were predisposed to like it," Newman says, "but Amsterdam is where we met the real world. The Paradiso is a big place and ticket prices were quite high, and they wanted a classic night out, and what they got was not long enough and not very good. So they were pissed off. It was an issue of the quality. They didn't just not like it because we played so short; they didn't like it because we were fucking shit."

Newman's assessment of Wire's Paradiso set highlights what he considers their unfounded arrogance. "We were up our own fucking arses. We thought we were important. We were the band who'd done *154* – nothing else had come out yet. After *154*, we were insanely confident but also fucking good; we were now overconfident but not very good. The Year Zero Beat Combo premise was a thin premise. There was nothing there that could stand up to what we'd done in the late 70s, and we were reminded of that. Our reaction was: oh you're just on about the past. But the reality is that we weren't that good. We played a lot of crap gigs. We got better, but it took two or three years to start to be good with that material, and some of that material was a bit iffy. It was a hard lesson that took a long time to learn. That's not to say that there weren't good things that came out of the 80s, but a lot of it came out of an overarching arrogance."

Gilbert's memories of Amsterdam are more positive. "As always with Wire, we weren't sure what the audience was expecting, and we tried to make sure that they should get the unexpected. I think we put a very efficient, very dynamic set together, that we were pleased with. It made sense." Still, he concedes that it wasn't an unalloyed success. He had enjoyed the MoMA and Bloomsbury Theatre settings, finding them more conducive and appropriate to Wire's work, but at the Paradiso he felt he was back in the sort of music-business context he'd wanted to escape in 1979, one with very narrowly defined conventions and expectations. "The Paradiso was a bit of a reality check, I suppose. The audience was waiting for something to happen. I'm not sure what it was, and, obviously, it never happened. And when we came offstage, the first thing the promoter said was: you should have played for five minutes more. There was no encore. I hate the ritual of the encore. Sometimes it's genuine, sometimes it's just about people wanting their money's worth. It's very difficult to judge that. It's another part of the institutionalisation of the process."

Bryan Grant, who had returned to the fold as Wire's manager, finally replacing Mick Collins, remembers the Paradiso vividly: "They did 45 minutes, and that was it. They didn't come back for an encore, and the audience went nuts. This guy came backstage and told us he was going to burn all his Wire records, and we had to be hustled out of the dressing room." According to Lewis's analysis, this insistence on the encore could also be explained in more specific cultural terms. "We learned an important lesson," he says. "The Dutch are liberal, stoned hippies, but also pragmatic merchants. Deep in their psyche is this merchant mentality, and it says: if you play the Paradiso, you will play for an hour. They were absolutely fucking furious."

The lack of old material in that short set didn't help matters. In the context of the punk era, during the initial phase of Wire's career, not catering to audiences had made sense. "It was more punk than punk," Lewis explains. "That's what was great about punk – there had to be some sort of confrontation, undercutting people's expectations. That's what good work does. It's not quite what you expect." It should be remembered, however, that although Wire often favoured unreleased work in the 70s, there was always something familiar for the audiences to hang onto in live sets; in 1985, in true Year Zero fashion, Wire made no concessions.

Newman maintains that the 1985 strategy differed in intent from the subversive impulse of the punk years. "It wasn't a calculated wind-up in the 80s. That would be pointless. We were doing it because we thought that was the logical thing to do." Lewis agrees about the clean break with the 70s material. "We felt it was the right thing to do, although it wasn't the easiest thing to do." At the same time, he expresses some reservations about Wire's modus operandi when it came to starting again, suggesting that there still was a "calculated" aspect to it. "The idea of not playing anything old turned out to be an incredible weight, very heavy baggage to carry. As a strategy, we felt that we had to confound people's expectations. It was part of the brief. There was supposed to be some kind of encounter with the audience – and that was probably one of the more misguided ones. We made life much more difficult for ourselves than perhaps we needed to. If we were arrogant about it, we certainly paid for it."

Despite Wire's unswerving commitment to new work in the 80s, they did make an exception for Michael Clark. He asked them to provide live accompaniment for his piece *Swamp*, commissioned for Ballet Rambert's 60th anniversary celebrations at Sadler's Wells in June 1986. The band obliged, performing *Pink Flag*'s 'Feeling Called Love' in the orchestra pit.

### Snakedrill

Although Wire were now active again, throughout 1985 and 1986 the band-members continued with their own projects. By June 1985, Newman was based in Brussels, where he produced Minimal Compact's *Raging Souls* and recorded his fourth album, *Commercial Suicide*. In July 1986, he married Minimal's bass player, Malka Spigel. Lewis, working as He Said, made his first solo album for Mute (*Hail*), and Gilbert continued to potter away with his noise. It wasn't until mid 1986 that they set about recording the material they had been developing as Wire.

In the meantime, they had signed to Mute. Daniel Miller was an admirer of the group and had met Mick Collins at the Factory Club in Manchester in 1979. "They were a guitar band," says Miller, "but they didn't think like a guitar band, which I thought was very interesting. And they had great pop songs, whether they liked it or not. 'Outdoor Miner' was the Number One that they never had. That track, more than anything, alerted me to their pop potential." His first social encounter with Wire came after they'd finished *154*. "I had a drink with them in Covent Garden. They'd just come from the playback of *154*. It was after the Roxy Music tour. I thought they'd be more aloof about it, but they were quite rock'n'roll in the way they described how much fun it was – being in a van, staying in hotels and stuff." In view of their familiarity with Miller as a Duet Emmo accomplice and as a label boss, Gilbert and Lewis were comfortable with Wire being on Mute. "When we felt things were good enough to record, Mute seemed the natural place," says Lewis. "We couldn't think of a better place to be. It was a fantastic record company – very stimulating, and Dan was a fan of what we'd done. Why should we go somewhere else?"

With an EP planned, they began to think about a producer. By now, Lewis, Newman, and Gilbert all had some production experience, but doing it themselves wasn't an option. Lewis felt it would have been difficult to achieve consensus, "given the problems we'd had with *154*" and given the diversity of their individual projects while the band had been on hiatus. "Our ways of working and making records had changed so fundamentally. We'd had very different experiences of that." Newman puts it more succinctly: "If we'd produced ourselves, it would have been an almighty scrap." Gilbert was keenly aware of the need for a neutral figure. "Because people had been doing their own thing, they were confident in their own bits and pieces and their career, so it was more about needing a referee and having Mute as a referee. We were still vaguely institutionalised. We needed a structure of some description."

Miller himself was an obvious choice as producer. From Newman's perspective, it was a case of cynical pragmatism to ask him. "It was a way of sucking up to Dan. It had a logic to it!" Miller was also eager to involve Gareth Jones, with whom he'd worked on Depeche Mode's *Construction Time Again*, *Some Great Reward*, and *Black Celebration*. "Gareth's a first-class engineer, as well as a producer," says Lewis. "I think it gave Dan security going into what he knew was a loaded situation: he was very sensible to bring someone to ride shotgun. It worked extremely well." Jones agrees: "I enjoyed it; I really enjoyed their energy. It was a pleasure and a privilege to get to know these legendary characters."

The *Snakedrill* EP was made at Strongroom studios in Shoreditch. This was the beginning of the band's transition to the digital realm. Developed through live playing by the Beat Combo, the tracks were then constructed by Miller and Jones mostly using Steinberg Pro-16 software (the grandfather of Cubase).

When the *Snakedrill* sessions began, Wire had an album's worth of material in utero; 'A Serious Of Snakes', 'Advantage In Height', 'Drill', and 'Up To The Sun' made the EP. 'Ambulance Chasers' would appear the following year on the 'Ahead' 12-inch single, while several tracks destined for 1987's *The Ideal Copy* already existed in one form or another, such as 'Cheeking Tongues', 'Madman's Honey', and 'Over Theirs'. 'Kidney Bingos' and 'Come Back In Two Halves' would find a home on *A Bell Is A Cup … Until It Is Struck* in 1988. 'Harry Houdini' never made it into the studio.

'Drill' (much more of which later in this book) was in an idiosyncratic class of its own. Its eccentric lyrics fuse the corporeal and the mechanical; the clipped, chanted vocals create a similarly cybernetic effect. Likewise, the music suggests a repetitive process set in motion and maintained by the band, with occasional tweaks. This melody-free minimalist exercise was about as far from pop music as Wire had travelled thus far and was unlikely ever to trouble chart compilers.

'A Serious Of Snakes' and 'Advantage In Height', on the other hand, were Wire repackaged as shiny, state-of-the-art pop. They even had a hint of the anthemic about them: 'Advantage In Height' was destined to become one of the band's most enduring live numbers. Continuing an established Wire tradition, these songs forge an improbable yet successful marriage of catchy pop accessibility and obscure lyrical content – 'A Serious Of Snakes' notably featuring choruses composed of inventive insults. These tracks, in particular, promised great things from Wire in the 80s. Not so, 'Up To The Sun'. Stuck somewhere between 'Happy Birthday To You' and 'The Rivers Of Babylon', this almost a cappella anti-jaundice duet starring Lewis and Newman found Wire at their self-indulgent worst. Witnessed once in performance, it made for a moderately amusing spectacle. But once was definitely enough.

"*Snakedrill* was good; people loved it," says Newman, but that didn't allay his concerns over the way Wire had been working since the start of the Beat Combo phase. The crux of this, again, was Newman's feeling that the methodology used to create the work – a move away from written songs toward a more intuitive rehearsal-studio approach – was conceived by "the commander" to marginalise him. For Newman, the weakness of much of Wire's 80s output stems from this devaluing of songwriting as the foundation of the work: "What suffered was the writing. In the 70s, I brought songs to Wire, and we played them. That broke down in the 80s because that was no longer considered acceptable, and things had to be done in a different way. But it was never really said in what way it was supposed to be done. That was one of the things that made it very difficult for me: I had no idea what we were supposed to be doing. It didn't seem to have any logic to it."

Newman believed that the process Wire benefited from most, and which, in his opinion, produced their best work, was being inverted, with songs now being made almost after the fact. "Everything got made in a certain way. It wasn't Graham handing me a pile of words and me showing up with a bunch of written songs that the band would learn. There was no preset material.

177

We had to develop more material together in the studio. We had to develop something we could play, that would be invented totally. And it was a hard call, because Wire is not a jamming band." He returns to the example of 'Drill': "'Drill' was the only thing that had come out of that. Maybe 'Ambulance Chasers' – jazz with weird chords and no structure – and 'Over Theirs', which was different every time you played it, because it had no structure. The rest of the things started to be written because that was the only way a piece could be made. 'Drill' wasn't written by any one person, it was just a rhythm, an idea that came with reductionism, with very little formal structure. Formal structure got imposed on it. It's not a song. It got formalised into a song."

Despite what he says about being sidelined as a writer, though, Newman notes that he composed the melodies for three of the four *Snakedrill* tracks, well in advance of recording at Strongroom: 'A Serious Of Snakes' and 'Up To The Sun' (in early 1985 when he was still recuperating from hepatitis in Heaton Moor) and 'Advantage In Height' (in Brussels in 1985).

If Newman felt locked out of the creative process as a songwriter, he didn't feel 100 per cent comfortable with the production model on *Snakedrill*, either. As he describes it, the band had little control over the material that was being generated for *Snakedrill*, because of Miller's approach, which didn't involve the kind of collaboration he'd experienced with Thorne: "*Snakedrill* came out quite well, but it was almost like we hadn't been involved in it. Daniel did the music with what we'd played, and I was like: I don't like this as a production method. With Mike, we'd built the music together. Daniel wasn't interested in overdubs or doubling tracks."

If the modes of developing and recording the material for *Snakedrill* were new, so too was the artwork. This was the first front cover of a Wire record to feature a band-member. Predictably, it's not a standard portrait. It's an arresting image, recognisable yet unsettling – a human body de-familiarised by the composition and the lighting. It's also vaguely erotic, in a severe, fetishistic way. Gilbert recalls conceiving and experimenting with the idea: "It's Rob in the bath, doing one of his martial arts poses. [Grey practised aikido.] I wanted something that was sort of enigmatic – something very physical-looking but slightly ambiguous. So I did some photos with Rob. I made him put oil on his body and changed the lighting to have this sort of effect. And I thought it looked so much better upside down – more odd, more peculiar."

The final cover image was made by the photographer David Buckland, who offers a different recollection. "The session took place in my studio in

Camden Town and was more an extension of friendship and experimentation. I was working with the designer Russell Mills. There was no brief at all for the session. The strong cross-lighting was a signature of my work at the time, and through various visual attempts with the band, I worked just on this solo image. The aim was to provide total tension and hence the body is fully 'wired', strong electric lighting breaking down the form and highlighting muscles and features. The hands held in this way accentuated this tense activity. The final image used is upside down, giving it a more 'constructivist' historical context."

## Sulphurous clouds and enormous cabbages

Following a brief European tour in autumn 1986 and the release of *Snakedrill*, Wire went to Berlin at the end of November to make their first album since *154*. When talk had initially turned to producers, Eno's name had been raised again – and rejected again, for the same reasons as before. "I was against it in the 70s, and I was against it in the 80s," says Newman. Miller was offered the job but declined due to scheduling issues. In the end, everyone agreed that Gareth Jones was the right man (joined by engineer André Giere). Jones, who lived in the city, had previously convinced Miller that it made economic sense for Mute artists to record there. "We worked out early on that we could get a good studio, flights, and accommodation for about the same cost as the labour if we'd stayed in London – because the pound was very strong against the deutschemark, and West Berlin had tax breaks from the government to encourage businesses to stay there at the time the Wall was up."

Wire were enthusiastic about the prospect of working in Berlin. They had a bond with the city, dating back to 1978, and the location appealed to their sense of Europeanness – something that had become heightened in reaction to the Thatcherite Englishness of the 80s. "It was about being a European citizen," Newman says. "London was Thatcher. There was a lot about London in the 80s that wasn't very attractive. I, for one, didn't want to be in London any more. And Gareth was in Berlin, so why not record in Berlin?"

Jones found the place stimulating, in terms of both work and play. "It was a wonderful atmosphere. Late-night bars had a massive allure, and the idea of being able to work late in the studio. And, obviously, the studio itself was very inspiring to a lot of artists. So the whole thing came together: cost-effective, great atmosphere, cool rock'n'roll lifestyle, and a wonderful studio." That "wonderful studio" was the Hansa Tonstudios complex on Köthener Strasse in Kreuzberg, close to the Berlin Wall and Potsdamer Platz.

It was where Bowie had made some of his most powerful, innovative recordings, and where Jones had already worked with Depeche Mode, among others. "It was a chamber-music hall before World War II," Jones explains, "and it was used for entertainment during the War. And *Low*, "*Heroes*", and *Lust For Life* were recorded there. Hansa's drenched in history."

Hansa – with its imposing Doric-columned façade and the grand Studio 2 – also made symbolic sense to Wire, as it marked a return to the kind of large, state-of-the-art facility where they had recorded their first three albums. "There was a feeling of going back to recording in Advision," Newman says. "We were making a big, serious record in a big, serious studio: 48 tracks, two tape machines running together. We were back to where we should be. We were back to being important. There was an element of: We're the kind of people who go to a foreign city to record because we're a famous, established rock band. And we record in famous studios where Bowie recorded." Indeed, the Bowie–Hansa association bolstered Wire's sense of (self-) importance. "We knew damn well where we were," says Newman of the venue. "It was extremely fitting for Wire, this proper place. And," he adds, "we wouldn't have wanted anything less than Depeche Mode got."

Gilbert was fascinated by the studio and by Berlin. He's sure that this environment made its presence felt on the recording. "The general atmosphere of Berlin had an influence, and Hansa was steeped in history, not only musical but other, stranger history." Everyone from communist artists to Nazis had made themselves at home at 38 Köthener Strasse. The avant-garde Malik publishing house was originally based in the building and, between 1918 and 1920, had hosted soirees for Berlin's Club Dada, one of whose founding members, George Grosz, also had a gallery on the premises. Later, the main ballroom – which would become the renowned Studio 2 – was used by the Reichsmusikkammer (Reich Chamber of Music) for classical concerts, as well as for Gestapo parties.

Gilbert was particularly taken by the way history lay exposed, the old erupting amid the new, the two colliding and converging in strange, provocative ways. "Hansa was a wonderful, shabby old building, but the studio was glistening and new. There was this very odd contradiction between the fabric of the building and the technology that was there. Apart from the studio space, which had been smartened up, the rest of the building was as it was, war-damaged. It was inspiring in a strange, decadent way. There were still weird bits of stuff around, bits of wood with holes in, where great big knobs had been, bits and pieces left lying around from earlier studio setups. It was like a hotel, and there were all sorts of nooks and crannies and this huge performance space, which was like a theatre."

Newman was also conscious of his surroundings. "Hansa was bleak. Miserable. Freezing. We were next to the Wall. You had to walk right past it to get to the café, opposite Zoo Station. You were standing in the wreckage of what had been central Berlin before the War. It was a wasteland. It was a very different place then. Round the back of the studio was a patch of bombed-out granite. You didn't get out of that environment. You were stuck in this heavy Berlin winter atmosphere."

From a creative and personal viewpoint, this place was ideal for Lewis. "A relationship I'd had for nine years had broken up. I'd thrown my life up into the air to see what might happen to it, and Berlin being a 24-hour city was quite convenient for me. And from the text side of things, Berlin enhanced the atmosphere of the record: I think it's a very edgy, very dark record. An uneasy record." Gilbert's observations on Lewis during the Hansa sessions are intriguing: "Graham was having a strange old time. He was enjoying Berlin. Creatively, he was going off the scale. He was going out and coming back with six enormous cabbages and making little installations in the studio."

Grey remembers Berlin – entering its last three years as a divided city – as claustrophobic and, at times, unreal: "Quite apart from the politics, history, and geography of it, the position of Berlin gave it an oppressive atmosphere. Because of the sulphurous coal burning in the East, there was a constant smell of smoke and sulphur in the air that added to the alien, slightly threatening atmosphere. Most of the time we were at Hansa, there was a cloud constantly hanging over the city, and you had no view of the sky. The weather conditions added to that alien feeling."

If the oppressive nature of the city impacted Grey and Newman, their experience inside Hansa intensified the sense of claustrophobia: this was a residential studio, the band-members staying in apartments on the upper floors. There was also onsite catering, so they didn't even have to leave the building during their stay, if they chose not to. Jones feels this didn't help the project: "Living at Hansa would have contributed to the intense, claustrophobic nature of the whole session, which is reflected in the record itself: it sounds gloomy, doomy, turned in on itself somehow. It would have added even more to any tension in the group when they were all just living upstairs, very close to each other. I've done some great, really creative sessions in residential studios where everyone's living there, and somehow it works, but for *The Ideal Copy* – where me and the assistant were leaving every night, and they were living in the studio – I don't think that was good. They

181

didn't get out properly. That must have only contributed to their frustrations with each other."

Grey certainly felt confined by the residential setup. "Was it a year? It was probably only two or three weeks, but it seemed like a year because the general interaction wasn't particularly good. There was the feeling that you never got away from the place. When we were at Advision, it was different – you had a break. I did quite a lot of reading and walking around Berlin. There was a gallery within walking distance of the studio. That was a good place to get away from things."

Jones thinks the decision to record over Christmas made matters worse. "*The Ideal Copy* was the first and last time I worked through a Christmas vacation. We thought it was a good idea, but it wasn't. I'd never try that now. Graham disappeared into a bar for a few days." For their part, Lewis and Gilbert don't report any dissatisfaction with the arrangements. They entertained themselves by decorating and transforming their lodgings and made the most of the local hostelries. "I decided to stop drinking at that point, which was slightly irrational, really," Gilbert recalls. "We found this quite interesting sleazy bar. It was very weird – it had tablecloths. To come down from the sessions, I just drank water and watched Graham get drunk. It worked very well."

At the outset, there had been a collective feeling that Berlin would offer Wire a chance to make a fresh start and to do things differently in a place where they were appreciated. "It was all connected to SO36 and Europe being more interested in the things Wire did," says Grey. "The Berlin vibe and the idea of it being a big change and being new and exotic all added to the attraction. And there was the idea that people would behave differently if they were in Berlin, that things would feel different and turn out differently."

Things did turn out differently for Wire in Berlin. They got much worse. The old tensions were still there, now exacerbated by new factors: a creative process that was grounded less in written, formalised songs and had more to do with the in-studio construction of tracks; and an inability to find a way to work together with the new technology at the centre of that process.

## Computerland

When Wire arrived in Berlin, all the tracks for the record (except 'Still Shows') had already been performed live in some version, and 'Over Theirs', 'Cheeking Tongues', and 'Madman's Honey' were now more than a year old. During the first phase of Wire, the development of songs on the road and in rehearsal had proved foundational to the eventual studio process. Now, however, although working drafts of the material appeared to be in place in advance of the sessions, the recording itself turned out to be a major stumbling block.

Having set up at Hansa, the band had begun working on the songs in a traditional manner, but it quickly became clear that this was unsatisfactory. "For the first part of *The Ideal Copy*," remembers Lewis, "we'd gone into the studio and tried to record in a fairly straight way, with the group playing. But everybody felt the results weren't going to set the world on fire, so we revised the process and committed to the sampling and sequencing method."

Newman was comfortable with the change, as this methodology dovetailed with his own interest in new technology and opened up possibilities for the band to get more directly involved in the making of the record – something he felt was necessary. After *Snakedrill*, there was agreement, according to Newman, that Wire needed to engage more in the production side of their work, as they had done on *Chairs Missing* and *154*. "Dan did it all [on *Snakedrill*], and so the feeling was that we had to figure out a way to be more involved in putting it together." As Newman had produced several records – "I was the only one who'd produced a record that had *sold*," he stresses, referring to … *If I Die, I Die* – he was keen to explore this avenue. "I was very excited about the possibility of reclaiming the production process. That's what excited me about *The Ideal Copy*."

Newman believed that his experience with his own Atari 1040 ST and familiarity with sequencing equipped him well for *The Ideal Copy*, for which Steinberg Pro-24 software and the new Akai S900 sampler were used. "Everything had changed. There was a sense in the mid 80s that this was a new and dramatic time in recording, a new way of working. You could take a sound and have it sound exactly the way it'll sound on the record. It's not a demo. You're working on the final thing all the time. It's a big psychological change in the way of working. I was excited by it, but it was about having it in my hands: technology is only interesting to me in terms of what it puts in my hands. The fact that you could bring this technology into your home was exciting beyond anything." In this regard, Newman felt better qualified than Gilbert and Lewis, who, although they'd used the Fairlight CMI's Page R sequencer with Dome, had not been involved in the nuts and bolts of it. "We were approaching the same thing from different angles. Bruce and Graham had started working with sequencing, but they didn't do it themselves: they had people who operated it for them."

That's not to say that Gilbert wasn't excited by the potential of the digital recording technology – what he quaintly calls "computerland". He felt, however, that it was still not developed enough to be used seamlessly in a broader, collective creative process. "From my point of view, we went from the initial primitive thing with *Snakedrill* and descended, very fast, into computerland. I loved what it could do – it was a very powerful tool – but it was in its infancy. Everybody was learning, and it became a little tedious, to be honest. With Dome, we'd done some sampling with the Fairlight, but in a much more playful way – not entire songs and structures. There was a lot of hanging around and programming now, which Colin and the producers we worked with were totally obsessed with. And I have to say it seemed much more about Colin's desire to find out how this technology worked, rather than be creative."

Lewis, too, found the new hardware and software somewhat leaden and awkward, at the same time as he recognised that it was what the band needed. "When we'd started working with Steinberg sequencing, it was clear to everyone that, although it was initially a tedious and time-consuming way of recording, that was the way it had to go. Gareth had just taken delivery of the latest technology, and there was a lot of seeing what would work and what wouldn't work, and of course, then things were taking unexpected directions. So it was about having to be spontaneous and working with a process that was quite slow at times."

## Boxing Colin

Ultimately, it wasn't disagreement over the programming and production technology that made the *Ideal Copy* sessions so divisive; rather, it was differences over the material itself. If Newman was eager to work with the technology, and the others had to bear with him, Gilbert and Lewis's approach to making the songs in the studio was one that Newman, in turn, found problematic and frustrating.

Despite his impatience with some aspects of "computerland", Gilbert is positive about the creative experience of *The Ideal Copy* and speaks with some enthusiasm about the results. "I suppose it was still an intermediary period, really. It still had elements of a very primitive approach and ideas about noise, and it's very raw. I think it's a good record. Graham and I were experimenting. We were in Berlin: let's make something physical, serious, unusual; let's be creative. It's not about making a pop record, it's about taking advantage of what we're seeing around us, the atmosphere, the lovely old studio." Essentially, Gilbert and Lewis gravitated toward the sort of process they'd pursued with Dome, exploring the material in a more spontaneous, open-ended way, constructing the songs as they went. "We were improvising in the studio," says Lewis, "rather than writing something before and recording it as a piece. Once that started, I found it extremely comfortable. Bruce didn't really play much. He just sat around and passed comment."

Making a Wire album for the first time with this methodology was appealing to Gilbert, most of all because there was no road map, the creative direction being determined in the moment, by intuition. "The only guiding principle for me was that we should make this interesting for ourselves and try not to go back to old Wire habits. We were delving into unknown territory in many ways. Although there had been some preparation, and there were some songs, there hadn't been an awful lot of rehearsal-room cooking up of stuff. So it was like jumping into the dark."

Inevitably, difficulties quickly arose. The new working method was anathema to Newman's more formal approach, which required the songs to be 'written' and arranged before initiating the recording process. As Lewis reports: "It became a large conflict because this was an area that Colin hadn't worked in." From Newman's point of view, such open-endedness was not viable for a Wire project; moreover, he felt increasingly that his bandmates were simply recording random instrumental parts that often bore no relation to one another or to the songs on which they were ostensibly working. To him, the band's failure to adhere to a shared, practical "guiding principle" made the project impossible to execute. "There was no fucking chance," says Newman. "Nobody knew what record they wanted to make – or everybody wanted to make a different record."

The problem, as articulated by Lewis and Newman, derived from such a fundamental issue that, in hindsight, the idea of Wire in 1986 seems utterly misguided. Creative tensions have produced great records but, in this instance, the basic philosophical difference regarding what the work is and how it should be done suggests that the band-members would have been better off sticking to their solo projects. Lewis says as much. He doesn't actually believe it was possible for the band to have had a common vision at this point, given that the genie had been released from the bottle years before: "I don't think we could have wanted to make the same record. At the end of *154*, people started to have different ideas of what they thought was the priority and what they thought the group was doing. I was uneasy with Colin's presumption that there was a specific way of making records. My experience told me that wasn't the case. It certainly wasn't the case with this one. The work I'd been involved in was about the creative process and collaboration, and it was very much about making and creating on the spot and in the moment. Colin's uneasy with that. It doesn't suit him. It's about how he composes, how he writes. He does like to feel as though he's in control, that he's written something."

Gilbert, too, thinks that Newman's discontent with the making of the record had to do with an inability to assert himself in this more fluid process, either as a songwriter or as a producer. "It was pure music coming out of four human beings, which I don't think Colin could really cope with, because he couldn't manipulate it in the same way he was able to do on *154*, and it was slightly out of his control. I think he found it very, very difficult. The work was being made at too fast a pace for him to get a grip on it and appreciate it for what it was. We were working at such a pace and laying down tracks that were less melodic than Colin would have liked. He didn't really have a chance to do his overlaid, chorus-y guitar stuff over it. It was all a bit too stark and brutal for him."

Newman reiterates his belief that underlying Gilbert and Lewis's insistence on this methodology was a desire to minimise his role – although he also believes, paradoxically, that the others depended on him. "Making *The Ideal Copy*, I felt I was marginalised, but they kind of realised they needed me. I was in the strong position by the end of the 70s, and when we got to *The Ideal Copy*, I'd done stuff, and I'd been really far and done something really different. They'd only done what they'd been doing before. I could see now that perhaps they saw me as a threat – Bruce more than Graham. I think there was an element of putting me in my box."

## Bandmaster versus gang leader

Newman grew more and more despondent as the recording progressed. "He was very, very unhappy," says Gilbert. "The more unhappy he became, the more difficult it was to work. Graham and I were enthusiastic, but Colin was in a constant state of frustration, I think. I think he hates the album because he had no control over it. Colin will never be satisfied with anything anyone else does. He thinks he's the only person who knows how to do Wire."

This question of control that seems to be at the core of *The Ideal Copy* was, according to Newman, a recurring preoccupation of the Wire narrative. "You can see the entire history of Wire as Bruce maintaining and keeping his pre-eminence in the band as the gang leader. That's what it was all about. Bruce would never admit to that for one second. If there was two people it was between, it was between Bruce and myself." Lewis agrees, identifying *The Ideal Copy* as a moment where that ongoing competition declared itself most clearly. "There was a clash between Bruce and Colin – a control thing. I was just getting on making the record."

Gilbert, too, frames the issues that surfaced during *The Ideal Copy* in a larger context, tracing his perception of the problems since Wire's birth: "At the start, Colin had fairly free rein because he was teaching me chords, how to play the guitar, basically. So he was very used to being the 'bandmaster' – I actually called him that, and I think he took it a little bit too seriously at times. But then again, someone has to be the bandmaster. Someone has to say: we'd better do this now – or – why don't we do that? Because he was singing, and it's important for the singer to know the band is going to start at the same time. I think he missed that early control he'd had with *Pink Flag* and *Chairs Missing* – and with *154*, when him and Mike worked very closely together."

For some perspective on the picture painted by the band-members, it's useful to hear views from outside the group. Daniel Miller went to Hansa to see how things were going. "There was a lot of tension. I remember each of them pulling me to one side and trying to tell me their side of the story, particularly Graham and Colin. Bruce seemed to have a much more pragmatic view. I can't remember what the issues were exactly, but it was all about control. Whatever happened, it turned out really well, though."

Another visitor was Bryan Grant. "I went to see how they were getting on. It was tough. There was blood on the walls. There was immense tension." Although Grant accepts that such situations can generate fine work, he's not convinced that was the case here. "Did it make it a better record? Probably not. I think they make better music when they're collaborating than when they're fighting. The tension had spilled over from the creative side. It had gone further than that. They were always a dysfunctional family, I have to say. I don't know if that's been a good thing or a bad thing, but I do feel they could have gone further in terms of public acceptance or commercial success if they'd had a common purpose. I'm not sure in those days that there was a common purpose." Within this "dysfunctional family", Grant singles out the relationship between Newman and Gilbert as a major factor exacerbating the band's problems: "Colin wasn't on the same wavelength as Bruce, and therein lay a lot of the tension. Bruce had an enormous amount of influence on the others because he was older. In some ways, he did dominate the direction of the band and what they were doing. That's where a lot of the confrontation came from and a lot of the tension and a lot of the uncertainty of what they were about and where they were going."

Gareth Jones watched things at much closer quarters, on a daily basis, as his comprehensive observations on the personalities and their interaction show. Jones considers the conflict primarily in terms of the old narrative of

Gilbert's experimental sensibility versus Newman's pop leanings; it's unclear whether those positions actually did become more polarised as a result of the uncertainties of the song-making process on *The Ideal Copy*, or whether that oversimplified account just gives Jones a way to make sense of something more complex:

"There was a lot of shit going down, far more than I probably realised. As far as I could see, a lot of the energy and creative drive of Wire comes out of the tension between the members. There was massive tension between Colin and Bruce, as well as between Graham and Bruce on one side, who were super-big drinking mates, and Colin, who was Mr Pop, on the other side. It was obvious that Bruce and Graham were frustrated with Colin. He had his problems with them, and they had their problems with him. They were embracing a noise aesthetic, and Colin was embracing a melody aesthetic, and we were obviously struggling on that record. There were a lot of frustrations, and it was joked about – Colin's 'prettiness' and Bruce and Graham's 'ugliness'. Their musical tastes were constantly banging up against each other. Rob was struggling because he felt he was getting replaced by the drum machine, by sampling his sounds and triggering his drums live. And Graham was going through a terrible personal crisis.

"There was also a great deal of fencing and pushing going on between Graham and Bruce, raising each other's game. They were super-critical. Bruce didn't let anything pass if he thought it was lazy thinking or untidy. You can't run the show with Graham and Bruce. It's impossible. There's no way you can tell Bruce what to do in the studio. Bruce does what he feels is appropriate. And he was older than the others. There was the sense that he was the grey eminence.

"Colin likes everything cut and dried. He likes to know exactly what he's doing. He would like nothing better than to be told that the session is beginning at 11:00 and will finish at 7:00, and he'll be there between 11:00 and 7:00, whereas Bruce and Graham will be comfortable just turning up and seeing what happens. They're super-different personalities. They can all attend the same meeting and describe it so differently. Colin is a control freak. I've experienced it in many other artists, and I recognise the personality traits in Colin. That's not to criticise him. Some control freaks make great art."

While Newman believes *The Ideal Copy* suffered from a lack of shared direction on the band's part, he also feels the production, or absence thereof, compounded problems. He had been keen for a less top-down process – away from Miller's method ("he 'does' the production to whoever he works with"). Newman saw the potential for greater band participation in the context of what he calls Jones's "more collaborative-psychological approach", which sought "to make everyone feel part of the process". However, Newman now suggests that he would have appreciated a firmer hand and that Jones's unassertive style contributed to the difficulties. "There wasn't a producer, really. That was the reason *The Ideal Copy* lacked direction. It was just a bit of a mess. Gareth isn't really a producer; he's an engineer. He could take certain decisions about how something ought to be. He had a certain amount of authority, but unlike Mike, who played the old expert, Gareth wasn't an authority figure. He had nothing about him that was an authority figure. You can't be annoyed with him about the process that happened. He was making records how he'd made Depeche Mode records, a similar kind of approach."

Lewis has no complaints. "I think Gareth did an exceedingly good job. He really looked in the corners and brought out as much atmosphere as he could. It would have been very easy to have given up."

For his part, Jones says he would tackle the album differently now. "Hindsight's a kind of meaningless thing but, looking back, I can see many ways in which we could have improved the record." To begin with, he would do more homework beforehand. "Who knows why they came together again – I didn't even ask them. That would be the obvious question now: So what are you guys hoping to achieve? You've been away for years – what's the game plan? There was no game plan that I knew about, at least. I'd spent time in studios with people arguing, so there was a sense in which a lack of shared vision didn't necessarily seem inappropriate. I'd done work with Einstürzende Neubauten where there didn't seem to be a game plan either, and some of that turned out wonderfully." Nevertheless, the absence of a common cause among the musicians puts the onus on the producer to help the band realise their potential, and Jones feels he might have fared better in that regard if he'd familiarised himself with their work and given himself a clearer understanding of what he could help them achieve.

"The producer's responsibility is to bring the best out of the artist, even if they can't see it themselves," says Jones. "My production experience at the time wasn't sufficient to be able to evaluate the group's work so far and to be able to say: What was great about that? Let's make sure we bring as much of that into this production as we can. We broke away massively from the band's original sound, with some interesting results but, to me, also to the detriment of what they were in their early days. Now, if I look back at that time, I would have probably encouraged them to stay much closer to their original sound."

Jones's realisation came some 15 years later, when he saw Wire playing in 2002 during their *Read & Burn–Send* phase. "I was kicking myself. I thought: now that's what I should have got out of them. I should have said: Fuck all this technology shit – let's go in the rehearsal room and make a big noise. It's going to be wonderful." Indeed, he feels it was a huge oversight not to rehearse the material with the band. "I didn't go into rehearsals with them, again, because I was inexperienced. It was the start of my career, and I can see now that I was making a lot of it up as I went along. Now I would never go into a recording studio with a band without going into a rehearsal room with them for a while first. You've got to get to know each other. I was doing projects back-to-back, I was a real studio animal. I didn't make the time to do that. They just turned up, and we went into the studio. So there we were, day one, off and running."

## Like an uncontrollable animal

Newman is the only member of Wire to have effectively disowned *The Ideal Copy*. "It was the first time I'd felt dissatisfied with the aesthetic the band was producing. I wasn't happy with it at the time, and I still don't like it." His discomfort with the creative direction at Hansa grew as the recording process unfolded, finally becoming intolerable amid the making of 'Ambitious'.

In Newman's view, things had begun to go awry during work on the taut, driving 'Ahead', one of the strongest numbers and the obvious single. "That was the start of it. It was the first thing we did totally sequenced. Gareth and I had recorded the riff from a MIDI guitar, put it in time, and sequenced Graham's bass. It was a different sample for each note – it was a long and complex procedure, and it took us a day to put together." As Newman tells it, the others weren't impressed. "Graham and Bruce came back from the bar, pissed, and said it sounded shit. So we had to go through the whole process of sticking it through a bunch of other effects and sticking it through an amp to try and make it sound great – which didn't get used on the record. And it was my vocal melody, the whole tune was mine, and suddenly Graham is in the studio at 12 o'clock at night doing an absolutely awful vocal. Horrible, pretentious crap. It went downhill from there."

The sexual charge of Lewis's lyrics on 'Ahead' finds no counterpart in the music, and is lost in Newman's mostly affectless vocal, but eroticism resonates throughout the atmospheric 'Feed Me'. The song centres on the dramatic interplay of Gilbert's jagged, anxious guitar and Lewis's unsettling, tranquilised baritone – punctuated by crash chords and a minimal, rolling rhythm track (both assembled out of samples from a Casio SK-1 – a source of much of "my noise" on the album, Lewis reports). Essentially spoken, 'Feed Me' is a distant, more sinister relative of Roxy Music's 'In Every Dream Home A Heartache', although while the latter resolves itself climactically, 'Feed Me' is a six-minute exercise in sustained tension.

This was a highpoint for Gilbert, a near-primal encounter with his beloved visceral, electrified noise. He recalls overdubbing his guitar part in the yawning, cavernous darkness of Studio 2 in the small hours. "It was like a weird call-and-response thing. I wasn't doing a lot, just a note here and there, but I could hear this immense sound in the big playing space. I was just crouched in the corner, and the guitar was like an uncontrollable animal. It felt nervy and dangerous. It was a very physical, emotional thing. That was the way it was made. It felt like it was something quite special." This was Newman's turn to be unimpressed. "I absolutely hated 'Feed Me'. I gave up. I had no idea what it was supposed to be. It was just awful." 'Feed Me' remains a divisive piece. "I wrote the text, the rhythm track, and the crash-chord sequence," says Lewis. "Colin came up with the original vocal melody." Newman isn't having this: "Definitely not! It's all yours, mate!"

This exchange raises the issue of songwriting credits. For *The Ideal Copy*, and for all their subsequent Mute releases, Wire reverted to a group credit. This reflected the difficulty of itemising the contributions to what was – especially by the time of *Manscape* – a complex process of collective, studio-based assemblage. However, discussions for this book of both *The Ideal Copy* and *A Bell Is A Cup* often established who had supplied the key elements on most tracks, with claimants stepping up for the tunes, the riffs, 'noise', vocal melodies, and words. In view of this, and also bearing in mind Newman's sensitivity to the recognition of his own individual role, it seems odd that they should have readopted the format used on *Pink Flag*.

'Over Theirs' is a companion piece of sorts to 'Feed Me', in terms of a shared dark, tense ambience. But whereas 'Feed Me' is amorphous and fluid, 'Over Theirs' is rigid and defined (despite Newman's description of the original version as structureless). While 'Feed Me' seems to emanate from an internal, deep libidinous space, 'Over Theirs' is more immediately rooted in the external environment of its creation, lyrically suffused with images of division, fracture, and liminality, as well as a sense of menace looming at those liminal points – on the edges of awareness. It encapsulates the aesthetic in which Lewis was enveloped in Berlin.

"There was a change in the writing process for me," he says. "The film *Bad Timing* had struck a chord. There were occasions where it was very much about things happening in the periphery of your vision, not a straight

191

narrative. That's what I was envisaging for *The Ideal Copy*: different locations and timelines occurring in the same reality. A lot of the locations of the pieces were peculiar places. I suppose it had to do with how my life had changed, finding myself more on the edge. It wasn't a domesticated life, so the things I was observing weren't as straightforward."

That fragmentation in the lyrics was enhanced by Lewis and Gilbert's tendency to approach writing as a collaborative game. "Bruce and I used to play a sort of Consequences," Lewis recalls, "pushing texts backward and forward: a cut-up between two people. Someone would write something and someone would write something else. That was useful because Bruce was interested in the notion of a fractured reality, too. And there we were, in Berlin, right by the Wall."

There's a depth to 'Feed Me' and 'Over Theirs' that draws listeners in, that *otherness* that's often at the heart of Wire's best work – a quality absent from much of the material on *The Ideal Copy*, which is largely flat and affectless, failing to create compelling atmospheres and devoid of any emotional resonance. In general, there's little substance to the sound and none of the expansiveness of Wire's 70s recordings, as Jones notes: "*The Ideal Copy* is super lo-fi in the sense that it's really noisy and doesn't have a lot of bass on it. That's partly the lack of vision on my part and not making it as big and bold as it could be. I was very focused on the mid-frequencies – that was very much an 80s thing." (Newman picks up on this same detail: "*The Ideal Copy* sounds way too lo-fi for me. It's got no bottom-end, basically.")

Tracks such as 'The Point Of Collapse', 'Cheeking Tongues', 'Still Shows', and 'Madman's Honey' sound over-constructed, clinically cut-and-pasted, shunning interesting noise and texture for unimaginative and at times random-seeming loops and samples. 'Madman's Honey' is an egregious case, with its sickly prettiness, plucked-string effect, clean acoustic guitar sound, and polite vocals. There's often a sense of parts failing to coalesce convincingly. This contrasts with *Chairs Missing* and *154* where, thanks to Thorne's vision of that "integrated electric sound", songs were far more than the sum of their parts. On *The Ideal Copy*, songs often sound like little more than a collection of parts: each sonic component or instrument remains separate, surrounded by space, rather than integrated into a larger whole.

In his extensive reflections quoted earlier, Jones identifies one source of the weaknesses – the fact that he was working with a blank slate and didn't have a feel for Wire or where they were coming from artistically. Consequently, he was unable to preserve what had made Wire's previous work distinctive and successful. Thorne had had the benefit of seeing Wire develop their artistic identity from the ground up, even watching them learn their instruments. As a result, he was deeply attuned to their sensibilities and able to guide the sound in new directions without losing its connection with that ineffable something that always made it Wire.

For Newman, 'Ambitious', a song in which he had some initial involvement, proved to be the nadir of his experience on *The Ideal Copy*. "It was just 48 tracks of undifferentiated noise. How could that be made into a piece of Wire music? Then Dan arrived one weekend, and they worked on it, and Dan made it into a song. Graham ended up singing it. They hijacked the song, and I felt sidelined. That was the general direction in which things were going. They weren't planned out, thought out. There was no logic. It was just random crap." Lewis begs to differ. He feels that the track "is, in many ways, the signature piece" of the album and takes pride in it. He particularly relishes one of Gilbert's unconventional contributions: "the slide-guitar solo on a prepared plastic toy guitar, using a contact mic".

In one sense, Newman, too, saw 'Ambitious' as "the signature piece", since it characterised everything that was wrong with the record and the sessions. It prompted him to sign off, leaving the studio, the city, the country, and, apparently, the band. "You've got someone going mad and someone desperately trying to make it all work and someone else giving up on it. I thought: well, if no one wants to do anything even remotely sensible, anything that's a good idea, then why would I want to stay doing that? I remember thinking: I don't think I can do this anymore. That was the point at which I left." He did tie up some loose ends, from his home in Brussels. "I was even conned into doing parts over the phone," he says, referring to his spoken section in 'Ambitious'. (Newman reclaimed 'Ambitious', after a fashion, by preparing two alternate versions, each with his own vocals. One would appear on the 'Silk Skin Paws' 12-inch single in 1988; the other surfaced on the 1997 *Coatings* compilation.)

According to Grey, "Colin went home saying he'd had enough of Wire. There was a general feeling that this wasn't good." Jones wasn't aware of anything dramatic ("I seem to remember Colin leaving early in a huff"), and Miller doesn't remember it at all: "Everybody was threatening to quit all the time. If he did, we probably thought: oh well, that'll be fine then." Predictably, Lewis and Gilbert didn't pay much attention. "Well, conceptually, he'd already left," says Gilbert. "He might have gone out of the door muttering 'I quit' – but I don't think anyone took it seriously. I just remember him being unhappy, but I don't think we socialised enough for him to be in the pub moaning over a pint of beer."

193

## I generally felt there wasn't much point in me being there

Aside from Jones's brief mention, the elephant in the room in the discussion thus far is Robert Grey. Drummers – whose engagement in music is the most physical – faced the greatest challenge in the 80s, as new technology demanded the highest level of machine-like uniformity from their playing. To Grey, whose investment in drumming is absolute, and for whom Wire is the live, real-time physical interaction with three other people, this posed difficulties that would escalate over the next four years, until he felt his position had become untenable.

At the start of the Beat Combo phase, live playing involving Grey had been the engine for the material's development, but for most of *Snakedrill* his drums were sampled and sequenced. Initially, Grey wasn't too uncomfortable with that process, since *Snakedrill* was only an EP, and he was performing the material live for gigs throughout this period. In Berlin, though, immersed in the recording of a full album, he began to find a completely digital process less attractive. "In 1985," he says, "it was still basically human; when we got to *The Ideal Copy*, more time was spent programming the computer in that session than anything else, like playing. I don't think we did any playing as a four-piece for *The Ideal Copy*."

With the project underway at Hansa, Grey started to find the removal of live drumming from Wire's recording process especially difficult. Unable to play to a click, he contributed samples of his drum sounds, which were then programmed. "It was suddenly all about sync," says Newman of the approach. "So we just took copies of Rob's basic patterns so that everyone could be playing along with the drum machine – so everything would be in time, and we could add other sequences running along with it."

Grey's participation was therefore reduced to a minimalist gesture, although not a variant of minimalism that excited him. "The bass and snare was sampled – just one note of each – and a pattern made of samples that I probably had something to do with writing would be played by the computer. And I'd play the hi-hat along with the computer, so I was accompanying the computer. But I missed the feeling of playing-as-four, which had always happened live and in recording an album before. The new method of working didn't seem like a substitute for how it had been before. Some people could adapt to programming and using drum machines, but it didn't work for me, so I felt that I was much less involved in making the album than I had been before. I generally felt there wasn't much point in me being there."

Ironically, Grey's attempt to engage with the technology only gave him a deeper appreciation for kit-drumming itself and a more acute understanding of his original affinity for his instrument. "I remember talking to Gareth, telling him how I wanted to express music, which is physically rather than through programming. Compared with the way we'd made the first three albums, this was too extreme for me. Until you try programming, I don't think you fully realise what it is that attracted you to an instrument or a method of playing in the first place." Still, the fact that Grey didn't quit Wire at this point suggests that he wasn't completely discounting a new role within the electronic environment that he knew was going to be crucial to the band's new direction. "I didn't feel it was the end of the road for me. I still thought that it was a workable situation, and that if I became more technically able with drum machines, it could still be made workable."

Lewis recognised the daunting nature of this paradigm shift for Wire but stresses that the general attitude was to make the technology part of the process, rather than resist it. "Everybody was in a similar boat. The technology wasn't easy to work with, but that was the challenge that was there." Moreover, he maintains that, despite its newness, the technology actually enabled Wire to accomplish an objective that had always been central to their aesthetic – a prioritising of discipline and accuracy that goes back to the post-Gill rebuilding of the band. These priorities were also key to his work with Gilbert: "We had a fascination with accuracy. You couldn't ignore it. You had to use it. And we'd been working with machines for the last five years or so and got very used to the accuracy, to the point where you could actually start to ignore the technology." If Grey felt live playing was the essence of Wire, Lewis focuses on commitment to the new as another core element – one that required a constant exploration of technology to expand the band's canvas. "The nature of what Wire had done all along was to embrace the available technology. You have to engage with that. That's how it stays relevant."

Lewis was frustrated with Grey. He had seen other drummers make a seamless creative transition in the 80s, and he didn't understand why Grey couldn't follow suit. "It was an extremely exciting time in the area of drums and beats. People like Keith LeBlanc were extremely good musicians who embraced the technology. They thought of it as an extension, and Robert didn't. He didn't engage. It was a big problem, and it certainly put him in a difficult situation. My attitude would have been that I'd like to understand it or to prove I was better than it. That would have been a sounder creative position to come from. But he didn't seem to want to take that on board. He disliked the click. He felt it undermined him. But he undermined his own position, and that made things very difficult for everybody else."

Jones is more generous: "We didn't work hard enough at getting Rob comfortable with playing to a click, so he was marginalised through our mutual lack of experience of how to bring the drummer into the sequenced world. Having not played with Wire for years, then having to play to a click, and not being confident, would have been difficult. We hadn't realised how challenging that might be. He got sidelined – not in terms of his rhythmic ideas, which are used – but in terms of him playing the drums, which he does so well. We didn't talk about it a great deal. It just didn't work. Now there's sufficient technology to do it, but then it seemed like there was no match between Rob's drums and machine rhythm, which was funny because Rob is a motorik drummer." Lewis, meanwhile, insists that the band did make a concerted effort with Grey. "It's not as if it wasn't discussed at considerable length. Everybody tried their utmost to explain to him why they thought it was good, how he could go about it, and how they thought it could be used. But he was completely resistant. I feel he made himself redundant."

As a footnote, it should be emphasised that although Grey found his role as a drummer all but eliminated, he did contribute to the album in a different, non-musical way, on the song 'The Point Of Collapse'. This is an historic Wire track as it includes Grey's only effort as a lyricist, albeit an unwitting one. "After badgering Rob to write, for years," Lewis recalls, "I made the decision to incorporate his entire output/offering – 'death in the living room' – into a text." Grey clarifies this, somewhat: "The word 'death' was written on the wall of my living room in Tulse Hill – I'm not sure by whom."

Whereas *Snakedrill* had suggested a healthy outlook for the new Wire, *The Ideal Copy* left two members of the band in serious uncertainty: it appeared that Newman had quit the group, and Grey was wondering if he still had a part to play. Differences of opinion had not stood in the way of *154*'s success, but the differences became destructive during the *Ideal Copy* sessions, and the album pales in comparison to its predecessor. Gilbert and Lewis still talk in positive terms about making the record, but while the process may have been absorbing and energising for them, the final product is all that the rest of us can access – and it's far from compelling. From the listener's perspective, the record does suffer from the lack of a commonly held creative vision, the whole band rarely seeming committed to or involved in each track. In the past, of course, there had been instances of this, but the strength of the material usually carried the day. That doesn't happen often enough on *The Ideal Copy*.

In keeping with the record's contents, the sleeve of *The Ideal Copy* featured Wire's weakest artwork thus far – particularly in contrast with the striking sleeve of *154*. During the Hansa sessions, Lewis had free run of the studio's photocopier, making and manipulating images. For one experiment, he used a beer-mat sized advertising card that he'd found inside a package of bed linen. Fascinated by the scene depicted on the card – a sort of still life with bed, pillow, bottle of wine, two glasses, and plant – he photocopied and enlarged it. He'd also scanned Gareth Jones's keys and was struck by the unusual chiaroscuro quality of the copy. He then combined the two images. This composite became a fetish object of sorts – or at least some kind of arcane blueprint for the band to follow in the recording of the album: when Jones saw it, he taped it to one of the machines in the studio and advised the band-members to keep in mind that *this* was what they were seeking to make. It therefore seemed logical to put it on the front cover.

The construction of the image – as well as its conceptual function in the studio, as *the ideal copy* – was undoubtedly engaging and stimulating, but as a cover image for the record, it's unsuccessful: it's slightly odd, granted, but not in a way that provokes, intrigues, or stays with the viewer. It's just bitty, dreary, and forgettable. Above all, it embodies the notion of the process being more interesting than the end product. As such, it's a fitting metaphor for the album. (Russell Mills and David Coppenhall, who designed the record's inner sleeve, also submitted a prospective front cover – but, as Mills recalls, it was rejected by Lewis.)

*The Ideal Copy* raised questions about Wire's immediate future, since the tensions had gone beyond the creative realm, as visitors to Hansa had noted. "There was some real vitriol going on," says Bryan Grant. "I was quite surprised that they continued after that." They did continue, but only after a five-month break, during which, in April 1987, the album was released. When they reconvened, their first move was to tour in support of the record, which was surprising in view of their previous refusal to promote their work in conventional ways. However, it would be misleading to imagine that this rather traditional album-tour approach meant that Wire had had a significant rethink since 1979: they would remain as uncompromising and wilful as ever.

**CHAPTER 7**

# 1987–89

## A Gift from God

In spring 1987, Wire had a record to promote, but they now appeared to be a man down. "When I left, I left," says Colin Newman. "I wasn't intending to come back." He did, of course. "I was lured back to help Dan out. It was his money. It cost a fucking fortune to make *The Ideal Copy*, so not supporting it would be bad. I did have a sense of responsibility. It wasn't like being with EMI. So for Dan's sake, I agreed to support the record and tour."

Activity began with the release of the 'Ahead' single in March 1987, the sleeve featuring a detail from a page of automatic writing by Graham Lewis. 'Ahead' confirmed Miller's belief that Wire had a knack for pop songs, and throughout their time on Mute, there would be an emphasis on singles. "One of the things Dan signed Wire for," says Newman, "was our ability to turn out a decent pop tune." At this point, though, it was no longer simply a question of coming up with "a decent pop tune" – there was the video to think about. One of the many changes in the eight years since the band's last studio album had been the rise of the music video, and with the genre now well-established Wire took their first steps in that medium.

Directed by Edwin Maynard with the assistance of Angela Conway, the 'Ahead' video is definitely of its time and, surprisingly, doesn't come close to meeting the band's high standards of inventiveness and originality. Literally and figuratively dark, it centres on two backseat passengers on a night-time car ride: Newman and a glamorous woman, played by Wire associate Christine Wertheim. Other band-members make fleeting appearances. While there's a suggestion of menace and danger, there's no narrative development around the characters to flesh it out. Random images from film shot at Hansa during the *Ideal Copy* sessions are intercut (monitors, oscilloscopes, and corridors), but most memorable is a recurring slow-motion sequence culled from security-camera footage at the June 1985 Oxford gig: a strikingly hairless individual – resembling football referee Pierluigi Collina – throws his head back, eyes rolling up, seemingly transported. "I absolutely hated the video," Newman says. "It was awful. It just looked really wrong, and I couldn't understand why Graham appeared to be singing part of it. It was the first video we'd ever made, and I didn't feel like it represented the band at all – how I, visually, saw the band."

Three concerts were scheduled for early June in Lausanne, Switzerland, as a warm-up for Wire's maiden North American tour. Back in 1979, when the band played already-released material in live sets otherwise given over to newer work, their catalogue wasn't extensive, so the old and the new were able to coexist fairly seamlessly. In mid 1987, however, to play old material (apart from the *Snakedrill* tracks) would mean reviving songs from nearly a decade ago. This would have been problematic for Wire, whose vocabulary didn't include the word 'nostalgia'. Although they were now very much a band from a previous musical generation, they were starting from scratch, with a new sound. And despite their own differing views on the new album, they shared the conviction that Wire could still be an innovative presence on a musical landscape that had shifted enormously since the late 70s. "Whatever you say about *The Ideal Copy*," observes Lewis, "it's unashamedly modern. It was bloody hard work for us to reinvent this thing and look forward. It wasn't looking back; it was trying to find a way forward. That's what we were trying to do. The priority was to keep the band's integrity: a band that changes and does new stuff. Besides, there had been such a long gap between going out of the door to get a packet of fags and coming back – in that time, we'd forgotten about all that other stuff."

Wire remained as staunchly committed to performing only new work as they had been since the band's re-emergence in 1985. To do anything else would have been self-defeating, as Robert Grey explains: "The focus on new material had become so entrenched in the way we worked that it would have been a backward step to say: we're going to play *Pink Flag* because we're touring America. If those had been the conditions, we wouldn't have gone." (Not until the 2000s would Wire feel able to comfortably mix 70s and 80s material.) With the benefit of hindsight, Newman thinks that Wire's fierce commitment to the new was all well and good in itself, but it led them to overlook other important issues. In particular, he believes that Wire, for all their 'modernity', had no real sense of recent history and no understanding of the context in which they were attempting to relaunch themselves. "It could have been more artistically successful if we had some sense of the bigger picture, how we fitted. We didn't have it. Between 1980 and 1985, things had changed so massively in terms of pop and music culture – Wire were aware that it had changed but hadn't worked out all the ways it had changed. And we just weren't united enough to have a common strategy."

If in 1985 and 1986 Wire's insistence on playing entirely new material
had challenged European audiences, the problems raised by such a policy
became more acute in the USA in 1987. With labelmates Depeche Mode
enjoying commercial success there, Mute hoped Wire could follow suit. But
to present themselves exclusively as a contemporary band wasn't a
straightforward matter, and they were caught between two stools: the new
incarnation of Wire was not the reason people were coming to their gigs. In
the mid 80s, a new generation of American listeners had just arrived at their
70s work, thanks to name-checks from a diverse range of artists like R.E.M.
(who would record 'Strange' on their 1987 album *Document*), Minutemen,
Hüsker Dü, Big Black, Mission Of Burma, and Minor Threat. Given that
Wire's policy regarding old work was, for the most part, unknown to
American audiences, the early material was what the new fans, as well as the
first-generation fans, were expecting.

Newman now recognises the near-impossibility of what the band were
seeking to do: "You can see the beauty of the Year Zero concept as a pure
idea," he says, "but when we hit the world, especially America, where people
were only just discovering Wire from the 70s, it was as if we were from Mars.
We were met by an audience who'd paid to see a classic band from the 70s.
We hit reality. It was like a car crash. How come we were sounding like a
completely different thing? How could that work? How could we not play all
those things that made us famous? It was a big fuck-up. But the even bigger
one was what happened at the end of the 70s: we shouldn't have stopped –
we should have just had a short break. Had we not stopped then, we
wouldn't have needed to completely reinvent ourselves, and we could have
slid into something. We could have had the modernity of the new stuff, and
we'd still be keeping in touch with the things we'd done before."

Bruce Gilbert doesn't second-guess the choices the band made, and he
has no misgivings about the way they tackled the American tour. "Our
mind-set was: We're bloody-minded. We do what we do. It was perfectly
natural for us. Bryan suggested playing old stuff, but he knew we were
stubborn about that sort of thing. And he knew we hadn't rehearsed it, so
we couldn't play it. With me, it could never happen. I had to relearn things
all the time. It would have been impossible – apart from 'Drill', of course."
On this tour, not only did Wire play exclusively 80s tracks but also, true to
their 70s form, they included unrecorded work that would appear on their
next album ('Kidney Bingos', 'Come Back In Two Halves', 'Silk Skin Paws',
and 'It's A Boy').

Grant didn't think this was wise. With his first-hand experience of the

North American market from various tours and his familiarity with the expectations of US rock audiences at the time, he knew that Wire's approach was more or less suicidal. "I love them dearly," he stresses, "but they're very perverse. I tried to get them to play old stuff, but they'd gone in a new direction with *The Ideal Copy*, and the answer was a very firm 'No. We're not a jukebox.'" Grant knew better than to question Wire's artistic choices. His strategy was to accept their decisions, tell them exactly what the consequences would be, and then advise them how to make the best of the situation. In this case, he suggested a pre-emptive media campaign, as Lewis recalls: "Bryan was never one to meddle, but he did say that we were going to make things very difficult for ourselves. His attitude was: on your heads be it – and no whinging. So, before we did the tour, he said: 'Some of you – and I'm looking for volunteers here – are going to America in advance, and you're going to spend a week doing interviews, and you will explain that you're not going to be playing old stuff. Because if you don't, you'll spend all of the tour explaining. It's going to be hard enough as it is. You'll go crazy answering the same questions over and over again.' Which we did anyway, but it wasn't as bad as it could have been."

Newman and Lewis spent four days in a hotel room in New York City, doing phone interviews, the monotony broken up by the occasional face-to-face chat with local journalists. "That was intense," says Newman. "From 8am to 8pm. It was full on. Neither of us had experienced anything like that. That's what it must be like to be mega-successful. Everybody wanted to talk to us, and they all asked the same questions. We lost reality after a point. It was surreal." Lewis agrees: "It was quite mental."

Among those who came to see them in person was Jim DeRogatis, who would later become the *Chicago Sun-Times*'s pop music critic. He had just started his first job as a city reporter for the *Jersey Journal* but also wrote about music for other venues. On this occasion, he was interviewing Wire for the Philadelphia magazine *The Bob*. This was a propitious meeting. "I maintained my professional demeanour for the interview," DeRogatis remembers, "and, at the end, I told them I was in a band and that we covered *Pink Flag* in order, in its entirety. I said: that's how much I love your work, I just wanted to tell you – and they both looked at each other conspiratorially and said: we might have some work for you." Indeed, DeRogatis's appearance was an unusual piece of synchronicity, since Wire had already discussed the possibility of having someone else play 'the old stuff' as a tongue-in-cheek way of meeting audience expectations.

DeRogatis's band, The Ex-Lion Tamers (also featuring Mick Hale, John

Tanzer, and Pete Pedulla), were eventually offered the support slot on the tour. Fans would get to hear the old songs after all – but not played by Wire themselves. From Wire's perspective, this was too good to be true. The Ex-Lion Tamers were the perfect readymade or, more pertinently perhaps, the ideal copy. Not surprisingly, Wire had fun with the concept throughout the tour. "It's a gift from God," Gilbert told *Contrast* magazine in San Francisco. "What they do is two pieces, basically: one is called side one and the other is side two. They just do the entire record, including the gaps. They do the gaps as accurate as the rest of it." DeRogatis even recalls Gilbert telling journalists that "the only band Wire had ever been influenced by was The Ex-Lion Tamers".

**Not driving in an American way**

The 20-date tour kicked off in Philadelphia and (bypassing the South) stopped in most major US cities, as well as Toronto, Montreal, and Vancouver. Manager Bryan Grant's recollections provide some insight into the experience. "We drank heavily. There were two factions in the band: Robert is very disciplined and does a lot of sightseeing and so forth, and Colin's not a party animal, but Bruce and Graham and I used to party. Graham more. When I say that, it wasn't an Ozzy Osbourne type of partying. They were never into that rock'n'roll folly." Grant knows what he's talking about when it comes to such matters, having done tours of duty as a Led Zeppelin crew-member in the mid 70s.

Even for an old hand like Grant, travelling with Wire was eye-opening. "I've toured America many times with a number of bands, in other ways, but the joy of touring with Wire is that you saw a completely different America. It was about the people they attracted. It was always interesting people, whether they be visual artists or musical artists or writers or photographers. There was always that side to it, those offshoots. And when I say we drank heavily, it was really just a lot of late nights in bars, clubs, and people's homes, just talking about things other than the normal boring stuff, because they're very curious. To me, that's what makes them an interesting band. They draw from their curiosity about life. That's one thing about Wire: they're not successful in the accepted sense, but I think they've had a much more interesting career than many, many bands who are a lot more commercially successful."

Grey enjoyed the tour. "I don't remember the experience being bad. I don't remember group tensions. Bryan was experienced, and he liked being on the road. It was good being with him: he knew his way around and he had everything sorted." Grey, however, didn't know his way around, and came very close to missing Wire's gig in Boston as a result. "I'd taken a car and gone back to the hotel after the soundcheck but got lost coming back. I got onto a highway, and a sign told me that I was going to Canada, which wasn't where I wanted to go. It was only by pure luck that I found my way back to the club and just made the show. The others thought maybe I'd been stopped by the police for not driving in an American way."

The tour doesn't seem to have been rewarding for Newman, personally or professionally. "It was mainly awful. Because I was doing that tour basically as a favour to the band and a favour to Dan, I didn't feel that comfortable about being there. It all became absurd. Graham and Bruce's idea of how you prepare for a tour was, basically, get to New York and stay up all night drinking tequila and then stay up again all night drinking tequila and then do the gig the next night. Half the band was in no space to do anything. It was still that colossal arrogance that we knew everything. We were awful as a live band, and the whole thing was kind of depressing. Graham was impossible. That was the first of many tours that I returned from, thinking: I don't want to speak to any of these people again for the rest of my life. In spite of the bad experiences, though, I enjoyed being in America."

Grant's observations supply more context. "Graham was halfway through a nervous breakdown. He was having a tough time with that first tour. I think it was the whole impact of America – the place, the sheer vastness of it all. He seemed to be overwhelmed by it." Lewis himself says little about the experience, other than to note that "it wasn't a very steady, settled time for me". He does point out, though, that Newman seemed to be having difficulties of his own. "Colin kept saying: I can't pretend in front of people. It was quite entertaining in parts. For some of us."

As for Gilbert, a coast-to-coast trek wasn't something that appealed, and he found it hard-going. "It was very seldom that I enjoyed touring, but my philosophy was that there was no escape, so it was eyes down and try and do your best. If you get into that cycle of being miserable, when all you can think about is stopping, it's very hard to get out of it. So I'd go into a frame of mind where it just had to be done. The drudgery and the travelling was the worst part – the getting up. I'm an early riser normally, but this is a constant routine, which is wearing. It was interesting seeing new cities, but it was more or less impossible to enjoy places. And there were few opportunities to enjoy local bars: being in a bar you find out more about a city."

One way he coped was to focus on the performances themselves, which he saw as a refuge of sorts, a space for artistic experimentation amid the day-to-day grind. "Because we were playing live on a regular basis, it meant we were finding out things: every time I played something, I found out something new about it – or a little touch to put in. So touring was always interesting from that point of view."

## The greatest thing ever

For Jim DeRogatis, the chance to tour with one of his favourite bands was a dream come true. Wire travelled by plane, and The Ex-Lion Tamers followed them around in a $500 van formerly owned by a fishmonger, which made the long, hot drives challenging. But it was worth it. "We had a contract that guaranteed us a pizza, two six-packs of beer, and $100 at every show," remembers DeRogatis. "I thought that was the greatest thing ever." At each gig, they performed Wire's first album. "We wouldn't say anything onstage: we'd just come out and play. The only thing we'd say was: Side Two." As an encore, they'd perform 'Dot Dash'. The Ex-Lion Tamers even joined the headliners onstage in Minneapolis for a version of 'Roadrunner'– a vast improvement on Wire's earlier jam with Steel Pulse.

The unique bill confused some audience members. "After our set at St Andrew's Hall in Detroit," DeRogatis says, "some people stomped out and demanded their money back because they thought Wire really sucked." For their final gig of the tour, The Ex-Lion Tamers added a new twist to their performance. "We decided to dress like Wire for the Los Angeles show," explains DeRogatis. "Graham had this sort of weird jogging-suit look, and Colin would wear a black T-shirt, black pants, and red braces. So we went into a thrift shop, and we came out looking like Wire." In her review of the gig for the *NME*, Jane García – clearly not in on the joke – wrote: "Colin Newman came out dressed as the lead singer of Ex Lion Tamer [sic]." Grey recalls another anecdote: "I heard that some people said they enjoyed Wire but couldn't understand that group that came on afterwards; they didn't know who they were and couldn't understand what they had to do with it." *The Ideal Copy*, indeed.

In her *NME* piece, García wrote that The Ex-Lion Tamers "were certainly a lot more interesting than what followed … because what Wire now play live is difficult music to listen to. Solid slabs of sound in a kind of controlled chaos that could never be described as enjoyable". And while other reviewers weren't quite so dismissive, few seemed unreservedly enthusiastic about Year Zero Wire. A notable exception was the late Jane Scott, of the

*Cleveland Plain Dealer*, then aged 68. She was one of a minority of critics to accept and appreciate that Wire were uninterested in recreating the past and were at least trying to do something new and original: "Wire showed that although it inspired many groups of today, it is also much different from bands of today."

According to DeRogatis, Wire were "very paternal" toward him and his bandmates, something he puts down to them trying to avoid duplicating the poor treatment they felt they had received from headline acts such as Roxy Music. Concerned that The Ex-Lion Tamers weren't eating properly, Wire even had a barbecue for them. DeRogatis singles out Bryan Grant for praise. "Some of the clubs would stiff us, like the 9:30 Club in Washington DC. We didn't get our pizza, we didn't get our beer, and [club owner] Seth Hurwitz didn't want to pay us our 100 bucks. I remember standing sheepishly outside his office, and he was jerking me around and didn't want to pay. Then Bryan Grant came over. And he was like *Peter* Grant – he's a very large and imposing man. He was like six-foot-four and 280 pounds. He asked what I was waiting for, and I told him I'd been waiting for an hour and a half to get paid. Then Seth Hurwitz asked him to come into his office to pay *him*, and Bryan said: 'No. You're going to pay my mate Jim DeRogatis first.' Every once in a while he'd wield the sabre and take care of us."

One of the most memorable gigs for DeRogatis was at the Ritz in New York. "I was with Colin when he met Joey Ramone. Of course, Joey didn't say anything, and Colin was being like a fan-boy, gushing and telling him how much the Ramones had meant to him. And my parents came. I brought my mom backstage to meet Wire. My mom told them: 'Thanks for doing this for James. If you boys had more time in town, I'd make you meatballs. And we'd have pasta. I could cook you guys a real meal. It would be wonderful!' And she knocked over Colin's white Ovation guitar. I was absolutely mortified."

The following year, when Wire returned for a second tour, The Ex-Lion Tamers reunited and opened for them on their first night at Maxwell's in Hoboken, this time enlisting an extra member and performing *Chairs Missing* from start to finish. "The role of Thorne was played by Speed The Plough keyboardist John Baumgartner," recalls DeRogatis, while Thorne himself watched from the side of the stage.

## If you want to hear it, go home and play it

During the tour, Grey became more sympathetic toward those who were keen to hear Wire's earlier work. While he was attuned to the band's emphasis on originality and innovation, he also understood the concertgoers' perspective. "The idea of saying how important new material was to us – that was fine for the band, but not for the audience. It's not considering the audience in any sense. They couldn't understand why we weren't playing songs they knew. I think we were testing their patience." This again highlights one of Wire's fundamental contradictions as a group choosing to operate within an orthodox rock environment but not abiding by its conventions or meeting the expectations associated with that environment. While their commitment to the new may have been unimpeachable in purely artistic terms, it was self-destructive in the immediate context of a first North American tour – the point of which was to build an audience with a view to garnering commercial success.

Grey gave this issue much thought. "The creativity is so important, but if the creativity becomes alienating for people who want to see you … how much can you ask them to adapt to what you're doing, if they don't think they've seen the group that they paid for? There was a feeling on Wire's part that if the performance was good enough, it would be OK – they could accept the new material, and they wouldn't feel short-changed, because they'd think the new songs were as good as *we* thought they were. But that's impossible. It's commercial suicide, really."

Grant definitely wouldn't argue with Grey's last remark. Much as he admired Wire, he was managing them as a business, and he was less than impressed by what he was seeing on this tour, with regard to both the content of the shows *and* the quality. Like Grey, he sensed a disregard for the audiences. "When they started touring again, Bruce said: We want white light. Nothing else. Stark. And I said: Bruce, it's dull. It's almost like they didn't want to be there, like they didn't care about the audience, who'd paid their money." Grant found it frustrating to see them eschew the very characteristics that, to his mind, made them such a great band. "They were going away from being what they were, which is a bloody good live band, a really good rock band, for want of a better term. There was almost an embarrassment. They didn't want to be a rock band. They didn't see themselves as a rock band. Actually, they didn't see themselves as musicians! It was as if they were saying: We're better than that. We're artists, not musicians. They wouldn't say: I've made a record; they'd say: I've made a piece of work. I'd say: get over yourselves. Sometimes Bruce would tell me: Bryan, you wouldn't know art if you tripped over it."

Although Grant saw this attitude as indifference to the audience, it wasn't as clear-cut as that. More accurately, it was – for some band-members – a refusal to view the engagement with the audience (the rock concert) as anything other than a pure artistic encounter, divorced from the milieu of rock'n'roll. Gilbert, for one, approached it in this fashion, resolutely focused on the gig as an artistic opportunity. He saw no contradictions and no problems. "As usual, there was a good deal of confusion," he says of a typical gig on the tour. "There was a contingent who would have gone to the venue anyway to see a rock band, and we weren't a rock band, so they were puzzled. And those who did know Wire were puzzled that we weren't playing the old stuff. People would say: why didn't you play this or that? And Graham's answer was: well, if you want to hear it, go home and play it. People thought: how selfish, how self-indulgent, if a band plays a new song. Of course, we thought it was the other way around: people deserved to hear things they hadn't heard."

## One of the hottest British rock groups in the world today

It was on this tour that Wire discovered the importance of college radio, for which there was no counterpart at home. "Wire had never been on the radio in the UK," says Newman, "so the idea of radio stations playing us was totally fascinating and weird. We were used to radio that was sectioned off in terms of its content. The idea of a radio station playing a genre like 'modern alternative', or whatever they called it then, was totally ludicrous. We were doing well on college radio." This meant more interviews. So great was the demand that even Grey ended up fielding questions for the band on a handful of occasions. "It was exhausting," Lewis says. "It was a tough tour as it was. There wasn't much spare time. College radio really got behind the record. It made a tremendous amount of difference. It even crossed over into commercial radio. That's what led to getting the late-night TV show spot."

The TV spot in question was *The Late Show* on Fox, on July 1 1987. The programme was being hosted by Suzanne Somers, a temporary fixture after the recent firing of Joan Rivers. Somers had been one of the stars of *Three's Company*, the American version of *Man About The House*. At this point, she was enjoying success in infomercials (as the spokesperson for the ThighMaster) and was about to relaunch her sitcom career in *She's The Sheriff*, which would be put out of its misery after just two seasons. It's baffling that Wire – a band with no hits and no mainstream media profile – were invited to appear on such a programme. Clutching *The Ideal Copy* with her black elbow-length gloves, Somers introduced Wire, somewhat inexplicably, as "one of the hottest British rock groups in the world today", adding, again somewhat inexplicably, that "their new album, *The Ideal Copy*, is hitting the top of the music charts".

Rather than introduce themselves to their largest audience thus far with one of their more accessible, melodic numbers, Wire played 'Drill'. The initial plan had been to perform two tracks, the single 'Ahead' and 'Drill'. However, the producers limited them to one song because of time constraints. "It was such a meeting of different cultures," recalls Grey. "I'm sure the people in the studio were told: 'It's just another pop group coming to play. They'll play a prearranged two songs, and it'll all be normal.' We played 'Drill'. There was definitely a confrontational element in that. It was testing their patience, coming and saying: we're the artists, and we decide what we play – and this is what we're playing. I thought it was right that we choose rather than be told what was suitable. It spread a certain amount of confusion in the studio. That was quite pleasing. We wouldn't want to behave like a pop group. That wasn't our motivation. That wasn't our motivation in quite a lot of ways."

Wire's first foray into American television didn't pass without incident. When the band played two rehearsal versions of 'Drill' of different lengths, the show's production staff became uneasy. For things to run to schedule, they needed to know the track's duration, but the band were only able to say that it varied from performance to performance and was unpredictable. This wasn't what the TV people wanted to hear. On top of that, Wire were threatened with having their sound manipulated to make it more palatable to the audience. There was even a contretemps between Grey and the studio crew, who vowed revenge when he – against labour regulations, apparently – made some adjustments to his kit. "They did the soundcheck, and they were all well-behaved," Grant remembers. "And then Rob took his tom away, and the union guys said: You're on our shitlist, mister. We're gonna fuck you up." Grant attempted to explain to them that they'd be wasting their time if they tried to sabotage 'Drill'. "I said: I don't think you can. It's not that sort of song. Whatever you do, it won't make much difference."

Although Grant appreciates why Wire decided to play 'Drill', he also sees this as another instance of their wilfulness. "'Drill' was not the best choice for national TV. Did I fight it? Did I try and pull them up? We were doing these clubs, and they'd do 25-minute-versions of 'Drill', and it wasn't what those audiences had come to hear, either – so why not? I mean, it's got some very serious grooves going. In another way, though, if you think of it as a straight performance, it was possibly just a little, well … silly. Again the word 'perverse' keeps cropping up in my mind because that's what a lot of what they did was. There was a slight knowing arrogance to them." For Grant, as the band's manager, the unfortunate downside to their adventurous creative spirit was the paradoxical self-destructiveness that often accompanied it. "There's an underlying urge, just when success is within their grasp, to destroy it. There were elements in the band who really were afraid of that success. And it's easy to destroy it."

Grey understands Grant's disappointment at the band's choice of material on this occasion, but by the same token, he believed that Wire fans would enjoy it. "I suppose it was another example of commercial suicide, but I'm sure it appealed to a few people who knew about Wire, and they would have thought it was funny. At the time, I thought it was funny."

After the performance of 'Drill', things went downhill quickly for all involved. It's painful to watch now as Somers, nervously flouncing around in her black tutu, tells the audience that Wire are "getting great reviews all over the world" and tries to engage the band in some vacuous banter that, to be fair, was the norm for TV shows of this kind. However, she's met with spokesman Gilbert in deadpan mode as he introduces Lewis as "our anthropological expert" and Grey/Gotobed as "our agricultural consultant"; Newman, he claims he's only just met. All the while, Lewis films the proceedings with a video camera. Somers, confused, tells Wire: "You're sort of a far-out kinda group, you know?" Gilbert replies: "I doubt it." The segment peters out as the uncomfortable host goes to a commercial, informing the audience that, after the break, "I'm gonna sing too, so don't come back!"

Of this post-performance segment, Newman says: "It was very much a Bruce thing. It was a bit taken over by Bruce. It was decided that Bruce would answer the questions. Not me. It was surreal. We didn't have the context for it. It was somebody else's TV stars. It was all kind of meaningless. I think it was funny. In some ways, it was a great moment of absurdist TV." Still, he does add: "It didn't feel that funny at the time."

The interaction with Somers isn't one of Wire's finest moments. To have played 'Drill' and left it at that would have been a strong statement – forcing on an unwitting public something that few would have recognised as pop music, or music at all for that matter. That alone would have been a subversive gesture, and would have provoked the desired confusion. Their post-song exchange with Somers shows how badly they misjudged the context – their efforts to be funny, 'absurdist', or subversive were really just awkward and embarrassing. They lacked the charisma and presence to pull it off. And besides, to pick on Suzanne Somers is rather like rolling a drunk. Ultimately, the effect of these shenanigans on the majority of viewers, who had no idea who Wire were, was to frame them as a novelty band and 'Drill' as a novelty song. In short, it was an opportunity squandered.

## The Oslo Accord and the Treaty of Berlin

Having returned from the USA, Wire played three dates in Europe. Prior to their last gig of the summer, at the Høvikodden Festival in Oslo, Newman – who had now fulfilled his obligations to support *The Ideal Copy* – issued what was effectively an ultimatum. "I'd agreed to do what had been planned. We had a band meeting where negotiations took place as to what would happen next. I was asked not to leave. I said I had conditions if I was to stay. I said: I'm not making another record like *The Ideal Copy*. I had no problem with Gareth [Jones]. I just wanted to make it differently and do something that was more like a Wire record: I would have more input into how the records were made, I didn't want to be marginalised, I wanted to have a central role and people should take seriously what I do. I told Bruce: you have to start trusting me." Newman was also eager to reintegrate Grey. "I wanted to involve Rob more. I'd been working on *It Seems* [his fifth solo album, released in 1988], and I'd come up with a plan for how to do drums in a MIDI environment, so we could have full-kit information. So that was the plan that was agreed on. That was the deal struck in the hotel in Oslo. That was what I thought was needed for the thing to work." Gilbert says he has "a flicker of recognition" when asked about these summit talks; Lewis simply says: "I don't remember that."

After an autumn European tour, Wire went back to Berlin in December 1987 to make their fifth studio album – *A Bell Is A Cup ... Until It Is Struck* – again bringing in Jones, who was joined by engineer David Heilmann. They didn't return to Hansa, though. Jones thinks this may have been down to Newman: "Colin was so gutted by *The Ideal Copy* and said he didn't want to go back there." Instead, the band had booked into Preussen Tonstudio, a very different establishment in a very different neighbourhood, a more bohemian part of Kreuzberg, populated mostly by Turkish immigrants, students, and artists. "It was a cool place," says Newman. "It was much more fun working there." He also felt far more positive about the recording environment itself. A far cry from Hansa, this was "a down-home, funky studio" built into a converted factory complex. "Hansa was actually much more 'Prussian'. Hansa was very cold; Preussen was very warm and cosy. There was even daylight in the playing room."

There was to be none of the claustrophobia that the band-members had experienced the previous year. This time they stayed in rented apartments in the city. "Colin and I were sharing a flat a little way out from the studio," remembers Grey, "so it wasn't 24 hours in the same building. That made a big difference." The pair came and went on public transport, which sometimes entailed a stop on the other side of the Berlin Wall. "You could take the S-Bahn from the apartment to the studio," says Newman, "and you could get out in East Germany and buy duty free at the interchange."

Jones enjoyed the studio and noticed an improved atmosphere, the band appearing more laid back. "I'd suggest that they'd got over their growing pains of coming back together. That was clear on *A Bell Is A Cup*. There wasn't so much of a stand-off." To Jones, the more intimate physical setting enhanced the interaction, whereas Hansa had amplified the band-members' alienation from one another. "It was a smaller studio. It was more contained. Hansa was so huge that people could be in their own spaces and then wander back. But Preussen was a more contained working environment. Also, they'd toured *The Ideal Copy*, so they'd come back together again – somewhat. I'm not saying there was harmony, but they knocked along with each other easier: partly because of the nature of the studio, where we were closer together all the time, and because of the touring they'd done. It gelled into some kind of compromise."

The band-members even spent some time together outside of the studio. "There was a bit more social interaction," says Gilbert. "There was a nice bar-restaurant nearby. Quite often we all had a drink and ate together at the end of a session." Lewis agrees that things ran more smoothly, although there is an ironic edge to his comments, indicating that this new bonhomie was partially legislated. "There were less bodies, definitely. It was bound to be more harmonious. One took one's responsibilities seriously. If I didn't feel I was any use, I'd retire to the bar down the road with Bruce and play pool. We were sublimely good by the end of the sessions."

Along with a general veneer of harmony and civility, there even appeared to be a shared creative vision, at least from Newman's perspective. "There seemed to be a general feeling that we were trying to achieve something as a band with everyone as involved as they could be. Me setting the tone and direction isn't about excluding people. It's the other way around. It's about being as inclusive as possible."

Grey noticed a difference in the mood, but he too hints that the situation was a little artificial. "It was better than it had been at Hansa. You've got to have diplomatic relations. You shouldn't have to engineer that, though,

211

should you? It suggests something was wrong, if it had to be mentioned to get through the recording. But it did seem less tense." He puts some of the improvement down to the band growing more comfortable with the digital path they were taking. "When we reformed in 1985, there wasn't so much of an idea of how we were going to do things – except for doing things differently. The electronic direction had become more accepted by the time of *A Bell Is A Cup*. It wasn't the same as *The Ideal Copy*. Maybe we'd gone through the worst shock of it." (That may be the case, but the Preussen sessions wouldn't see much change in Grey's dissatisfaction with his role as a drummer who didn't really do any drumming on his band's records.)

### The Pope of Pop

*A Bell Is A Cup* saw a new expression enshrined in the Wire lexicon: "Think pop." This was a mantra bestowed on the band by Daniel Miller when he visited Preussen during the recording of the album. "We asked Daniel for his words of wisdom regarding what we were supposed to be making," recalls Lewis. "And he said: think pop." "So for the whole session, the message was: think pop," continues Newman. "That was the line we had to take. Within the Wire way of talking, it became a phrase. It was used in every circumstance possible." (For *The Ideal Copy*, the label boss's bons mots had been "every one's a classic".)

Obviously, Miller's instruction for *A Bell Is A Cup* had been given ironically, but Grey can see that there was a certain psychology to it. "Daniel and Gareth would be saying, in a partly serious way: come on, think pop! Wire has always had this pop element, so that was what they wanted to bring out, with a view to being commercial – but you couldn't say that to Wire explicitly. That wouldn't work. But saying it in a jokey way got the message across without causing a confrontation."

While Miller had long recognised Wire's gift for pop, he wasn't interested just in their potential as a straightforward chart band. "I always thought Wire could be everything," he says. "Wire could be pop and experimental at the same time." Moreover, he saw that the band's capacity for merging those two sensibilities was in sync with the contemporary UK zeitgeist, according to which, as a legacy of punk, challenging or leftfield music was achieving mainstream visibility and even commercial success. "It was the last hangover of post-punk," Miller explains, "and people were more open in terms of what they listened to, and the radio was more open in terms of what it played. You could get away with a lot. I thought it was a very good time for unconventional pop music, and Mute had had success with other bands like Wire. I don't know if I encouraged it with Wire, but we certainly talked about it."

In appreciation of the 'think pop' mantra, Wire reciprocated with a treat for Miller. "We did a spoof video to horrify him," says Gilbert, "a fantastic video for 'Kidney Bingos', with a hideous puppet-bird thing that Graham had. It was called The Pope of Pop. It was ridiculous. Daniel was horrified." Lewis elaborates: "I bought a hideous, feathered, fluorescent pink puppet – it was superb in its grotesqueness. And we made a fake video with the puppet singing and playing my Casio keyboard. Dan was taken in for about ten seconds, which was worth it. There was a horrible moment where you could see him thinking: oh no …" As Newman observes, this in itself was a strong indication of the improved band dynamic – all very different from what Miller had witnessed the year before: "That was a big contrast with him seeing the atmosphere at Hansa for *The Ideal Copy*. The absurdity of it was very high."

Whether or not Wire were actively thinking pop, that aspect of *A Bell Is A Cup* is its most immediately striking characteristic – the songs are largely melodic, textured, and cohesive, with two very catchy singles among them. Lewis is certain that this facet of the band's sound was entirely organic – "It came out of the material" – and not the product of a concerted, conscious effort. He also sees this new emphasis as a by-product of their increasing confidence. "The way we were playing had changed, and we were more comfortable than we were before *The Ideal Copy*, when we'd had to learn to play again."

As far as Jones is concerned, if anyone was thinking pop it was Newman, who had in mind a more standard, chart-friendly record. "I remember a lot of work with Colin," he says, "a lot more layering. It came from a more pop sensibility." Jones himself wasn't altogether happy with this new direction. "This is the flowering of Colin's pop sensibility, which is all well and good, but it's not quite noisy enough, really. I don't think *A Bell Is A Cup* was noisy enough for Graham or Bruce or me in the end. That was one of my frustrations with it. I loved having that pop sensibility in there, but I'd also have liked a lot more noise on that record."

Noise aside, Gilbert had conceptual concerns about Wire's ascendant pop sensibility. This was nothing new, of course: on previous albums he had absented himself from the band's strongest pop moments or minimised his role. As he explains, he lacked enthusiasm for Wire's most accessible, melodically attractive work not because he was averse to pop, but because he never really understood the concept of 'pop' and what determined that a particular sound was 'pop': "I have a big problem with the term. I don't know really what it means. Is it pop because it's popular or is it pop because there's an identifiable genre in any given decade that is pop music? Here, Colin had a very firm grip on what he thought was pop, and I had no idea. I didn't understand it at all. I don't think it was as simple as 'commercially viable music'. I've had lots of discussions with Colin about it. To him, it was some sort of concept of a music that encompassed everything that had been pop. I think sometimes he meant it in a pop-art way, where you're using all the images and clichés of what is popular but expressing 'culture' in some way by using them. I understand pop art, but I don't understand what he means when he says perhaps we should make it 'a bit more pop'."

Now finally "setting the tone and direction", Newman sought to give songwriting and songs a more foundational role in the process, as opposed to the kind of improvised, in-studio creativity and construction that had been favoured by Gilbert and Lewis at Hansa. In advance of the recording, he'd made home demos of 'Follow The Locust' and 'Free Falling Divisions', plus two other tracks that didn't make the album: 'Plague Dances' and 'Let's Get Longing' (also referred to as 'Rat-tat-tat').

"We did actually have the material this time, and that helped," says Lewis. "There were a lot of songs that were finished – or at least the scheme of things was there. It had a more conventional approach." When Wire began work at Preussen, many of the tracks had been played live, as well as worked on in rehearsal studios: 'Kidney Bingos' and 'Come Back In Two Halves' obviously dated back to 1985; 'Silk Skin Paws' and 'It's A Boy' had been added to sets in summer 1987; 'Free Falling Divisions', 'Boiling Boy', and 'Follow The Locust' began to see regular live action during Wire's winter 1987 European dates. With Newman now playing a more decisive part – as per the terms of the Oslo Accord – the translation of this material into recorded tracks in the studio went more smoothly.

Against the grain of the separation that had taken place on *The Ideal Copy*, for *A Bell Is A Cup* Newman was also keen to reintroduce an element of group-playing in the recording of the material. They had again begun with some preliminary studio work to get a feel for the process, and it was more successful than the false start at Hansa with the *Ideal Copy* sessions. "We did some recording in the original Worldwide, upstairs in the old Rough Trade building in Ladbroke Grove. We recorded the original version of 'Kidney Bingos' there with Gareth. That gave a sort of indication of how we might be able to move forward. It developed as we worked on it." Consequently, throughout the Preussen sessions there was a greater sense of the songs being framed in advance by already worked-out ideas that were more closely tied to the sound of the band playing, in contrast with *The Ideal Copy*. According to Newman, "*A Bell Is A Cup* was partly played as a band or mainly constructed around drum tracks that were put together out of the band playing live. A couple of tracks were put together in the studio around sequences."

Although Lewis mentions the more "conventional approach", based on material that had already been worked up, he emphasises that there hadn't been a complete methodological overhaul, and there was some balance. "It was more song-based, but there was still a lot of creativity in the studio. Everything had got a little easier – but the groove was still quite square." At any rate, he adapted to the process and found himself concentrating more on the melodic dimension of the material, shifting his attention away from traditional bass duties. "As it was songs, I found a new place to be. On *A Bell Is A Cup*, the bass is more synthetic, rather than played. I started writing a lot of melodies. There's a lot of melodies on this record, a lot of keyboard stuff." (He had 'previous' in this regard, having tickled the ivories – a grand piano, no less – on *Snakedrill*'s 'A Serious Of Snakes'.)

Nevertheless, Lewis's remarks on the making of the record tend to sound guarded, in this case giving the impression that he didn't feel 100 per cent committed to the project that Newman was guiding. Indeed, he seems to have been more creatively engaged in his solo work, specifically his second album, which he was recording concurrently. "It was all about control, really," he says. "It didn't bother me so much, because I was making *Take Care*, and there were sonic questions that I could get answered where I was, in my own work." (*Take Care* would be released by Mute in February 1989.)

As with *The Ideal Copy*, Gilbert had reservations about the impact of technology on the Preussen sessions. "There was a lot of computer stuff going on again, and I suppose I was sitting back a bit. I don't think I was really playing enough; I wanted to be playing more." To him, the studio had become less a place of spontaneity and exploration and more a waiting room, with the attention now centred on the workstation. This was where a disproportionate amount of the activity appeared to be taking place. "A studio situation is a very creative one and, having done my own stuff, I wasn't used to having to hang around. I was used to executing an idea or experimenting with an idea as it occurred." In the past, even if work was going on in which Gilbert wasn't involved, there had sometimes been opportunities to piggyback off it, to use it as a springboard to pursue other ideas. "There always have been situations – and I think they're quite valuable," explains Gilbert, "where the track is being played or fiddled about with, and it's useful to have what they're doing coming out on the headphones in the playing studio – just to experiment with various noises that could be part of another song." However, the approach taken at Preussen precluded such a possibility. As Gilbert sees it, this limited his creative options in ways that recall the experience of making *154*, when Thorne and Newman worked separately from the rest of the band.

## I don't think I enjoyed it any more

Grey's role in any Wire studio recording from now on was always going to be problematic, but Newman was optimistic that the compromise he had worked out for the drummer on *It Seems* could also be applied to Wire. "Rob couldn't play along with sequencers, and we wanted to use sequencers because that was the shiny new pop stuff. So developing a method for doing it was important. I'd come up with the solution to make a hybrid – being able to record with live drums and then use that as the basis with the machines. We'd worked it out – triggers on his bass and snare drum that went through a device that turned them into MIDI, so the information from the drums could be recorded into a sequencer: where the hit was, how loud it was (the rhythm and velocity). So we got full-drum information from him. It was about getting as much from Rob as possible, so there was the feel of a drummer actually playing on it as well as a live band – that was the general idea."

Jones agrees: "I think on *A Bell Is A Cup* we moved forward a bit with drums. Rob was more involved, because there's a much clearer drum picture of him on the record." To Newman, this was part of the plan set forth in Oslo, to include Grey. "It looked like Rob was holding up the process, but there was no attempt to engage him. The idea for me was to integrate Rob back into the band. I've always tried to be inclusive. If someone's not happy, I think: how can we get someone more happy and involved?"

Despite Newman's intentions, Grey's recollections of making *A Bell Is A Cup* don't sound like the words of someone who felt particularly included or involved. "I don't think I enjoyed it any more. There was less sympathy toward group-playing than before. But I had got over the shock of the difference between *154* and *The Ideal Copy*, so I had, to a degree, got used to it. I think the conditions were a bit better. I approached it feeling that it wasn't my first choice, but that, if this was the way we were going to do things, I should see if it could work – if this is what Wire want to do, then I should try contributing through programming, not playing. It still sounds very computer-based, but good things came out of it." Notwithstanding these "good things", the picture Grey paints is a little depressing. "I think Gareth tried to involve me more. He tried to find me things to do to fill my time. He gave me the job of trimming the drum samples. It was done manually then. You had to choose where it started and finished. Maybe he thought it would help me get into the idea of programming."

Lewis's memories are of his own continued frustration. "Rob's resistance to technology hindered creativity. He certainly wasn't involved with the programming. When you're working on a record, you've already made a pragmatic decision as to how it's going to be. That's the baseline. You can't undermine something – all you can do is start where it is and accept where it is." Ironically, Lewis implies that he didn't really participate in the programming either. "I found it so tedious. I didn't think it was very intuitive. In my own work, I got around my impatience by working with someone who did the programming so I could get on with thinking about what might happen next. It was interminable."

**Eyes down**
'Kidney Bingos' was a jumping-off point for the album – one of the oldest songs in the *A Bell Is A Cup* repertoire and the one Wire had already worked on most extensively. Lewis remembers the band rallying around this track as it took shape. "Everybody thought it had a good pop feeling to it." In Gilbert's account, though, it began as something quite different. "I had this riff, and it was almost rock-y," he says, "and I was struggling to make it less so, to subvert it. But it was subverted in a different way, into something quite melodious and pleasant. I was trying for something nasty, but it just went out of my hands. Colin commercialised it."

Confirming Lewis's instincts, 'Kidney Bingos' became another of Wire's pop classics, again marrying an opaque text to a sing-along tune. The mostly monosyllabic, listed words display no immediately obvious connection to one another, forming only three or four meaningful phrases. They're nevertheless organised into three verses composed of four stanzas (with numerous internal rhymes) and a one-line chorus. Although it might appear otherwise, these lyrics are more than randomly generated verbiage, and they stand up to a close reading; it's not exactly that they make meaning, but that there seem to be puzzles one can unravel in the text. Many of the words can be rearranged – by inversion of their order or by the juxtaposition of words from disparate parts of the text – to reveal recognisable phrases or to resonate with each other through association, suggestion, or simply rhyme. Take the third stanza: "Gold street spy fleet scandal food poor treat / Fire run club gun rule mob burn some / Bomb time pop crime stock frame steady climb / Fresh name donor game fair meat all the same." Some jiggling around yields: Fleet Street; mob rule; fire/burn; time frame; time bomb; time/crime; gold stock; fresh meat; fair game; game meat; and so on. It's an entertaining word game that attests to Wire's love of language and linguistic play.

Gilbert's starting point for the song had been an imagined, and typically macabre, scenario. "The *Sun* newspaper had just started their bingo game," he recalls, "and I thought that at some point in the near future the first prize would be a kidney." The structure of the lyrics, with their internal rhymes, does replicate something of the bingo caller's phrasing of numbers and nicknames: "Dressed pints demon shrinks bread drunk dead drinks" isn't a million miles away from "52, Danny La Rue, 87, Torquay in Devon." (Gilbert's spoken rendering of fragments of these lyrics on his 1997 solo record, *The Haring*, makes that connection obvious.) Beyond the fictional *Sun* bingo game, Gilbert was also inspired by something very real and even more unsavoury that he'd been noticing in news reports: "There were stories around this time about people being kidnapped and having their organs stolen and traded."

In spite of the anti-representational nature of the text, the emphasis resting mainly on the playful structure, a deeper, political unconscious can be teased out of 'Kidney Bingos'. If various words are grouped together, they evoke the specific socio-political and economic climate of Britain in the 80s: "pit", "striker", "dole", "axe", "fleet", "street", "spy", "scandal", "drugs", "crash", "mob", "rule." One can almost imagine Gilbert (and Lewis, who contributed the second verse) clipping them out of newspaper headlines for use in this text.

Beneath its seeming randomness, then, 'Kidney Bingos' suggests a knowing process: the layers of ambiguity, the absence of a conventional narrative, and the denial of fixed meaning are all very deliberately constructed, so that the text remains open and fluid. This was clearly a priority in the lyric-writing language games that Gilbert and Lewis enjoyed, and it echoes in some ways Gilbert's comments on the construction of an *apparently* random process at the 1980 Electric Ballroom performance, with its seemingly "unrelated actions". He confirms this intent in his discussion of 'Silk Skin Paws' – another of his collaborative, text-trading efforts with Lewis. "Graham had written quite a lot of words and showed them to me," says Gilbert, "and I edited them and changed some of the phrases around to make them more ambiguous. That happened quite a lot."

Newman's vocal on 'Kidney Bingos' is almost saccharine in its sweetness, especially on the choruses – an element that reinforces the vintage Wire tonal dichotomy between lyrical content and sound. The wordplay resists listeners, keeping them at a distance, while Newman's singing is uncharacteristically intimate and inviting. Despite this tension, though, there's nothing inventive about the way Newman's vocals are handled on *A Bell Is A Cup*. This is true of Wire's 80s recordings in general – a change from the band's work in the 70s. The creativity of the early Wire albums, in terms of their attention to the voice as an instrument, is often notable in its absence in the 80s. From track to track on *A Bell Is A Cup*, there's a sameness in the presentation of Newman's voice in particular. While it does no harm to the songs, it does suggest a lack of imagination. Previously, the band explored the creative possibilities of almost every component of their sound – everything had potential as part of their expansive sonic canvas. Here, the vocals seem to have been left largely to one side.

## We were told that only one of you would speak to us

Insofar as the lyrics for 'Kidney Bingos' point the listener toward Britain during the Thatcher years, the song forms part of a broader narrative threading through *A Bell Is A Cup*. Lewis's texts in this vein, while hardly literal, are easier to unpack. Take, for example, his vignette on conspicuous consumption, yuppies, and Thatcher herself in 'The Queen Of Ur And The King Of Um': "Tainted Matthews in car-key relations / Gilt invitations to the blue queen's ball / They stare at themselves, there's a need to be seen / Talking pillars in the blue queen's hall." Gilbert's contributions to the same song document his encounter with an entirely different 80s tribe – another instance of his discovering something *other* in the banality of the everyday. "It was a vision of what I think might have been *goths* on a Tube train," he recalls. "They looked like some sort of bizarre royalty from a very strange country, but I was earwigging their conversation, and it was all words of one syllable and grunts. Hence 'ur' and 'um'."

Musically, 'The Queen Of Ur And The King Of Um' "was written on the session and came fully formed," says Newman. However, while Newman had recast the sound that Gilbert intended for 'Kidney Bingos', in this case Lewis remembers some creative interference with Newman's original ideas for the track. "Colin came up with the tune for 'The Queen Of Ur And The King

Of Um', and it took some time to figure out how to subvert it – because he did it in waltz time, and we turned it into 12s or something. Which is why it has that peculiar rolling feel to it." The rhythm is crucial, giving the song its relentless, almost triumphant, processional gait, in turn enhanced by Lewis's horn and string samples.

'A Public Place' renders 80s Britain in a more chilling, austere fashion – a sonic and lyrical evocation of how an authoritarian society constructs space: controlling personal movement, organising the distribution of individuals, and ensuring visibility and surveillance. In the mould of 'Feed Me', and in contrast with the rigid march of 'The Queen Of Ur And The King Of Um', this is a drifting, inhospitable soundscape, assembled from clatter-y reverbed percussion improvised by Grey, Newman's droning synth textures, and Gilbert's persistent chiming guitar, which nags away like a toothache. There's even a jaws harp, courtesy of Lewis. The main structuring device for the album's least conventional number is Newman's vocal melody, as he almost croons Gilbert's dystopian psychogeographical vision.

Again, Gilbert draws on images that had presented themselves to him. "It's a little vignette from something I saw in Euston Station. There was a very old woman in a bit of a state – a drunk who'd tried to mount this litterbin in order to piss in it. [The unfortunate woman would appear explicitly in a subsequent song, 'German Shepherds'.] And at the same time, in another part of Euston was this massive pile of vomit, and all these pigeons were crowding around it." It's not exactly appetising, but Gilbert imbues it with some unlikely poetic gravitas: "Pigeons move busily / Through the contents / Of a man's life / In this public place / His last mortal remains / Reflect a private lake / In this public place." This text emphasises the deeper, more sustained and substantive engagement with ideas and images of which Gilbert is capable.

While 'A Public Place' sees Gilbert returning, in a fairly direct way, to his choice theme of the sorry state of humanity, 'Boiling Boy' comes at the same subject matter from a more oblique angle, with less for the listener to hang onto. Indeed, the chorus-cum-warning, "lock up your hats" – an allusion to German Dadaist Hans Richter's 1928 short film *Vormittagsspuk* (*Ghosts Before Breakfast*) – alerts the listener to the fact that he/she shouldn't expect any concessions to realism here. We're in the more febrile realm of the unconscious and the irrational, and Gilbert conjures up the suitably fevered character of the Boiling Boy to enact his by-now familiar worldview. "It was the usual thing of *it's all hopeless and dysfunctional*," he explains, "and this idea that human beings carry on and on forever despite the horror. I had this image of this boy blithely carrying on and being almost unaware of the horror. I think the line about 'his atoms were excited and he glowed in the dark' was also to do with someone who was mentally ill. That was my original thought."

Like Gilbert, Lewis is also on good lyrical form for *A Bell Is A Cup*. Although the record often seems focused on contemporary Britain, two of Lewis's most memorable songs look elsewhere: pumped along by massive synthetic bass, 'The Finest Drops' celebrates Berlin's distinct, cool scene, whereas the relentless 'Follow The Locust' looks to hyper-real America (here dubbed "the gambling museum"). It's an unsettling, speedy trip across the continent, inspired by the previous year's jaunt, a companion piece, of sorts, to 'Map Ref. 41°N 93°W' (there may be an echo in the "map a chart" phrase) – although the 1979 song sounds almost sedate in comparison with the mad-rushing paranoia of Lewis's 1987 experience. It's a harrowing travelogue, almost Ballardian in its portrayal of fragmented psychology and subjectivity amid gleaming technology and artificial landscapes, the narrator adrift and decentred in modernity. ("Stay on your feet / And get collected / Enjoy and explore / The gambling museum / The flight nurse attends me / But I can't wait to see the doctor.")

If the album title itself – a possibly apocryphal Zen saying remembered by Gilbert – was enigmatic, then the cover imagery was equally so in its juxtaposition of a horse's head (from the Parthenon marbles collection) and a filing cabinet. It's certainly no less idiosyncratic than the artwork for *The Ideal Copy*, but it's an improvement, if only for the clarity and simplicity of the image. Gilbert adopts the old surrealist and Dadaist strategy of combining divergent signifiers to open up new possibilities for meaning. He explains the thinking behind his choice of images for the sleeve: "I've always liked putting two disparate images together. In this case, they're both containers in their own way. I like the idea that one is a container of information – Greek history – and the other is a container of differently consumed information."

Bryan Grant recalls a meeting in Los Angeles, in the run-up to the album's release, at which representatives of the band's US label, presumably concerned about sales and marketing, became flustered about the title and the cover. "They were asking: So what is it? What's 'A Bell Is A Cup'? What's the significance? There was always a little bit of fear from the record companies." He recounts another (unrelated) incident, this time from the late 70s, which implies that Wire's reputation went before them: "When we went over to do *Rockpalast* in 1979, we arrived in Cologne, and we were met by two young German record company people. They seemed incredibly nervous. It was only later, when we were having a few drinks with them, that we found out what was going on. One of them said: But you are lovely people! We were told that only one of you would speak to us – and that he would hate us. But you are not like that."

## Stop me and buy one

As an attempt to realise a more song-based, pop-oriented version of Wire, *A Bell Is A Cup* is successful. It vouched for Wire's increasing facility with technology and, unlike *The Ideal Copy*, it suggests that they had found a way of working together, with the material, to produce something far more satisfying – for the listener, at least. The band-members weren't convinced. While Lewis was happy enough with the material that went into the record, he was not pleased with the final product. "I don't like the mix. It doesn't sound cohesive to me." Gilbert was also disappointed with how the album turned out, but he's philosophical about it: "You can't please everyone. Everyone can hear a potential mix in their head, but whether that can actually get onto tape, or onto record, you can't always predict – especially with a band situation, where everybody might be pulling in different directions, wanting something different, something more interesting."

Although the band-members weren't involved in the mix, Jones points out that they could have been, as it was very much part of the overall process. "The band could have been there for the mixing, if they'd wanted to be. It would still have been built into the session. It wouldn't have been like: OK guys, you're finished, you go home. It wasn't like that at all." Still, Jones notes that, years later, he listened to the original multi-track recordings and reached the same conclusion as Lewis with regard to the end result. "They sounded amazing, but I didn't have that feeling from the finished record we'd made. So I thought I'd like to remix it, not for a fee or anything, but if I'd mixed it differently that doesn't mean it would have made Colin happy, either."

Jones, like Gilbert and Lewis, believes *A Bell Is A Cup* is a weaker record than its predecessor. "For all its faults, I think we got out of *The Ideal Copy* what we put into it. It's more coherent to me, but *A Bell Is A Cup* didn't quite become the record I felt it was going to be from everything we put into it. It's not reflected. I don't think Colin shares that feeling. But, of course, it's much closer to Colin's vision of what he wanted than *The Ideal Copy* was. *A Bell Is A Cup* didn't seem strong and ballsy enough to me." The producer also speculates that the record might have benefited from being recorded at Hansa: "We could have had the Hansa scale and darkness on the record, along with all the interweaving pretty stuff that Colin was doing."

As a final observation on both albums, Jones suggests that the organisation of the recording process – above all on *The Ideal Copy* – may have contributed to the band's creative fragmentation; it alienated them from each other, as well as from the projects in which they were engaged together. "So many bands start because they all have fun being in the room together making a noise at once, and we did an extreme thing on those two records, which was stripping it right down and doing layering, one musician at a time." At the end of the day, Jones is under no illusions about the records he made with Wire. "Those albums were wonderful experiences to make. It was inspirational to meet these musicians – I was in awe of them. But they were both abject failures, really. It's clear that those two albums are not going to go down in the pantheon of their work like *Pink Flag* and *154*, but that reflects a number of things: my inability to pull it out of them, their inability to work together, and the lack of shared vision."

"*A Bell Is A Cup* is a more coherent record than *The Ideal Copy*," Newman says. "People tend to think it's the best Wire record of the 80s, flawed as it is by its awful, big snare drums. Technically, what's wrong with *A Bell Is A Cup* is that the snare drums are too loud: it's got 80s big hair and shoulder pads. That's what's wrong with it. And it sounds a bit plastic." As much as Newman himself seems critical of the record, he still manages to be mildly offended by Gilbert's assessment of it: "Bruce considered *A Bell Is A Cup* not to be a major contribution to Western Culture." While Gilbert doesn't put it in quite those terms now, he does comment that the album "ended up having an ice-cream van sound" – his negative characterisation of its melodic orientation.

Ultimately, the album draws Newman back to his narrative of what went wrong with Wire in the 80s, problems he had already identified during the making of *154*. "*A Bell Is A Cup* isn't a patch on any of the records we made in the 70s. We'd lost it in the 80s – because everybody had got too concerned about their own thing. I remember thinking at one point: if they don't give a fuck about it, why should I? It was like a cash cow. You get the foreign trips, the money, and the attention, but you treat it like shit. You have to treat Wire with the respect it deserves. That means looking at yourself as being separate from the band. The band is an entity in its own right, and it deserves to be treated with respect. Don't put yourself before it. Nobody is bigger than the band. Nobody is more important than the band. It has to be fucking good. In 1977, we discovered in a rehearsal room that we were good – and we lost sight of that in the 80s."

### Not something that will make people go: *Nice song!*

In February 1988 – three months ahead of *A Bell Is A Cup* – 'Kidney Bingos' was released as a single. The B-side of the seven-inch edition, 'Pieta' (which began as an improbable attempt at bhangra, also recorded at Preussen), contains another rare Gilbert vocal outing: the spoken line in the chorus, "Which way, Michael?" The Bacon-esque homunculoid cover image is a processed Xerox of Newman's face, originally captured, according to Gilbert, in a photocopying shop in New York City.

The accompanying video was messy and amateurish, and not in a good way. Whereas 'Kidney Bingos' is a cryptic, playful song, its visual rendering is woefully literal and obvious, marred by the use of hackneyed, heavy-handed imagery to represent the climate of 80s Britain. Fleshing out Gilbert's inspiration for the song, the dominant image is meat, and lots of it: displayed, chopped, and cooked throughout. Added to that are verité sequences (mostly shot by Gilbert) featuring crowds of shoppers milling about the streets, people using a cash dispenser, derelict individuals sitting in a doorway, and the occasional piece of advertising slogan-style text, encouraging people to "Come on. Win it once. And again. And again" (evoking the Thatcher era's casino economy). Amid all of this, a shirtless Grey floats across the screen with a plastic kidney on his chest and The Pope of Pop himself even has a cameo (culled from the Miller-teasing Preussen video). Newman lip-syncs and does some choreographed hand movements, although, by the end, he appears to have given up the ghost. You can't blame him. EMI might have had a point when they refused to allow Wire to make a video in 1979.

Lewis insists that the imagery was all perfectly appropriate to the contents of the song, embodying the social context surrounding the lyrics, but Newman disagrees: "It's the wrong video for the song. If you're going to have a video for a song, you don't have a video that basically consists of people cutting up meat – that's not an image that's going to go well on primetime, if you're in the business of doing pop." That's true enough, but then it's not as if Wire had taken advantage of promotional opportunities to sell their work up until that point. Nonetheless, Newman sees the video as sabotaging the single itself. "The video was the defeat of the song, in a way: to show it in the worst light. It's very Bruce. It's such a completely uncommercial video. It's lo-fi. People chopping up meat in a very brutal way is not something that will make people go: *Nice song!*" Newman may have been unhappy, but it could have been worse – Gilbert would have liked to see Wire approach videos from a much more radical perspective: "I think they were far too normal, really."

Wire recorded their fourth John Peel session on April 24 1988. Peel didn't seem to have held 'Crazy About Love' against them, although nine years had elapsed since that last, unconventional appearance. On this occasion, Wire played more than one number: the already-released 'Drill' along with 'Boiling Boy' from the forthcoming album and a new song, 'German Shepherds'. (These recordings would feature on the 1997 *Coatings* compilation.)

In June, to coincide with the 1988 North American tour, 'Silk Skin Paws' was released as a single. The cover image, titled 'Magnet Man', was prepared by the artist Richard Mackness. "My work looks at the tension between people and technology," he explains, "and this image was one of a series of pieces using the human torso as a metaphor for instinctual, gut-feeling 'humanness'. There's a force field around the form, like the lines of magnetic resonance you can see with a simple bar magnet and iron filings on a piece of paper. So the image was intended to convey the sense of electrical power, industrial energy fluxing around the organic human form – energising, enabling, and yet consuming it. Like a Faustian pact."

A video was also made for the 'Silk Skin Paws' single, but it was shelved due to concerns over the content – a shame, as it was superior to its predecessor and far more entertaining. It was filmed in the lighting storeroom at Bryan Grant's Britannia Row headquarters. "The conceit was that everyone was going to get very drunk, and we were going to make a 'performance' video," says Newman by way of explanation, adding: "It's probably not a good idea to give me lots of alcohol when I'm very annoyed with Graham." This refers to sequences showing him and Lewis locked in physical combat. Other highlights include Gilbert wrapped in what looks like clear tape and Grey wearing a jacket composed of torn-up newspaper ("in a feathering effect," the drummer stresses). Newman is surprisingly positive about this video. "It's the only one I actually looked any good in. I look dead cool. It looks very 90s, very ahead of its time." Of all the Wire videos, it was also the only one that found some favour with Gilbert. "It was interesting because it was quite dark and quite grotesque," he says. (This suppressed item is viewable on YouTube.)

### La cerveza más fina

For the 1988 North American tour, the support slot went to New York-based Band Of Susans. At the time, they were signed to Mute's Blast First imprint – run by Paul Smith, who would manage Wire in the 2000s. Band Of Susans guitarists Robert Poss and Page Hamilton were unfamiliar with Wire's music, so they had gone on a crash course. "I got *Pink Flag*, *Chairs Missing*, *154*, *The Ideal Copy*, and *A Bell Is A Cup*," says Hamilton. "I loved it all. Actually, it became an unhealthy obsession." Poss did some further research. "When we learned we were going to tour with Wire, I got hold of an – I believe – *Alternative Press* article about the prior tour, and I recall reading about these persons and band as strangers, trying to get a sense of who they were. I remember looking at a photo of Graham and thinking ... *I wonder about this guy*."

This opportunity had come at just the right time for Band Of Susans. "This was our first real tour with our first LP," says Poss, "and there was a level of excitement and earnestness and energy on our part that probably was amusing – and possibly nostalgic – for Wire, who were tour-hardened veterans at this point. It was very important for us since it was our first 'out-of-town' experience, and we were largely unknown in the US. John Peel had played our records, and we'd gotten some great press in the UK, but the US was new territory to a large degree."

Things got underway on June 12, at Maxwell's – "a great place to arrive and get up to speed," says Lewis. As it turned out, Band Of Susans didn't join the tour until June 22 in Minneapolis: Poss's mother was killed by a drunk driver on June 1, and the group pulled out of the first dates. "For me, it was some of the best times of my life combined with its worst event," Poss says, reflecting on this period. Once on the road, he and his bandmates quickly fell in with the refreshment-oriented culture of Gilbert and Lewis. "I drank a lot of tequila and Corona, which was a nice combination," Hamilton remembers. "Bruce would ask me: would you like a small brown one, Page? And this was at 11 o'clock in the morning." Poss has other stomach-unsettling memories. "I recall bathtubs full of Coronas, and me never wanting to see that brand of beer ever again by the time the tour was done."

Poss and Hamilton made the most of the chance to see Wire play during the tour. "Susan [Stenger] and I watched every single show," says Poss. "I recall being very much in awe of Robert's skill and finesse at his snare-hat-kick drum set and being amused by the pedals array that Graham had for his bass. We forged a long-term bond and friendship with the band, particularly with Bruce."

Musically, Gilbert made the biggest impression on Hamilton, who was struck by an aspect of Gilbert's approach that seemingly limited his options and constrained him as a guitarist, but which in fact generated ideas. "Bruce was playing in drop-tuning, and I thought: what a pain in the ass! I was too lazy to do that. And he said: that's how I do it – because I'm lazy. I still thought: what a pain in the ass – because you can't play this and you can't play this and this. But, then, if you play in drop-tuning, you realise that it makes you start listening to your musical ideas, rather than just playing the guitar. And that's what I always thought Bruce was so great at. It was about his musical ideas, rather than just being about his 'guitaristic' ideas. It was very musical. Some of those guitar sounds, *man* – those great grainy, fucked-up sounds, with simple little dissonances going on. It was so artful and so cool." Socially, Hamilton gravitated more to Lewis. "I was like Graham's stalker," he laughs. "I hung out mostly with Graham because he was closer to my age and party-oriented, and we were both athletic. I taught him how to throw an American football, and in return he taught me some soccer shit. I really bonded with him."

By the time Band Of Susans met up with Wire in Minneapolis, Wire had completed their West Coast dates. The highlight of that leg of the tour had been the strange experience of playing three times in the Los Angeles area in the space of 24 hours, in progressively smaller venues: their first engagement was at the Rose Bowl in Pasadena on the afternoon of June 18, followed by a midnight show at Scream, in the Park Plaza Hotel overlooking MacArthur Park; the next evening, they performed at Club Lingerie on Sunset Boulevard. Wire had played huge indoor arenas on the Roxy Music tour, but the experience of an outdoor sports stadium like the Rose Bowl was new. They opened for labelmates Depeche Mode (on the 101st and final date of their *Music For The Masses* world tour), albeit fourth on the bill – beneath Orchestral Manoeuvres In The Dark and Thomas Dolby. By evening, 60,452 Depeche Mode fans would have assembled, but Wire took the stage in broad daylight, with the crowd only starting to trickle in.

"It was a bizarre experience," says Lewis. "There wasn't much of an audience there yet. Some people were in the far distance, and the seats up front were mainly occupied by people we knew. It was like playing a rehearsal in a rehearsal room outside, to friends." He adds, inscrutably: "It was like being watched by a postcard." Gilbert enjoyed it. "That was very odd. It was very hot and very big. People were still taking their seats while we were playing, but right at the front there was a contingent of British journalists like Jon Savage, trying to make us feel at home." Grey relished playing in this setting – but only on his own, beforehand, and not during the gig itself. "It's such a totally un-Wire thing, playing in an arena,' he says.

"I can't remember the actual set. I remember the soundcheck more than the gig. It seemed bigger when it was empty. It conveyed the size and the massive power of the PA: I was just playing the drums on their own and enjoying the volume in the open air and the scale of the place. I loved that it was just so big."

Bryan Grant again accompanied Wire on this tour, and in his opinion they were now reaping what they had sown on their last visit. "The core of people who'd been waiting for Wire to turn up for ten years had been disappointed. So when we toured again with *A Bell Is A Cup*, a lot of that core audience had gone away, and the press weren't as interested. The audience numbers were less on this tour, and that disappointed the record company. I think they did themselves quite a lot of harm there." Grey echoes this: "We were going back, but we weren't really playing bigger places. We'd sort of blown it, as far as American audiences were concerned. It was a only a hard core of fans that were prepared to put up with us when we came back." (Although numbers were down, those who did come to the gigs were more committed to the new version of Wire and less fixated on the band's first incarnation.)

Ironically, although broader interest in Wire had waned, as a live act they were now at their strongest since reuniting three years earlier. "That was the best they'd ever played," says Grant. "They were much more accomplished as musicians, and they'd calmed down. They'd been there once and knew what to expect." The group's increased live prowess is evident on concert recordings from this period – particularly their July 21 1988 London Astoria gig (released in 2010 as part of Wire's Legal Bootleg series). Lewis singles out the Astoria set as an indication of how *A Bell Is A Cup* might have sounded, had the final mix been different. He also agrees with Grant that this tour was less of an ordeal. That Wire had one coast-to-coast adventure under their belts made the 1988 excursion easier, and he enjoyed himself. Newman, too, found it less intense ("It wasn't as crazy. It was more relaxed"), but he still had reservations about the experience ("I felt just as a terrible afterwards"). "Colin didn't want to be there again," says Lewis.

Although Grant suggests that Wire's profile was lower than it had been the previous year, Lewis recalls several interesting prospects being discussed. One was the possibility of Wire opening for Neil Young. "It came about via Bryan, who did the PA for him. We weren't definitely offered it, but the talk was that we could have toured with him. Wire held Neil Young in respect from the beginning. My thought was: if we can get on this tour, maybe we can get him to come on and play 'Drill' with us every night. I'd have been willing to put up with anything to hear that for 20 nights. It would have been a marriage made in heaven." Gilbert agrees that it would have been an intriguing proposition to tour with the man "who invented the one-note guitar solo". According to Lewis, there were other options: "We could have toured with New Order and with Public Image. Opportunities like this were coming up. We were still making headway."

### Wire on the Moon

In September, Wire made their first trip to Japan, with concerts in Tokyo and Osaka. "It was really very, very different," says Newman. "It was amazing. I remember Mike [Thorne] had told us that going to Japan was like going to the Moon. And he was right." Newman vividly recalls arriving at Narita airport. "They had HDTV – 1988! I thought: is that a window? I'd heard of HDTV, but there was no way you could actually see it in Europe or America." Until now, Wire's experiences abroad had been straightforward, given that there was generally some framework of shared reference points, culturally and linguistically. In the Far East, without even a common alphabet, it was difficult for the band-members to get their bearings. "It was very alien," says Gilbert. "There was no starting point with the language and the signs. There were absolutely no clues whatsoever." For him, the only downside to this was having to depend on others in the most basic situations. "It meant that we relied totally on people to take us around. It was a bit odd having an escort everywhere. We also had an old friend, luckily, [the artist] Shinro Ohtake, who dug an escape tunnel for me and Graham a couple of times. It was all rather odd."

Gilbert was surprised by the courtesy and formality of the audiences, as well as by an overwhelming sense that protocol was being followed at all times – things Wire hadn't experienced before. "The audiences were terribly polite. They didn't seem sure whether they should clap or not. They were very serious. At the end of each track there was just a polite murmuring, but at the very, very end they clapped." Lewis remembers some remarkable attention to detail on the part of their crew for the dates: "All of our equipment was put in exactly same place in Osaka as it had been in Tokyo – right down to my ashtray."

The Japanese gigs saw Grey branch out somewhat in performance. Although he was not an aficionado of percussion, the chance to do what he calls "mobile percussion" was more appealing. His 'clatter' had been an important ingredient on 'A Public Place', and so he explored ways to recreate that in the live setting: "There weren't any drums on that track, so

229

I did atmospheric percussion. I was walking around the venue, hitting things that I thought would make a good background noise. I used bits of metal that I'd found, or taken from the backstage area. At the Ink Stick in Tokyo, the tables had metal legs, and they had quite a good sound."

After Japan, the band flew to the United States, where they were scheduled to play more dates – including a co-headlining spot with Pere Ubu at the Hollywood Bowl. However, things didn't go to plan, and they were denied entry by the immigration service in Los Angeles because of visa issues. Enigma (Wire's US label) mobilised its lawyers and even a friendly senator to lobby for the band, but time ran out, and they returned home to London.

The following month, amid a handful of European dates, the band visited Portugal for the first time, with gigs in Lisbon and Porto, but the trip ended up being fairly pointless because the shows received practically no publicity. "I think the promoter woke up to the fact that we were coming only the day before," says Gilbert. As a result, the concert venues remained largely empty. Newman estimates an audience of about 150 at the Pavilhão do Restelo, a 3,000-capacity indoor-sports arena in Lisbon. "We played anyway," he says, "and, in classic Wire fashion, we played a brilliant set." Which was just as well, as it was being recorded and would be used for the band's next studio project. Newman reports that "only about two people" showed up in Porto. Gilbert is more precise: "It was literally one man and a dog."

Gilbert and Lewis stayed on in Portugal for a few days to do interviews – most memorably with a Catholic radio station. This wasn't very successful, but they did behave better than the previous guests. "The Stranglers had been there before us," recalls Lewis. "They'd ripped down the crucifixes in the studio, tied them to pieces of string, and run around. Which wasn't good. And there was a 20-second delay in the headphones. We tried to answer the first question four times, and eventually the interview was abandoned." They also did a television interview but ran into more difficulties ("the mics didn't work, so they couldn't record"). Still, their stay wasn't a complete waste of time: Lewis bought a postcard that would be the basis of the artwork on the *Manscape* album.

### A cross between guerrilla warfare and the Boy Scouts

Wire started recording their next studio project, *It's Beginning To And Back Again* – or *IBTABA* – in November 1988. They opted for Kitsch Studio in Brussels to accommodate Newman, who didn't want to be away from home as his wife had just given birth – plus he was already committed to collaborating with Alain Bashung on Bashung's album *Novice*.

Paul Kendall co-produced *IBTABA* with the band. He had been with Mute since 1984 and had first encountered Wire at Strongroom during the recording of *Snakedrill*. "My responsibility at that time was to nanny Daniel's Synclavier around London and Berlin," he remembers. He had helped out on Lewis's *Take Care* and had recently worked with Gilbert on *One Of Our Girls (Has Gone Missing)* by A.C. Marias, which would be released in 1989.

His journey to Belgium was not without incident. Travelling by minibus, with Lewis and Gilbert and the band's gear, he had been singled out by border guards for a strip-search – "possibly due to my total leather apparel," he confides. Lewis recalls that it didn't end there: "Later that evening in Brussels, when Paul, Bruce, and I were wandering the town looking for somewhere to eat, squad cars appeared from nowhere and stopped and searched Paul, not Bruce and I. I've often wondered if this was to do with our respective dress codes, Paul in head-to-toe black leather and Bruce and I in our Dome-wear: sober business suits, collar and tie."

Kitsch was within walking distance of Newman's house. Hansa this was not. Newman characterises it as "something of a budget studio", and what's more, when the band showed up for work, it was still being built – "in the throes of construction by a crack team of Spanish builders", according to Kendall. Since the concrete floor had only just been laid in the studio, the band had to investigate other options for a live room. "We were assured," remembers Kendall, "that within 24 hours all would be ready for the recording. It seemed unlikely. Eventually, we installed ourselves. The band would play live in a fine galleried hall reminiscent of a small medieval banqueting room, linked by video feed to the control room [at the bottom of the garden] – which was quite novel in those days." Gilbert found the unusual surroundings attractive, especially the improvised live room. "It was in a lovely old Belgian house. It was quite odd. It was like having your own small ballroom to play in."

The sessions got off to an ominous start when Kendall's attempt to switch on the control-room air-conditioning resulted in a power failure, with Wire in the middle of their second number. Kendall also recalls that the studio staff didn't seem to be quite up to speed with some of the finer points of the recording process. "Due to the interruption, I wanted to edit the two performances together (a two-inch analogue tape edit). The studio didn't own a proper editing blade – they gave me a Stanley knife. After a little explanation that the cut was critical, I was supplied with a cutthroat Gillette. Effective, but highly dangerous."

Lewis was put out by the conditions at Kitsch. "What an absolute nightmare. Talk about trying to bail a boat out with a cup. They'd only just laid the concrete! We would have been perfectly within our rights to have just packed our bags and gone home, really. But being the reasonable people that we are, we decided to keep going. So we had to camp out in this ghastly apartment at the studio that wasn't finished. The experience was like a cross between guerrilla warfare and the Boy Scouts." Gilbert saw the conceptual potential in this situation – the idea of constructing an album in a studio that was itself also in the process of construction: "It was interesting that the house we were using as a studio was being turned into a studio while we were still there."

Other than that accidental mise-en-abyme aspect, *IBTABA* did actually have a conceptual framework, established by the band beforehand. This was to be an exploration of the 'live album' convention. Wire were obviously no strangers to such an endeavour: *Document And Eyewitness* had been an atypical live record that made no attempt to finesse the material for listeners. For *IBTABA*, Wire again avoided the standard route of preparing and polishing recordings of their performances for release as a live album. This time, their adventurous strategy was to strip down those recordings and use their basic components as a foundation on which to make *another* set of live versions of the same tracks – in the studio. For this experiment, they worked with concert recordings made in Portugal and the USA of four numbers from *A Bell Is A Cup* ('The Finest Drops', 'It's A Boy', 'Boiling Boy', and 'A Public Place'); one from *The Ideal Copy* ('Over Theirs'); plus 'German Shepherds' and 'Eardrum Buzz'. A new number, 'Illuminated', was put together at Kitsch. (On the eventual album, 'The Finest Drops' and 'A Public Place' would lose their respective definite and indefinite articles.)

The idea, as Gilbert saw it, was to set up another "artistic opportunity", a situation that emphasised the material as a work still in process – not a finished product. "Bands do live albums," he says, "and I thought it would be interesting to revisit some of the songs in a simple studio and see if there was any more dynamic we could squeeze out of them – making it as live as possible, avoiding overdubs if possible, but still in a studio." Gilbert envisaged a combination of the in-the-moment interaction and spontaneity of live playing with his own extreme ideal of remixing – which entailed subtracting as much of the original as possible, instead of adding to it. "When I'm mixing things, I'm looking for things I haven't heard before, rather than enhancing or bringing out certain elements. It's about something a bit more creative and dynamic. With dance-music mixing, obviously there's a creative element, throwing something into the mix, which could change the whole thing entirely. But *emptying* the track totally, I think, is always an interesting thing to do. Getting it down to a couple of elements, almost throwing away the elements that had been there, and starting again. That can be very stimulating."

Newman explains the process in more detail: "We took the recordings from the Metro in Chicago and Lisbon and took off everything but the drums and vocals, and played along to it, playing everything else again. The concept was that it was a band doing 'a remix-by-playing'. That was the idea. It was a strange thing. It seemed interesting." Initially, Lewis, too, thought this could be a promising venture. "It seemed like a good idea to try out. It was another version of how to make a live record. We started erasing things and seeing if we could come up with alternative ways of going about it. We thought: this hasn't been done before; let's try it. Some of it came out of Bruce's dissatisfaction with the previous record."

On that topic, Newman maintains that *IBTABA* was very much Gilbert's project: "*A Bell Is A Cup* was my record and *It's Beginning To And Back Again* was Bruce's record. *A Bell Is A Cup* was my bribe for getting back in the band. But Bruce said that wasn't a contribution to Western culture, so then we did *It's Beginning To And Back Again*, which was Bruce's idea of what a contribution to Western culture would be." Gilbert sees it a little differently: "I can't say it was 'mine', but I did think it was a good wheeze because it was something we hadn't really done before. I can't remember being particularly pushy about it. I just thought it was an interesting idea."

Grey's role on the album remains vague. "I remember going to a studio in Brussels, but I don't remember doing any recording," he offers. It doesn't seem to have made much of an impression on Lewis either – at least not a positive one. "We were there a month, but it was a pretty long month. We were doing the best we could in crap circumstances, really. It's not a record I listen to." Newman goes so far as to discount it as a 'real' Wire album. "I don't regard it as being a proper album. It was kind of a filler. We did only fillers from then on." Gilbert is ambivalent: "I can't say it was a life-changing process. I'd probably consider it a bit of an oddity. It was just an idea. In the end, one can't claim that it does anything special or different from anything else. I think it was worthy of an experiment. And it didn't cost much to do." (The final observation is also true of the 'found' cover artwork – a photograph of a white paint splash on the underside of the platform wall at Westbourne Park Tube station, the stop for the Mute offices.)

Measured against the exciting idea the band was seeking to execute – the notion of a radical "remix-by-playing" – the results are ordinary. It's one of those instances in Wire's work where the practice doesn't live up to the theory or the narrative around it. Most of the numbers sound like routine live-in-the-studio renditions, rather than bold reimaginings of the original work. However, if the theoretical back-story is ignored and the tracks are framed simply as fresh versions of existing studio recordings, then this is a worthwhile record. The material isn't dramatically overhauled or transformed, but the band do bring new dimensions to the pieces: 'Finest Drops' achieves greater fluidity, remedying some of the "square" feel that Lewis mentions regarding *A Bell Is A Cup*. More expansive drone-textures increase the menace of 'Public Place', while the foregrounded acoustic guitar introduces an intimate, tactile element at the heart of the austere, impersonal soundscape. 'Over Theirs' is especially compelling, extended here to nine-and-a-half minutes and occasionally straying into noisier, more exploratory areas. The retooled 'It's A Boy' loses Newman's climactic guitar attack that ratcheted up the urgency and drama of the original, but it compensates with the addition of some frantic piano-hammering. Also noteworthy is the previously unheard 'Illuminated'. Built from the ground up at Kitsch with a drum machine, it anticipates the dance-influenced direction the band would pursue on *Manscape* and *The First Letter*.

## The rush to pop

Given the unorthodox nature of *IBTABA* – in terms of concept and execution – the project was always unlikely to yield any chart-bound songs. Realising this, Daniel Miller had asked the band to come up with some potential singles, separately from the recording of the album. Prior to the Kitsch sessions, therefore, they had convened at Terminal 24 Studios, with producer Rico Conning. They delivered 'Eardrum Buzz', 'The Offer', and 'In Vivo', which would appear as bonus tracks on the CD release of the album. "We had three days, and we did those three things," says Lewis. "It was pretty extraordinary to produce them in a short time, to order." Newman, though, thinks there was something artificial about the situation. "This was the only occasion when Wire set out to make a single and, while it kind of worked, there's a bit of a sense of what Gareth used to call 'attempt-a-pop' about the whole thing."

From Conning's perspective, the band worked harmoniously toward a common goal during these sessions. "I wouldn't say there were any opposing axes, and they seemed to have a unified vision for these songs. Like all great bands, once they played together a whole new beast emerged."

Conning, like Miller, was attuned to Wire's pop sensibility and jumped at the chance to work with them on material aimed at a wider audience. "I was thrilled to get these songs, as I really thought they stood up to their best early work, and I certainly was concerned to maintain their pop purity. Unfortunately, 'Eardrum Buzz' is the only one I got to mix. I took so long over it, I wasn't able to complete the other two. I thought they'd give me more time, but they decided to mix the other two themselves." Even so, it was an experience he values. "They are amazing characters," says Conning, "a completely unique band."

But, as so often before, Newman was dissatisfied with the production and felt his contribution wasn't given enough weight. "I found working with Rico Conning very unsatisfactory. He seemed to have little or no interest in the vocals. He wasn't interested at all in getting good vocals out of me. It seemed all a bit weird to me." Lewis offers his perspective: "Rico was his own man. He wasn't willing to bend over for Colin." Newman does value the tracks, if in a slightly backhanded way, considering them the only above-average material on the CD version of an otherwise mediocre record: "The thing that made *It's Beginning To And Back Again* was the singles tacked on the end."

Released just before *IBTABA* in April 1989, 'Eardrum Buzz' – the band's second-biggest 'hit' – reached Number 68 in the UK charts. This was a classic pop-song-as-irritant, in the mould of 'I Am The Fly' – complete with an annoying, highly contagious chorus. As with 'Kidney Bingos', the basic idea had been Gilbert's, but his founding guitar part, which leaned toward the metallic end of the riff spectrum, was forced out and the song taken in a different direction by the band. Lewis and Gilbert assembled the artwork for the single, collaging photocopied images to replicate the dominant finger-in-the-ear gesture of the subsequent video. While 'Eardrum Buzz' was a brilliant throwaway pop song, 'In Vivo' – released in July 1989 – was more durable, a driving, harder-edged number in the same vein as 'Ahead'; also like 'Ahead', it had something of mid-80s New Order about it – and, insofar as that's shorthand for great electronic pop, there's nothing wrong with that. (The cover of the 'In Vivo' single was a picture made by Lewis, composed of multiple images of the Hindu goddess Kali.)

Taken alongside 'Kidney Bingos', 'Eardrum Buzz' and 'In Vivo' underscore Wire's pop prowess during the Mute years. Miller still swears by them: "'Eardrum Buzz' and 'Kidney Bingos', in particular, are great pop tracks. They got on the radio. Maybe they were just a bit too weird? But people were still quite open to it." Regarding Wire's lack of commercial success, Miller feels that perennial divisions within the band over the pop side of their identity may have ultimately been their undoing. "They made great pop records. They didn't undermine it in the records," he points out, suggesting that the problems resided in the decisions made around the work. "They wouldn't play the game. I think the band didn't really want it. Well, I think Colin wanted it, but I don't think the others did. Colin wanted to be a pop star, Graham secretly wanted to be a pop star, Bruce had absolutely no intention whatsoever of being a pop star, and Robert would have probably gone with the flow. If they'd had a lot of success, it would have been problematic for Bruce – that's my sense of it." Miller's comments appear to support Newman's contention that the Gilbert-driven 'Kidney Bingos' video may have been devised to scupper the track's chances as a single.

Far from undercutting the songs, the 'Eardrum Buzz' and 'In Vivo' videos (directed by Angela Conway) complement the tracks perfectly. The first of these was shot in the theatre at the Magic Circle's London headquarters – on the legendary stage where prospective members perform their conjuring acts before the Magic Circle's examining committee. The sight of the band framed by a small stage and proscenium arch is an almost cartoonish allusion to the *Chairs Missing* sleeve. Indeed, this was Gilbert's concept, the video evoking something of the music-hall aesthetic – a reflection of his broader interest in the cultural curiosities of the Victorian and Edwardian era. In this cramped setting, the band mime with minimal instrumentation as props: Lewis with his Rail bass, Gilbert with a tambourine, and Grey with a snare and cymbal, while Newman camps it up at the front, singing and dancing. The boxed-in, claustrophobic feel accentuates the absurdity, the video demonstrating a cardinal rule of comedy: the humour of a situation is enhanced or magnified if the characters are placed in an environment that imposes constraints on their movements, rendering them almost mechanical.

The visual claustrophobia is also apt as this is one of Wire's most self-referential songs, with three of the band-members making covert appearances in the lyrics, amid an odd dramatis personae – Adolf Hitler, Marco Polo, Buffalo Bill, The Louisville Lip, Hannibal, Captain Flash, and Custard Jack. "'Custard Jack', aka Jacques Cousteau, is Bruce," explains Newman. "Bruce had a dark-blue knitted hat, which caused Graham to dub him 'Jacques' because, well, it was very funny at the time. You had to be there, really. 'The Louisville Lip', aka Screwy Lewie, is Graham." Lewis adds: "Colin was 'Marco Polo' – a reference to his pathfinding and map-reading skills."

Alternately wearing white and black 'ear-shirts', Newman plays two parts in the video, which was intended to hint at the traditional doppelganger narrative of good-versus-bad. The idea isn't pursued beyond that visual coding, which is unsurprising as there was literally no room to develop a story. Lewis and Gilbert also dress up for the occasion: the former sports a Tyrolean-style jacket while the latter wears a chin-length wig, sunglasses, a Homburg and lipstick. Adding another level, the video is intercut with a star-studded cast who make blink-and-you-miss-them cameos, grimacing and rubbing at their ears with their fingers – and in the process mirroring the irritation experienced by the listener. It's quite a list: among others, it includes Björk, Bernard Sumner, Robin Guthrie, Michael Clark, Howard Devoto, John Peel, Vince Clarke, and even Sir Michael Tippett (an appearance secured by Mike Thorne, a Tippett acquaintance and collaborator). This is the complete package – a quirky, charming video for a quirky, infectious number: the pleasurably annoying, repetitive structure is reproduced in the video's confined space, leaving the viewer boxed-in with Wire and their song, unable to get away from it. "It was shown on MTV more times than anyone would want," says Newman. "Enough to make you really sick of it."

The video for 'In Vivo' offers an ideal antidote to the cramped interiors of 'Eardrum Buzz'. Although it's set largely in crowded urban areas, it nevertheless conveys the impression of wide-open space, with sunlight, blue sky, and constant movement. In keeping with the sweeping, anthemic tune, it's vibrant, colourful, and joyous. Filmed on location in London (Speakers' Corner) and Manhattan (Chinatown and a brief sequence atop the Empire State Building), it features Newman as a street-preacher figure, with sandwich boards, declaiming the song's lyrics (also written on the sandwich boards) to passers-by. Lewis appears as a spectator in the New York sequences; in London, Gilbert, wearing an eye-patch, heckles Newman ("I played the sceptical onlooker"), while Grey can be seen, in extremely short shorts, with his dog, Prince ("He was promised a part in it").

While Mute was endeavouring to present Wire as a modern pop band, in July 1989, EMI returned the focus to the Harvest years, releasing *On Returning (1977–1979)*, the first major compilation of the group's work. In a similarly retrospective mode, six months later Strange Fruit released the band's complete Peel sessions from that same period.

Looking back at the burst of activity that spawned the 'Eardrum Buzz' and 'In Vivo' singles, Newman expresses some uneasiness, again suggesting that there was something a little forced about Wire's volte-face. His remarks

237

further complicate the familiar binary view of Wire as a group divided between his own commercial, pop aspirations and Gilbert's absolute resistance to anything of the sort. "For a band that prided itself on its avant-garde attitude, there was a rush toward pure pop. There was even talk of getting Stephen Street, who was good at 'popping-up' old bands. It was a serious suggestion. I was completely against it. It was all about having a hit. After all these great avant-garde pronouncements, suddenly it's reduced to 'having a hit'." As he tells it now, he found this attitude, which he associates particularly with 80s London, difficult to comprehend. "I was divorced from the way people were thinking in London. Brussels was gentler, more weird and dark. It was quite arty. There was a feeling of being part of an underground. I didn't really get London at this point. I didn't understand where people were coming from."

Although Wire's late-80s singles took them further into mainstream territory than they'd been before, they now beat a sudden retreat. What followed would be their most uncompromising, and unusual, venture yet – an electronic, minimalist album with zero commercial potential: *The Drill*.

**CHAPTER 8**

# 1989–90

## The difference between duggaing and widdling

The track 'Drill' is a chapter unto itself in Wire's history and an enduring testament to their perversity. Having played a foundational role in the (re)creation myth of 80s Wire, it took on a notorious life of its own in the live context – sometimes extending to stamina-testing lengths. This track eventually became the exclusive focus of the band's next studio project, *The Drill*, a record composed entirely of 'Drill'-centred experiments. (Although it was completed in summer 1989 – before Wire began work on *Manscape* – its release was postponed until April 1991.)

When asked what he considers Wire's finest achievement, Bruce Gilbert's response is immediate. "I tend to think it's 'Drill', really, because it's so idiotic and says everything about Wire – or Wire as was. And because it doesn't fit into any category. It's a thing on its own." In his opinion, it captures the essence of the band's creative interaction just as some of their earliest work had done. "I think it grew from '12XU' in many ways. It's Wire at its most fundamental." Colin Newman concurs, supplying some (non)musical context: "'Drill' is just '12XU' without the chords. Like 'Underwater Experiences', it comes in the category of Wire things that don't have a lot to do with music."

The constitutive element of 'Drill' – and a core, onomatopoeic entry in the Wire lexicon – is *dugga*. "Dugga is a pet name for the rhythm of 'Drill'," says Gilbert. It's also a verb, as Newman demonstrates, outlining the phenomenon in more technical terms: "Duggaing is playing in 16ths on the guitar." And, according to him, it's not something that just anyone can do: "Being able to dugga is a skill." Not so, responds Gilbert. "Duggaing is the least skilful thing you can do: you hear it in metal stuff – that one-note chugging thing."

Newman and Graham Lewis beg to differ and, in the process, make the case for an illustrious genealogy of talented dugga practitioners. "Once you get into dugga, you come to Bach, who was a big duggaist in his time," Newman explains. "And Dollar Brand [Abdullah Ibrahim]," adds Lewis.

"He used to play dugga – top dugga. And The Master Musicians Of Joujouka. They dugga." Newman concludes: "So you can see we're part of a grand tradition." Returning to Gilbert's mention of heavy metal, though, surely it could be argued that, if you can trace a direct line from Bach to dugga, then Ritchie Blackmore is also a master of the art. "No," comes Newman's curt answer. "That's *widdling*. There's a big difference between duggaing and widdling."

One rendition of 'Drill' could differ from the next, as the producers of *The Late Show* had learned. "When 'Drill' was going very well, you wouldn't know how long it was," says Gilbert. "It was open-ended. When someone found a new noise or when a new sound was developing or when someone was going to a different position on the fretboard, the interweaving of the dugga had all sorts of possibilities and was always different." Gilbert took great pleasure in the performance of 'Drill', ascribing unique properties to the piece: "Some of it has to do with the trance-like state you can find yourself in. I'm drawn to repetition, to the beat, in a very primitive way, and although it's repetition, it doesn't seem to mark time; it seems to stop time. I like things that stop time and become their own reality, their own universe. I find that very, very attractive."

Lewis, too, notes the way in which 'Drill' can affect his temporal awareness onstage. "Peculiar things start to happen. You really do have the sense of things slowing down and speeding up – a swerve in perception. It was a very attractive thing to be engaged in." To him, the performance of 'Drill' has an even more explicitly transcendental dimension. "The experience is similar to what people describe with going through the pain barrier: you come out on the other side and get into this 'no-mind' state and, incredibly, you get another energy, and you're not certain where it came from because you thought you were exhausted. That's extremely exciting and addictive. It's an extraordinary thing. Once we played it for 29 minutes and 30 seconds."

However, the indeterminate duration could make 'Drill' very challenging in performance, as Gilbert emphasises: "It was physically demanding. The record length was around 30 minutes, I think. When you're doing it for a long time, and people are happy to keep it going, it can be very wearing. You feel like your hand's going to drop off. I have an absolutely hopeless guitar technique – I have trouble with my wrists." (This is the crux of the dark art of duggaing, apparently. "It's all in the wrist," confirms Lewis.)

Robert Grey, ever the minimalist, preferred the more economical variants of 'Drill'. "In the 80s, it went through a period of extension and improvisation. It was testing how far you could go with it. That was all right, but I prefer concise and brief, rather than extended and improvised." If for Gilbert and Lewis the taut, mantric repetition unlocks something greater – making the song a conduit of sorts – Grey finds none of those mystical overtones. He doesn't derive that same sense of release from the rigid, repetitive structure ("there's a tension about it that's not in other songs"), and for him, the performance doesn't lead away from the track and resolve itself in an experience beyond the physical here-and-now. Rather, it focuses him firmly on the moment and on the task at hand, heightening his consciousness of the physicality of drumming and intensifying his concentration: "Even though you're doing the same thing, it has to be played well. Repetition sounds easy but it's not."

In Grey's view, to have "played well" is to achieve an awareness of connecting with the essence of the track: "It's certainly not every night, but sometimes it seems to work as it should, and you express what it is you like about the song – and it can apply to any song." Above all, that sense of having "played well" is about establishing a bond with the other performers and experiencing his ideal of Wire as four people playing. "The idea of it being well played is the most important thing, and that should involve everybody else to make it work."

Sometimes, at least, 'Drill' provided Grey with a route to what he most valued in Wire – as it did, differently, for Gilbert. Much of Gilbert's conceptual fascination with 'Drill' comes from its fluidity. It was not a written musical piece, and there was no single author or composer. It had grown out of a rhythmic idea, randomly generated by experimentation. There is no authoritative template or version of 'Drill', and its first recorded incarnation on the *Snakedrill* EP was just one instance in an already evolving work. As such, it was a paradigmatic work-in-process, a simple idea open to manifold iterations. "The reason I liked it so much was because it only really existed live in its proper state," he says. "It only really works live. It's not something you put on a record player. That's why we always went back to it. It was one of the few opportunities we had in the set to have something that was open-ended: it was a chance to explore the sonic landscape."

Lewis also appreciated the occasion afforded by 'Drill' in the band's live set to experiment and to engage in research and development. "It's so elemental. It has such a simplicity. It's kind of indestructible. It took on a useful role as an R&D vehicle that was always there. It gives you that possibility to improvise around one thing. It's the nature of improvisation: when you know things inside out, you've got that security that gives you

241

the opportunity to let go. And you've always got that rock or anchor that you can return to: when someone plays a theme you know, you come back to it again."

Nonetheless, Newman has reservations about the research and development value of 'Drill'. "'Pink Flag' was the original research and development track, and 'Drill' was regarded as being the R&D in the 80s. But I don't know what kind of R&D it was, because everybody forgot what they did by ten minutes after the gig. It sounds impressive to say it in interviews, but there's got to be some 'D' as well as some 'R'!" Despite the prominence of 'Drill' in Wire's work over the years, Newman now seems less excited about it than his bandmates. "I'm probably the person who is least fascinated by 'Drill'. Most of what 'Drill' developed into in the 80s was overblown, but I think the basis of 'Drill' is fascinating. It's really cool when it's very small. In the 80s, it turned into this massive great excuse to play for 30 minutes. There was an element of humour to playing it for half an hour, but most people will be left cold by that. The first five minutes is cool – but endless noodling? It's too much, really. Hippie-noodling is hippie-noodling."

### Dugga, by fair means or foul

The Drill was Wire's first studio album to be recorded in Britain since 1979. It was made at Worldwide – which had relocated to Mute's Harrow Road headquarters – with Paul Kendall again co-producing. "*Dugga dugga dugga* was the modus operandi of *The Drill*," he explains. "From this grew the concept of creating an album's worth of variations on the dugga theme – not remixes but distinct versions with completely different instrumentations." Or as the small print on the record itself advised: "This collection of recordings represent [sic] an exploration of 'DUGGA' – ie, monophonic monorhythmic repetition."

Newman describes *The Drill* as another Gilbert venture. His tendency to categorise projects from this period as either Gilbert's (*IBTABA*) or his own (*A Bell Is A Cup*), and to consider the 'Gilbert projects' less essential to Wire's catalogue, indicates how divided their aesthetic visions had become. "*The Drill* was one of Bruce's ideas as well," he says. "His disgruntlement with *A Bell Is A Cup* was so great he had to have two albums to make up for it. The basic premise was that we were going to do versions of 'Drill' because Bruce said: there can never be enough versions of 'Drill'."

Gilbert doesn't feel he should take all the credit for this album. "I think Graham and I cooked this one up together, actually," he comments. Lewis agrees, stressing that it was an outgrowth of the pair's work, both in Wire and in their extra-curricular activities. "Bruce and I kicked the idea around for some time. We loved 'Drill'. The album felt like a very natural development of the way we were using the studio at the time – sampling and sequencing. It seemed like a good idea, something obvious to do with the technology available – and it seemed like fun."

From Gilbert's perspective, *The Drill* was an attractive enterprise since it was another laboratory in which to explore the potential of dugga – giving ample opportunity for him to indulge two of his key criteria for a worthwhile artistic "wheeze": pleasure and the perverse desire to pursue an idea to extreme ends. "I thought: wouldn't it be fun to make as many 'Drill's as possible? Just to push it as far as it would go." Like Lewis, he also considered this a logical step in Wire's broader, ever-increasing engagement with the electronic environment. He saw this technology as a means of escaping the constraints of the musical tools with which he was accustomed to working. "I was interested, if possible, to avoid using guitars – to use loops and computer sampling to create rhythms." Of course, this wasn't a new inclination – as far back as *Chairs Missing*, Gilbert had begun to look to effects as he tired of all the "thrashing" that the guitar required. Bearing in mind the rigorous demands of duggaing for up to half an hour on the guitar (with wrist issues to boot), it's not surprising that this avenue would seem appealing.

*The Drill* was sample-based, the band making use of the newly available Akai S1000, one of the first stereo samplers. The pieces were, for the most part, constructed collaboratively in the studio. "It was like an intellectual exercise," reflects Newman. "It was all programming. It was like *making something*, not like recording an album of songs – because there weren't really any songs on it."

Gilbert recalls the overall approach: "The process in the studio in some ways was very similar to my own work in that the *Drill* things were very spur-of-the-moment. It was spur-of-the-moment ideas, working quickly, thinking on one's feet. We'd cook up a sampled rhythm of some description and walk around, saying: try that. And then, if anybody had any ideas about what else could go on top or how to create a dugga of some description, by fair means or foul, then that would be added. PK [Paul Kendall] was very much up for that: he had a background in experimental music – not afraid to push the technology or the effects in the studio until they broke or cried." And just as the band strove to reimagine 'Drill' in different musical ways, its original lyrical component was subjected to a parallel process. "As the recording went along, it was noses to the grindstone," says Lewis, "and Bruce and I hammered out a bunch of text to go with the pieces."

For all of the focus on the synthetic, there was also an effort to incorporate some traditional organic instruments as sound sources. "We hired violins, brass, and percussion," Kendall remembers, "and proceeded to emulate the Portsmouth Sinfonia, nobody having the technical ability to actually play any of the hired arsenal. We would sample fragments and sequence them, as was the way in the pre-Pro Tools world." Ironically, Newman had been working on a 'Drill' in advance of the sessions that seems to have anticipated this direction. "I'd actually prepared one beforehand at home, which was a sort of orchestral 'Drill'."

While Grey played practically no part, Kendall does recall him contributing some rhythmic ingredients, albeit in an unorthodox fashion: "One particularly fond memory of these sessions was Robert producing a seminal bass-drum sound by hitting his chest, a resonant beauty – the sound or the chest?" However, he continues: "It was clear that, in general, Robert wasn't particularly impressed with technology. Sadly, he became marginalised in the recording process. Robert was a joy to watch live; he should never have been put in a position to battle it out with programmed rhythms and beat boxes."

Newman goes so far as to suggest that the album was conceived to exclude Grey. "After all my efforts with *A Bell Is A Cup* to get Rob involved, it seemed that *The Drill* was absolutely designed to not include him. There was nothing for him to do. He was completely superfluous to the recording. It was like saying: there's no job for you. It wasn't a bad piece of work, it was an interesting thing to do, but, in the end, what we were doing was excluding a member of the band. The argument was always that he was holding us to ransom, because he'd only do what he wanted to do, and I couldn't really counter it. Rob was there the whole time and absolutely hated it."

Lewis rejects the idea that there was any deliberate exclusion of Grey. Quite the opposite, in fact: "We thought it might be an opportunity to seduce Rob – for him to understand the potential of working in this way." And Kendall does remember Grey making some effort with the technology: "For a brief period, he tried to embrace using pads to trigger sound, but he felt more comfortable with the actual physicality of drumming." For his part, Grey says he has no recollection of working on *The Drill*.

## A curious object

Newman reports a muted frustration with the studio methodology pursued by Gilbert and Lewis on *The Drill*, which at times reminded him of what he had found unworkable on *The Ideal Copy*. "One of Graham and Bruce's stock-in-trades was to record something and then find the one part that was good – but that's how you end up with tapes full of crap, because everyone's just playing general stuff, and nobody's got the time to figure out what bits are any good. For me, and a lot of people who do production, it was a lazy way of working. Of course, you can get magic by letting someone do a mad track and then taking the very best bit – but you do that *once* in a piece, with one crazy, interesting element. You don't do that over 24 tracks."

Newman is talking about the role of chance in artistic endeavours, a subject on which he feels that he and his bandmates held irreconcilable views. "It's about the application of intelligence to what you do. The use of only chance in a creative process is problematic to me. Of course, it's all part of what we can use in the process, and sometimes chance really throws up fantastic things, but [it only works in terms of] the contrast between that one chance thing going against all the other things that aren't left to chance – which makes the chance thing sound magic. If it's all chance, it doesn't work."

Newman's verdict on the record is familiarly ambivalent, ranging from measured appreciation to damning with faint praise. "It was a one-trick pony, that album. It was fun to make, and it's not bad. I don't think *The Drill* is a record that many people return to. It's a concept. It wasn't terrible. The cover's interesting. You can't really talk about *The Drill* as being an album. It's just some tracks." Although coming from a different set of values, Gilbert agrees with Newman on that last point. "Is it an album? No, I think it's another curious object."

"It had something in common with dance music, but it wasn't really dance music," says Newman of *The Drill* – a comment that provides a useful way of looking at the project. He and Lewis had both taken an active interest in dance music as it evolved in the 80s: they talk enthusiastically about early New York hip-hop, Lewis waxes lyrical about Chicago house and Newman recalls that, by the time of the sessions for *The Drill*, he was listening to records from closer to home that were coming out on Rhythm King and the Belgian R&S label. While that wider context might seem to offer a frame of reference for *The Drill,* its relationship with contemporaneous dance music is oblique and refracted as opposed to derivative or imitative. These tracks aren't literal exercises in dance style but, rather, playful experiments that typify Wire's healthily detached interest in the pop climate around them – drawing elements from it but in the greater service of 'Drill'.

The sonic possibilities of dugga are the focus of attention here, multiplying rhizome-like through material that holds up a distorting mirror to dance music's past and present (and even its future), sometimes within the same track: the arpeggiated pattern on the perky 'Jumping Mint' is Moroder-esque; the bassline of 'Arriving/Staying/Going?' might be a compacted 'White Lines', while its cut-up vocals forecast glitch; keyboard sounds from Chicago house (as adopted by European artists) echo on 'Did You Dugga?'; and 'Where Are You Now?' forsakes beats for minimal ambience. There's even a proto mash-up with the 'Drill'/'12XU' hybrid of 'In Every City?' (A live approximation of this would be aired on their 1990 post-*Manscape* tour as '12 Drill U', alongside 'Eardrum Bingos', a conjoined twinning of 'Eardrum Buzz' and 'Kidney Bingos'.)

If Gilbert dismisses the notion that *The Drill* was 'his' project, he's willing to take the credit for the cover design, which was based on an old piece he'd made at art school. "I thought the *Drill* thing should be fairly industrial, brutal-looking. That seemed to be a solution. It actually went back to something I did when I was a student – a brutal, twisted pop-art approach to making a painting. I took black-and-white or red-and-white chevron shapes, with part of a face cut out as a butterfly. That was all it was: something very simple, very stark. I'm a big sucker for chevrons and things like that." Lewis is unhappy with the cover, feeling that Gilbert took it over somewhat, after the two had initially discussed it. "This is an example of Bruce hijacking something. We'd said that the cover should look like something from Black & Decker, but Bruce hijacked it. It was a bit of a fait accompli. I've never been happy with it. I wanted it to look more hardcore, more tool-like. I always thought it was candy-striped, a bit lightweight."

Kendall's final take on *The Drill* is a positive one: "The process of making *The Drill* was a pleasure. There were moments of great experimentation, and we weren't spending vast amounts of money, as everything was recorded and mixed in Mute's in-house studio. Days would normally end around 7pm, leaving plenty of time to ruminate over the work, over a pint." Once work was finished, however, *The Drill* was kept back for almost two years, as it turned out not to be the type of album Mute was eager to release. "My understanding," says Newman, "was that it was not considered a commercial-enough product to be the 'new' Wire album – and after *IBTABA* there was a need for something that could give us the 'access' that some of the singles had enjoyed."

While it's a minor work, *The Drill* is a success. Idiosyncratic, perverse, inventive, and occasionally irritating, it bears many of the hallmarks of classic Wire. Key to that is the sense that the band-members are being led more by their imaginations than by the technology. On the subsequent

*Manscape*, the opposite would be true. Unlike the often crowded, over-busy tracks that populate *Manscape*, the pieces on *The Drill* benefit from an understated, less-is-more aesthetic. Most of all, *The Drill* was an example of Wire balancing concept and practice: in this case, there's no impression that the former outweighs the latter.

Between recording *The Drill* and commencing the next studio album, Gilbert and Lewis revisited one of the more divisive and contested *Ideal Copy* tracks. They had been commissioned by American choreographer and dancer Stephen Petronio to contribute music for his piece *MiddleSexGorge*. They settled on an extended version of 'Ambitious', which they assembled with Kendall at Worldwide. With time running short and the premiere looming, the completed track had to be sent to New York, where Petronio's company was based. In a world before file sharing, this was easier said than done, as Kendall explains: "We had to produce an extended version and get it to New York for the company to rehearse to ASAP. This required Michael Clark – Petronio's partner – to purchase an answering machine in New York, so we could play the music down the phone onto the cassette tape. Their cassette version was used for the rehearsals, and there was even a possibility that, as they had become so used to the tape, they would use this rather than the full sonic purity of the original."

**The train set**

If 1985 had been touted as Year Zero by Bruce Gilbert – an appropriately austere and severe marker for Wire's return as the ascetic Beat Combo – the band also developed a narrative casting 1990 as a reset moment. According to Newman, *Manscape* was viewed very much as "the 1990 album", highlighting the idea of the new decade as the start of a new chapter for Wire. This phase would see them make the latest digital technology central to the composition and construction of their work, aligning the band with the broader, mainstream intersection of rock and electronic dance musics that would be a defining characteristic of the 90s.

Work on *Manscape* began at the Sunday School rehearsal studios in Elephant & Castle in late autumn 1989. Skylights and natural light in the room made for an amenable setting, one the band felt would be conducive to creativity – "It was chosen as a place to compose for that reason," says Lewis. The sessions went well, despite the fact that Big Audio Dynamite were working next door.

For *Manscape*, the band opted for a new producer, David M. Allen, who had been recommended by Bryan Grant. "He'd been successful at producing The Cure, who Bryan worked with," recalls Newman, "so the idea was that maybe he'd be successful at producing Wire." Lewis adds: "He'd also been involved in making *Dare* with The Human League. He was smart and affable. He knew our work, and he was someone who was very au fait with current technology."

Newman conceived of *Manscape*, like *A Bell Is A Cup*, as a project on which the band-members would develop and record the material together, as much as possible – in contrast with what he characterises as the more exclusive approaches to *IBTABA* and *The Drill*: "We'd done two albums of what Bruce wanted, so I thought: let's try and do something different and include everyone." This time he was keen to integrate the technology more seamlessly into the creative process and, with that in mind, he equipped the band with Casio MIDI guitars. "The original basic recording was done in the rehearsal room. I'd set up all the technology for it so that we could actually record in real time together. We had a central sequencer with a MIDI cable going out, and we had MIDI guitars so everyone could play into the sequencer. So the radical thing about *Manscape* was that we recorded all the information in a rehearsal room to play back the audio. That was a different way of working: we were programming, writing, and recording. We were working out arrangements like that. It was an interesting record; it was made in an interesting way, because it was quite a democratic process as to how the pieces were made."

Lewis thought this was a brilliant idea. "The concept was absolute genius. The possibility of working with the computer and sequencer – being able to run the sequencer and record information and material into the computer while it was running, so you could jam along with it – that was genius. You could record and play back digital information to drum machines and synths, and everything would sync together. Each of us had a box, and we could choose different signals and try different sounds. And the computer would record the information." The added attraction for Lewis was that this methodology seemed, by the very nature of its design, to have chance and spontaneity built into it. "It was interesting because there were random qualities to it. There were some great accidents. It really was like having a train set – that was the way it felt. Everybody had a signal box, and you could nick trains that were going down another line and see what might happen. You could hack into signals and take sounds out, take the MIDI that was going to control the kick drum and plug into that and set off a synth sound, a trumpet, or whatever, because the information is an on-off signal – it's not the sound."

Energising as this may have been, it quickly became a challenge to stay on top of the prodigious amount of material that was being generated and stored, and the band had to resort to copious note-taking to keep track of what they had done. "After a couple of weeks," recalls Lewis, "the pile of paper was gigantic because we had to notate where every one of these MIDI channels was going to and from, through and back. It was so complicated." To complicate matters further, in their enthusiasm for this process, they'd catalogued the material in terms that gave little indication as to what it consisted of. "Because we were in such a confident mood about this," Lewis explains, "we hadn't bothered to give anything names – someone had the bright idea to give all the pieces numbers instead of names. So we had all the information, but we didn't know what the sounds were." The numbers are preserved in some of the song titles: 'Sixth Sense' was number six and 'Who Has Nine?' – which failed to make the album but appeared on the US-only 'Life In The Manscape' CD single – was, obviously, number nine.

The shortcomings of the numerical system became only too apparent when Wire packed up their maze of equipment and sheets of A4 and moved the entire operation to Mickie Most's RAK Studios in St John's Wood for the main phase of the recording. "After a very productive session at the Sunday School, we were very optimistic and decamped to RAK," recalls Lewis. "We set up the train set again, and Dave said: so what does everyone want to start with? And we started to choose numbers, like a takeaway menu: Ah, I think number seven was quite good. What about 19, anyone got a good feeling about 19? And, of course, nobody could remember anything, and it became extremely abstract. But we gradually set up a system, and it did have a lot of possibilities and a lot of interesting things did happen."

Lewis still sounds excited about the inspiring yet complex process. "Some stuff had been written beforehand, but there was an awful lot of writing still to be done, because things were in a fluid state. There was a lot of data, and we were trying to corral it and recreate what we'd had at the Sunday School. There was a very good spirit about it. We were trying to do something that I don't think anybody else was trying to do." He remembers a shared enthusiasm, with his bandmates commenting that the experience was akin to the burst of studio creativity that had spawned their second album in 1978. "Having survived the primitive technology and the, shall we say, less-than-happy processes [of the 80s records], there was a sense of adventure about it. A number of times, somebody would say: oh, it feels a bit like doing *Chairs Missing* – when suddenly we'd got more understanding of the process, and there was a greater confidence."

249

The situation, as Lewis depicts it, suggests that Wire were reconnecting with the studio and its technology as a stimulating environment in which they could work together as a band. That view wasn't in fact held by everyone. Wire's new identity for the 90s maintained the embargo on live drumming in the recording process and Grey worked independently, programming drum patterns for his bandmates. Prior to *Manscape*, he had coped with his decreasing role on the records in part by focusing on the drumming that was still involved in the group's live work. Now, though, a decision had been taken to banish kit playing from concert performances, too, and he was left wondering what his function would be at future gigs.

Gilbert, meanwhile, became less comfortable as things unfolded. Although he favoured spontaneity and improvisation and gravitated to the random, he describes feelings bordering on panic as the band struggled to keep control of the ever-proliferating menu of musical parts that, as far as he was concerned, didn't seem to be coming together in any workable format. "My main memory of it is: Oh God, we haven't finished *that one* yet. We've got to press on. There was a sense that time was running out very, very rapidly, and there were sheets of paper all over the wall and things didn't really resolve themselves for ages, which was a bit nerve-wracking."

Gilbert's unease went beyond the simple notion that the material never took coherent shape; rather, he was becoming frustrated with the technology that had made this the case. What, for the others, was the beauty of the process – an ability to generate, store, and play back ideas with great facility – contained a fundamental flaw in Gilbert's view. He believed that the essence of the material was being lost in its translation to pure information. As Gilbert saw it, the technology was filtering out the interesting elements of the band's work: he felt that the most intriguing sounds they were creating – that he could hear coming from the speakers in the studio – didn't make it into the digital realm. He outlines his dissatisfaction with the MIDI process: "It was a fait accompli in many ways, because using computers became very important to Colin. We'd gone into the rehearsal room with a computer, and we all had the MIDI guitars, so we were cooking up songs, developing songs. We were playing through amplifiers and effects and stuff, but the musical information was going to the computer. So the information was all on file, but none of the sounds were." It wasn't just the original sound itself that was missing but also – and crucially, for Gilbert – all of its idiosyncrasies. To him, these aspects were often the work's creative core.

Again, Gilbert seems to adhere to a surprisingly Romantic viewpoint, suggesting that artistic value hinges on the presence of certain essentially human, authentic elements – errors, imperfections, or flawed sounds – which digital technology eliminates. "The MIDI guitar was sending note information, but some of it was a little bit impure and slightly off and, with MIDI guitar, the notes have to be right on the button before the computer recognises them as specific notes. So there was a lot of editing, and strange chords or non-chords were struck because nobody knew what they were. Some of the songs sounded really convincing in the rehearsal studio, but when they were transferred to the computer, then the notes had to be changed into digital information, into synthesizer noise, and that had none of the urgency or texture of the effects that Graham and I had worked quite hard on to help the songs along – to make them more interesting, interesting for ourselves. That was all gone. It was as if it had never existed. All it was was musical information, which was really quite depressing. Apart from the odd noise here and there, it all seemed sterile, and it was a bit difficult to get enthusiastic about it, to gee oneself up to press on with it."

Gilbert's ultimate concern was that, since the material was being reduced to a lifeless, one-dimensional digital format, in the end the record would not actually be made by Wire, recording and working with the sounds they were generating. Instead, the album would be made after the fact, when they had finished their work. "I had that sinking feeling that it was all going to happen in the mix, which was obviously the common method at the time for doing things. And I think Dave was known for remixes. His most comfortable position was to have all the information and then cook up a mix."

## Splurge

While Newman had been hopeful about the approach to *Manscape*, he feels that the record didn't live up to its potential. That failure wasn't so much linked to the technology but, once again, to the absence of pre-written songs at the heart of the process. "It's an amazing missed opportunity. It tells you that we just didn't understand how to do the record. It was easy enough to do *The Drill* because it was a very specific thing. *Manscape* was the first attempt, as a band, using the same technology we were using personally, to compose pieces together, to make pieces together and do vocals on top of them. That's the essence of the assembly method; it's not writing the song first and then performing it – it's writing the song after, having assembled all the stuff. What we should have done was produce the songs, and then say: now let's make the record – what are the elements that are needed to go with the voice to make that song work?"

251

To an extent, Gilbert agrees with Newman. Despite his affinity for more intuitive, spontaneous working methods, he found this process unsatisfactory because he had no sense of there being any substantive foundational material with which to engage. "By doing it the way we did it," he says, "we never really rehearsed the songs, never really played them properly, because we couldn't – it was all in the computer."

Newman lays much of the blame for *Manscape*'s flaws at the producer's door. In his opinion, Allen's inexperience with a group featuring multiple songwriters meant that he was unable to get the best out of Wire and keep the work in focus – eventually losing control of what they were creating. "He was less musical than Gareth, and he wasn't a facilitator. He was used to working with a band like The Cure, where basically one person does everything, and you've got to subvert them so they come up with interesting, different stuff – so that they keep from doing the same thing. That's not really the problem with Wire. You've got four people coming up with stuff. So very quickly the pieces developed into splurges, like *The Ideal Copy*, where you had tapes full of unrelated stuff."

Lewis, too, reckons that the work was let down by a lack of initiative when the emerging material needed a firm guiding hand. "There should have been severe editing and rearrangement. You should start to focus and cut things away, but it just wasn't possible, which is a real shame because there are some extraordinary things there. Which is revealed later, when you come to Wir – the seeds of it were there. Potentially, it's got such fantastic things on it, but it didn't quite get the editing and finishing it needed."

With the situation already precarious, the wheels began to come off as the producer became distracted. Lewis explains: "From the start, Dave was in a pretty pressurised situation. We had a process, and it was developing, and everyone was trying to keep faith with it. But then Dave's life unravelled. The most extraordinary things happened to him. Around him there were nervous breakdowns, deaths, robberies, and pregnancies during this period. I'd been through quite a rough period, but I felt blessed by comparison to what he was going through – because it was the most unbelievable set of events. What had been his life wasn't his life at the end of making the record. He did offer to resign. He said: get rid of me – it would be understandable. But we said: how on earth can we bring someone else into this?"

Gilbert's recollection differs slightly. "It turned out to be a bit of a nightmare because Dave Allen's father died a couple of days into the recording, or his father was ill. He was obviously having a problem, so we said: you should go. We more or less kicked him out of the studio because it was a ridiculous situation. You can't just carry on working in a situation like that. He obviously couldn't keep working, because it affected him greatly, and he was coming and going a bit. So it got a little bit out of focus and panicky at times." Nevertheless, the band soldiered on, with the engineer, Roy Spong, taking up the slack.

For Newman, the final blow to *Manscape* was the mix. He had assumed that Allen – in addition to stopping the band from amassing "splurges" of unwieldy material as the composition and recording moved forward – would formalise and arrange the tracks in the mix stage (Gilbert's nightmare scenario of the record, out of the band's hands, being made after the fact). "We trusted Dave Allen to mix it," says Newman. "The mixing could have been the arrangement that would make the album, but I don't think he really knew what he was supposed to do. He was used to having something that was an arrangement that worked and then getting that to sound good. That's what anyone who mixes can do, but he didn't even know what should be loud and what should be quiet. I expected somebody, when they were mixing, to have some sense of perspective with the pieces, how the arrangements are going to work. But he didn't seem to have any idea. The mixes are just terrible. I could have made a much better job of that." (Ironically, one song unwittingly predicted the fate that would befall the material in post-production: during 'Goodbye Ploy', Lewis refers to a "third-rate butcher's dance-hall mix".)

## Not being part of the piece

That Grey was no longer working alongside his bandmates is the clearest indication that the creative process didn't turn out as Newman had hoped: in spite of the purportedly inclusive structure, Grey was not contributing in the room with the others. But that's not to say that he didn't participate. Grey had actually begun to engage more than before with the digital tools. "We were rehearsing before going into the studio, and there was no live playing – I didn't even have my drums at the studio. We were writing new tracks, and I would do programmed drum patterns on my own, one or two each day. I was using a Roland R-8 drum machine, but I combined it with an Octapad – you could assign each pad to an instrument on the drum machine, and then you could trigger the drum machine through the pad. So that could be a bit of playing: you could play just one or two bars through the pad into the drum machine, and then the drum machine would remember it."

Grey's account of his composition process is intriguing. Although working in a digital environment, he drew on a deeply organic context: while the other members of Wire were immersing themselves in modernity, embracing new technology in their own work and in their vision of the band, Grey was moving in the other direction. He had started attending African (Ghanaian) drumming classes, where he learned about the role of drumming in its traditional ceremonial or cultural milieu: in religious and ritual practices, tribal communication, storytelling, and dance. And he brought some of that knowledge to bear when he set to work with his R-8. "I started quite a few of the tracks with a bell pattern. In African drumming that's the timekeeper, and it tells you which dance you're doing – it has a basic pattern to it. So when I was working those tracks out, I generally started with a bell pattern."

However, he used these patterns only as a form of creative scaffolding that enabled him to engage comfortably with the technology, and when each rhythm track began to take shape, he removed that original framework. "I took the bell pattern off afterwards, having built up something that sounded more like rock drumming around it. I used it as a guide in the first place. It gives you a way to find a rhythm you haven't found before, which is what I like to try and do. It gives you a starting point. Once I'd got the bell pattern worked out, then I'd move to the hi-hat, and then work the snare and bass drum in."

Grey did get some satisfaction from programming, although he emphasises that the process had nothing to do with drumming, because there was no technique required and, most importantly, no physical involvement. "What I programme often doesn't sound like what I play on the drums, because programming allows you to leave behind your technique – you don't need any. It doesn't even have to be playable in a real sense – it can just be something you find interesting. It can go more into your imagination, just using anything. I agree that there were some good things about it, but there's no performance in it." Rather than provide even a minor sense of physical engagement, using the Octapad only heightened Grey's feeling of alienation from the development of the band's material. "Yes, playing through a pad is slightly more natural for a drummer than pressing the keys on the drum machine, but it's not like being part of the piece. It's just tapping things out – it's just a method of recording it."

Not "being part of the piece" was the pith of the matter for Grey, as the band would create each track without him, after his drum pattern was complete. At this point, his long-held ideal of Wire as four people in a room, playing together, seemed irretrievable. And beyond not *playing* in the same room, they rarely shared the same space at all now. "I'd leave my tracks for the others, if they were interested to have them or not. They'd use them however they wanted. I didn't stay around for the rest of the rehearsal. I was already in the process of leaving, really. I couldn't see any point in being there. Once I'd done the programmed track there wasn't anything for me to do, and I didn't feel a part of what was going on."

## Haus music

As *Manscape* was a studio-based, collaborative musical construction, there's generally no clear sense of the tracks having been written by individual members. "Because of the technology, there was a blurring of the composition," says Lewis. "It was quite a mix-up." Newman agrees, although he believes he played a more significant role than the others. "I'm not sure who wrote anything. We sort of made them together, but in some ways I kind of wrote all of them – apart from 'Torch It!'. I had quite a strong hand in the way some of them developed, but I wasn't very happy with how any of them turned out."

With regard to lyrics, Lewis also talks about "a mixing of texts" that paralleled the musical teamwork. "I wrote a lot of them," he says, while stressing that the pieces were shaped by a familiar "joint-writing" strategy. As Gilbert explains: "There's a lot of Graham in this, but I edited a lot of his stuff." Gilbert still found this routine appealing, especially the opportunity it offered to experiment with Lewis's syntax, in such a way as to open up further semantic possibilities in the texts. "I enjoyed it. Chopping the phrases up a little, the sense of the song can still be there, but the words will be slightly unusual in terms of placements and juxtapositions. And if you do it in that way, new levels of meaning emerge." As well as working on Lewis's words, Gilbert was also mostly responsible for naming the pieces. Instead of devising titles that summed up the subject matter or resonated with a central idea, Gilbert took a more random tack. "I usually came up with the titles. We'd ask: what are we going to call it? And I'd stare at the text and put two things, two words or ideas, together – it wouldn't necessarily mean anything."

Collaborative lyric-writing on *Manscape* wasn't the sole province of Lewis and Gilbert: Newman had also become more involved in the words, and 'Other Moments', for instance, was written by him and then reworked by Gilbert and Lewis. Lewis also worked from the lyrics Newman had begun for the track 'Goodbye Ploy'. "Colin started it," he says, "and I thought it was another one of his whines about London and the UK, now that he was living

255

in this heaven that was Brussels. But I'd moved as well [Lewis had relocated to Uppsala in late 1988], and I wanted to turn an eye on the UK. Mine was more of an Alan Bleasdale version." Another, more personal take on Britain, 'What Do You See? (Welcome)' expands the collaboration, with Lewis's wife, Liv Elvander, contributing to a travelogue composed of oneiric snapshots from a trip the couple had taken to all the places he had lived in England.

Britain in the 80s is a less explicit thematic concern of 'You Hung Your Lights In The Trees/A Craftsman's Touch', where some of Lewis's lyrics evoke the climate of the Thatcher era via an allegorical blend of consumerism and the practice of false-light wrecking. (A composite of two separate songs, this had been Number 15 on the studio menu.) While Grey was dissatisfied with the way the band were functioning and felt he wasn't participating in *Manscape*, he is fond of several of its songs – and he singles this one out for the highest praise. "'You Hung Your Lights In The Trees' is possibly my favourite Wire track, which is interesting because it's not 'played'. There's some competition with 'Brazil', but it's got that melancholy tone about it that I like." He also appreciates the intricate, shifting beat. "Listening to the rhythm, it's difficult to know where you are in the pattern. There seem to be rhythms coming from different directions. You can listen to it in more than one way: you can concentrate on one rhythm, but other rhythms come across and subvert the basic rhythm."

'You Hung Your Lights In The Trees/A Craftsman's Touch' is one of the few *Manscape* songs on which Wire display real mastery of the arrangement and the technology. It's no coincidence that it's one of the more minimal pieces (even though, at ten minutes, it's the longest album track the band have recorded to date). With vocals by Lewis and Newman, it's a beautifully understated electronic folk song: melodic, affecting, and hypnotic. Despite the band-members' criticisms of the record's post-production, everything here seems to be in proportion, particularly Lewis's vocals, which are perfectly placed in the mix to yield one of his finest moments. It's the best track on the album and also one of the few that hasn't aged too badly.

None of the above can be said of 'Torch It!', which is far less successful in its combination of melody and beats. If Wire were drawing some ideas from dance music on *Manscape*, 'Torch It!' isn't so much *house* as *Hofbräuhaus* – an unremitting, industrial-Oompah rant. Grey remembers that the drum pattern was modified once he'd left it for the band to use, in the process losing some of the nuance he'd written into it. "Sometimes I noticed that things I'd put in had been taken out, and the drum tracks had been altered. Most of the patterns remained as I'd done them, but 'Torch It!' was changed. They'd removed bits: the way I'd written it, it sounded, to me, more Turkish originally – although there was an Oompah beat and toms on top. But when it came to it, it was only the kick and snare that was used, so you could say the Turkish influence had been rejected."

Notwithstanding Lewis's extraordinarily spirited vocal performance, Newman is not a fan of 'Torch It!'. "I was really annoyed about 'Torch It!'. Bruce and I did this fantastic bit with all these interlocking guitar parts, and then I came in one morning and Graham had shouted all the way through it: a stream of verbal abuse. We'd spent four days making this, and I was going to do a great vocal, but Graham came in and just shouted all the way through it. I fucking hated it." Newman's displeasure with the direction in which his bandmates sometimes took songs is a leitmotif in the Wire narrative, and this instance only reinforces the notion of the band at this juncture as a fragmented entity. "I don't know how it happened," he says. "We're still in classic Wire territory where nothing ever really gets discussed – people just do what they want to do."

"'Torch It!' I have to take responsibility for," says Lewis – his ambiguous remark open to interpretation almost as an admission of guilt. The track's manic, splenetic tendencies do make more sense when Lewis describes some of the inspiration for the piece, but his explication doesn't necessarily make the track any more enjoyable for listeners. "It was about the period when I was really depressed in 1984/85, when basically all I was listening to was Howlin' Wolf. That's where 'Torch It!' came from. It's definitely out of that: 'I asked her for water, she brought me gasoline'."

Talking about the album as a whole, Gilbert identifies a vague conceptual, or thematic, unity. The title *Manscape* (his choice) was intended to suggest the idea of the contemporary world suffering under the blight of humanity. "It's the usual: doom. We're all doomed. The political atmosphere of the time. Dissatisfaction. The destruction of global assets, of nature, of the environment – *Manscape* being the world, the way we've made it." He also mentions that he was keen for this record to be 'relevant', even topical, although he was aware of the perils of such an enterprise, especially for Wire. "I thought we were going to make something that had an element of social comment in it, but not political. It's a bit of a tightrope, that one – to remain as an observer without getting dragged into political statements."

Contemporary events certainly seem to inform the first two tracks on the CD release of the album (absent from the vinyl version, which was three songs shorter). The opener, 'Life In The Manscape' – made at Worldwide with Paul Kendall when the album sessions had failed to yield a single –

hints, in its chorus at least, at the changes underway after the fall of the Berlin Wall but reduces it all to an execrable refrain: "Free speech and more TV / Distribute liberally." The obviousness is reinforced by the track's unimaginative anthemic plod. And although The Pope of Pop makes a fleeting appearance in the lyrics, it's not enough to redeem the song. 'Stampede', meanwhile, renders the ideological and political reconfiguration of Eastern Europe in a more substantive and creative fashion, only to sink deep into 80s musical cliché and come up sounding not unlike The Thompson Twins.

One of *Manscape*'s more egregiously anomalous musical moments comes in the shape of 'Small Black Reptile' – a track which, sadly, requires the name 'Wire' to be used in the same sentence as the phrase 'pleasure-cruise reggae'. Equally unworthy is the insipid piano-tinkling on 'Morning Bell'. But it's worse than that for Newman and Lewis, who cite 'Morning Bell' as a track that epitomises the album's basic failings with regard to arrangement and mixing. According to Newman, "'Morning Bell' is a plaintive, simple tune, which in the right context would have people with tears in their eyes listening to it, but Graham plays a guitar that comes in in the intro, which is way louder than it should be. The part works. It's not the wrong notes, it's not the wrong sound – it's just too loud." Lewis agrees: "It's supposed to be in reverb and set at the back – it's supposed to be a wash, a dream sequence." In Newman's assessment, such issues mar the material throughout. "It completely changes your perspective," he says, again referring to Lewis's noisy intervention, "and suddenly you're looking for drama. It's supposed to be quiet, it's supposed to be reflective. That track could have been carried with just the beat box, the organ, and the voice. Have that, and you'd totally have the complete track. Anything else should be just colour and detail."

A couple of other numbers do come closer to that desired integration of core elements with supplementary "colour and detail". Like 'You Hung Your Lights In The Trees', 'Other Moments' benefits from its simpler, less busy arrangement – centred on skipping beats, distorted, spectral guitar, and Newman's rueful vocals. That simplicity allows the sonic ingredients to cohere, giving the track a distinct identity and mood. The same is true of 'Patterns Of Behaviour', featuring lyrics by Newman that were inspired by the sequencing process itself – an apt conceit for a technocentric album such as this.

Newman stands by much of the material, albeit not in its final recorded and mixed form. "'Small Black Reptile' was massive; 'Other Moments' was unbelievably beautiful, in interesting ways; 'Morning Bell' is an anthem; and 'Patterns Of Behaviour' is a great piece, but it's not. Those pieces never came out how they should have come out."

## Glimpses of something quite interesting

As an album that was resolutely modern in its conception and construction, *Manscape* hasn't travelled well (ubiquitous cheesy xylophone-type sounds alone see to that). Wire had ended the 70s anticipating the 80s with *154*; with *Manscape*, they began the 90s by looking back, sonically, to the 80s. Even more acutely than with *The Ideal Copy*, there's a sense of the work being driven by the technology and the songs being put together only in terms of what could be achieved within that framework. As a result, it's often leaden and lifeless, melodies in particular sounding plugged-in rather than having grown organically with the songs. Returning to Newman's comments on the methodology, however, there aren't actually many fully realised songs here – at least, not ones that manage to define and sustain any unique, interesting character. The fact that the band had to reconvene expressly to record the US single underlines that idea. Ultimately, *Manscape* feels unfocused and unresolved – ideas are lost in the numerous tunnels, sidings, and branch lines of the train set, and the occasional promising sonic directions are rarely pursued.

And if a substandard Wire record weren't bad enough, the afterlife of its title only added to the indignity: within a few years, the verb 'to manscape' and the art of 'manscaping' would be common terms, undermining, for posterity, any gravitas the title may have once had.

Lewis's final appraisal of *Manscape* concentrates on the album's unfulfilled potential. "Listening to it today, I can still hear the extraordinary record I think we were trying to make. Again, it was a very modern record, the way we'd gone about it. But it got lost. You hear the essence of so many good things, and some things do come off. There's a fragility and some very strange atmospheres, but we just didn't manage to pull it off, because of circumstances." He revisits the notion of the producer as the weak link, although he concedes that the band should have been more proactive: "I don't want to dump this on Dave – we should all have been able to take responsibility – but his life situation was so difficult that I don't think he was in a position where he could have been as assertive as he needed to be – to edit, to be really brutal, to cut and stand up and say: No. I'm going to do this."

Daniel Miller was also disappointed with the end result, but he feels the band bear as much of the responsibility for *Manscape*'s failure as Allen. By his reckoning, it was a lacklustre effort that raised questions about Wire's continuation as a functioning creative unit. "I thought they'd lost direction, and Dave was struggling with them. There was a slightly unambitious feeling in the studio around that record. The band *as a band* wasn't working. Sometimes when there are lots of problems, a band is still working as a band. They all seemed to be working very individually at that point." This last comment echoes Newman's general criticism of Wire in the 80s. Miller's observations are also interesting since his impression of the studio atmosphere contrasts with how Newman saw it – having planned the MIDI setup specifically so that the band could work together.

While Newman expresses dissatisfaction with all of the band's Mute-era albums, he doesn't dismiss *Manscape* quite as categorically as he does *The Ideal Copy*. Yet precisely because he can see more clearly how *Manscape* could have succeeded, it's the album about which he feels the most frustration – to the point of being unable to listen to it in preparation for an interview for this book. "It's no good for me to listen to it, because I'd just be annoyed about it. If there's a record in the world which is full of stuff that's totally annoying, it's *Manscape*. It's the definition of 'not mixed' – in my method of working." Like Lewis, he stresses what the record might have been, again highlighting the difference between what it promised and what it delivered. "The people who like *Manscape* have fought through the production and say they like the songs, which is pretty noble work to have done. I stand by the idea that some of the material is really great, but it came out sounding not very interesting. It was, potentially, the best Wire album of the 80s – if we could have figured out a way to develop the material."

The disappointing gulf between 'what was' and 'what might have been' is also encapsulated, to some extent, in the artwork for *Manscape*. The full potential was embodied by the limited-edition version. Working with Lewis's roundabout-monument postcard image from Portugal, designers Neville Brody and Jon Wozencroft fashioned a gorgeous, tactile package, composed of a matte cardboard envelope and various inserts. But the econo version used for the regular CD release was bland and without character – its front cover featuring the band name, title and a grainy detail from Lewis's photograph, as if viewed from the wrong end of a telescope. The only attractive aspect is Brody's font for the band name itself, which dominates the small space.

"I wasn't terribly thrilled by it" is the highest praise Gilbert can muster for *Manscape*. He agrees that it contains the germ of something worthwhile.

"I think there were moments, glimpses of something quite interesting, but essentially, I think it was slightly dull." He returns to his critique of the technology deployed in the making of the record and its tendency to sap his creative excitement. "The creativity got swallowed up in computer code: none of the nuances, no weird noises, none of the sound. It was totally flat. That is what Wire in the 80s is about, for me: a lot of interesting ideas about subject matter, a couple of interesting ideas musically but, essentially, fairly arid. It was sad because I think there were some interesting ideas around, but the effect in the end was very sterile. Impersonal. Where there had been a guitar, now there was a keyboard sound. Forced melodic elements. Forced into something because they fitted, rather than because they were actually saying something. It kills any enthusiasm for the song, the piece. And quite often it ended up being that plinky-plonky sound which Colin was very fond of, because they were pure notes. They were something he could pitch to, something he could understand, relate to; whereas for me it was that sterile ice-cream van sound again."

Grey's view of *Manscape* is more complex, since he's being asked to evaluate an album in which he feels he played no creative part. "I agree that there were some good things about it, but there's no performance in it." In seven words, Grey's final judgement speaks volumes: "It's more Wir than it is Wire," he says, implying that on *Manscape* the band had already begun their next phase without him.

### Options Rn't

Grey quit Wire in May 1990, just before the band were due to set off on a short UK tour to promote the album. The fact that he left it so late to formalise what, to him, had been clear for some time underscores the difficulty of the decision. Nothing had changed since the start of the *Manscape* process, and he had known from the outset that he would not be drumming in live performance, but that did not make the final, logical step any easier to take.

As the tour drew closer, Grey had still been exploring possibilities for how he might participate and endeavouring to reconcile himself to an entirely new role that he had mostly rejected thus far: his options came down to playing electronic percussion as a supplement to his programmed drum tracks or executing what was essentially a live mix of the latter. Percussion, in any shape or form, remained anathema to him. He reiterates the position he'd held since joining Wire in 1976: "I have a distinction between drumming and percussion. That was one of the things I don't like about *Pink*

*Flag* – it's the added percussion. There's such a difference between playing drums and playing percussion. Playing a tambourine is percussion. When you're playing drums, you have a whole kit and a range of sound from cymbals to kick drum, and you're involved in everything about the song. I see percussion as decoration. I don't like adding percussion to live performance, and I didn't want to play percussion on the programmed tracks. It didn't interest me at all. It was pressing buttons rather than playing. It was like being in the studio – the drums were a background track, and other people could add their bits to it while it was playing."

Newman still thinks this was a missed opportunity. "It would have looked cool! He could have had a fantastically innovative array of electronic percussion. Rob can be quite innovative in his approach – look at his minimal 80s kit. He would have got a lot of work then." Obviously, none of this made any difference to Grey and, with percussion off the table, he felt that his remaining option was quite absurd. "I couldn't see the point of doing a live performance in which all you did was basically turn the drum machine on."

As Grey saw it, to describe the timing of his decision as 'last minute', in relation to the start of the *Manscape* tour, would be to miss the bigger picture. As far as he was concerned, his decision was in fact irrelevant to Wire's commitments, because he was never going to be involved in the tour as a performer. His bandmates were in no way dependent on his participation, since he'd finished his work and programmed his drum patterns for them to use. "All the things that interested me about drumming had become less and less. I'd been building up to the decision for a long time, so it wasn't as if I'd suddenly thought: I'll leave today. Anything but. It wasn't as if I was thinking: What's the nastiest time I can leave? Just before the tour starts? I mean, the drums only needed switching on and off, so that confirmed my final decision – why should I go on tour to do that? It made it as obvious as it could be that there was nothing to stay for. I just couldn't see the sense of it. I remember talking about it quite a lot with the others. It seemed this was the direction Wire was taking, and that's what everybody wanted to do. So Wire was now three people."

His situation had indeed been a frequent topic of discussion, and the other band-members were more than aware of his views. From Lewis's perspective, things had now become profoundly frustrating. "I'd heard what he felt he wanted to do so many times. We were rehearsing for a tour, and we all spent time talking to him again about the same issues, and it appeared in the end to have made the same progress as we had before. With

*Manscape*, you're starting to hear and understand the possibilities of working with a mixed technology. We weren't a pure synth band. I don't know where Rob was, but everyone else was still wanting to play. We were playing with and in the technology. He decided the technology was against him and was excluding him – that was his choice. Everyone else was trying hard, and on *Manscape* you can hear some successful and unsuccessful attempts. We'd tried to help Rob understand how the technology worked, how he could interact with it, how he could be part of the process we were all excited about." This was the key point for Lewis, who felt that Grey no longer shared Wire's vision and was, to an extent, holding them hostage to his minority view of what the band should be.

Given the way that the band-members had, over time, reinvented their own roles and explored new creative avenues with a view to pushing the Wire project forward, Lewis may be justified in feeling some impatience with Grey's unwillingness to try different creative options. "I was exasperated, quite honestly. I just couldn't understand why he couldn't understand our concern about what we were trying to do. That's what exasperated me most. Dealing with Bruce and Colin, they had arguments about their own axes that they wanted to grind or furrows that they wanted to plough, but with Rob it meant that he didn't want to engage in what we'd invested a lot of time and effort in."

At this point, in Grey's opinion, there was no way around the fundamental issue: Wire were now, and had for some time been, an entity whose work was possible without his participation. The live setup for the forthcoming dates simply marked the conclusion of a process that had started in 1985 when Wire had come back together for *Snakedrill*. Grey does recognise the effort made by his bandmates to include him in the new version of Wire, and he notes that he attempted to rethink his role – but to no avail: "They had encouraged me through *The Ideal Copy* and *A Bell Is A Cup*, and I sort of adapted to it, but I just found it wasn't what I wanted. I found it alienating listening to the drums being played by the drum machine." He even implies that rejoining Wire in 1985 may have been a misjudgement on his part, and that his bandmates, if they were planning to fully immerse themselves in a digital environment, should have thought more about the logic of inviting him back as a drummer. "If that's the sort of group you want to create, it should be like that from the beginning so you'd have somebody who wanted to programme, who didn't want to play drums."

Gilbert had been aware that the impasse was becoming increasingly acute. "It did seem to be reaching a pitch. It was clear Rob was getting more and more frustrated, and he wouldn't engage with the technology. I did feel sorry for him because he'd set his drum kit up and just sit there, and that would be it. He enjoyed the physicality of live drumming – anything else was percussion, which he wasn't interested in. He was confident in what he was there for. He was there to drum. He needs to feel that he's the heartbeat; he needs to play the bass drum. He is drum." Like Lewis, however, Gilbert emphasises the group vision for a way forward, which had to be the priority. "It was the plan, but it was a plan that Rob didn't like and didn't feel he could fit into or have any meaningful part of. From his point of view, it was all going on without him."

Gilbert maintains that there were ways in which Grey could have adapted his role while still expressing himself as the band's rhythmic backbone, but the stumbling block was always the issue of physical involvement. "He's the drummer: one would hope he might have a very interesting view of using MIDI percussion or using extraneous noises – views on where to place certain sounds in the rhythm. But he didn't really like hitting bits of plastic. He wanted the physicality of it, which is his thing."

## Mr Suit

The endgame was played out at an ironically fitting location: the Fridge in Brixton, run by Andy Czezowski, former manager of the Roxy, the site of Wire's live debut as a four-piece band. Because they were taking a computer on tour for the first time, they felt the need for a full production rehearsal. Grey was in attendance, recalls Gilbert: "He just kicked over a cymbal or something and started packing up, obviously furious. I thought: this is serious. One didn't know quite what to say."

Newman remembers Grey visiting him prior to the tour and making it clear that he was about to quit. Newman had tried to dissuade him. "Rob came over to Brussels. He told me he was going to leave, that he felt there was nothing to do, that he'd had enough. I begged him not to leave. I didn't think it was a sensible thing for him to do. We'd done *Manscape*, and there was one more album to come in the Mute deal, and it was the one for the biggest advance. So I said: stay for that, get the money, and then we'll decide what we're going to do. I fought with him quite hard about it. I really, really wanted him to stay. In the end, he worked on programming everything for the live set and said: 'I've done all my work. I'm leaving.' It was just before we were about to go on tour." Lewis continues: "He quit a week before the tour – at least it was a week and not two days. Suddenly we were in a very fragile situation. What we were trying to do was not easy – to take a computer and a sampler on the road. They weren't built for it then. But it's what we thought we should do. It was another one of those things we thought we should try to achieve."

Even though Grey's parts were programmed and his presence wasn't required, the impact of his departure was considerable, according to Newman: "The shock of it, a week before we were due to go on tour, was immense – the idea that we'd have to go onstage as a three-piece and be totally dependent on Paul Kendall to mix it live and make it sound good. I think Rob leaving made it impossible, but we couldn't pull out." Given that the issue had clearly been moving toward this critical point, the apparent sense of shock is hard to understand – especially in Newman's case, as Grey had told him what he was planning to do. "It just shows how much we were paying attention," says Newman. "With hindsight, of course Rob was leaving. He was preparing everything so he could leave. He made it so that he didn't have anything to do."

The tour went ahead with a live version of the MIDI setup, detailed by Newman: "There was a sequencer driving the show (running on an Atari) with an S1000 sampler at the desk, being driven by the sequencer. The three of us had MIDI guitars, which were played live, driving our own modules. Then, live vocals. The whole thing was dependent on the person mixing, as what was being played onstage was fundamentally an 'accompaniment' to the main body of the music coming from the sampler. We weren't really playing that much. We were just jamming on top of prepared tracks, really." Overall, Newman wasn't happy. "Those dates didn't work very well, and PK's live mix was pretty awful." Lewis is more upbeat: "It went down really well in Manchester because they were all off their heads on drugs: they completely got it!"

Meanwhile, the band's Sheffield gig ended in Spinal Tap territory. "We finished the set with 'Underwater Experiences'," recalls Newman, "and we had a lighting person with us who wanted to use smoke. Bruce said he could only use it on the last number. And he did. He released all of it at once. There was fog and smoke absolutely everywhere. We couldn't see a thing. We went down to the dressing room under the stage, and you couldn't see anything at all. It was quite dangerous, actually. It was one of those mad moments."

During the tour, Grey's absence was palpable. "It was strange," says Newman. "It didn't feel like there was enough of us to be a group. Wire has always been four people onstage. It has to be four people onstage. It just is. It wasn't horrible or arduous – it was quite fun – but it felt wrong. It was just odd." He also remembers the band adopting an unusual symbolic strategy to make up the numbers: the purchase of a suit that was almost big enough to accommodate an extra person. "I was like: How can we go onstage without Rob? It's going to be weird just being three people. It's going to be like someone's missing. So before the first gig in Edinburgh without Rob, we went to a second-hand shop, and I bought an oversized suit because Bruce seemed to think that would make it easier. It was another piece of classic Wire logic."

On balance, Lewis believes the tour was successful. "The dates were mixed, but I think we did well, considering. I understood what we were missing, which was the live drummer – something both visually interesting and propulsive. It's not something you can easily fill. But we had no choice, so we had to deal with it. We were as entertaining as we could be." Gilbert is less sure, feeling that the band's performances left something to be desired. "Generally speaking, we all knew there was something definitely missing – it was verging on the sterile. There seemed to be less room for the creative mistake. Quite often, it felt like we were simply executing the songs, rather than playing them."

For Gilbert, the absence of Grey was crucial, although what he sensed was lacking was, paradoxically, no longer a part of the version of Wire to which he, Newman, and Lewis were now committed. "There was a feeling of: where's the other one? And having this feeling of looking around and having Rob be there. There was a concern: Would the computer work? Is everybody ready? But with Rob there was always an organic feeling that he would know, that it was ready to go. With the computer, it didn't flow. And Rob would always start the song with that drumstick click. So it was all rather never-wracking without him, really."

| CHAPTER 9 |
| 1990–2000 |

## Under Erasure

Following their UK excursion in May, Bruce Gilbert, Graham Lewis, and Colin Newman were scheduled to play a series of summer dates in the United States. Rather than headline their own gigs, they had signed on as the opening act for Mute labelmates Erasure, who were on a world tour, still promoting their *Wild!* album from the previous year. This had been difficult to arrange since Wire's US record company (still Enigma) was unhappy with the band's lack of success and refused to provide any support. Nevertheless, Bryan Grant had managed to secure funds, and the tour was due to go ahead.

Erasure were acquaintances of the band (Vince Clarke had appeared on Gilbert and Lewis's fourth Dome album, as well as in the 'Eardrum Buzz' video), but Wire quickly began to doubt the wisdom of this undertaking. The question of funding gave Gilbert pause as he feared it might compromise Wire's creative freedom. "Bryan negotiated quite a lot of tour support, and I felt we were putting ourselves in an incredibly vulnerable position. You know what Americans are like – a little bit of power, and they will use it. I could envision a situation where somebody, some executive, would say: You really should play some of those old songs. This really isn't working for us – one of *those* phrases. So I expressed my doubts about whether this was a particularly happy way to approach a tour of America. All my instincts told me we shouldn't go."

As far as Newman was concerned, several factors conspired against this proposition. Spending time away from home wasn't very appealing. He had a young family and he was involved in his own projects in Brussels, having formed Oracle with spouse Malka Spigel and her Minimal Compact colleague Samy Birnbach. Moreover, the headliners and Wire were ill-matched. Erasure were a globally successful pop band, putting on elaborate arena shows for audiences who probably wouldn't have heard of Wire. It felt like 1979 all over again. "Erasure were just not the kind of group we should have been supporting," says Newman. "It seemed like the wrong thing to be doing. The more I thought about it, the more I hated the idea. I thought we should be with someone who might like what we do – and their audience wasn't going to like what we did. It was like going back to the Roxy Music tour."

More substantively, Newman had reservations about Wire's viability as a live band at this point. "The issue was: can we physically do it? We'd only recently lost Rob, and we weren't a stand-up band. We were so totally dependent on someone out front to make it sound like it was supposed to sound. It was fragile. We could make a record, but I didn't think we could be a live band. It was so dependent on a network of technology. We couldn't just do what Wire had always done, which was stand on a stage and play, and have it go through a PA, and what we play is what it is. So, the idea of a month and a half on the road in America just didn't seem possible, technically."

According to Newman, it was only Gilbert and he who were against the tour. "Graham just saw it as a chance to get more famous. He doesn't think about the practical details, about how you make something work – just about what it means. Bruce and I were more focused on the technology, and it didn't seem doable. Graham was royally pissed off and felt like he'd been betrayed: he thought it would have been good for him because he was more or less becoming the lead singer." Lewis doesn't articulate it in that way, but he does believe this may have been a missed opportunity for the band. "I'm still scratching my head about that one" is all he says.

Having gone to great lengths to make sure that the tour went ahead, Bryan Grant wasn't pleased to hear that the band wanted – at the 11th hour – to withdraw. "Bryan had worked incredibly hard to put it together, and it was the last straw for him," Gilbert recalls. "He just said: That's it. You've embarrassed me, so I think it's better we part company." Newman continues: "Bryan was royally pissed off as well because it was the final chance we had to do something for the mainstream. So he quit. He felt there was nothing for him to do anymore."

To Grant, the cancellation itself wasn't so much the issue; rather, its significance was as part of a wider pattern of dubious band decisions that had made his position as manager progressively less tenable, if not completely meaningless. There now appeared to be no way around his paradoxical status as someone whose job was to foster success for a band who, seemingly, didn't want to succeed. "I was exasperated. I couldn't see it going anywhere, because of this *perversity*. They're perverse as fuck! They wouldn't listen to what I said. There was a frustration with them. And

Britannia Row was getting more and more demanding, so it was like I couldn't afford the hobby – much as I loved them."

He called a meeting with the group at which he explained how absurd his role had become. "I sat down with them, and I said: What do you need a manager for? One: you need a manager to talk to your record company – but you know Daniel [Miller] better than I do, so you don't need me for that. Two: you need a manager to give you advice and steer your career, and you don't listen to a word I say – so you don't need me for that. And, lastly, you need a manager to manage your money – and you *certainly* don't need me for that! If you ever need me for anything, then give me a yell." (That parting shot was no empty pleasantry: Grant would answer a call almost 20 years later, during a time of crisis for the band, and offer assistance that would prove invaluable to Wire's continued existence.)

While at the time Grant found his position understandably frustrating, he recounts this last meeting with humour, and he has positive recollections of his tenure with the band. He describes what made it all worthwhile, again emphasising that Wire were a magnet for inventive, imaginative types: "They always had interesting people coming to shows – like Eno, painters, or someone quite unexpected who'd picked up on them. People got very much drawn into that 'thing' that was Wire – you felt you were inside something very special. They attracted interesting lighting or sound people like Simon Sidi, a well-known lighting and production designer now, and Simon Miles." (Sidi went on to work for the likes of Elton John, P. Diddy, Roger Waters, and Kanye West; Miles made a niche for himself in US television, doing lighting design for major shows such as *Dancing With The Stars* – a far cry from Wire's 1980 Electric Ballroom concert.) Grant recalls how these individuals found common cause with Wire and were attuned to the band's innovative outlook, exploring creative possibilities with scant resources. "Simon Miles was doing stuff with very little, but very dramatically – like gobo venetian-blind effects, black-and-white, and so forth. Very interesting stuff. And there were sound engineers, too, who went on to greater things. We were always experimenting. I remember when we surrounded the audience [at the Ratinger Hof] with the PA system, rather than having it just on the stage. We were always trying different things."

Grant's fondest memories are of being on the road in the late 70s – a place and a time he especially enjoyed. "It seemed like we were driving around for an eternity, in this white minibus – those interminable drives around the UK and Europe, listening to Bowie and Eno, and strange conversations that just went on and on. And it was always cold. Germany in the winter, Holland and Belgium. All dressed in black and looking grim, wearing these funny fur hats made of plastic and leather – Urtyp hats we called them [cheap promotional attire for a German beer company]. We looked like terrorists. They'd probably have shot us now. We used to smoke about 100 cigarettes a day. Dear, oh dear. How did we survive it? Heady days. The world was exciting. It was a good time in my life. Wire had a big effect on me. I just wish that during the time I managed them, I'd been able to do more for them ... but they weren't having any of *that*!"

After the cancellation of the US tour, in August Wire made a couple of live appearances in England: one at the Mean Fiddler in London and, two days later, at the Reading Festival – an afternoon slot on the main stage, at the foot of the bill between The Young Gods and Psychic TV.

## The triangular trade-off

Regardless of their mixed feelings about live work, the band pressed ahead in 1991 with a new studio album, *The First Letter* – to be released under the name Wir. The record was assembled in the Worldwide programming suite at Mute, where the band had done much of the preparation for the *Manscape* tour. They felt this was the perfect workplace for their trimmed-down, electronically oriented incarnation, as Newman recalls: "Because we'd been programming there for that tour, it seemed logical. We were programming, putting the material together, and what we needed was somewhere with samplers, synthesizers, some computers running Cubase, and minimal recording gear – just somewhere we could put our ideas together and then make them into a production. The programming suite had everything we needed for that. It was eminently sensible. It had a great buzz about it. It was nicely scruffy. It was a great place to work. Everyone worked there – well, maybe not Depeche Mode."

Recording as a three-piece, the band-members immediately noticed Grey's absence, just as they had done in live performance. Unsurprisingly, Lewis highlights the rhythm tracks on *The First Letter* as a component that would have benefited from Grey's expertise, had the latter chosen to investigate that creative avenue. "The three of us composed without a drummer, and I think you can hear that – it has its strengths and weaknesses. We weren't drummers, but we had to compose rhythms. I thought Rob would understand that, being a drummer – he would know how to programme rhythms with this technology. I don't. I always look to people who specialise in punctuating, creating melodic sounds from percussive materials."

Gilbert also missed Grey's contribution: not in terms of how he might have reinvented his role and helped Wire come up with more convincing rhythmic patterns, but on a more essential working level – often at the core of the music's genesis. Again, it's interesting that what he felt was lacking – Grey's intuitive, human presence as a drummer – was something the band had decided was no longer part of Wire's identity. "When we were cooking things up in the studio," he remembers, "we were using a drum machine, just to get things going. It's different. Quite often, Rob's input was quite subtle: if it didn't feel right to him, he'd slow it down or speed it up, until it was at its correct speed for the way he was feeling about the song. If we wanted to, say, do it really fast, we could now just turn a knob, but with a drum machine it just wasn't the same dynamic." Consequently, Gilbert wasn't brimming with confidence about the sessions. "We were determined to make an object of some worth, but because it was created in a different way, we were fairly unsure of what we were doing. It felt very worthwhile to do it, but it felt terribly different."

Newman believed that Grey's absence from this project made an even more profound difference, fundamentally changing the nature of their endeavour. In addition to it no longer being Wire, to Newman it was no longer really a group. "With Wir, it always felt that there was someone missing. It really did feel incredibly fragile in a way that made it seem it wasn't ever going to last. It was fun doing *The First Letter*, but it didn't feel like it was a band. It was like the feeling of the first gig we did, and there being a gaping hole in it. It just wasn't 'it' any more. Rob has always been almost invisible within the band, and he's not always had the highest status and not always been given the most respect, but he proved his point with his absence. It wasn't Wire without him. So let's not pretend it was Wire."

Beyond the challenges of making and performing music as a trio, there was now another important issue that Wir had to face: the potentially destabilising effect of Grey's departure on band politics and decision-making. Given Wire's fractured history during the 80s, which had already seen Newman quit because of his dissatisfaction with Gilbert and Lewis's approach to the work, a three-piece line-up didn't seem very promising. Insofar as Lewis and Gilbert had traditionally formed a strong bloc within Wire, it appeared that Newman's minority status in Wir would make his situation impossible. "You would have thought so," he says, "but there's something weird about a triangle. Triangles are a bit more stable and, strangely, in some ways, my position was more secure than it had ever been. It was quite a democratic process with three."

271

Newman's democracy, however, hinged on what he perceived as Gilbert and Lewis's weaker position. In Newman's view, they were now conscious of the fact that they were in a precarious situation, knowing that he could end the band by leaving, if he chose to do so. As he explains: "You're getting down to pay-dirt here. If you want to be totally brutal, if I'm gone, they've got Dome; they haven't got Wire." He adds: "I didn't think in those terms, but it must have occurred to me in some way that I had some sense of power."

## A more modern process

Working in Worldwide's programming suite made sense to Newman especially because it facilitated the kind of creative approach that was increasingly prevalent at the start of the 90s, as electronic dance music infiltrated the pop mainstream. While *The Drill* and *Manscape* were hardly mainstream pop records, they had obviously been influenced, in concept and execution, by this change in sensibility. *The First Letter* reflected a more fully realised exploration of the new working methods. "Compared to *Manscape*, it was a more, as it were, *modern* process," observes Newman, who felt in sync with this shift toward the production culture of dance music.

He was particularly interested in the way the digital culture of dance music de-emphasised the conventional studio environment as the primary site of creative activity. With the right equipment, most of the work could now be done at home, the studio only necessary in the later stages. "I had exactly the same equipment at home as you did when you made a record," says Newman. "That was already a firmly established idea with me, going back to the late 80s. I wanted to have the same thing. It was how a lot of mainstream dance-music production was done: you'd make all the music in your bedroom, and then you'd take it into the studio to finish and mix it and put vocals on it. That was the model. For Wire, it seemed the inevitable way of working."

To Newman, despite their "fragility", Wire as a three-piece were potentially a very contemporary concern. Now more than when they had reformed in 1985, they were in step with the zeitgeist. "It wasn't a period of rock music," he says, "and Wir wasn't really a rock band." Mute's programming suite was therefore ideal since it was an in-house version of the bedroom studio, with all the necessary tools, in which the three members of the band could make the album.

Dance music's working methods and technology were attractive to Newman above all because they blurred the orthodox division between producer and artist, facilitating a much more direct role in the development of the material from the outset. This was just what he wanted. "Wir was now a different band, the dynamic was different. I didn't care that much about being the front man now. I wanted to be the producer. I was starting to take more of an engineer/producer type of role. That was what I really wanted. I didn't like the way *Manscape* had been mixed, but I'd guided it into really interesting places through a long process of production starting with the initial making of the pieces."

Newman considers the making of *The First Letter* a key phase in his continuing apprenticeship as Wire's producer. Although Paul Kendall would be brought in to co-produce and mix the album, Newman was at the centre of the process from early on, preparing rough mixes as the band worked alone at Worldwide. "I sort of fell into that," he says, "because I was quicker with the machines. I was the only one with my own studio. It was similar to the way *Manscape* was done, but it was very much me making material or 'playbacks' out of what the others were giving me. It's 180 degrees from *A Bell Is A Cup* – that was about songwriting. This isn't about songwriting; this was about production. I was very excited that I could do that, that I could do it with my hands, that I could make those things. I was basically acting like the engineer. You can see that with what I was putting together at this point, through all the rough mixes. Those are very much things that I'd put together from Bruce and Graham's content. I was recording everything they did and then figuring out ways to make it work within the piece we were working on."

Newman's account of the band-members' differing attitudes to the methodology, and his description of how those attitudes informed the division of labour, underscore Wire's long-established creative dichotomy. Gilbert and Lewis were focused on the process; Newman was more concerned with the end product. "I was in charge of all the equipment. What I discovered through *Manscape* and *The First Letter* was that what really mattered to me was the way it was done, because the way it was done was going to influence the final outcome. That didn't matter to Bruce and Graham. They didn't seem to care about that at all. They were just happy to do it. So with *The First Letter* and with *Manscape*, which I also didn't mix, I was preparing the way which came to fruition with *Send* – that is, using Wire as raw material to make compositions out of. That was how they liked working. That's how they worked with other people when they did Dome stuff. There wasn't really any opposition to me organising it all. They'd just say whether they liked it or not. As long as I could make something that was

273

convincing for everybody, then it seemed to be OK for me to do that. So on one level, it was all my material."

Lewis confirms Newman's centrality in the making of the record, but also stresses his and Gilbert's roles. "Colin ended up at the workstation end of it, banging things in, but in terms of where rhythms or whatever came from, it was a mixed thing. With sampling, it comes from various directions, and Paul was involved later on. It wasn't just one person's responsibility. The process felt very natural to the three of us. We knew how it worked. It kept revealing things, and it kept expanding. It felt creative – and there's some fantastic songs on it."

It's interesting that Lewis should use the word 'songs' in relation to this project: the band's revised strategy for making a record, as Newman conceived it, actually abandoned a song-based process. Ironically, this didn't prevent the band coming up with songs, as Lewis suggests. One of them, 'So And Slow It Grows', would be another Wir(e) hit that never was.

The decision not to approach this album in songwriting-and-arranging mode was a significant about-face for Newman, after his discomfort through much of the 80s with the band's efforts to compose in the studio and the resultant depriviledging of his role as writer. *Manscape*'s flawed attempt to make songs had been a pivotal experience for him. "I wasn't thinking of it in terms of songs now," he says, "they were just pieces. Each one began with just a different mood. We'd start with an idea, and I'd build it up and take it somewhere where I liked it. It wasn't about writing songs." It's possible that what enabled him finally to become comfortable with this method was that he no longer felt a loss of control and importance, thanks to his increasing participation in production – directing and shaping the material.

### An odd fish

Newman's enthusiasm for *The First Letter* ends largely with the completion of his rough mixes of the material – before Kendall took a more prominent role. In conversations about the album for this book, Newman generally brought the focus back to its pre-Kendall incarnation. "What I remember more than anything was the pre-production," he says. "That was fun. We worked pretty hard to put things together. I didn't like the final result because I didn't like the way that PK mixed it."

Newman had never been keen on having Kendall involved in the first place, believing he wasn't up to the job. "I thought it was a terrible idea to have Paul Kendall produce it. He was a mate of Bruce and Graham's, and I

274

was outvoted on it. You've got to have someone you trust to mix it. I wouldn't have been allowed to mix it. It's obvious. Gilles Martin could have done it, but he'd worked on my late-80s solo records, so he couldn't be included, because of the politics of the situation."

Chief among Newman's concerns was Kendall's musical know-how – or, as he saw it, lack thereof. "I like Paul as a person. He's an odd fish. He's not really interested in music. He likes to do stuff that's really experimental. He had his own label [Parallel Series] in the 90s, through Mute. It was all far-flung electronic, not the most listenable sort of thing. That's what he was into. He had no business mixing a Wire record, really. I don't think Mute wanted to spend any money on us. It was all done in-house, and Paul was cheap because he was on the payroll." From Newman's perspective, Kendall's predilection for more extreme experimental approaches aligned him with the Gilbert–Lewis axis of the trio. His participation in the record therefore posed a threat to the balance of Wir's triangular democracy.

Kendall certainly gravitated more to Gilbert and Lewis. They were accomplished drinking companions (he and Newman rarely socialised), and more importantly, he had forged a solid working relationship with the pair. Even within the context of Wir, Kendall tellingly refers to them, collectively, as "Dome", as he discusses their contribution to *The First Letter*. In addition to reinforcing the sense that they came as a bloc – often with common ideas and opinions – by referring to them with the name of their other project, Kendall is alluding to a creative philosophy and to practices that didn't always square with Newman's vision of Wire.

Kendall was closest to Gilbert, with whom he shared a broader artistic sensibility. Indeed, he confirms one of Newman's observations, remarking that he wasn't drawn to Gilbert's work "*musically* [but], more accurately, *artistically*, as music has never interfered with the process of experimentation". Kendall admired Gilbert as an artist and enjoyed working with him. "Bruce's role within Wire was an *oblique strategy* – not exactly true but in essence very close. He would always find a sound that, while seemingly oblique, was absolutely perfect. Sessions with Bruce could shoot off in many directions, and if there were blockages there was always the possibility of a couple of beers to mull over life. Bruce always gave me space to express myself, acting as an editor of the Chinese takeaway – two of number 43 with a dash of 31. As much as he knew what he liked, he wouldn't be averse to saying if something was wrong. Communication was always easy, even without the ale. It was similar with Graham. I always felt the freedom to be creative, which is not always the case when engineering for artists.

Graham and Bruce were always easier for me to understand and communicate with."

The tension between Dome and Newman during the sessions was something of which Kendall was well aware, and while his artistic sympathies lay with Lewis and Gilbert, he was mindful of the need to balance the competing orientations. As he recalled in a 1996 interview with the Wire Mail Order newsletter: "Colin was the only one who knew how to operate the sequencer. And because of their different approaches it was a trifle unfair, and I think there was quite a lot of frustration from Graham and Bruce that they weren't more involved. There were a lot of battles between myself and Colin … I suppose, in the end, I knew that Colin was looking over my shoulder so I had to do something that would keep him quiet, and at the same time make Graham and Bruce happy."

Kendall was also aware that this dichotomy was a vital part of Wire's successful creative identity and that his role was not to resolve that tension but to accommodate and sustain it. "I can't say specifically that there were any fractures in the band at this point, because there were always polarities," he comments, "Colin on one side, Dome on the other. Daniel Miller has said the beauty of Wire came from the ebb and flow of these polarities. I cannot disagree."

## Self-consuming artefacts

*The First Letter* attracts a similar level of critical opprobrium to *Manscape*, albeit unjustly. While it's not in the same league as the band's 70s recordings, it deserves more credit than it receives. After Wire's inconsistent 80s output, *The First Letter* is a breath of fresh air, balancing experimentation and a pop sensibility in the spirit of some of their most enjoyable work: it sounds like serious fun.

As the band-members recount it, there was a ludic, adventurous aspect to the way they had created *Manscape*, but it ultimately sounded as if they were working in a technological straitjacket; *The First Letter*, by contrast, gives the impression of a freer, more unrestrained process. Here, the technology functions not as an impediment but as a tool and a means to an end. In those terms, the record has more in common with *The Drill* than with its immediate predecessor. Like *The Drill*, *The First Letter* preserves the feeling of creative freedom that lay at the core of the process, a more direct link between the ideas and the execution – compared with the Byzantine technological mediation of *Manscape*. As a result, it's not surprising that there should be noticeably more range and diversity to this material, the

BLOOMSBURY FESTIVAL

SUNDAY 21 JULY 1985

THE SHIVERING MAN

BY ANGELA CONWAY
MUSIC: B.C. GILBERT
CAST: MICHAEL CLARK
JULIE HOOD
A BIG MAN

INTERVAL

WIRE

TONIGHT'S PERFORMANCE IS AN EXTRA EVENT TO THE
BLOOMSBURY FESTIVAL

**RIGHT:** The programme for Wire's gig at the Bloomsbury Theatre, July 1985.
**BELOW:** Four people in a room: a portrait of the band taken in Kings Cross, London, in around 1987; Newman and Lewis performing 'Up To The Sun' at the Messepalast in Vienna, Austria, October 1985.

**ABOVE:** The Ex-Lion Tamers, who toured with Wire in summer 1987. *LEFT TO RIGHT*: Jim DeRogatis, Mick Hale, John Tanzer, Pete Pedulla.
**BELOW:** Newman and Gilbert onstage at the Rose Bowl in Pasadena, California, June 1988.
**FACING PAGE ABOVE:** The three-piece Wir, photographed in 1991 by Stefan de Batselier.
**FACING PAGE BELOW:** Wir in London, 1991.

**FACING PAGE ABOVE:** Wire self-portrait, Chicago, 2003.
**ABOVE LEFT:** Postcard sent out by the band – now with Grey back in the line-up – with mail order copies of the first *Read & Burn* EP, 2002.
**ABOVE RIGHT:** Gilbert and Lewis in conversation at the Angel pub in Soho, London, May 2007.
**BELOW:** *flag:burning* at the Barbican, London, April 2003, with each member of the band performing in his own plywood box as part of Es Devlin's stage set.

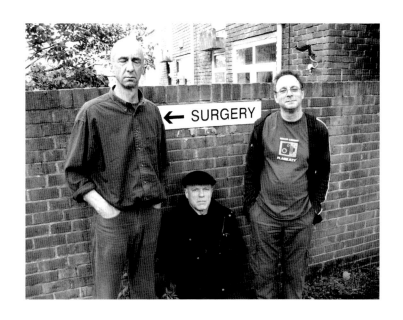

**FACING PAGE ABOVE:** Grey, Lewis, and Newman in Southfields, South West London, 2007.
**FACING PAGE BELOW:** Newman, Grey, and new recruit Matthew Simms at the Bowery Ballroom, New York City, April 2011.
**ABOVE:** Newman, Lewis, and Grey at La Machine Du Moulin Rouge in Paris, May 2011.

**ABOVE:** Newman at work on *Change Becomes Us* at Rockfield Studios near Monmouth, Wales, April 2012.
**BELOW:** Lewis and Grey during the Rockfield sessions.

band-members liberated to go off in all sorts of directions, able to pursue ideas with greater spontaneity.

The first track, 'Take It (For Greedy)', encapsulates the album's modus operandi. Not only was it constructed out of samples, but they were all lifted from Wire's own music. The title of the original work file for the track – 'Strange' – makes no secret of the starting point, as the chunky riff-fragment introducing the number is instantly recognisable as Gilbert's. Also somewhere in the piece are residual elements of 'Straight Line' and 'Another The Letter', among others.

"'Take It' I did basically at home," says Newman. "It's basically all samples out of Wire records, virtually everything – definitely things off *Pink Flag*. Graham just sang all over it. I got so pissed off about it, but I remember being very excited by the original version. Making a track out of Wire samples seemed to me to be an extremely funny thing to do."

The departed Grey appears on this track in sampled form. "The snare was a Rob snare," recalls Newman, "taken from wherever I could find one on its own on one of the 70s albums." Grey has never listened to *The First Letter*. "Definitely not!" he says. "It's not really something I want to be reminded of." Since he was no longer a member of the band at this juncture, his continued virtual presence puts a different spin on the Wire axiom, 'You can't leave Wire'. Usually, this refers to the notion that, even if a band-member quits, there is no escape: no matter what he does beyond the group, he will always be defined by his work with Wire. "Everyone apart from Graham has left at least once," jokes Newman, "and the only reason he hasn't left is because he didn't think of it first."

While 'Take It (For Greedy)' is deeply self-referential in musical terms, with its echoes of 'Strange', it ends up sounding almost completely other – more like a chilly reimagining of Robert Palmer's 'Addicted To Love' than Wire. Newman's self-quoting approach to the music would prove ironic a couple of years later, when Elastica appropriated elements of 'Three Girl Rhumba' and 'I Am The Fly' for their songs 'Connection' and 'Line Up' – coming back for more in 2000 and taking 'Lowdown' as the basis for 'Human'. In light of this conspicuous consumption of Wire's work, Gilbert's lyric (a litany of phrases involving the word 'take') was prescient. "It's about greed and some people's capacity to take everything that's not screwed down," he explains. "I don't mean that just literally but conceptually as well."

But Gilbert had no objections to Elastica's use of Wire's music. "I thought it was amusing and flattering. I thought it was fascinating," he comments. Newman was less pleased, mostly because it was reported, falsely, that he

285

had given Elastica his blessing to borrow from 'Three Girl Rhumba'. Contrary to popular myth, Wire did not initiate any legal action over this: their music publisher, Carlin, had simply approved the appropriation after consulting with a musicologist provided by Elastica's publisher. (Wire didn't receive any significant payment and only learned about the deal after the fact. Not only was 'Connection' a successful single, but Elastica also did well from advertising deals with Budweiser and Garnier hair products, who soundtracked US television commercials with the song; in the UK, Channel 4's *Trigger Happy TV* used it as theme music. 'Three Girl Rhumba' itself was adopted for a European H&M commercial in 2004.)

From the opening track of *The First Letter*, the handling of the vocals is striking. In general, Wire's 80s records had been unimaginative in that respect, the vocal parts often sounding like little more than placeholders – for the most part one-dimensional and occupying the same prominent, clean space from one track to the next. The difference here is bold and refreshing, the band re-embracing the voice's possibilities, investigating its potential in terms of processing and manipulation, as well as its placement and emphasis in the mix. On many tracks, this contributes to a deconstruction of the straightforward 'lead' vocal, which in turn undermines the material's conventional narrative point-of-view. The album benefits enormously from this. From *Pink Flag* onward, Wire's lyrics themselves (above all Lewis's) regularly displayed this sense of fragmented perspective, but it was seldom enacted or represented in the sound and arrangement of the vocals. An early, dramatic, exception was *154*'s 'Indirect Enquiries', of course, on which Newman's voice had spawned "mad munchkins" to bring the song to its unbalanced conclusion; while not included in the written lyrics, Lewis's interjections during Newman's lead vocal on 'I Feel Mysterious Today' have a similar effect of destabilising the main narrative voice. *The First Letter* revisits these strategies: rather than being centred around a single, discrete vocal part, the songs tend to be *decentred*, owing to their disjointed, sometimes competing voices.

On 'Take It (For Greedy)', Lewis's lead vocal is split into two distinct voices singing the same words – one almost falsetto and detached, the other huskier and more foregrounded. The feeling of fragmentation is heightened by moving the two in and out of sync and by occasionally having one voice drop out and yield to the other – for the aggressive, in-your-face "take the lot" line, for example.

Although Lewis is the album's dominant vocal presence, Newman adds to the proliferation of voices. The interplay of the two is accentuated on

'Looking At Me (Stop!)'. This is one of the more pronounced instances of the album's inclination toward fractured narratives: the schizophrenic tendency intensifies with the combination of Lewis's voice – coming from different spaces within the track – and Newman's contributions, particularly in the contrast between his chirpy nonsense ("Up down here there nowhere / Bus stop hope stop all flop") and Lewis's clenched-teeth, end-of-my-tether tone.

Playful levity runs throughout, often amplified by this inventive approach to the vocals: the rather perfunctory dance beat on 'Looking At Me (Stop!)', for instance, could be cited as evidence of the album's weak rhythmic foundations were it not for Newman's wobbly refrain sending up that aspect of the song ("I'm looking at life and I'm looking at rhythm / I have two left feet, can't do nothing with them"). 'Footsi-Footsi' is another good example of how the arrangement of Lewis and Newman's vocal parts enhances the uniqueness of this record, as Lewis's dark impressions of capitalism vie with Newman's singsong melody. (With its title referencing the *Financial Times*–Stock Exchange index [FTSE], the song is, thematically, very much a companion piece to 'Take It'.)

### All the same, the songs remain

Beyond the vocal component, the tracks display further schizophrenic impulses, leaning again toward the eccentric rather than the centred and cohesive. At its most exploratory, and in keeping with the construction method, *The First Letter* diverges from traditional song structure to embrace experimentation in the best way – not in po-faced, alienating terms, but in a mischievous fashion that goes right back to *Pink Flag*. The old tactic of the manipulated frame, for example, is reprised on 'A Bargain At 3 And 20 Yeah!' This 2:55 track is essentially all introduction: a 2:18 preface composed of looped noise and a Lewis monologue builds tension, increasing the listener's anticipation of what will come next. When the moment of release arrives, the actual body of the 'song' – Newman's word-associating spiel – is compressed into the final 36 seconds.

'Naked, Whooping And Such-Like (Extended On And On)' is the most noteworthy non-song, thanks to the involvement of the late French music writer Claude Bessy, a member of the highly select club of guest vocalists to appear on Wire albums. Like some dissolute Gallic cousin of Quentin Crisp, he recites Lewis's text as memorably as he held forth on the subject of new wave in Penelope Spheeris's *The Decline Of Western Civilization*. Lewis felt that Bessy was the right man to deliver his mostly indecipherable prose. "I wrote the text using an Old English dictionary of slang, which is why there are so many archaic nautical terms in it. Unless you knew the translation, you had no idea what it meant. What kicked me on was the idea of getting Claude to read it, because I knew we'd get something really special."

Adding another layer of oddness to the disembodied voice and its enigmatic words is the distressed sound of the medium itself – Bessy's part is a distinctly lo-fi analogue affair, taped at home. "I sent it to Claude," recalls Lewis, "and he recorded it on an old cassette player. Then we chopped it up. We originally set it to the music, but Dan said: don't do that, it's such a waste – separate it. That was a great idea." Bessy's monologue lasts less than a minute and a half, after which the track morphs into something else entirely: a motorik instrumental passage stretches out for another five minutes, with some fleeting punctuation from Bessy's sampled wheezing snigger. Far more than a postscript to the spoken section, the unrelated second part has a life of its own. It's also forward-looking, in a retro sort of way – its streamlined Teutonic pulse anticipating a later strand of techno that would mine the more electronic side of Krautrock for inspiration.

At the other end of the spectrum, the lush, melancholy 'So And Slow It Grows' is unmistakably an outstanding *song* – despite the emphasis on assemblage and construction as the album's basic methodology. This is a Lewis vehicle, displaying strong sonic ties to the cool, dark electronic pop of his 80s solo albums. It could be described as Wire's 'Avalon' moment – as 'Avalon' is to 'Re-Make/Re-Model', so 'So And Slow It Grows' is to 'Pink Flag'. For Lewis, it represents what the album might have been. "If all of the tracks had been given the amount of money and attention which was given to 'So And Slow', it would be a record that people are still talking about. I'm so incredibly proud of that track."

As with *Manscape*'s 'You Hung Your Lights In The Trees/A Craftsman's Touch', the odd track out on this album is also one of the most memorable: in this case the unsettling electro-ballad, 'Ticking Mouth'. Sung-spoken by Bruce Gilbert, it eschews the fragmented narrative that dominates much of *The First Letter*, in favour of a coherent, unified, and consistent voice (although Lewis does burst in midway through to proclaim in Swedish, "Jag vill ha dej!").

The rigid inevitability of this song's clockwork mechanism suits the grim inexorability of its subject matter – a variation on the Floydian "hanging on in quiet desperation is the English way" theme. This is the most nakedly emotional track Wire have ever recorded. Obviously, there's no shortage of emotional content in their work, and they do have songs of love and hate, but they rarely approach such themes in a literal or unironic fashion. 'Fragile', for example, is a love song, if a slightly obscure one; a more extreme instance is the notorious 'Three Girl Rhumba' – a Newman song actually inspired by three real women, but you'd never know it. Although it's challenging to tackle emotional material head-on (and in rhyme) and to emerge with your artistic credibility intact – given the instant perils of maudlinism, cliché, self-indulgence, and sentimentality – Gilbert carries it off here. It's a further testament to his skill as a lyricist.

Part of the song's success derives from the gap between Gilbert's understated, matter-of-fact vocal and the raw, intense feeling he's articulating – it's a bare-bones vignette of a doomed relationship, with scarcely a hint of emotion in his neutral delivery. His command of stark, concise imagery is crucial: he portrays barely controlled, violent emotion ("Smiles like bullets"; "A raging silence"), as well as a broader, chronic sense of the relationship's implacable decline ("A numbing cold that weakens the will"). The refrain, "I hear a ticking in your voice" (and its variant, "I hear a ticking in your heart"), is a powerful evocation of finitude and time running out; the image's time-bomb nuance, with its more extreme implications, only intensifies the emotional charge. Gilbert is even able to use the clichéd metaphor "looks that could kill" without it sounding remotely clichéd, also attesting to the simple power of the song's scenario. In this context, he somehow reinvests the hackneyed figure of speech with its original signifying powers, as if we're hearing it for the first time.

Gilbert talks about the track: "I did a demo for 'Ticking Mouth' at home, and they said: you've got to sing it. It was about a relationship, like 'Two People In A Room' – but taken to a conclusion where the clock is just ticking, and you know it's going to end. You're aware of someone's patience running out and the changing exchange, the changing tone of conversations, with someone you've known for a very long time. It's a bit like a ticking clock that you know at some time is going to crack."

Throughout his tenure in Wire, Gilbert was unwilling to provide vocals, mainly because of a concern that, if he sang on a studio recording, he might then have to perform it onstage. "I'd be required to sing live," he says, "and that would be an impossibility" – due both to his shyness and to the fact that just playing his instrument was an ordeal in itself. Nonetheless, he did perform 'Ticking Mouth' in concert. "I think we only did it once. It was a ridiculous notion because I can't sing. I've never been so terrified in my life. To get around the horror of it, I sat on a stool, and

I had a cream suit on – I had to get into a mind-set where I could take the piss out of it. God, it was appalling. Absolutely appalling. It was always hard enough for me to concentrate on playing the guitar, because I'm not very good. So after a diversion like that, I need to sit down and have a cigarette and a beer – not carry on playing. The one advantage was that we had a setup with the computer doing the backing track, but it was eventually too fraught with potential disasters, especially with the state of computers then, which were very, very delicate. The slightest surge from the club's electricity, and it was disastrous."

Newman singles out Gilbert's performance on this track as something unique. "I recorded the original of that vocal, and I remember being quite close to tears. Bruce has something in his voice which is really quite disturbing. There is an emotional depth there, but he doesn't reveal it very often. Maybe he doesn't like to sing because it's emotionally too revealing."

## Tweed jackets, buckets, and freaky guitars

When they reflect on *The First Letter*, some band-members sound characteristically unconvinced by their own album. Newman again chooses to damn it with faint praise, describing it as a marginal improvement on their weakest work. "It's a peculiar record. It's only better than *Manscape* because it's not as horribly mixed. There are some good bits." Not that he's happy with the mix on *The First Letter* either, of course. He returns to this issue: "I absolutely hated the way PK mixed the Wir record. That was a way better record than how it turned out, because PK thought he needed to make it sound more weird. And it wasn't weird. It was interestingly constructed, but it wasn't an obviously weird record. He made it less musical because he wasn't a musician. I always said that I could mix it better." His final remark about the record seems to address the band's Mute period as a whole: "Why did we manage to make such a pig's ear of doing pop music?"

While he doesn't talk explicitly about the mix, Lewis feels the material was never properly realised. "It's so full of great ideas and harmonies, different angles that didn't get hunted down completely. You need time and money to do that. It would have been an incredible record." Nevertheless, he's more pleased with it than Newman. "It still sounds special. A couple of things perhaps aren't quite as good as the rest, but the range is astonishing. It reflects how hard we really did try to put our differences away and concentrate on the work and get it right." Gilbert is more economical in his evaluation. "I thought it was OK. I didn't think it was a masterpiece. It was adequate." Producer Kendall is even more succinct: "It was nearly a monster."

Designed by Gilbert associate Russell Haswell, the cover art for *The First Letter* was plain and simple. For the vinyl edition, the bare white outer sleeve had a functional, anti-design appearance: it was styled as a white-label release, in a fake generic bag with a rectangular sticker affixed, bearing the band name, title, label information, and catalogue number – all in the same distinctive font. The label on the record itself (visible through the sleeve's cut-out centre) matched this aesthetic, displaying only the catalogue number. The rendering of the group's name on the artwork was subtly inventive: the *first letter* of the name Wir is not actually a letter but a horizontally placed '3' (Lewis's idea), self-referentially stressing the number of band-members. Inside the sleeve was a folded poster (with a centre cut-out), one side bearing a colourful computer-generated collage of beagles, a bee, and an Indian postage stamp, the other featuring the song lyrics and an image of a Greek sculpture. All of this worked well in the 12-inch format, but the condensing of the poster's contents into the confined space of the CD booklet wasn't as effective, and the vinyl white-label look didn't translate to the CD packaging.

Haswell also designed the sleeve for the 'So And Slow It Grows' single, incorporating materials supplied by Lewis: a modified postcard image of a squid drying on a clothesline and a photograph of a life belt. 'So And Slow It Grows' was the most obvious choice for a single, and it was the last of the band's Mute era. Supported by the obligatory video (directed by Angela Conway), it again seemed destined to bring the band some commercial reward. 'Kidney Bingos' this was not. Although the video is not particularly creative and lacks any interesting substance, it's an attractive, polished promo clip. Moody, monochromatic images pass by in a dreamlike, seamless flow, composed largely of the band in stylised music-video-mime mode, while some de rigueur stock footage of plants growing enacts Lewis's words (another tired, overly literal music-video trope). The fleeting slow-motion appearance of a pristine dove is presumably intended as a poignant symbol of something or other. However, the bird's presence unavoidably calls to mind another less dignified feathered friend from the 'Kidney Bingos' video – The Pope of Pop – thereby instantly undercutting any of the poetic gravitas it might have.

Of interest to Wire buffs is a glimpse of Newman, who had previously favoured a short back and sides, now sporting a luxuriant shoulder-length mane. Gilbert, meanwhile, is attired in a white suit and white gloves and injects absurdity into the otherwise sober proceedings by miming a guitar performance in a non-realist fashion. But even with this appealing visual calling card, the single failed to make any impact.

Wir did little to promote *The First Letter*. In July 1991, three months before its release, they played a one-off gig at the Mean Fiddler; more auspiciously, at the Kilburn National on October 24, they opened for Blur, then in the first flush of success with *Leisure* (and managed by none other than Mick Collins). Wir didn't go down well. "They came on wearing tweed jackets and tied buckets up with rope," remembers Blur guitarist Graham Coxon, "and the audience were very rude to them. They had freaky guitars rigged up to freaky noise-making boxes. It was pretty difficult stuff, and the audience were telling them to go away."

Newman didn't enjoy the evening. "That was weird. Suddenly, from being quite an important band, we were just some other group. We were very much the support band." He spoke briefly to "Him" from Blur, who waxed enthusiastic about his band's plans. "I've never had a huge amount of time for 'Him', but we were kind of talking and he said: we're all 60s now, but we're going to be 70s soon – we've been listening to a lot of your stuff." It was a strange encounter, to be sure: Wire doing their utmost to move forward and produce original work, with very little to show for it, and Blur – a band inspired by Wire – looking backward, on the way to millionaire-dom.

Gilbert wasn't concerned with Wir's status, but like Newman he did feel some ambivalence about what they were doing. "The trio was OK. It changed the sound. It developed into a wall-of-sound kind of approach, which seemed the best way to approach it since we had this pre-recorded drum track. But it was almost like we were over-compensating, so people wouldn't notice that there was a rather sterile backing track. I think we just did it naturally, as a reaction to being a three-piece with no human being to back us up." Grey's absence continued to nag at Gilbert, with specific regard to the band's live work. "I think there was a constant sense of something missing. Not just the music. His physical presence. Rob was probably the most interesting thing to look at in Wire."

Eventually, Wir came to a halt. For Newman, this was inevitable because it had been a flawed undertaking from the beginning. "It sort of petered out because it couldn't exist. It was the wrong thing. I don't think it should have gone on. I think it was misguided." Lewis didn't see Wir in such fatalistic terms. From his perspective, the band was simply eclipsed by a need for him to pursue his own work, a feeling that had become more acute since his relocation to Sweden. "I had to get on and engage somehow because I was finding it quite difficult to be here. The thing to do was to start building some kind of network – to start doing work and see where it led."

As for Gilbert, he saw it as the end of a cycle, just as 1980 had been. He believed this was the right moment to set the band aside and to shift attention to other artistic opportunities. "We generally agreed it was time to give it a bit of a rest and have a rethink about what Wire could be – should we want to do it again – and to give ourselves enough time to think about it and enough time to get on with our own stuff." For Newman, too, this wasn't necessarily the end of Wire, just the conclusion of a chapter. "I didn't think that, because the 1990s wasn't the time for Wire, that was the end of what one could do."

## Hobbies and extra-curricular activities

With Wire out of commission again, their profile was boosted by a couple of retrospective releases. In 1993, Mute's *Wire 1985–1990: The A List* collected 16 tracks from the band's time on the label; *Behind The Curtain*, a 31-track CD issued by EMI in 1995, assembled then-unreleased live tracks from the April 1 1977 Roxy show, along with demo recordings from 1977 and 1978 (mostly *Pink Flag*, *Chairs Missing*, and *154* material).

The flame was also kept burning during the 90s by the fan-run Wire Mail Order (WMO) newsletter, launched in 1994 to report the band-members' activities and to relay sundry bits of Wire information. With the band's blessing, it evolved into a record label that made unheard Wire nuggets available and reissued various Gilbert and Lewis-related projects. The most notable WMO ventures were *Turns And Strokes* (1996), *Whore* (1996), and *Coatings* (1997). The first of these covers the tail end of Wire's time at EMI, via hitherto unreleased live numbers (including a few from the Jeannetta Cochrane and Electric Ballroom shows) and a rehearsal track – plus 'Catapult 30' and 'Second Length (Our Swimmer)' from the 'Crazy About Love' 12-inch. *Coatings* gathered alternate versions and marginalia from the band's 80s incarnation. *Whore* compiled 21 Wire songs covered by an array of artists, among them My Bloody Valentine, Lee Ranaldo, Lush, Godflesh, Bark Psychosis, Mike Watt, Main, and The Ex-Lion Tamers. (Another WMO release, *Dugga Dugga Dugga*, followed in 1998, consisting wholly of 'Drill' covers.)

Although on hiatus, Gilbert, Lewis, and Newman did reconvene for a couple of Wir performances that took place in April 1992 and February 1993. These were part of two larger events, both titled *I Saw You*, featuring Dome, Paul Kendall (as Piquet), and Jon Wozencroft and Russell Haswell (as

AER). Newman even reprised his massed-guitars ensemble, which had last seen action at the Jeannetta Cochrane gig. "It was Bruce's thing, a sort of 'let's assemble the gang'," says Newman of the *I Saw You* shows. "Wir was only a part of it. There was a whole performance. It was fun, but Wir didn't seem central. It had just become something Bruce wanted to do – and we just appeared in it. That's how it felt. It didn't seem very important. It wasn't Wire. It wasn't a big thing in your life any more, just something you did sometimes. It seemed like a bit of a hobby. The 90s wasn't really Wire's time in any shape or form."

The first *I Saw You* event was staged at the Clapham Grand on general election night, with a poor turnout; the other was held with more success the following year in Vienna, as part of the tenth birthday celebrations for the Szene club. During their stay, Wir also visited the ORF, Austria's public service broadcaster, recording two tracks for the *MusicBox* programme: the pumping 'Sexy And Rich (Janet)' and 'The First Letter', a 16-minute industrial-tribal onslaught on which Newman shouts his way through a passage of 'Reuters'-like reportage. (These were released by the Touch label in 1997 on the CD single titled 'Vien'.) "It was completely absurd, but it was fun," says Newman of the Vienna trip. "It was all funded by the ORF and – and this is classic Bruce organisation – nobody made any money."

Throughout the 90s Newman, Gilbert, and Lewis further bolstered their credentials as artists outside the band, pursuing wide-ranging projects – again, anything but a schematic account of these is not within the scope of the present book.

Newman had moved back to London from Brussels in August 1992, setting up his own studio (Swim) and record label (*swim ~*) that would concentrate primarily on instrumental dance-oriented music, with him producing. He also put out a solo album, *Bastard* (1997), and worked with Malka Spigel on projects such as Oracle, Immersion, and her solo records. Most importantly for Wire, Newman's *swim ~* productions gave him more hands-on training that would be vital to Wire's future activities.

Gilbert had continued to work at the abstract-experimental end of the electronic spectrum, releasing *Insiding* (1991), *Music For Fruit* (1991), *Ab Ovo* (1996), and *In Esse* (1997), all on Mute, as well as *Orr* (with Robert Hampson and Paul Kendall) on the Parallel Series label in 1996 and the spoken-word album *The Haring* on WMO in 1997. He began performing solo for the first time in late 1993, albeit from a garden shed erected inside venues – one engagement in 1994 found him installed inside the Piccadilly Circus Tower Records store, much to shoppers' consternation. That same year, Gilbert became involved with Disobey, a club night organised by Blast First's Paul Smith, devoted in large part to extreme interrogations of the conceptual possibilities of noise. There, alongside techno renegades and noiseniks like Richard D. James (Aphex Twin), Russell Haswell, and Mego's Peter Rehberg, he DJ-ed as The Beekeeper, subjecting listeners to obscure *musique concrète* CDs, often played simultaneously. In order to work with a blank slate and to enhance the randomness, he would black out the discs' identifying information with a marker pen in advance. Thus he entertained and terrorised club-goers from Moscow to New York, administering severe aural pleasure, even DJ-ing on the opening night of composer Magnus Lindberg's 1996 Meltdown at the Southbank Centre, billed as "The Godfather Of Avant-Disco". Beyond 'music', he found time for installation work and also gave a talk and performance at The Royal College of Art.

Working under the acronym H.A.L.O., Lewis released a solo album, *Immanent* (1995), and pushed ahead with his plan to forge alliances in Sweden. He enjoyed various electro-acoustic and ambient-minimalist collaborations: Ocsid (with Carl Michael von Hausswolff and Jean-Louis Huhta), Hox (with Andreas Karperyd), and He Said Omala (with Andreas Karperyd and Mattias Tegnér). He also joined Gilbert at Disobey in December 1994 for a rare Dome outing; a Dome album, *Yclept*, was released through WMO in 1999, featuring both new material and work dating back to 1983.

### It's my party, and I'll drill if I want to

In September 1995 – at the invitation of Gareth Jones – Gilbert, Lewis, and Newman met up for their first post-Wir studio session together. The occasion was a remix of Erasure's 'Fingers & Thumbs (Cold Summer's Day)', which resulted in a sublime version titled 'Figures In Crumbs'. A more significant event took place the following May, when all four members of Wire gathered for the first time in six years, to perform 'Drill' in honour of Gilbert's 50th birthday. The location was an unnamed club under the arches of the Hungerford Bridge on London's South Bank. It was instigated by Paul Smith. "I'd been knocking around with him," recalls Gilbert. "We first met when he was managing Band Of Susans, and we got pally. Always in the back of his mind, I bet he was thinking: if I'm very patient, I'm sure I can get Wire back together again. He was very fond of Wire and thought that we weren't as 'big' or as respected as we should have been – this is where he came up with this concept that we'd end up playing the first three albums in their entirety at some point, as special events."

For now, however, Smith was focusing on something a little more manageable. "He was determined to make a bit of a fuss about my birthday," continues Gilbert, "although I didn't realise just how much of a fuss until very close to it. Sitting in the pub with him one day, he said: What do you want to do? Do you want to play? And I said: definitely not. But he said: Wouldn't it be a wheeze if Wire played just once and played 'Drill'? You wouldn't have to learn anything. I was amazed everyone agreed to do it. I suppose the blackmail situation was that it was my birthday – and I was getting very, very old."

This invitation-only event, under the auspices of Disobey, was intended to be a small affair, with DJ sets from G-Man and Aphex Twin – "there was more emphasis on the birthday party than on Wire playing," says Grey. But things turned out differently. The KLF's Jimmy Cauty parked his Saracen armoured personnel carrier Audio Weapons System outside, its bass frequencies potent enough to "violently shake the temporary portaloos in Waterloo station to shocking urine-soaked effect", as Lewis reports enthusiastically. Among those in attendance were Him from Blur and Her from Elastica and rising art-world stars the Chapman brothers, who were also part of the Disobey orbit.

To cap it all, Wire's performance was filmed and broadcast as their 'final appearance'. "Paul Smith sold it to MTV," Grey remembers, something that didn't sit well with Newman, who felt the occasion had been hijacked. "I was incensed that Smith touted it as 'Wire's last-ever gig'. He had no right to do that. It was supposed to be a proper 'do' for Bruce's 50th, and 'secret' – at least the Wire part. MTV filmed it, much to my horror." After this, everyone went their separate ways again – although the germ of an idea may have been planted.

Grey's participation at Gilbert's birthday was surprising, given the circumstances in which he'd left Wire and the distance he'd put between himself and the group in the interim. Once he'd quit in 1990, Grey experienced some relief at having removed himself from an untenable situation. "I'd been carrying on doing something only as a compromise, so that didn't make me feel very good about it. Eventually, you find that you're doing what other people want you to do more than what you want to do yourself, and there's only so long you can do that. It's depressing to be doing it in a half-hearted way."

After leaving, Grey had also begun to feel, fundamentally, that his investment in Wire had been a mistake, in view of the way everything had finished. He found this difficult to come to terms with. "It seems strange to say it now, but it seemed like I'd made a wrong decision in 1976. I felt that all the work I'd put into Wire had been a waste of time – that it hadn't really led anywhere. I thought: why did I bother if I became redundant at the end of it? It was a couple of years before I drummed again. I remember going through a phase of saying I wouldn't play any drums at all. Then I came to the conclusion I would play for my own interest, rather than contribute to anyone else's schemes. Which seemed rational at the time."

Grey was now farming full-time, having abandoned music as a career. Adrift from Wire, he paid less attention to pop and rock and listened mostly to classical music. "I'd had enough of bands. I thought that was enough. I didn't think I would want to join another band." That said, he did join one, for an evening at least. In November 1996, six months after turning out for Gilbert's birthday, he was lured back to London for a one-off performance with The Brood. This was a group featuring Robert Poss, Justine Frischmann, Peter Kember (aka Sonic Boom), and Susan Stenger – put together by Stenger to play Rhys Chatham's 'Guitar Trio' at the Purcell Room, on the South Bank. (This was also propitious as it was Grey's first appearance under his birth name, having now definitively discarded 'Gotobed'.) Two years later, in October 1998, Grey was recruited to perform John Cage's 'Ryoanji' with Stenger and Gavin Bryars at the Barbican Centre, as part of its American Pioneers series. This piqued his curiosity about Cage's work. "I became interested in what he'd done, but that was more about ideas than listening to the music he produced – looking at things in different ways and coming up with new ideas for ways of presenting music."

Grey's eventual full return to kit-playing had come about in an unusual fashion for someone who had been a professional musician – he started taking lessons in the basics of drumming. "African drumming led me to this," he explains. "After I left Wire, I was still going to my African drumming classes in London. I kept that up because that was drumming in a completely different context. That was still an interest. But then I moved back to Leicester, and when I was leaving the class, they emphasised that I should find a new teacher. In African drumming, it's important that you have a teacher – and finding the right person was a very important part of the process: if you join a class, you're adopted by that teacher, and they pass on their knowledge and rhythms to you, finding out what you're good at playing, improving your technique, and talking about the history of African drumming." Grey had again begun warming to the idea of kit-drumming at around the time he left London, and it occurred to him that, just as he'd learned from his African drumming teacher, it might be useful to reapproach rock drumming by following a similar process. "I'd understood about the benefits of having a teacher who could pass on their knowledge to you, so now I thought it'd be useful for me to find someone who taught more from a Western perspective, so that I could learn from that, and it could also help me to get started again."

Having found a teacher in Leicester, Grey attended lessons on a weekly basis. He was more or less starting over, eager to access the knowledge he, as a self-taught drummer, had never acquired. "The instructor was teaching drums as a proper musical instrument and preparing people to take their grades. That was my first encounter with proper musicians, learning drumming as a musical instrument. It was totally orthodox. I went for about a year, and it did help me re-establish contact with playing. For example, I'd never learnt the snare-drum rudiments, which is what you're supposed to do when you start, and I worked my way through the book of rudiments. That gave me a direction of some sort and was quite an interesting process to go through – learning what drummers are traditionally supposed to learn."

Grey finally stopped going to the classes when they began to lead in a direction that he felt wasn't worth pursuing. "The teacher's idea was to train you to be somebody who could play in an orchestra or who could sight-read a part, which is what I suppose a professional musician would aspire to – but I'm just not one of those people. He was very keen on me learning to read music and take music exams, which was a bit of a stumbling block. I can't see that it would have been of much value to the way I play. To other musicians, that probably sounds like a terrible thing to say: I suppose it's like being illiterate. If you don't read music, you have to pick it up by ear. That's a more natural way of playing, and I manage with that. So I did pursue the lessons for a while, and that gave me some insights into how drummers relate to other musicians, but then I decided to go back to working out my own ideas on the drums." Grey believed that playing alone was just as vital to his reacquaintance with the drums. "I still had a desire to play, and you have to learn to play your instrument on your own anyway before you can engage with others' playing."

## The South Bank show

A new phase began for Wire in 1999. David Sefton, head of contemporary culture at the Royal Festival Hall (who had been at Gilbert's 50th birthday), invited the band to perform a retrospective set on October 30 – billed as "Living Legends" – and to curate the rest of the evening's entertainment.

Regardless of Sefton's offer, however, Grey speculates that a reactivation may have been on the cards since the 1996 get-together: "There was no mention of continuing then, but maybe the idea of the birthday party was just to see if we could all be in the same room together without it being unbearable. Paul Smith had obviously been talking to Bruce about reforming Wire. I remember Bruce or Paul Smith saying: Why not? Why don't you do it? Why don't you think about it? It was a slower process than saying: shall we restart?" Gilbert recalls that he had certainly been thinking about the group's possible future. The Royal Festival Hall show offered a specific, immediate objective for Wire, but more broadly, he was interested in exploring their continued viability beyond the unique context of that gig. To him, it was a chance to see if another cycle of work was in the offing. "It was curiosity and, I suppose, I thought there might still be something to do. There might be new things to make. I wanted to see where it went."

Although Gilbert, Lewis, and Newman were enthusiastic about the Festival Hall invitation, Grey was cautious. "I did have quite a lot of doubts about this being a good thing, and the first time I was asked, I just said I wanted to think about it. Not make a decision." Given what had happened at the end of the 80s, the decision wasn't as straightforward for him as it was for the others. "I wasn't feeling very positive about Wire," he says. "I felt that I'd moved away from it, and I was doing other things. Having had ten years without Wire, I thought we weren't going to work together again. I thought Wire was finished. Ten years is a long time: I had doubts that we'd be able to recreate the working relationship. And I was still feeling that it was somewhat unjust that Wire had become a three-piece. I had mixed feelings about how much I was wanted. But if Wire were going to play the Festival Hall, then I couldn't see that I could not play drums."

Grey recalls how it was pitched to the band: "Paul Smith put it forward as an offer we couldn't refuse, really – to do the Festival Hall and be well paid for it. Why would you not do it? Apart from: can we work together? That was the only difficulty." There was another difficulty, of course: after steadfastly refusing all manifestations of nostalgia, Wire were committing to an event that was devised expressly to focus on their early work. In the 70s, they had rarely played anything more than six months old and in the 80s they had played nothing from the 70s; now they were entertaining the prospect of a performance devoted exclusively to oldies. It was a risky enterprise at this point in their career, especially if they were considering continuing as a serious band and moving ahead with new material – as opposed to throwing in their lot with the punk cabaret circuit. The Royal Festival Hall appearance could condemn them to the latter: surrendering to this sort of museumisation could be taken as the band's acknowledgement that they were now obsolete, their most significant and influential work little more than a dusty artefact. Even so, they agreed to do it.

Various aspects of Wire's identity made it possible for them to play a seemingly unthinkable retrospective gig while retaining their credibility as an ongoing concern. Their contrarian reputation, for instance, preceded them and, in this case, worked in their favour: precisely because the Royal Festival Hall concert was an unthinkable thing for them to do, it made absolute sense for them to do it (since they had always specialised in doing exactly the opposite of what was expected of them). Moreover, their meagre past success and their low profile also helped considerably. They'd never been famous. They'd never had a hit. They'd never really been part of a scene. They weren't reforming to promote or commemorate anything. They were active as artists outside of Wire. They'd never officially broken up and gone away. In short, this was no comeback: there was nowhere to come back from and nothing to come back to. All of this made the potential pitfalls easier to negotiate.

If Wire's established character automatically enabled them to undertake the Festival Hall show, they were also aware that, in order to make the most of this opportunity, they needed to take other deliberate steps with regard to framing the performance and controlling the tone of the proceedings. In particular, they understood that the attitude with which they presented their material would be decisive: to be avoided at all costs was any sense of a self-congratulatory, triumphalist return to the old songs. The nature and structure of the evening were conceived with these issues in mind. The result was an event titled *It's All In The Brochure*, which combined their set with a diverse, humorous, and playful bill involving various collaborations and different media.

Although Wire took care to ensure the successful execution of this endeavour, there's also a sense in which they were never actually in danger of losing any credibility: even if Wire weren't averse to nostalgia, they could never be nostalgic – even if they tried. The fact is that no one would believe them. Nostalgia can only be done in an unironic manner – with some investment in the notion of authenticity. But Wire's work – always infused with an arch sensibility and a feeling of remove – was grounded in a rejection of authenticity. This undercut any possibility of nostalgia, in much the same way that the greatest deadpan comedians can never play dramatic roles.

Just a month before the Royal Festival Hall show, however, the Wire jinx struck, as Grey injured his shoulder, requiring the event to be postponed until February 2000. At the time, a press release attributed the mishap to "hay-baling". The truth was less picturesque and pastoral. "I was actually pushing the car out of the garage," the drummer remembers. "It wasn't anything dramatic – I wasn't trampled by a bull or anything like that." During this enforced hiatus, further activity was planned, including an April performance at the first-ever All Tomorrow's Parties Festival (curated by Mogwai at Pontin's in Camber Sands) and, more importantly, a North American tour in May. For both ventures, it was announced that the band would play a retrospective set.

The Royal Festival Hall concert finally took place after low-key warm-up gigs in Nottingham and Dublin. Wire drew on material from *Pink Flag* through to *A Bell Is A Cup*. They also played 'He Knows' (a new track) and 'Art Of Persistence', a number that had resulted from the band's efforts in rehearsal to revive the long-fallow 'Ally In Exile'. The performance was prefaced by and interspersed with myriad attractions: video of their 1979 *Rockpalast* appearance; an Immersion set (with Newman and Spigel); a short film scored by Lewis, who also performed as He Said with Susan Stenger and Andreas Karperyd; a Daniel Miller–Seth Hodder DJ set; a Michael Clark dance piece during 'Heartbeat'; and a video reprise of the 1987 Suzanne Somers incident. Among the merchandise on offer was *Third Day*, an EP documenting a rehearsal for the gig, released on the band's own newly founded pinkflag label: this featured 'Blessed State', 'Mercy', 'Art Of Persistence', and two renditions of 'Pink Flag'. (Highlights from the Festival Hall, including half of Wire's set, would appear on another pinkflag release, *It's All In The Brochure*.)

The formation of pinkflag and the launch of the band's own website (pinkflag.com), along with the upcoming live dates, were encouraging signs for Wire-watchers. Added to this, the news that Paul Smith had now come on board as manager seemed to confirm that Wire were an active entity again and that a recording project was on the horizon.

Nevertheless, the band kept their focus on the task before them: the completion of the US and Canadian dates. Gilbert, who was always particularly resistant to playing the older material, isn't sure why he agreed to continue with the retrospective set beyond the Festival Hall engagement. "It may have been an act of perversity," he concedes. At the same time, he does note that he made a point of guaranteeing that the touring set wasn't too arduous. "I decided I wasn't going to be playing proper chords, just open-tuning, so that meant that certain things just wouldn't work. Anything with a minor chord was out. If we were going to play old things, it shouldn't be a struggle. It should be enjoyable. We did the easier ones. It was more relaxing." Lewis, meanwhile, took the tour as something of a challenge, on various levels. "I think it was basically: Could we actually do it? Could we actually go on the road? Could we actually bear to be with each other for that length of time? Could we produce something that was worthy of our name? There was still an awful lot of pride involved."

Grey emphasises Paul Smith's importance in this part of the Wire story. In his view, without Smith's belief in the band and their worth, the Royal Festival Hall gig and everything that followed may never have happened. "There's always been somebody who was a conduit, a person who kept the peace or was a referee or who was able to channel different opinions into something constructive – rather than the whole thing breaking down. Paul took on this task. He convinced us that Wire had a value in itself, rather than being a destructive force. It had a value in the music world. It seems stupid to say that, but everything just seemed to have a tendency to fall apart. I mean, Wir, the new Wire, only lasted a year, didn't it? If Wire had fallen apart and then Wir had fallen apart, you wouldn't think there was a great future in it, with the four of us involved. It needed someone from the outside to say that, musically, Wire has a value – and he even dared to say it had a future. At the time, I think everybody believed it was more likely to fall apart than work. So we needed someone there to tell us that it could work."

There was a genuine buzz about the May 2000 North American tour, with Wire generally received as returning heroes – in marked contrast to their last visit, in 1988. The New York show was memorable. "Before the gig, we had a visitation from Mr Bowie," recalls Gilbert. "It was all rather odd. These American clubs and venues have a dressing room and a roped-off area for people you don't know, but who are VIPs, and somebody came in and said: somebody wants to meet you – and so he drifted in. He seemed a decent bloke. He was very pleasant. He seemed to know everything we'd done. But he was very disappointed we weren't playing more from *Chairs Missing* – very disappointed. It was a very short visitation. He didn't come back afterwards, probably because he was *terribly disappointed*." (Bowie had been brought along that night by an old Wire associate, Page Hamilton, who had recently finished a stint as Bowie's touring guitarist.)

While on the road, the band also spent three days at Steve Albini's Electrical Audio in Chicago, recording a version of their live set. The combination of Wire and the maverick anti-producer was an interesting proposition. However, the traditionalist studio approach, with its emphasis on repeated playing in order to get the right take, felt anachronistic and oppressive to Newman. Wire may have been playing old material, but Newman didn't think a retro methodology was required in order to document it. "It was the awful pressure, which goes back to *Pink Flag*," he says. "When we did that recording with Albini, I thought: this is awful! We were really examining each take, and there was no feeling of freedom in the playing. You just felt like a bloody machine – everyone's got to get all their parts right, and if anybody stops, then that's fucking up everyone else. It's really hard work."

"I did one session where they were playing the old material," Albini recalls. "I don't know what the intention was. Maybe it was just to make a document of the band at that stage. Then everything was left hanging. I never received any further instructions – but I didn't want to pester them about it either. I figured that if they had a plan, I wanted to let them pursue their plan." To date, these recordings remain unreleased.

Lewis was happy with the way the tour turned out. "There were still four of us at the end. We'd healed certain aspects. There was a definite sense of achievement for ourselves, that we'd managed to do that." Crucial to that feeling of accomplishment was the notion that they hadn't simply been performing karaoke, but rather, they'd started to bring fresh perspective to what was, in some instances, very old work. "It sounded contemporary," says Lewis. "That's what was important. We weren't trying to emulate what we were doing before. We weren't trying to play the songs as they were played; we were playing them in a way that felt contemporary. It was strong; it was powerful. It was convincing."

Above all, the experience seemed to put the band in a place to move forward with new work. "We'd all survived, and it was still in one piece," continues Lewis, "so there was a feeling we could do something else. We gained confidence from doing that tour – and there was now something of interest to explore. There was definitely something in the sound. Everybody thought it was very impressive, and the way it sounded suggested there was work to do: there could be new material."

## CHAPTER 10

# 2000–03

### The Disobey table

By the end of 2000, Wire had completed an improbable process, having spent the year looking back on their career. EMI even topped it off by releasing the first boxed-set compilation of the band's Harvest albums. However, all of this retrospective activity could hardly have been less indicative of the direction they were about to take when they began developing new material: their next project would emphatically dispel notions that Wire's 'living sculpture' had breathed its last and was being crated up for storage. For this new phase, which ran through 2001 and into 2002, Wire didn't focus on making an album but instead concentrated on the EP format, releasing *Read & Burn* volumes one and two in 2002; the following year, selected numbers from these EPs, along with several non-EP tracks derived from the same recording cycle, would be compiled on the *Send* album. This body of work made an ironclad case for the band's continued vitality and inventiveness. Which was no mean feat. On the face of it, the musical landscape at the time didn't leave much room for Wire, who like many bands of a certain age might have been best advised to apply for their pensioners' bus passes. But rather than retreat to the safety of the karaoke circuit, Wire launched themselves right into the contemporary musical discussion.

After the group's 90s break, Bruce Gilbert and Graham Lewis came to post-millennium Wire as participants in a vibrant pan-European experimental scene. At the same time as Lewis had pursued his ambient-electronic interests with Hox, Ocsid, and He Said Omala, as a listener he had gravitated toward the more extreme manifestations of guitar-based music in Sweden. "Rock music and thrash metal were still important culturally here – particularly thrash, which I'd really enjoyed: The Entombed and people like that." Gilbert had persisted with his ear-unfriendly endeavours, shedding, beekeeping, and disobeying in and out of the art world. While his relationship with rock had always been ambivalent at best, by now he seemed completely, and happily, estranged from it, approaching his work from the outer reaches of the abstract-noise realm. On the surface, this augured badly for a new collaboration with Colin Newman. If they had previously encountered difficulties regarding process and objectives, the two now appeared to inhabit irreconcilable creative spaces, suggesting that any productive alliance was unlikely. That wasn't the case, though.

The fact that Gilbert's noise proclivities currently situated him amid a radical outgrowth or mutation of techno gave him something in common with Newman, who was immersed in dance music, albeit in (comparatively) more mainstream terms. Their interests didn't converge on the dance floor itself but somewhere on its margins. Newman paints an amusing and revealing picture of the relationship between their two very different areas of electronic music in terms of the contrast between Gilbert's Disobey and another significant 90s club, the Electronic Lounge. The latter, with which Newman allied himself, and where he and Malka Spigel DJ-ed on occasion, was devoted to socialising and networking – the music was played relatively quietly to facilitate this; Disobey was the polar opposite, with social interaction practically impossible because of the harsh, inhospitable nature of the aural environment.

"The Electronic Lounge was in the ICA bar, every two weeks for two years," explains Newman. "You could meet anyone you wanted to. Anyone who was making music you liked was there in that room, and you could talk to them. Bruce, Paul Smith, and Russell Haswell had Disobey upstairs at the Garage – a room with horrible acoustics. It was full-on noise stuff: people went with earplugs." Nevertheless, Newman remembers that the Disobey crowd used to put in a grudging appearance at the Electronic Lounge. "The people who ran Disobey – Bruce and Paul and anyone from Mego who happened to be in town – had their own table at the Electronic Lounge: the Disobey table. They all sat at the Disobey table, and they all scowled at everybody. They looked like idiots, really – sitting at that table scowling while everybody else was getting on with what they were doing. They looked at everybody with scorn – but they still went. I used to see Bruce there often, and he would come away from the Disobey table and we'd have a chat."

Newman arrived at Wire's *Read & Burn–Send* period after spending most of the 90s focused on dance music. At this point, he was particularly energised by the angsty, austere subgenus of drum'n'bass known as 'dark', but it was the production experience garnered from his own *swim ~* releases that would prove crucial in shaping Wire's forthcoming work. As the story thus far shows, since Wire's return in 1985, Newman had been closely following the advances in production technology that had changed both how records were made and who made them, and he had been keen to bring those advances to bear on Wire. He reiterates his fascination with this: "In the mid 80s, there was a revolution in music production as people started making records in their own spaces that sounded like proper records, not like a homemade record. One of the things that excited me about dance music was the fact that people didn't need to go cap-in-hand or get the men in the white coats in to make it sound like a proper record. You could do it yourself. The first time I heard Aphex Twin's 'Digeridoo' in 1992, I thought: This is what this guy does fiddling around at home. It's liberating. It's really exciting."

## A Rolls Royce for Mini money

By 1999, Newman had produced various *swim* ~ projects, in his own studio, realising what had been an ambition since Wire first entered Advision in 1977. "In the 70s, it was like your dad took you in the studio, let you play with the toys, and recorded your songs. When we started in the recording studio, there was an element of: 'You musicians, you children, are out there on the other side of the glass in the playing room, and we're in here in the control room. We've got all these knobs and dials, and we can make you sound great, but it's *our* place, and you need us. And we're expensive. It's going to cost you the price of a house just to be in here for two weeks.' That was how it was. Then, in the 80s, it was like trying to work out how you make records, but in a very expensive studio and with people not really having much idea." For Newman, the dependence on the professional producer and his expensive playground definitively ended in December 1999 with Digidesign's release of Digi 001. The potential that this rack, with Pro Tools software, placed in his hands was the final piece in the jigsaw. "I bought it, and this was when this whole process started. It was the first Pro Tools you could buy for your home studio: it was your Rolls Royce for Mini money, champagne for lemonade money."

This upgrade laid the foundation for the *Read & Burn–Send* cycle. "It was really the first big Pro Tools production I did," says Newman. "It was about learning to use that. *Pink Flag* was recorded in the same studio where Yes recorded *Tales From Topographic Oceans*; *Send* was made at home in a garage. It's about getting the means of production. The *Send* era is the band figuring out how to make a record for themselves. I'm a firm believer in the idea that as soon as you get the experts in, your ability to figure something out goes out the window. I didn't want to have someone else offering me choices. I wanted to see what the choices were myself. *Read & Burn* and *Send* are really the story of that."

Another key factor impacting Wire's new work on the cusp of the millennium was the return of rock, as the orbits of London and New York – generally out of sync – aligned for a post-post-punk collision of beats and noise, in tandem with a wider resurgence of BIG guitars. While Gilbert was committing acts of abstract-noise terrorism and Lewis was listening to thrash metal in Sweden, Newman was finding kinship with a newly revitalised milieu of rock – as an habitué of London's Sonic Mook Experiment and an enthusiastic attendee of gigs by the likes of Mclusky and Liars. "We used to play the Sonic Mook record before going onstage in 2000," remembers Newman. "That's pretty much the aesthetic for the *Read & Burn* and *Send* stuff: dirty electro, new-millennial post-punk, fast-loud stuff. But we were going at it as if we didn't have anything to do with post-punk the first time around. There was an aesthetic there that made sense in both New York and London: that was an interesting moment, a moment in which Wire could operate as a new band."

For Wire to "operate as a new band" – to be contemporary – was essential, and even more challenging than it had been in 1985 and again in 1991 (as Wir): they weren't getting any younger, and the problem of being credible and 'modern' was only more difficult. "We could have said: OK, it was successful to tour the hits – let's continue," says Newman. "We took a risk, but it's a risk seen from the perspective of someone who's not in the band. From the perspective of someone who's in the band, it's a no-brainer. Doing the new thing is more interesting." This time, their reinvention would meet with unambiguous success.

Lewis, for one, had a clear idea of what it would take for Wire to be convincingly new and modern in the early 2000s. "There was no way we were going to be accused of being tired old men. It was going to be bulletproof: hard-as-rocks and extremely fast and tough. It was a time for this aggressive sound, and what emerged very early on was that it was not about songs or melody, really. Writing strategies came from that. It was more like writing copy for noise than writing songs as such: it was going to be barked, so the words worked differently."

As Newman saw it, the aesthetic was – in a nutshell – a hybrid of rock and dance-floor values. Ironically, although Wire were committed to that forward-looking sound and eager to move away from being a band playing their 'greatest hits', the new phase actually began with a return to *Pink Flag*. While in some ways *Pink Flag* had haunted Wire – it's the yardstick by which punk fundamentalists still insist on measuring all of the group's diverse work since 1977 – they now realised it could be a source of innovation. The *Send*-era output signals a reconnection with the foundational, pared-down sensibility dramatised on that debut release.

The first building block in the reconstruction of Wire for the 2000s emerged – before any real plans had been made for a new project – when Newman reworked a specific and unexpected part of the band's history: *Pink Flag*'s short-sharp parting shot, '12XU'. The track had a chequered past, as the number that, for many, embodied Wire as merely a punk band; it was the one that everybody wanted to hear played live. Consequently, its inclusion in their retrospective sets was inevitable, if only as a comedy turn. In the same spirit, and for the band's further entertainment, Newman prepared two versions of a live recording of the song from a May 2000 gig at the Garage. "I did two mixes of '12XU', like I would do my own stuff. I did them totally to amuse the band. I didn't do them for any other reason. But not only did they think it was really funny, they also thought it was really good and got really excited about it. They immediately picked up on the aesthetic. That's where it all came from. It's using the methodology of dance music inside rock music."

These mixes catch Wire at their most brutal and hard-edged – as filtered through Newman's dance-production sensibility. They were the precise route by which Wire discovered how to present their sound in a wholly up-to-date manner. "We found a way, from within the band," says Newman, "to produce items that represented Wire in a way it hadn't ever been represented before: it sounded contemporary because of the way it was being produced. It was all loops, chopped-up elements: none of it was done with proper recording."

Working with the tools and methods of dance-music production was, of course, nothing new to Wire. From *The Ideal Copy* through to *The First Letter*, this had grown increasingly important as the band concentrated not on conventional songwriting, group-playing, arrangement, and recording but, more and more, on a sampled, sequenced, cut-and-paste model of construction. Now, however, the pivotal difference was that Wire were approaching this mode of production explicitly as a rock band. "A lot of the stuff on *Send* is derived from how you build a dance-floor track, but doing it with rock music," emphasises Newman. "I certainly wasn't the first person to do it, but within the context of Wire that was a new discovery." From that starting point, the brief was straightforward, as far as Newman was concerned. "The aesthetic was: if Fatboy Slim was making punk-rock records, what kind of punk-rock records would he make? That was the idea. It wasn't done with a high aesthetic. It wasn't an attempt to make something cerebral. It was deliberately 'anti' the way in which Wire might have worked in the past."

The release of the two '12XU' mixes – as a single titled 'Twelve Times You' – was also significant: selling a surprising 1,500 copies, the record gave the band some idea of how they might present any new material, if it was completed. Despite the successes of the previous year, in 2001 there was still uncertainty surrounding the band and their future – and a new album seemed like an enormous step. As Lewis recalls: "We didn't know how we were going to go about it in terms of a process, with me being in Sweden and nobody knowing if Colin and Bruce could bear each other for long enough. So rather than take on a whole album, which would have been quite daunting, the idea of doing an EP or a few tracks came up." Newman attributes to their manager the idea of releasing the new work as a series of EPs, culminating in an album. "Paul Smith's plan was to put out a couple of limited edition EPs and then compile them on an album. It wasn't done to get the maximum money out of the fans. We genuinely thought we'd only sell 2,000 of the first one and 2,000 of the second one, then we'd have a bigger sale on the album because it's the major medium."

## Two people in a converted garage

A couple of tracks that would appear on *Read & Burn 01* had begun to take shape in performance, in advance of the studio work: a version of 'Germ Ship' was played at the Queen's Hall in Edinburgh in December 2000, and the same concert featured a renewed approach to 'Ally In Exile' – by now on its way to becoming 'I Don't Understand'. Early 2001 would also see some rudimentary recording at Ritz Studios in Putney, but while *Read & Burn 02*'s 'Spent' originated in group-playing there, the session's main objective was to capture Robert Grey's drumming as raw material for the subsequent development of the tracks. The band weren't pleased with what Lewis calls Ritz's "claustrophobic dead-drum sound", but this would in fact enhance the work's sonic signature – adding to its distinctively severe, menacing, intense feel. Some rough guitars were also recorded at this session, with similarly claustrophobic results. In this case, the effect was reinforced by Gilbert's determination to keep the sound as dry as possible. "Bruce insisted on no reverb at all on anything," says Newman. "That was one of his things – along with 'no harmonies'."

With Newman now finally producing Wire for the first time, the material was put together in the converted garage space in his South West London home – aka Swim Studio. The logistics were unique for Wire, as the work was executed by Newman and Gilbert alone. "*Send* represents a coming-together in a way that had never happened before," Newman remarks. "There was an understanding between Bruce and me because we were both guitarists, but we'd never sat down and worked together quite like that. It's the only time we've ever worked that closely."

Although it made sense for Gilbert and Newman to work together at Swim, there was an element of 'needs must' to this decision since, at this stage, the band had little money and no label backing. "How else was it going to happen?" asks Newman. "We were a band who, even at the best of times, never had a good, cohesive social structure. Only two of us lived in the same town: Rob hadn't lived in London for a long time, and there was no real facility to record drums on a regular basis. And Graham was in Sweden, and we couldn't afford to keep flying him over here. Everybody sending parts to me by post and having me assemble them wasn't a way of making a record. So this was the only way we could devise to make it."

Grey also suggests that the two-man team was created, partly, to minimise the creative problems that had often arisen when Wire convened. "The idea came up pretty much between Colin and Bruce. Since we didn't need to be in the studio together, that made things easier as a working process: we wouldn't all be together, so there wouldn't be as many disagreements."

Initially, the mood was simply exploratory, as the pair set to work with no real expectations or objectives. "We didn't know if anything would come of it," Newman stresses. "It was a leap of faith. It revolved around me and Bruce working together a few days a week. Bruce was even allowed to smoke in the kitchen – anything in order to make this happen!" Lewis was kept up-to-date via periodic CD-Rs; in turn, he mailed ideas and parts or took them with him on his occasional visits to London. "I was working on things separately, waiting for the post," he says. "Now and again I'd get something on a CD. It was quite distant. I'd come to London for a day and bang down eight or ten basslines and make as fast a contribution as I could."

While he missed "being in the studio and having discussions in the pub with Bruce", Lewis tried to make the distance less an obstacle and more a productive factor, at times enabling him to push the work in new directions. "It was a peculiar situation. It was the first time I'd made a piece of work like that, very much looking from the outside in – but I think, on occasions, that was very useful because you're not involved in the same way. So you can bring some objectivity, something to stretch things and focus things." One of his examples concerns the pace of the tracks. Although, for Newman, accelerated tempos were a priority from the outset ("Everything had to be fast. That was the aesthetic"), Lewis takes credit for some of the speedier moments. "When we started, a lot of the stuff Colin and Bruce were suggesting was very medium-paced. In that way, my contribution to the landscape was 'Germ Ship', really early on, and later 'Nice Streets Above' – which were more sample-based, very dance-based, but more aggressive, with more distortion and feedback."

Grey, on the other hand, played no direct role. Apart from one drum pattern (for 'Raft Ants') that he sent by mail, the drum tracks came from the Ritz session and other pre-existing recordings – these were then processed and edited by Newman. "*Send* was my first encounter with Pro Tools," says Grey. "I wasn't really involved in the way it was made, setting up any of the rhythms. Colin used cut-up pieces from previous drumming I'd done and made loops out of them. So it was recycled rather than new things created. In a loose sense you might say, yes, I played that kick drum or snare beat or a few beats together, but, really, I wouldn't consider them my drum tracks. Even though Colin says it's my drumming, that's stretching a point."

Gilbert is sure that although Grey didn't physically perform his parts, the drum tracks did capture his singular identity. "They were reconstructed in terms of drum patterns that Rob would use. I don't think any of them were patterns that Rob would not use or had not used, but they were edited to give them that extra-urgent edge. Or if, say, the bass drum from one recording wasn't good, it would be replaced with the bass drum from another recording of his work. This is where Colin's skill comes into it. He never strayed from any of Rob's patterns." Grey doesn't think this was always the case, as various rhythm tracks seem alien to him. "I don't recognise many of the patterns there as mine. I remember listening to 'Mr Marx's Table' and thinking: I would *never* have come up with a drum part like that, because it only does one thing – it only does on-off!" Not that he had a problem with this. "It was good to bring in something I wouldn't have thought of. It also had that attraction of simplicity, which I like. I enjoyed the way it worked and the way it was arranged – that applied to the other songs as well."

If it's true that the two-man recording configuration was in part designed to limit tensions and disagreements, the identity of the two people in the room was nonetheless a little ironic. It certainly brought together the two strongest artistic personalities in the band, but their ability to forge a unified

311

strategy in pursuit of a shared creative goal had been a problematic issue since *154*. In short, this pairing didn't seem to be the most stable base on which to build an album. Surprisingly, though, everything ran fairly smoothly. Gilbert contributed most of the guitar riffs and lyrics, quickly getting into the swing of the process. "It was enjoyable for me, but not necessarily for Colin, who was beavering away when I wasn't there. I'd go two or three times a week and work for six hours and try and pack in as much as possible, even if it was unresolved. And I'd come home and work out parts for a song and put them on to DAT, making all the parts separate so it was easier to take off and edit."

## Speeded-up techno and funny noises

Newman talks in more detail about the collaboration with Gilbert, emphasising the piecemeal assembly process, making loops and pasting everything together. "Bruce would come with stuff, usually with some kind of dugga, and we'd work on it. There's some classic Bruce riffs on *Send*. It's probably got more Bruce riffs on it than any other Wire album. I'd play a bit of guitar, and I'd work around his ideas a lot, rather than just say: OK, I've got this song, we're gonna do it like this. We weren't working on songs and making them interesting in the arrangements – they're not songs, they're pieces stuck together." This was the essence of Newman's method, which made perfect sense for him in relation to his production work with the *swim ~* label. "By 2001, we'd had a decade and half of dance music as the dominant form, and everyone related to it somehow – even if Bruce was in the Disobey wing, that's still dance music, leftfield. It was definitely right at the time. It was the only route for me to go out of dance music into rock music. There's no way I could have gone from the mainly instrumental music I'd been doing – music that had a relationship with the dance floor – to just doing rock records with songs. That seemed like going back to the time of the dinosaurs."

Although in the previous decade Gilbert had strayed further than ever from rock, he does stress the importance of traditional, authentic rock values underlying the *Read & Burn–Send* process. In this way, he again shows his Romantic streak, valuing human agency and the work's foundation in unique, original played parts. "It was an opportunity to make one of those things that, on the surface, was machine-made but actually contained, shall we say, 'natural' sounds from guitars and stuff, and I think that was fairly inspiring, to come up to that standard, to achieve that sort of urgency. Obviously, Colin and I were using the kind of technology that you'd use with dance music, but with a human feel – everything was instruments originally. There's no synthesis going on. We'd use the live drum tracks from Robert, and Graham sent basslines and ideas, and Colin and I would jig them about and have some fun. But it felt a little strange because we'd been so used to being in a room as a band and knocking the stuff together. This was a little more abstract."

As the partnership between the two developed at Swim Studio, Newman felt that they settled into very specific roles. "I was getting stuff out of Bruce from recording, combining it with Rob's drums, and it sounds like a strange notion, but it was like I was producing Bruce." Gilbert accepts this characterisation, but also notes with some irony that there was a sense of inevitability about the direction the work took. "I suppose in the end that would have to be an accurate description. I'd occasionally put something structured down or leave behind a series of riffs, and next time I came there would be a whole track. So it was a fait accompli, but it kind of worked." Although he was observing from a distance, Lewis believes that this setup in Newman's studio, with Newman holding the production reins, was "a problem for Bruce, which I knew it would be, because of the nature of the individuals involved: their particular obsessions, their need to control, which everybody has, creatively".

Very much in producer mode, Newman recalls contriving ways to trigger creativity. Feeling it was vital to keep Gilbert engaged, he would come up with idiosyncratic ingredients to draw and maintain his bandmate's interest. "Something that's characteristic of the material is that the tracks have lots of tricks and funny noises in them, and a lot of that is because of Bruce's boredom." One shining example was 'DJ Fuckoff' (later collected on 2010's *Send Ultimate*, which compiled all the tracks from the two *Read & Burn* EPs and *Send*, plus other released and unreleased pieces from the era): "It's a remix of 'Drill' – just one bar. It's speeded-up techno with funny noises. I did it mainly to amuse Bruce. I thought he'd probably think it was funny. There's not much in the way of structure. It's kind of an assault, but it has a lot of humour. It goes insanely fast, especially for the time. Bruce liked it because he thought it sounded like it was done by a 14-year-old who'd never heard any records in his life. It's a bit like 'The Sabre Dance'. It hasn't got a lot of what you can call 'music' in it. It's what '99.9' realised better later on: that absolute collision of dance-floor and rock values, but in a very carefree way."

Newman's offering of random materials catered to Gilbert's preferred approach: reacting to sounds in the moment and working spontaneously.

This is what he'd always enjoyed in the more conventional studio setting with the band, as well as in his own projects – making use of whatever sounds presented themselves or building from other work that might be going on in the immediate environment. "What happened quite often," Gilbert recalls, "would be that we'd have a riff of some description or just a drum beat or a series of rhythmic noises, and, again, it would be a bit like being in the playing-room while other things were going on elsewhere – me pulling something out of the air, using an effected sound to go along with what I was hearing."

While Newman's efforts to allay tedium spawned ideas for tracks, he also remembers that, paradoxically, Gilbert's boredom in itself sometimes provided the impetus for key creative decisions. "I tried to get him to play when I could, and there was a lot of stuff that was got out of Bruce – but even if it wasn't his piece or if he didn't do the main riff on it, there's substantial contributions that he'd make just by sheer boredom. I used to fiddle around with the computer, and he used to just say: it should be like this or that or that bit's good and that bit's good – he didn't have to do anything."

The first scenario – Newman introducing "funny noises" and "tricks" – was, of course, completely in line with Wire's practice of building a track around a single, unusual sonic element; but it was also typically Wire for its involvement of humour as part of the band's lingua franca. Newman underscores the way these two factors intersected in the *Read & Burn–Send* process. "The pieces often started off as jokes. The great thing about it was that the more moronic and dumb it was, the more Bruce loved it. They started off with something that wasn't really anything at all, but were made into something. It was all about how to make as much as possible out of as little as possible. The music sounds quite serious and quite brutal, but we did laugh a lot, and a lot of the things did start off as: what would happen if you did … ?"

Interestingly, although the sound of the *Read & Burn–Send* work was quite far removed from Gilbert's abstract-experimental ventures, the general spirit of the project – particularly its 'what would happen if?' ethos – was really not that different. "In some ways it was similar to Dome," Gilbert observes, "in that we'd set the computer going and go for it and then pick out the best bit and then edit it, sometimes in a very free way, with the hope that a really good bit would emerge and then we could make the most of that by more editing."

Newman's production was a revelation to the band. Gilbert was struck by the facility he displayed as they worked together. "I'm still at a very primitive stage. I'm still just using my computer as a recorder, and my editing skills are extremely limited, whereas Colin was more advanced. Fast and skilful." Lewis is also complimentary. "For the time, and for what we were doing, Colin's production was perfect. The job he did was remarkable. He surprised himself, I think. Collectively, we all jumped off the cliff and tried to support what was going on. That was the first time this had happened for a very long time."

Despite the creative rapport between Newman and Gilbert at the core of this project, unsurprisingly, the two did not see eye to eye on all aspects of the work. The use of DI (direct injection) was one bone of contention. Newman found this invaluable: "I'd record guitars in plain DI, which means you hear the effects when you're recording it, but you also have a version of it which doesn't have any of the effects. So you can get that same performance and give it completely different treatment. And by layering those things together, you get enormous guitar tones. It's a great way of getting great guitar sounds. That's one of the things I learned from working on that material. But it's very much a case of 'if Bruce will let you do it'."

Gilbert wasn't convinced by this technique. Newman's use of DI could take the work in directions he didn't appreciate, marginalising his own contributions. "My biggest complaint about that process, the way Colin approached it, was that you'd have two signals. One was a clean signal, and one was things coming from my effects boxes. So there'd be two tracks. Which meant that Colin could then put an effect on top of the clean thing, which he was quite fond of doing – if from his point of view it wasn't satisfactory. So sometimes I'd come back the next day, and it would be different. And the one with my effects on it would be pushed into the background. It gave him flexibility, and I understand that it's very logical to do that, but sometimes I felt it took away from the more interesting nature of the thing I'd hooked up on my effects." Gilbert recalls responding with a mild form of subterfuge: "I got around that sometimes by doing stuff at home and putting it on a DAT, and there was no clean signal."

Overall, Gilbert was impressed with the technology and with Newman's expertise, but he was also frustrated by ways in which he felt Newman missed the opportunity to exploit the tools they had at their disposal. "Colin had a massively sophisticated effects processor – very, very powerful. And when you set certain parameters, you can take it to extremes that sometimes sound pretty boring on their own – but if you 'effect' the parameters while the sound is playing through the computer, changing it, modulating it, it can be really interesting. So I'd say: you should do that, Colin – and he'd say: But you can't record it live into the computer. It would have to come out of the computer and be recorded by a DAT machine and then be placed back into the computer. So I said: why don't we do that? And he said: oh no, you'd lose the quality. He didn't want to do it."

For Gilbert, the point was that, by using technology in an unorthodox fashion, they could push the work into intriguing areas; in his view, Newman remained somewhat constrained by the tools. "I thought: This is the power you have with the computer. It enables you to make some extraordinary noises, and it should be utilised. You shouldn't be afraid to go outside the computer and use it as a recording machine. That's the creative object that it could be."

Gilbert and Newman's contrasting sensibilities had obviously been integral to Wire's identity since 1977, the band's work both enriched by that tension and periodically undermined by it. The first two *Read & Burn* EPs and the eventual *Send* album would be a rare instance in which the two worked together and arrived at a highly successful artistic compromise. At the same time, however, the *Read & Burn–Send* cycle also reflects a creative – as well as personal – relationship concluding, it would seem, in irreparable estrangement.

Newman's attitude toward Gilbert in our interviews was complex, ranging from genuine admiration to animosity, and his feelings about this work are intimately bound up with that complicated relationship. "With Bruce, we got very close and we did some amazing things," says Newman, "but it was shortlived. And when it was finished, it felt totally miserable, the period afterwards. And then we fought about everything. Bruce won't let you get too close."

### John Lee Hooker on steroids

"Coppiced riff meets aphorism," barks Newman on '1st Fast', the earliest completed *Read & Burn* track, neatly summarising the aesthetic the band would pursue during the *Read & Burn–Send* phase. "This was the very first song after the '12XU' remixes," Newman explains. "It was an attempt to do something in that vein: totally reductive and simple. It's a description of the process. It's saying: This is what's required. It needs to go fast and be over fast; everything's got to be short and pruned in this process. The lyrics shouldn't be long and meandering, they should be short and aphoristic – one of the watchwords was that nothing was to be 'baroque' in any way." Lewis's own aphoristic assessment offers an appropriately concise characterisation of the track. "There aren't many notes in it, but there are an awful lot of them."

Gilbert's guitar, writ large by Newman's production, was the lifeblood of the *Read & Burn–Send* enterprise. "The stuff was very much about guitars," Newman reiterates, "making those big, huge guitar sounds, those classic Bruce riffs. He was very much in the texture of it." But while the guitar sound that Newman manufactured might have been original for Wire in 2001, that simple focus on the possibilities of the instrument was nothing new for the band. Just as the construction of tracks around a single sonic component was an established Wire tradition, the attention to guitars throughout this material also had antecedents, continuing the process begun on *Chairs Missing*, with its extensive use of effects in conjunction with the instrument. Upgraded technology and a revised working method didn't alter the band's aesthetic but reinforced and enhanced it, providing them with fresh ways to accomplish perennial artistic goals. "The technology facilitated the approach to using guitars again," says Lewis. "Before, we'd always been looking for a technology that was going to subvert the guitar in some way. Now, re-presenting the guitar was the central focus of it: that big John Lee Hooker-on-steroids sound. That's what it was based around. That huge guitar. Everything else was subservient to that." (There is also some precedent for this "huge guitar" as far back as *Pink Flag*'s 'Strange', for which Gilbert's basic riff was famously pumped up with a dozen or so overdubs to become a juggernaut blues-drone.)

The opening track on the first *Read & Burn* EP, 'In The Art Of Stopping', encapsulates the guitar-centric strategy, emphatically setting the tone for this new chapter in the band's work. "It's a totally blues-rock riff," says Newman. "That was the aesthetic we wanted. Bruce loves the blues. That's where he comes from. That guitar riff was made to sound enormous. That's the entire raison d'être. Bruce's riff is so inevitable. And it's the key to *Read & Burn 01*. Again, how to make as much as possible out of as little as possible: a huge great fuckoff guitar riff, with shouting and stops. There's really very little apart from Bruce's guitar, my voice, and drums on it. It's not really a tune. My only task was to make the guitar as big as humanly possible."

Newman gives some more context for this insistence on unremitting, super-sized guitar, as typified by 'In The Art Of Stopping': "It was in a slightly garage-rock sort of vein. I was listening to that first Black Rebel Motorcycle Club record – not their songs but the way that everything just sounded enormous. It's of its time. It relates totally to The White Stripes and whatever was happening around 2000. That's what its roots are. And there's no bass: groups without bass was very much an aesthetic at the time."

Notwithstanding its absolute simplicity and its unabashedly moronic disposition, 'In The Art Of Stopping' is also a classic example of a self-conscious Wire number that playfully suggests and executes its own concept. That concept is Gilbert's notion of Wire's simultaneously *creative* and *destructive* sensibility: they are creating this song only in order to destroy it or perhaps only in order to have something to destroy. Lyrically and musically, this track enacts the idea that the destructive moment – the *stopping* or ending of the song, and the transformation of its presence into absence – is actually the moment that creates the work of art. The title sets this idea in motion, the song serving purely as a preface to its own subsequent absence: that the music and lyrics are composed of three and a half minutes of repetition underlines the point that the song itself has no real identity or value and that the focus rests on its impending end and disappearance. Indeed, the largely undifferentiated sound accentuates the idea that it's a non-song; that it's not completely there to begin with. The fullness of the creative moment only appears in the song's absence.

A video was later made for 'In The Art Of Stopping', shot by Malka Spigel. The concept was Gilbert's. Low budget, simple, and effective, it features performance footage of Wire from 2002, supplemented with sequences of the band huddled inside what could be a broom-cupboard – Swim Studio, in fact. The tight camera work in that dark, confined space – with the emphasis occasionally and uncomfortably on Newman's lit mouth – graphically renders the claustrophobia of the *Read & Burn–Send* material.

## It's all about the riff

One of the few tracks to emerge from playing together as a group, 'Spent' is another prime example of the riff-centric methodology. "It came out of that very feeble jam at Ritz," says Newman, "but it's indestructible. I asked Bruce if he had any more riffs, and he said: I've got this one – and the band played it in a minute and a half. Really it's all about that riff. The entire thing was constructed out of that. It's all chopped up and made into something."

The working version of the track was titled 'Ten Years After', a reference to its unconscious origins in late-60s/early-70s blues-rock (the phrase "ten years later" appears in the lyrics). "I thought the riff was too close to a classic Ten Years After track," remembers Gilbert, "one of those fast two-note things. Colin saved it from sounding too much like the offending article by adding an extra loop. Which I'm very grateful for." For Newman, this track is a paradigmatic instance of the *Send*-era sensibility. "'Spent' is like a fluffy ambient track where you have a huge great long blissed-out build up before the beat drops. Rhythmically, that's where it comes from, but the musical elements are from blues-rock."

'99.9' is another track that epitomises the dance-rock hybrid. "It's unplayable," says Newman, "even though it has all the elements of a band playing. It's really the apotheosis of punk-rock dance music. It has all the elements of both, plus a strong smattering of heavy rock. You either love it or hate it." The words were composed on the afternoon of its maiden performance, at a memorial for This Heat's Gareth Williams in March 2002 – "just so we'd have something to sing," Newman recalls. "Lyrically it's as nonsensical as most Wire things are. It's a series of one-liners by Graham and Bruce. I put one or two in." While the lyrics for '1st Fast' articulate Wire's new aesthetic, the words to '99.9' reflect on the broader status of Wire in the early 2000s, referring to the open-ended nature of the undertaking in which they were engaged. "'The road ahead looks quite uncertain' described the process," says Lewis. "It was definitely something to pursue, but no one knew how it would end up."

This track would serve as the set opener for the band's live dates through much of the *Read & Burn–Send* period, performed by Newman alone onstage, backed by a CD, before the band launched into 'Germ Ship'. The sight and sound of Newman ranting on his own was at once a compelling and unsettling spectacle; it challenged and disoriented audiences, foreshadowing the punishing musical encounter that would ensue. As far as Lewis was concerned, it was the ideal preamble. "It was quite inexplicable that at the start you had the singer onstage, alone, going completely demented. Even if you knew who Wire were, you'd still wonder: What's going on here? What's happened? It was a weapon against indifference."

Throughout the *Read & Burn–Send* material, far from evoking Lewis's feared "tired old men", Wire go to the other extreme – and over-compensation has rarely sounded so good. In places, the effect is patently ridiculous and quite brilliant. 'Comet', which could be by Motörhead circa *Bomber*, condenses the general spirit of Newman and Gilbert's endeavours, combining humour and unforgiving execution. "It was a comedy song, really," says Gilbert, referring to the lyrics, "my usual doom-laden approach to everything. It's about the bullet that's got your name on it – a very big bullet – and the idea that whoever discovers the comet that actually crashes into the Earth, it'll be named after that person." The track's absurdity is heightened by its tempo. For Grey, the speed of the piece made it a favourite to perform, mostly due to the challenges it presented, almost as a limit experience. "I very much enjoy 'Comet' because it's something of a tightrope: being so fast, it gives scope for things to go wrong."

Wire have never wanted for fast-loud songs (from '12XU' and 'Two People In A Room' to 'Two Minutes' and 'Stealth Of A Stork'), but there's never been anything remotely macho about them. With their muscular, guitar-oriented attack, however, Wire were sounding macho for the first time in their career (notwithstanding Susan Gogan's comments about "cock rock" 25 years earlier at the Nashville Rooms). 'I Don't Understand' is a case in point. It might not be as fast and hard-edged as some of the other tracks, but its attitude is unmistakable – this is all about exaggerated strutting, flexing, and posturing. Of course, just as the arch, constructed character of Wire makes it impossible for them to do nostalgia, they can't really do 'macho' either, and it remains at the level of irony. With 'I Don't Understand', that irony was amplified by the song's afterlife as the soundtrack to a certain TV advertisement. "For it to have been used in a Victoria's Secret lingerie commercial is a stroke of genius," says Newman, "because it's so macho, in a stupid way."

With its roots in 'Ally In Exile', 'I Don't Understand' further exemplified Wire's long-established, Wombles-like recycling and reusing of their own discarded sonic artefacts. This approach was foundational to 'Nice Streets Above', for which Lewis revisited 'Drill'. "This was a gift, an *objet trouvé*," he explains. "It was a loop I made from a live desk-recording of 'Drill': [the line] 'could it be a, could it be a drill?' I changed the pitch of Colin's voice and, strangely, it sounded like me, singing, 'nice streets-a, nice streets-a, nice streets-above', which was an odd phrase. It ended up with that typically Wire, obsessive feel. Colin would call it 'moronic', but it's more of a completely insane concentration on a simple idea – and making that as absurd as possible."

If 'Nice Streets Above' evolved from Lewis's tinkering with Newman's part on 'Drill', Newman and Gilbert performed altogether more radical surgery on one of the pieces Lewis had submitted by mail, 'The Agfers Of Kodack', in the process transforming it into something new. Applying a vintage Wire method, they stripped it to the bone. "Graham originally sent this piece, and me and Bruce gradually took away all his elements, right down to the last bit, and suddenly this Black Sabbath-style guitar riff – which I'd played along with the general chaos – leapt out from nowhere, and the song became really good. It was one of those hilarious moments. It was totally absurd. Very moronic. Bruce and I burst out laughing because it was so absurd. The song suddenly became really good because of it."

Grey's solitary postal submission, the drums for 'Raft Ants', made it onto *Read & Burn 02* more or less intact. He didn't make life easy for the producer, given the nature of his original recording – but according to Newman, it does seem to have been aesthetically in line with what was being cooked up in the studio. "Rob recorded it on DAT at home, all in distortion. So it was totally brutal. Everything was in distortion." Newman remembers that his own contribution to the song was equally unorthodox: "The riff is what would happen if you made Lenny Kravitz nasty." This was one of the few tracks that the band were unable to perform live – not because it was impossible to transform it from a studio construction into a viable song, but because of fundamental creative differences. "Rob completely disagreed about where the 'one' [the downbeat] was," laughs Newman. "Technically, it's playable live, but we'll never be able to because Rob's idea of where the 'one' is is somewhere different from where I made it, and the rest of us can't find it – we're not on that 'one'."

No Wire record would be complete without a contested song and 'Trash/Treasure' was the example from *Send* – or not, as it transpired, since the track, from *Read & Burn 02*, was excluded from the album. "I wanted to write a pop song," says Newman. "It was sort of British miserablist in style. It also harks back to Nils Lofgren … but you've got to know your rock history really seriously to get the connection. It makes no sense that it wasn't on *Send*. It's one of the strongest tracks. Bruce refused to have it on there, because he thought it was too pop. There's a huge history of that in Wire. He was implacable on it. He just wanted noise." Gilbert clarifies his position: "It could well have been because it seemed too pop, but it just didn't feel cohesive with the rest of the material somehow." Like Newman, Lewis was disappointed that this song didn't make *Send*. "It's in a pop tradition that Wire has always subscribed to, but the discussion around it seemed to take a neurotic turn, and everything became an issue: Should it be a single? Will it unbalance the album? There were things that went onto the album that I would have certainly replaced with 'Trash/Treasure'."

There were other pieces, however, that didn't even make it as far as the *Read & Burn* EPs – most notoriously 'Aike', a Gilbert ambient-guitar interlude. "Paul Smith hated it," recalls Newman. "He called it 'sub-Pink Floyd rubbish' and said if we released it, he'd stop managing us." (The track almost saw the light of day on *Send Ultimate*, but Gilbert blocked its inclusion.) A set of Gilbert lyrics, 'Welcome To The Exit Museum', was rejected by Newman. "I refused to work with it. It was just so negative.

There's some pretty negative stuff in *Read & Burn* and *Send*, but this wasn't 'funny' negative, 'Mannequin'-type negative. It was just horrible and depressing – grumpy old men territory." Gilbert gives only schematic details of the content: "It was an absurdity: [about] a room or a building completely full of exits," he says, adding, as an idea occurs to him for a future artwork, "I really should do that at some point, unless some other bugger's done it." Newman also had reservations about some of Gilbert's other pieces: he felt 'Being Watched' was "slightly pervy" and deemed 'You Can't Leave Now' "a very cruel lyric" – but nothing else was vetoed.

## Coca-Cola and Émile Zola

Thematically and tonally, the material is unequivocally millennial – albeit after the fact – with the lyrics displaying a markedly apocalyptic orientation: ecological calamity, violence (real and threatened), death, greed, rampant consumerism, surveillance, an ambivalent relationship with technology, and even planetary disaster are all grist for Wire's dystopian mill.

Like the music, the texts fit with Newman's desired aesthetic, being neither "baroque" nor "long and meandering". In some cases, the concision is extreme. With the exception of 'The Agfers Of Kodack', Lewis's "copy for noise" is surprisingly unadorned. 'Germ Ship' – his "ode to dear old planet Earth" – is refreshingly succinct ("Germ ship / Aliens on board / Fatal attraction / Sponsored by Ford"). In turn, Gilbert pushes his own minimalism to new levels with the 13-syllable 'In The Art Of Stopping' ("Trust me / Believe me / It's all in the art of stopping"). Lewis, however, wins this competition with the ten-syllable 'Nice Streets Above' ("Nice streets, such nice streets, such nice streets above").

While the *Read & Burn* title of the EP series suggests espionage and intelligence-gathering, more significantly it alludes to a postmodern sensibility centred on the rapid recyclability and exchangeability of text and information. This title captures the depthless, self-conscious cut-and-paste feel of some of the lyrical content, which is characterised by its juxtaposition and listing of slogans, phrases, and individual words, randomly excised, it would seem, from the discursive fabric of everyday life. Such an approach perfectly matches Newman's production ethos, itself centred on collage, artifice, and construction. This is illustrated by 'Spent' – assembled from contributions by everyone except Grey ("Rob hadn't written any lyrics since 'Death In The Living Room'," notes Newman) – and Lewis's cut-and-paste, listed-word piece, 'Raft Ants', which scores extra points for rhyming "Coca-Cola" with "Émile Zola".

Overall, though, the lyric-writing during this phase of work offers little with which to engage, in terms of style and structure; there's nothing very noteworthy about the way the words work or the way ideas are presented. 'In The Art Of Stopping' is an exception in that the words function as part of the song's conceptual conceit – but it's an isolated case. That said, it's unfair to critique this material in conventional, traditional terms given the intent and design of the *Read & Burn–Send* aesthetic: it is very much a concept – all about surface and noise. To say that the lyrics are often slight and facile, without substance, disposable and unoriginal wouldn't be a criticism but simply a description of how they were intended to sound.

If there is a criticism to be made, it's a wider artistic one, about the shelf life of this sort of postmodernism and the staleness of its representational strategies: the recycling of cliché is a central postmodern trope, and it can still make for powerful and enduring artistic statements; however, the vast majority of its practitioners fail to do anything authentically creative with their clichéd materials and produce work that is merely clichéd postmodernism. Even by the standards of 2002, some of Wire's lyrics can be viewed in those terms.

True to form, Gilbert's words here tend to be more satisfying and substantive than those of his bandmates. As usual – and as Newman's remarks on 'Welcome To The Exit Museum' attest – it's all rather grim. More grim than usual, in fact. This is certainly an instance in which it could be argued that the tone of Gilbert's writing gives some insight into his state of mind as he neared the end of his tenure with Wire. His contributions are decidedly morbid, focused on departure, ending, decline, and demise (sometimes to humorous effect, as on 'Comet'). 'You Can't Leave Now' is especially dark, with its images of feral dogs, gluttony, and living death. Newman singles out this song, asking: "Is 'You Can't Leave Now' really him talking about himself?"

Whether or not there is an autobiographical dimension to Gilbert's work, it is fitting that he should give his final vocal appearance as a member of Wire on one of the bleakest tracks of the *Read & Burn–Send* period: the environmental-disaster ditty, 'Half Eaten', which ends with him unable to escape the horrors of the disintegrating world because he hasn't "got the fare".

### Giving imagery the finger

The simple-yet-striking artwork for each of the *Read & Burn* EPs and the *Send* album was devised by designer David Coppenhall, a Wire fan since

*Pink Flag*, which his friend Russell Mills had first played to him the week of its release. Coppenhall got to know the band-members in the early 80s, eventually collaborating with Mills on the artwork for He Said's *Hail* and the rejected *Ideal Copy* sleeve. He forged a close and lasting friendship with Gilbert, with whom he felt a strong artistic kinship, working on the covers for *Turns And Strokes* and Dome's *Yclept* in the 90s. By the time of Wire's *Send* era, he'd designed covers for an array of artists including Eno, David Sylvian, Harold Budd, King Crimson, and Led Zeppelin.

The *Read & Burn* EPs display a consistent aesthetic: they came in matching Digipaks – the first blue-grey, the second red – bearing just the band name and the CD title; the same minimalist approach was applied to the CD labels, plain white except for a coloured square at the centre containing the catalogue number. The effect was generic computer-software chic, in keeping with the *Read & Burn* title. (The inside-folds feature obscure retro-industrial images furnished by Lewis.) Coppenhall explains how it all came about:

"The time felt right for a deliberate move away from image. It was a time of tedious oversaturation – everywhere you looked was awash with imagery, every space felt filled … claustrophobic, over-busy. I felt a stark simplicity would be refreshing, and Bruce was all for a utilitarian feel. I'd always been aware of Bruce's general innate disdain for packaging, really – the dressing something up, selling it. It was something I understood and held an empathy with. With Bruce, there had been a mutual respect for the utilitarian approach adopted by, say, Penguin, with their uniform Tschichold book-cover series in the late 40s. This thinking carried through the series. The *Read & Burn* statement in itself alluded to mass production, copying. It seemed only natural that the covers might cynically reflect this process – and in something of a banal way. Colours were chosen specifically to conflict, with the aim to judder or feel slightly uncomfortable on reading. Veering toward an afterimage."

Although it shares the same minimalist, industrial aesthetic, the black *Send* sleeve also involves a figural element – a finger (Coppenhall's) emerging from the dark to press a touch-screen button, as if enacting the album's titular command. He outlines its genesis: "It was simply pushing my finger directly onto the scanner and scanning it. The cover came about in a bizarre way. In itself, the title presented a bit of a conundrum – another prescriptive action, an instruction which in many ways felt devoid of representation. It lay on the back burner for a week or two, and I recall the word rattling around my head endlessly and still nothing came and no thoughts from anyone. Colin sent me a couple of image options he'd sourced, but they somehow didn't feel right. I sorted a mail to him to say this, and just as I went to press … *send* … it flew into my head, and I just shifted that finger across to the scanner screen instead.

"The boxed graphic was following the *Read & Burn* link: to me, 'Send' had become the final instruction following the *Read & Burn* title, and it made sense to follow on. I liked the fact that it was both a simple and direct recording of the instruction and process. It also kind of cynically echoed the classic 'Your Country Needs You', yet also countered it due to its introspective nature. A finger-on-the-pulse suggestion, along with a 'fuck you' aspect. Obviously, the finger on the button could be seen to hold a more sinister aspect."

## The dreaded drum option

A traditional approach to the *Read & Burn–Send* material would have seen the songs learned by the band, rehearsed, then recorded in the studio and subsequently played in concert; in this instance, the band-members learned the songs in preparation for live work only when the recording was finished.

"I learned my parts off the CD," says Grey. "It was the first Wire album where I learned the songs after they'd been recorded." While in theory such a process wasn't challenging, when it came to this body of work, he felt some uncertainty regarding its live incarnation and his role in it. "I did wonder about that. As far as playing drums was concerned, I was encouraged by the retrospective work, but it was somewhat unknown as to how the *Send* stuff was going to be performed live – or even if it could be. I was worried that if my acoustic drumming was compared to the electronic version, it might sound like it was lacking a quality that made it good on the CD – that it wouldn't translate into acoustic drumming. So there were a lot of unknown quantities. Everything was a bit up in the air."

Gilbert believes that, despite the artificial assembly process, the intention was always to make something that could be played live in a standard band configuration. "From the outset, it was obvious that whatever methods we used to construct the things, it still had to be achievable onstage – especially using guitars and drums." Nonetheless, early in the planning stages Grey worried that history might be about to repeat itself – particularly when the band bought him some shiny new electronic toys. "After the Royal Festival Hall in 2000, I was encouraged to use an Akai MPC sampling drum machine and a mixing desk – as if that was what I was going to be using, rather than playing acoustic drums. The idea was that this was how Wire would look in the future. There was some hope – or some pressure – that this was what I was going to play, and there wasn't going to be any of that 'live drums nonsense'. It was as if I was being adapted to Wir, which was like going back to *Manscape* and programming. It was a second attempt to fit me into this formula. I don't think the dreaded drum option was on offer originally, but the sampling drum machine wasn't what I wanted."

Gilbert still emphasises that at no stage was there any suggestion of usurping Grey as a live drummer. Rather, he and Newman were just looking to expand the band's range by incorporating both playing *and* programming. "We were moving toward a situation where it could be a mixture." Newman goes further, describing it not as a mixture but as distinct projects: "We were going to have two kinds of Wire. We were going to have one that was more electronic." Gilbert remembers the band giving Grey his unwanted present. "We bought Rob the drum machine and said: Just have some fun, and come back with a few interesting patterns. They don't have to be drum sounds, just anything you like. It's a sampling thing – you can even sample yourself sneezing or coughing. But he took it home and never took it out of the box. We were just trying to stir it up a bit. There was no question of him not playing drums. We were just trying to enrich the mix with a variety of things we could play with."

As it turned out, Grey's antipathy to the drum machine almost became a moot point since the nature of some of the material seemed to rule out the possibility of kit-playing. As Grey saw it, the principal difficulty (as in the case of 'Comet') was to match the tempo at which his virtual self had played on the records. "There was a question as to whether some of it was going to be faster than I could play – so that would exclude played drums in itself." Lewis recalls speed being the main issue. "When the recording was done, the gauntlet was thrown down to Rob: do you think you can actually play this? – because the tempos are rather high. If he couldn't play along, it was impossible. Rob accepted the challenge." As a result, according to Lewis, the band settled on the conventional live setup: "The decision was made that it wouldn't involve other more sophisticated technology. It was going to be guitars and drums, and for costs it would be kept as a small mobile unit. It was a very good time to get back to that simplicity."

This stripped-down approach to performance, starting in 2002, was welcomed by Grey, who felt that a tendency toward over-adornment and embellishment had, in the past, begun to mar Wire's live work as a four-piece, eroding their traditional adherence to the values of precision, accuracy, structure, and discipline. "I don't think it had been a very convincing performance in the 80s. For a long time, it had been too imprecise. If we were going to relaunch ourselves as a live band, we had to simplify everything to basic playing, just to make it work – so that it wasn't just freeform like it was in the 80s." He makes a point that resonates with other criticisms of Wire during that period – as articulated from within the band (Newman) and from the outside (Daniel Miller) – suggesting that some individuals had lost sight of the collective endeavour. "It seemed more like people just doing what they wanted, without really worrying about whether this was making a whole." From his perspective, then, the *Read & Burn–Send* material held great potential as another reset moment for Wire. Although it had been made artificially, by two people in a room, it now offered Wire the chance to rediscover some of their core values in performance.

The band had taken their first tentative public steps at the Gareth Williams memorial in March, where they played a three-song set. The ink was barely dry on Newman's scribbled crib-sheet for the hectoring '99.9'. This was a beta version featuring live, slightly random playing from Gilbert and Lewis, plus bass drum from Grey – the rest of the rhythm track pre-recorded. 'In The Art Of Stopping' sounded more promising, if a little precarious, as it was clearly being held together by Newman's shouted "one-two-three-four" signposts. While the evening ended on a familiar note with 'Pink Flag', the track was bulked-up, more muscular than previous incarnations – benefiting from the band's new, anabolically enhanced sensibility.

"That was a kind of trial run," says Newman, "and I came away from it thinking we could do it." Which was just as well, since they had just scheduled further gigs. The first complete set of new material (with encores of 'Lowdown' and 'Pink Flag') was debuted a month later in Bristol; this was a warm-up for two All Tomorrow's Parties sets, on April 20 and April 27, again at Pontin's in Camber Sands, this time curated by Shellac. Between these ATP performances, the band also played a live session for Tom Robinson's programme on the just-launched BBC 6 Music. All of this was followed by the May arrival of *Read & Burn 01*, the first major release on the pinkflag label, which – to the band's surprise – began attracting considerable interest. "Suddenly we were pressing up in quantities that I hadn't been involved in with any release," recalls Newman. "It was great to feel part of something that had a life of its own. You could feel it in the work. You could feel it in the moment."

On July 20, Wire performed a one-off gig at the ICA and, the next day, visited the BBC's Maida Vale studios to record their fifth Peel session, the first in 14 years. For the occasion, they played '1st Fast' and 'I Don't Understand'

327

from *Read & Burn 01*, as well as 'Spent' and '99.9', which would appear on *Read & Burn 02*. Successful tours of North America (September) and Europe (November) followed, punctuated by the October release of the second *Read & Burn* EP. The live sets from this period concentrated on the new material, although four *Pink Flag* tracks were habitually aired as encores.

Amid all this activity, Wire had also revalidated their art credentials at *M25/London Orbital*, a multimedia event organised by Paul Smith at the Barbican in October to tie in with Iain Sinclair's *London Orbital* book and film (co-directed with Chris Petit). Gilbert, an associate of Sinclair's, had contributed the film's soundtrack. Others participating that night included Sinclair and Petit themselves, Ken Campbell, Bill Drummond, Jimmy Cauty, and Bill Griffiths. J.G. Ballard was scheduled to make an appearance but was ill and unable to make the trip into town from Shepperton. In keeping with the event's subject matter, Wire performed an automotively themed piece titled 'Dip Flash', built around their 1978 single 'Dot Dash'. This would later evolve into '23 Years Too Late', on the third *Read & Burn* EP. Gathered side by side at a table, the band-members eschewed their usual instruments to present the "more electronic" version of Wire that Newman had been envisaging. Lewis used a Korg Kaoss Pad, Gilbert added effects and noises here and there, and Grey tapped away on his Octapad, while Newman mixed everything with the basic tracks on his laptop.

### Sign me up!

Late 2002 saw the band start preparations for another unlikely engagement along the same lines as the Royal Festival Hall retrospective. It would involve performing the *Pink Flag* album, from start to finish, at the Barbican in April 2003. This was to be part of the venue's Only Connect series, which paired artists working in different media for one-time events. "The whole thing was very much a Paul Smith concept," says Gilbert. "He had his fingers in all sorts of pies, and an opportunity arose, with a little bit of funding, to collaborate with another artist, in another medium." Wire's co-conspirators on the night would be the 2003 Turner Prize nominees Jake and Dinos Chapman and the theatre designer Es Devlin.

As Gilbert recalls it, the idea of playing *Pink Flag* as a concert performance had been in the air for a while before they were approached by the Barbican. "It was some kind of grand strategy by Paul Smith. We were in my flat. He was racking his brains for what to do and had the first three albums out on the floor, looking at them, and he was saying: there's got to be something we can do, something creative, something Wire would never do –

which was of course playing the album in its entirety. So he said: isn't it time we did the whole of *Pink Flag* as the album? I wish he hadn't had that idea."

At this point, it was a fairly new, exciting notion; Brian Wilson, David Bowie, and Arthur Lee had all performed classic albums at the Royal Festival Hall within the previous year or so, but All Tomorrow's Parties didn't begin their Don't Look Back series until 2005. Newman remembers Smith making his pitch in the pub. The prospects were mouth-watering, to say the least. "Smith told me one night in the Angel that we should do *all* of the albums. We should do *Pink Flag* first, then *Chairs Missing*, and then we should do *154*." Newman looks back on this with some irony, given the way that their relationship with Smith would later deteriorate. "This was Smith the Magician in full flight: the colours that you see are fantastic! It's all absolutely amazing! And we're going to be a week in Los Angeles doing *154* at UCLA, and it's all going to be incredible! We were going to do everything. Even *154* on ice … and we'd find great collaborators, and we'd do it in art institutions. It all sounded fabulous. So I said: *Yeah! Sign me up!*"

Regardless of Smith's irresistible plan, there was some reluctance on Wire's part to perform *Pink Flag* as a standalone piece. "We weren't totally comfortable with it," says Lewis. By playing this album, they felt there was a danger of undermining all the work they'd been doing to reinvent themselves as a contemporary band. *Send* was due to be released the same week as the Barbican event and so, unsurprisingly, Wire were adamant that their performance had to involve that material. They arrived at a compromise. "We decided that if we did *Pink Flag*," Lewis recalls, "we would do the new album as well. Then it makes sense: we can contextualise everything again. It's our game, it's our history, it's our choice as to how we portray it."

Organising the collaborative side of the project wasn't straightforward. Es Devlin, whose name had been suggested by Paul Smith, was the band's first choice. Devlin, a former student of Beckett collaborator Jocelyn Herbert, had experience at diverse levels of culture, designing sets for The Pet Shop Boys, The Rambert Dance Company, Sadler's Wells, the BBC, and The Royal Shakespeare Company, as well as working with Harold Pinter and Trevor Nunn on *Betrayal* at the National Theatre. Gilbert was enthusiastic ("She had a reputation for doing quite radical things"), and Lewis was impressed by the Beckett and Pinter connections. However, Devlin's agent turned down Wire's proposal, saying that her client did not work with pop musicians, despite evidence to the contrary. ("She said: absolutely not – without talking to me," recalls Devlin. "I sacked her afterwards.") As a result,

Wire moved ahead with their second choice, the Chapman brothers. "They were stars," says Newman, "so it wasn't a bad idea."

Then matters grew complicated. After Devlin's agent had rejected the band's offer, Smith emailed the designer directly. "He said: it's such a shame you can't do it," Devlin remembers, "and I thought: wow, I never even heard about this! It sounds great, I'd love to do it." This took place with Wire in the middle of their November 2002 European tour: Devlin had received Smith's email one evening while she was working on an opera in Stockholm and, by coincidence, Wire were one block away, about to go onstage. She caught the end of the gig and, based on what she'd seen, told them she was definitely interested in developing something.

Wire were now in an awkward position. "So Es came back and said she wanted to do it," Newman recalls, "but we couldn't then say we didn't want Jake and Dinos." Indeed, the Chapmans had seemed like a better option – a known quantity, according to Lewis, who had first met them in the mid 90s. "Bruce and I knew Jake and Dinos. They were very much part of the Disobey scene. They were on the Disobey crew, doing postcards and flyers. They had been fans of *Pink Flag* when they were younger, and they'd come up with an idea."

The decision was made to split the Barbican budget between Devlin and the Chapmans, and the band quickly realised that this could work to their advantage: having these two very different creative teams facilitated the performance of two discrete bodies of work. Consequently, they planned the evening, titled *flag:burning* (a Gilbert–Lewis idea), around two sets: the first consisting of *Pink Flag* (with the participation of the Chapmans), the second composed of material from *Send* (working with Devlin). The sets would be linked by a second version of *Pink Flag*'s title track, played not in the style of the 1977 original but in the contemporary *Read & Burn–Send* style. "It was the bridge between the first half of the show and the second half," says Lewis.

The event's structure and its title (which connected *Pink Flag* and the *Read & Burn* era) embodied the band's "creative but destructive" aesthetic: not as a nihilistic process but as an ongoing cycle of remaking and reimagining. The performance, juxtaposing the two sets, would enact this cycle for the audience, celebrating Wire's iconic work but then immediately overwriting it. The concept hinged on the transitional reprise of 'Pink Flag', which encapsulated the evening's broader dynamic: acknowledging the connection between the old and the new but simultaneously expunging the past.

While this promised to be a memorable occasion and a significant validation of Wire's cultural worth – in terms of the way it allied their work with the work of their art-world collaborators – there was dissent in the ranks. Looking back, Gilbert maintains that, from the beginning, he was less than happy about the Only Connect project. Whereas the return to playing together as a band in 2000 had been appealing, as had the creation of the *Read & Burn* and *Send* material, this performance was another matter entirely. "I didn't want to do it. Everybody else wanted to. I didn't feel I could prevent them. Everybody seemed very keen and excited to do it. It was a good wheeze and quite a surreal event, so I couldn't stand in the way of it, as an idea. But I did not enjoy it at all."

The root of the problem for Gilbert was preparing the *Pink Flag* numbers. The mechanics of the process were unusual, as he had to relearn the band's own work from tablature posted online by fans who had transcribed the material. "Apart from one or two songs, everybody had completely forgotten it. Nobody really remembered what the chords were. We had no recollection of how they were played, so we went through the process of learning. I had to go to some sort of website to find what the chords were, and it became clear that, often, they were wrong. A lot of them didn't work. They were people's interpretations of what they'd heard on the record. What they were hearing was probably a clash of chords, and they'd picked the closest one."

Performing *Pink Flag* in its original format meant that all the guitar duties would rest with Gilbert because Newman, in 1977 mode for the first part of the show, would only be doing vocals. Gilbert was therefore confronted with one of his bêtes noires: the minor chord. "As far as I know," says Newman, "the only time Bruce used a regular tuning – possibly since the 70s – was for *Pink Flag* at the Barbican and the warm-up gig at On The Rocks [the night before]." Gilbert describes his preparation in intensely negative terms: "It was quite traumatic for me, actually. I had to learn all these old songs, songs with minor chords in them. At that point, I couldn't play guitar – I never could, really – because, by that time, I'd reverted to open tuning, so I had to learn how to play guitar all over again. I literally had to learn these songs and put my fingers in strange places. I was traumatised by learning it again. Totally traumatised. I thought I was going to have a nervous breakdown. I thought: I can't do this. I literally can't do it. It was a nightmare. An absolute nightmare."

He did manage, but only just. "I got through it with copious notes. And a combination of looking at the tablature and listening to the records. I actually practised at home, playing along with the records. There was no other way of doing it. I was just grinding through it, trying to get the physical memory going. That was the only way I could learn – the physical memory of it, rather than what proper musicians do. Just the physical repetition of playing those chord sequences was the only way I could do it. I don't know how I did it. At the end, I felt sick. I thought: that's the last time I ever do that – play old stuff. I was teetering on the edge of collapse. Loads of bloody notes. All over the floor. Shocking."

Things did improve somewhat for Gilbert when the band began rehearsing. "It felt a bit like when we first started, when there was a visceral kind of pleasure about making a lot of noise. I've always liked that anyway – it's just a pity one then had to do it in front of people." His spirits were lifted a little by the practice gig at On The Rocks. "I enjoyed the warm-up in that small place. The reason it was enjoyable was seeing the huge smiles on people's faces. They thought they'd never see Wire playing the old stuff in a funny little club. People were very, very happy. I was stunned. My terror got transcended by the smiles on people's faces. But doing it at the Barbican was gruesome."

### Samuel Beckett meets Spinal Tap

On the night, the band performed *Pink Flag* in front of an enormous screen showing exercise and aerobics videos, a different (but not different *enough*) one for each track. This was the Chapmans' contribution. Although it caused some initial amusement and surprise, it soon fell flat, making what was a revolutionarily brisk album start to feel strangely long. "Jake and Dinos had collected awful 80s exercise videos – Lycra, exotic locations," recalls Lewis. "And they Chapmanised them by stretching them and buggering them about now and again in unfortunate ways while we played *Pink Flag*. It was a bit of a one-trick pony. It was a joke that didn't really work." The Chapmans' piece foundered because they seemed to lack an awareness of how to translate their work to the context of live performance. "It was an idea that worked well for three minutes," says Newman. "Jake and Dinos are great with what they do, but they can't do real time. What Wire do live is time-based. You can't just have one idea: there need to be a number of ideas to sustain the length. We trusted the fact that Jake and Dinos were art-stars. We should have communicated more with them."

At the conclusion of the *Pink Flag* set, during the contemporary revision of the title track, dancers took to the stage. With the Chapmans' videos still playing, they did aerobics in front of the band – this was devised by the accomplished choreographer Aletta Collins (daughter of ex-Wire manager Mick). Lewis thought the live aerobics was a hoot. "It was good to see the look on the audience's face. Some people loved it, others were in complete horror. It was really fun." In the intermission, the Chapmans made a stab at DJ-ing in the Barbican foyer. "They just left a record playing," laughs Gilbert. "They didn't really pursue it."

Grey took a dim view of the first half of the evening. He had no objection to the idea of artistic collaboration, but he found this instance of it unsatisfactory. "I don't see why we needed a performance in front of us and behind us. Are the audience meant to be watching us, a video, or the dancers?" Essentially, he felt that the video and the dancers sent the wrong message about the work itself, their very presence implying an inadequacy in Wire's material and its execution. "If you need something to supplement what you're doing, it suggests to me that the thing that people have come to see is lacking – it's not interesting, so you need to add something."

The second half of the evening was far more successful. Newman sums up the difference: "Jake and Dinos had a one-minute joke, and Es had a proper idea, because she knew how to design stage sets." Devlin's concept reimagined and restructured what she considered to be the clichéd visual grammar of the rock band in its live habitat. This was something she'd been thinking about for years. "I'd been to see a lot of gigs throughout the 90s, and the only thing that I saw visually that really blew me away was U2. I remember thinking: someone's trying to achieve something visually here. But everything else I looked at, I thought no one was making an effort. As a person who interprets things visually, I was always disappointed. I was above all sick of the shape of the way bands looked, whatever the space was around them: whether it was an arena or a proscenium-arch theatre or just a club. I didn't understand why the drums were always on a little riser with funny little bits of scaffolding that always seemed to be there. I just didn't get it. It annoyed me that it was almost the law that you always had these ugly bits of kit – so I was determined to not have those."

Additionally, Devlin was eager to do something about the dead space that surrounded and often overwhelmed bands onstage. "In terms of framing, from working in big theatres and small theatres in my opera and theatre work, I'm always very interested in the negative space between the performer and the frame around them – and I wanted to tighten that with Wire."

As a means of deconstructing the unimaginative traditional choreography and framing of rock performance, Devlin placed each member of the band in his own small environment – separate boxes lined up side by side across the stage: "I had the idea quite quickly," says Devlin. "I must have been quietly scheming it for years every time I'd seen a band.

I was quietly thinking what I would do, without consciously knowing that I was thinking that. So it was almost instantaneous that I knew I wanted to do that shape around them."

The boxes that Gilbert, Grey, Lewis, and Newman inhabited for their set were ten-foot square at the front, eight-by-ten at the back and ten-foot deep. They were made out of plywood, with mirror-foil walls on the inside, so the band-members were unable to see one another. There was a grey projection screen on the back wall of each box, and the front was covered with a sheet of shark's tooth gauze – this became opaque when front-lit and transparent when lit from behind. Pre-recorded video was occasionally projected onto the gauze, showing details of the performers' faces (Newman's mouth, Grey's nose, Lewis's right eye, and Gilbert's left eye), as well as a digital readout of their heart rates (recorded on an ECG machine Devlin had borrowed from a hospital). Stock brain-scan images were projected onto the back walls.

"The idea for that content was to analyse 'the band-creature' in its box," explains Devlin. "Knowing what they're like, I thought it would tickle them that we were deconstructing them a bit – rigging them up to machines and trying to self-reference. I think they enjoyed the fun of that. I just flew in with utter ignorance and went completely on enthusiasm and instinct and, weirdly, I think there was more about it that was in tune with them than not."

Devlin's original plan had been to have the band hooked up to MRI and ECG equipment onstage, so that the information could be presented in real time. Live neuroimaging was a non-starter, as Devlin recalls: "Getting complex brain-reading machinery wasn't going to happen. We looked into it for about ten seconds." The idea of onstage heart-rate monitoring for each band-member was also swiftly abandoned. "I wanted to have the ECG attached to them while they were really playing. It was supposed to be live, but it dawned on us that we weren't sophisticated enough to make that happen. So we faked it. The heart rates were completely fake – and a lot of them flatlined at certain points throughout the show. But it wasn't to do with them actually dying, it was because we hadn't got the right Sellotape to stick the little nodes on – and they kept falling off. It didn't occur to me that people would see them flatlining and think they were dead. So in the end, it wasn't truthful. It wasn't quite the investigative approach that it was pretending to be."

While Devlin created a truly memorable, iconic spectacle, her concept was in part based on an erroneous assumption, as Gilbert explains: "When she'd seen us play in Stockholm, she was struck by how separate we all seemed to be – but, actually, Wire live rely totally on not being separate. We rely on subtle cues and signs and people's body language." They were surprised that she hadn't noticed their reliance on communication with each other onstage. Lewis took this as a compliment. "Everyone was flattered by that – that someone who came from the theatre world didn't see the cues or signals."

Devlin laughs when she thinks about this issue. "Although I'd seen a lot of gigs, I was utterly ignorant about what it took to play live. In my arrogant and ignorant self back then, I didn't even think to ask them: could you actually perform like this? Because I just presumed that they could. And I think they presumed I *knew* that they couldn't: to them, it seemed so self-evident that you couldn't perform like that, so they assumed I must have understood and taken all that into account – and that I would be supplying all kinds of kit and monitors to make it all possible for them. Gradually, I think it dawned on them that I was absolutely ignorant of what it took and that I hadn't made any provisions for how they'd play at all – or indeed how they'd even get out at the end."

Devlin's last comment alludes to the evening's unintended punch line. Notwithstanding some of the Beckettian nuances of her design, the show ended on a more lowbrow note, in a way that highlighted the similarities between Wire's boxed performance and Spinal Tap's infamous pod disaster. She elaborates: "It really was all done on a tight budget and, in the excitement, we'd commissioned it all – and the screens on the back of the boxes were supposed to have Velcro, and they turned up without any Velcro. So I just stapled the band into their boxes – and it just didn't occur to me in my ignorance and stupidity that they'd have to get out. So they couldn't get out at the end. They were incredibly long-suffering. They didn't even shout at me once."

While Gilbert doesn't mention this slightly undignified conclusion, he does feel that, overall, playing in this unique setting presented difficulties, mostly because of the removal of the band-members' ability to communicate with one another. "It was very strange being in a box," he says. "It was all rather abstract and odd, because we couldn't see each other. And the boxes were on a slope. Very nightmarish." A minor equipment malfunction made things even more challenging for Gilbert and, unfortunately, further cements the Spinal Tap comparison. "The strap came off my guitar, and it was a situation where I couldn't stop. There was no way of doing it up. I could have ducked out of a little bit, a few bars, and got the strap back on, but it was going fast and furious, and there was no time to do it. In the end,

I was playing on my knees." In contrast with Gilbert's normally understated and unobtrusive presence, this appeared to be the height of enthusiastic, rockist theatrics. From Gilbert's point of view, it was anything but. "I found it appalling. I hated it. I tried to keep myself going by thinking of the absurdity value."

The mood backstage at the Barbican wasn't good. Those present remember tension between Smith and Gilbert. Gilbert confirms as much: "It was the last thing I wanted to do, play an old record in its entirety – however amusing it might be, however perverse it might be. Paul was excited, and he was saying how great it was. I told him we shouldn't have done it. He was rather disappointed in my reaction because he'd obviously worked very hard and made it happen, and I was a bit of a wet blanket. I'd agreed to do it, but I just wanted to get it over and done with." This was just the beginning of a friendship-ending rift, which would have serious consequences for the band and their manager – and their respective legal advisors.

Smith had been more closely aligned with Gilbert than with the other members of Wire. There was a sense among those around the band that he had initially gravitated to Gilbert because he considered him the artist in the group, and he liked the idea of being involved with people who were serious about art. Their relationship had been a fruitful one, especially for Gilbert's solo career in the 90s, when Smith had opened doors for him and provided him with numerous artistic opportunities. At the Barbican, however, their alliance appeared to be faltering.

One backstage observer that night recalls an escalating exchange between the two, during which Gilbert denounced Smith in brutal and comic terms that the manager would have found particularly galling. "At some point, Bruce told Smith he was just a shopkeeper, that he didn't know anything about art. I don't think that was exactly what he wanted to hear. I think that might have been a turning point."

## The Triumvirate

By the end of the work cycle encompassing the first two *Read & Burn* EPs and the *Send* album, Colin Newman had noticed a marked change in Bruce Gilbert's attitude. In his opinion, the guitarist was intent on pushing Wire toward an even more extreme sound. "By the time we came to compile *Send*, Bruce was again reining back from any notion of being in a rock band, and the idea of songs was starting to be anathema to him." As far as Newman was concerned, it was as if Gilbert had taken a decision and was now on a fixed course from which he wouldn't be swayed – and in the process, he was trying to set the collective agenda in terms of his own interests. "I'd obviously experienced this before with Bruce but felt he didn't have the right to just decide the band's direction based on what I felt was a whim. It was like he arrived one day and announced it as the new direction. He seemed to be genuinely surprised that I didn't want to make an album of noise. It was suddenly: I think we should be doing noise. He'd turn up with noise loops, and I told him that this wasn't going to work within the context of Wire." Newman recalls Gilbert appearing somewhat taken aback: "How could that not be the logical conclusion of working with him for a year and a half? Hadn't I understood anything? Obviously, I was way too stupid."

As the band began to think about making the next *Read & Burn* EP, there was a definite sense that Gilbert was distancing himself. "After *Send*," Newman remembers, "there was some discussion that we should be having some new things, and there was a new tranche of material." But when the others started to develop ideas, laying the foundations, Gilbert mostly remained an observer. This time, it was Graham Lewis and Robert Grey, working by mail, who set the ball rolling. "Graham gave some bass ideas to Robert," says Newman, "who sampled them into his drum machine and then sent me loops of what he thought worked best. I then fed them into pieces which later became parts of *Read & Burn 03* and *Object 47*. I thought the basslines idea was something which was attempting to engage the band as a whole more, and I was getting some good results from it. Bruce never really engaged with any of these ideas. He heard all the new material, but he didn't really play on any of it."

Lewis recalls that he initiated this process, in response to the deteriorating alliance between Newman and Gilbert. "I put together those basslines just as a starting point because it was becoming obvious that the cosy creative situation that Colin thought he had with Bruce was starting not to work out. And Bruce was grumbling and moaning to me about that because he felt the direction he wanted to take things in was not being adhered to by Colin. I don't know why he was telling me this or why I was supposed to feel sympathetic about it, because until then, they'd been in cahoots. It had suited him before."

Newman's account of a post-*flag:burning* get-together suggests that his partnership with Gilbert wasn't in good shape: "We had a meeting, Bruce, Smith, and myself, in a nice restaurant in Shoreditch before the 2003 US tour – to celebrate the initial ship of *Send* and to talk generally about the future. I got very drunk – I'd just started on the Atkins diet, no carbs to soak up the booze, plus I'm useless at drinking anyhow – and Bruce was very negative about our 'future'. I'm sure I had a go at him. I don't remember much."

When Gilbert did contribute ideas to the new work, he now tended to pursue his own increasingly narrow, noise-oriented path. "Post-*Send*," recalls Newman, "there seemed to be only dugga loops coming from him. He seemed to be only interested in the duggas." Two of these merit a mention, if only for their ominous titles. "The main ones I remember," says Newman, "were 'Suicide Dugga' – definitely a working title, only named that because it sounded a bit like Suicide – and 'Senseless', with a sampled Bruce vocal, basically repeating the word 'senseless'. Make of that what you will! I had a sense that he felt he'd given me all his riffs. Maybe he was losing interest in the guitar again or maybe the whole Barbican thing had brought him to a watershed – and this was his push for a new direction."

Lewis agrees that the *flag:burning* event might have been a turning point for Gilbert. "I have a feeling that Bruce felt he'd been coerced into the Barbican show somehow. Something had snapped between Smith and Bruce." However, he also points out that problems had been building steadily. In his view, Wire's newfound success and the band's emergence as a viable business was something with which Gilbert was uncomfortable and, moreover, it had redefined his relationship with Smith, putting an end to their days as art-world co-conspirators. "Even earlier than *Send*, after the first *Read & Burn*," says Lewis, "the pinkflag label really started to develop, and there had to be some sort of structure because everybody was so surprised with its success. Suddenly there was something there to be managed, looked after and administered: it was the business side of it, there was money. And from Bruce and Smith being huge social drinking buddies – as well as cooking up various artistic plots together, in the thick of the YBA scene – those ties just seemed to fall apart. That's where problems were inevitably going to arise because Bruce does zero business. He doesn't really do that."

Gilbert says he expected things to change between him and Smith, once the latter became involved with the band in an official capacity. "We'd fallen out, and that was mostly because of the Barbican. I suppose I thought, when he started managing Wire, that it was going to be the end of our relationship as it had been. It would be more business-like." If Gilbert had balked at the idea of Wire-as-commerce though, Newman had embraced it. He had occupied himself directly with the creation and running of the band's label and was more attentive to the group as a commercial entity. For Lewis, the cooling of Gilbert's relations with Smith led to the formation of a new axis that eventually caused grave problems for Wire. "So things started to become a business, and that's when Smith's attention started to wander from Bruce to Colin a bit more – around *Send*. There was a shift in power, or activity, between the three of them. Things didn't appear to be quite as rosy between Bruce and Smith as they had been. That was my impression."

Throughout this period, Lewis and Grey seemed to be very much on the periphery of band-related planning and discussion, a great deal of which was taking place between Smith and the *Send*-era creative team of Newman and Gilbert, who were all based in London. Lewis wasn't pleased with this setup and with the tendency for decisions to be taken by what he calls "The Triumvirate". "I lived a long way from London and, from where I sat, things were not very transparent. Conversations and discussions that went on between Bruce, Colin, and Paul Smith, I obviously heard second-hand, and there were too many faits accomplis." While Lewis may have felt this acutely under Smith's management, the fait accompli had, for better or worse, been part of Wire's modus operandi since the band's inception. "Various aspects of Wire were democratic, definitely," says Gilbert, "but other aspects were more fait accompli. It's something that was employed to great effect in Wire sometimes, I think, because it pushed things along very quickly. Here it is: it's good for you." (In the interviews for this book, the term 'fait accompli' came up almost as much as the words 'perverse' and 'perversity'.)

Lewis makes a telling observation regarding his communication with the group's manager – the individual whom one would most expect to be a constant and reliable conduit of information between all band-members. "In all of the time Smith managed Wire," he says, "I received two phone calls from him. That was my experience of it – just to give you an idea of how informed he wanted to keep us – and he only rang me when he thought things were severely in jeopardy. He was always there at the beginning of tours, and he was always there at the end. What's around at the end which is not there at the beginning? *Money*. After that, he would drop in from time to time, when it best suited him."

In general, Lewis feels that there was a concerted effort to keep him marginalised within the band. "The whole thing had been set up in such a way that I was isolated, physically, in terms of the creative process and the rest of it. And Smith tried to keep that going by whatever means – flattering Bruce and Colin or turning the crew against me, or whatever. I was like an outsider in my own thing – I always had a sense of looking at it from the outside when it was going on."

Gilbert agrees with suggestions that communication between band and manager left something to be desired. "Paul's management style was to keep his artists in the dark as much as possible – not being terribly forthcoming with information all the time. That's a very old-fashioned way of controlling people. It was a bit too much."

## You've got mail

Despite Gilbert's apparently diminishing engagement with the band, Wire had moved ahead with live work after the *flag:burning* show at the Barbican and the release of *Send*. They played a handful of European dates in May and completed a North American tour in July – performing the *Send*-based set (plus *Pink Flag* encores) that would remain largely unchanged until August 2004. This was a unique situation for Wire. "We'd been doing the same set for a long time," says Lewis. "It was an interesting proposition because it was something we'd never done before. It gave you an idea of what it would feel like to be in a metal band or something. It was an extremely interesting sonic tool, the *Send* thing, but we just couldn't go on doing that."

When Smith showed up in New York at the end of the American tour, he appeared to concur with that statement, as Grey explains: "Around the time of the Festival Hall in 2000, Paul had been very keen for us to get back together and perform. I don't know if he saw it going any further than the Festival Hall, but he seemed very positive. After the Barbican, however, there was some sort of overhang of disagreement in the air. We went to

America, and he met us in New York, and he seemed to be in the mood for an argument. I'm not sure what had set this off, but having been supportive of Wire, it seemed to me that he turned against us. I remember him saying he thought we'd become 'boring' and that we should write a new set; he thought we'd been playing the *Send* set too long. If that was him putting his cards on the table, nobody was going to think that Paul was supportive of what we were doing."

Like Lewis, Grey had the impression that Smith had begun to ally himself primarily with Newman. Following the encounter in New York, this alignment grew more obvious to the drummer: "After that, it seemed like he became more interested in forming a partnership with Colin than managing Wire. There'd just been this big change of attitude."

Lewis also saw this as a pivotal moment. "It was now completely out in the open. He'd breezed into New York at the end of the tour and blithely said: that was a bit so-so – after we'd been working fucking hard for three weeks. I think Bruce started to understand that his buddy wasn't who he thought he was. I was happy to see that there was such hostility, quite honestly. I suddenly felt less alone because I thought: at last somebody's noticed that this isn't working out."

The year ended with a short run of gigs in Spain and Italy, during which Newman thinks Gilbert rallied a little. "He seemed to perk up a bit on the Italian tour, but when I tried to talk to him about future plans, he didn't seem very interested." In the New Year, the band visited Japan again and, for the first time, New Zealand and Australia. Gilbert enjoyed aspects of this, but he was definitely tiring of the routine. "The curiosity made it more interesting, but of course the same problem arose, as it arose all the way through our so-called career, which was: Why don't you play this? Why don't you play that? The cliché. Which is something we've lived through, throughout the various eras we've been active. It's something we've tried to discourage: please don't expect us to play old songs."

According to Newman, the trip to the southern hemisphere wasn't a positive experience ("The Australian tour ended very badly, with a lot of mistrust flying around"), but they kept at it and in the spring and summer played the Triptych Festival in Scotland and a series of larger events on the Continent. "Bruce didn't really approve of any of the festival shows," says Newman, "although I think he did quite like the fact that we played at Benicassim and Roskilde." In Newman's view, nevertheless, this was the end of the line for Wire. "We seemed, as a band, to be running on empty. There was no future, even though we'd had a very successful record."

341

Shortly after the Benicassim Festival, Gilbert met with Newman and Smith in London. They had gathered at artist Tom Gidley's home to watch a playback of what would become *The Scottish Play: 2004*, a concert DVD filmed by Gidley at Wire's April performance in Glasgow as part of Triptych. (Released the following year, this would also feature footage from the 'boxed' second half of the *flag:burning* concert.) They then adjourned to the pub, Newman recalls, for further discussion of the DVD and "some other things which were of general interest to the whole band" – including an invitation to perform in November at All Tomorrow's Parties in Long Beach (aboard the Queen Mary, no less).

"Bruce just issued a flat 'no' to everything," says Newman. "The ATP thing was quite a big deal, everyone needed the money, and it was not Bruce's prerogative to turn it down. I just saw red. I didn't think Bruce had the right to just turn down stuff which was in the band's interest. I called him something choice. He got up, went to the toilet then came out and went off in a huff. I had never spoken to Bruce so strongly in my life. No one did. He tended to be treated with respect by everyone. He obviously thought I was getting above my station."

Not long afterwards, on August 24, Gilbert informed the others via an eight-sentence email message that he was leaving Wire.

In its minimalism and concision, the parting missive was Gilbert to a tee. "It was a very short paragraph," says Lewis: "It was along the lines of: I'm resigning, it takes immediate effect, and I don't wish to discuss the matter any further – with the swishing of a cloak and the slamming of a door."

"I don't think it came as a great surprise," Grey says, "but seeing it in black and white made it a statement, whereas before it had just been disagreements." While the timing was a shock to Lewis, the actual decision wasn't unexpected, in light of the way things had been going. "It was out of the blue, but I can't say I was altogether surprised. The whole period had an air of foreboding." Newman agrees, emphasising the sense of decline over the preceding year: "The mood in the band had not been great since the end of the US tour in July 2003."

True to his email, Gilbert has never spoken to his bandmates about the exact reasons for his departure. When asked if he had sought any further clarification, Lewis replies: "No, because I think it's his responsibility to explain his actions. He's a grown-up." Grey was also left to speculate. "My feeling is that it had become this conflict between the artistic venture and the business venture; but also I think there was a separation between the artistic venture and the musical venture. I think, for him, it had steered away from the artistic venture more toward the musical venture – and that brought Bruce back to being in a 'beat group', which is where he didn't want to be. That's just my guess on what it came down to."

Newman, meanwhile, goes back to the context of his work with Gilbert during the *Send* phase. "I think it got to a point with Bruce where maybe we exhausted each other. I had that feeling he'd given me all his riffs, because in the end he was only coming with duggas, and there's only so many versions of dugga you can have. Sometimes I feel like I exhausted him, that I just took him for everything, that he doesn't have anything left to give a rock band because he gave it all in *Send*. There are lots and lots of reasons why Bruce and I fell out and why he left, but there's a core reason that I really don't know – and I don't think anybody knows why he left. In many ways, there's only one reason why Bruce won't ever come back, and that's his own pride. He painted himself into a corner, conceptually: how could someone who's more or less expunged Wire from his history go back to Wire? How could he be part of that? It's too compromised. It's too 'rock'. It's lots of things he doesn't like. In that *Send* material, there is the story of Bruce leaving the band."

## Getting on the floor with the children

Gilbert spoke to me in some detail about what led him to quit Wire. There was no one single reason. "It was very, very gradual," he says of his decision. "Bit by bit, I found it harder and harder to have, I suppose, conversations with the other people in the band about artistic intent and so on. It was a very gradual dissatisfaction on my part – and some personal issues as well." Nevertheless, Gilbert made it clear that the crux of the problem for him was the blurring of the lines between the group's identity as a creative endeavour and as a business endeavour, more and more under Newman's control.

The immediate catalyst, however, was the negative experience of playing live and the miserable ritual of touring. Gilbert had never been enthusiastic about performing but accepted it as part and parcel of being in a band. "Obviously, it's necessary when you're in a project that requires you to play in front of as many people as possible, but I always found it a bit weird playing in front of people, especially day after day, in different countries, different locations. It was something I was never really comfortable with." What had kept him going was the potential for his ideal of Wire to manifest itself in live playing. "There were always times and situations when the band really clicked together, not necessarily for a whole performance, but that's what I always loved about the band situation: when it suddenly gelled and turned into something quite other – a creature which we didn't have anything to do with in some ways. It has a life of its own." Such instances were now increasingly rare. "I don't think there were enough of those times," he says.

In the absence of those transcendent moments that made Wire a worthwhile creative activity, the routine of live work – focused particularly on playing abroad – became less attractive to Gilbert than it had ever been. That he was approaching 60 was also a factor, giving him a more acute sense that this was not how he wanted to spend his time. In the year leading up to his departure, the writing was on the wall. "I thought: this is no way to live life, really, a lot of mucking about and schlepping instruments. The whole thing just started to pall – especially when I'd been doing solo live performances with two small cases, rather than struggling up the road with three guitar cases and a bag to go on tour for six weeks. I just thought: I'm getting too old for this game. It's not what I need."

Festivals, above all, had become unbearable to Gilbert, and Wire's visit to Benicassim in 2004 represented a new low. It was here that he first began to think about quitting. "The first notion of it popped into my head in Spain: it was a classic example of soundchecking at 10am and then getting onstage at two in the morning, stooging around for hours and not being able to have a drink in between. It became gruelling. It was stupid. I thought it was absolutely ridiculous, waiting to get your couple of hours in a caravan, just to sit down and have a cup of coffee. I thought: this is no way to carry on. It was the last thing I wanted to do. I tend to go to bed very early. In the winter, I go to bed when it's dark – it's pathetic really – but it was incredibly boring. Nowhere to go. Not even anywhere to lie down and hide."

The obvious question is: why didn't Gilbert simply withdraw from live engagements but continue contributing to the band? "I had no feeling that that was possible," he says, "because the setup was not going to change." Crucially, Gilbert felt that the group's identity as an artistic project was now too compromised. For him, the evolution of Wire into an almost entirely self-contained entity – with its business dealings and recording/production now all being done in-house – meant the loss of the oppositional, outsider position that was vital to his artistic identity and to his view of the band's creative process. His central concern regarding the "setup" was the pinkflag label. "I think it's incredibly sensible to have one's own label, financially. Artistically, though, I don't think we ever had any real problems working with record companies, particularly Mute: it's four against one in that kind of situation, and we had a reputation for having our way. We had to convince people to put our records out or we could negotiate if there was a promotional idea or if there was something someone wanted to do – rather than it just being: this is the way we're going to do it because it's our business. I know it's not a very grown-up way of looking at it, but I just think a split between the creative and the business side can be very important. It should be two separate things."

With the band controlling its own releases, Gilbert felt not an increase in artistic freedom but, rather, a reduction. This wasn't just about being less able to resist commercial pressures on band decisions, with Newman acting as label manager; it also reflected the practical reality that Newman had, in addition, assumed the role of in-house producer. "When the record company or label *is* the people who make the things," he explains, "then obviously somebody has to take the responsibility for administration and, of course, Colin had the studio, so it all became a little focused in one area. And Colin's very, very good at it, but I think the issue of artistic control became a little bit strange because, although we worked together in his studio, I couldn't be there all the time, and so, obviously, somebody has to mix it." While Gilbert accepts the way that much of the *Send*-era production was a fait accompli, he was convinced that an independent producer would be imperative if he were to continue with Wire. "I've always been keen on having a neutral or somebody with a slightly different vision. Although it's a very old-fashioned notion – because the days of budgets, producers, and big studios are a thing of the past – I think quite often you get the best out of people with a referee."

The *Send*-period material had been successful, but by 2004 Gilbert was no longer interested in pursuing the same working method. With that approach, he felt the work had become divorced from his ideal of Wire as the stimulating encounter between four people. Wire, now essentially a duo, seemed to function as a rigid, mechanical rationalisation of the artistic process, in the service of the pinkflag business. His assessment is blunt: "Because of the way we had to develop and record new material, we weren't all together cooking stuff up in a rehearsal room where experiments could happen and good accidents could happen and turn into a song: it was just Colin and I, two or three days a week in a tiny studio, trying to be creative. In the end, we were just a mini-factory for making material – rather than it being an artistic expression."

At the heart of it all, then, was the fact that the increased concentration of responsibilities in Newman's hands just didn't fit with Gilbert's idea of making art. "Because Colin was running the label, he was thinking in terms of administration, publicity, promotion, what we should be doing. From my point of view, he was a split personality in terms of running a label, doing promotion *and* being an artist in the group. And it didn't sit comfortably with me because I think he started making decisions that we just went along with because it was easier that way. It seemed to be more of a business object than a creative object. I wasn't comfortable with that. Everybody seemed very happy with the situation, and there was no way around it: there is a label run by Colin Newman called pinkflag – and we work for it now."

If Benicassim had set Gilbert seriously thinking about leaving Wire, the final straw came a few weeks later at the meeting already described by Newman (with Smith and Gidley). "I had a little bit of a bust-up with Colin over *The Scottish Play*," recalls Gilbert. "Colin had mixed the sound. I was hardly ever on the video – and I don't mind that, it's not something I'm concerned with – but it appeared to me that Colin had more or less mixed me out of 'Pink Flag'. I was sitting there thinking: this is ridiculous. But I didn't want to be that person who says: I can't hear myself! I'd seen that happen in other situations. So I was feeling a bit raw about that, but I didn't want to bring it up as a 'thing', because the project was happening: it's a film, it's nicely edited, it's a good thing, and the fact that I wanted to whinge about a small part of it seemed to me symptomatic of bigger issues. And Colin was going on about some promotional thing, and I said it was bullshit, and we had a little contretemps – and I said: I'm not sitting here listening to all this."

Gilbert had come to the conclusion that any attempt to resolve things was no longer worth the effort, given the nature of the discussion that he felt would be required. "There were philosophical and artistic issues," says Gilbert, "and I found myself in a position where I had to be in either perpetual argument mode or negotiation mode – rather than it all being very natural and everybody's voice being heard in a proper way and being able to influence the situation without having to get on the floor with the children. The opportunity came to make the break, and I took it."

## I've been told they've got a young man now who is very, very talented

When asked if he has regrets about any phase of Wire's work, or if there is something he wishes had been handled differently, Gilbert returns to the band's loss of direction and cohesion in the 80s. "Unfortunately, the process was wrong. There was group loyalty – still very strong – but in a situation where the process is going a bit weird, it's not enough. It's touching to present a united front against the world, but if the process is off-beam a bit, you can't will something into being. It's not possible. The machine, the process, has to be working for everyone."

He feels that the process during the 80s was compromised most of all by the band's inability to engage, as a collective creative unit, with new technology. "The 80s thing with the computer seemed very exciting in one way. There were a lot of good ideas, but the way the process worked meant that they didn't achieve their full potential and lacked a certain something." He reiterates his belief that the fundamental problem through all of this was the shift in focus from the work itself to the workstation. "Having those MIDI guitars, for example, I thought this was a whole new avenue, but it was all the same thing: more control by the person who knows the most about the computer. When I realised the way it was going, I should have said: I don't think this is really working. Let's get back to basics or do it with the technology in a slightly simpler, more flexible way."

Regardless of the impact of technology on Wire's working processes in the 80s, Gilbert allows that, in the end, the band-members' diverging interests couldn't be accommodated or reconciled within Wire. "There was probably a bit of self-delusion about being able to reinvent oneself all the time, especially with a band where everybody is seeking different terms increasingly, despite how much it seems to be unified." He contrasts this with his experience of Wire at the start of the band's career – presumably before *154*. "In the 70s, the momentum was such that it carried itself. We weren't thinking too much about the future. It was about enjoying the creative part and making things without having to get into great long discussions and arguments about how the work is made. We were able to work together. Once it becomes fragmented, it becomes a different creature altogether. It becomes more abstract. Perhaps too much about ideas rather than: what's this noise we make when we're together?"

When he looks back now, Gilbert recognises the central role played by Wire in his broader work as an artist. "It is a major part – and not just because of the amount of time spent doing it. It introduced me to all sorts of things. Proper studios. It gave me a little bit of confidence in myself. It opened a lot of doors. And I was quite proud of it, in a strange sort of way. It was an avenue. I could feel I spent too much time on it, but each time it was one of those itches you can't quite scratch – it always seemed like unfinished business."

That sense of things being unresolved and incomplete appears to carry over to the way he now perceives Wire. He acknowledges a nagging feeling that he's lacking something. "I think something's been lost. I can't really put my finger on it." But that doesn't mean he's still interested in scratching the Wire itch. "It's a pity that it ended the way it did – my part in it – but when you're starting to make artistic decisions from a business point of view, then it's not healthy. I can't possibly imagine wanting to be in that situation again. It doesn't interest me." He goes even further: "I don't want to play guitar ever again, although I've still got the guitars I was using – I can't say 'playing'."

Gilbert mentions that he is kept apprised of the band's work: "I've been told they've got a young man now who is very, very talented," he says, referring to current guitarist Matthew Simms. "Good luck to them." He also confides that he almost attended a 2011 concert by the band. "I was tempted the last time they played in London," he laughs. "I was going to buy a ticket and show up, but then I thought I'd better not go. Someone asked me, and I said: no, I'd better not – I don't want to upstage Wire."

## Three people in a foyer

With Gilbert now gone, Lewis recalls, "It started to get really quite strange. In late 2004, I got invited to come to London for a meeting with Colin and Smith and Rob about what 'we' were going to do. This was the meeting where the realignment of writing credits [for the first three albums] was one of the things on the agenda. This meeting was about eight hours long, and eventually I realised that what it was about was that they were going to try to wear me down to the point where I would agree that we should continue without Bruce. They thought it would be a very good idea to get somebody else, and I said no. I wasn't going to enter into that as an agreement with Paul Smith on board. That was basically it: suddenly, Bruce was a totally irresponsible, stupid person, and for the first time in many years, I became the centre of attention. But all the time, it was obvious that what was going on was that Colin and Smith had the intention of continuing as a business partnership, which was basically then going to administer what relics or souvenirs were left over from the carcass which had been the living thing called Wire. The way they presented it to me, it looked as though they were just going to take it all, and we were going to get fuck all out of it. So that wasn't something I was willing to sign up for."

For Lewis, the meeting brought into sharp relief the serious issues facing the band. "They were really severe problems – of betrayal, basically. I suppose that's what it came down to. It's a hard thing, but it happens in groups on occasion, and everyone feels shame about it, but it was just awful to be there thinking: how on earth could it have come to this?" Above all, he felt that if Wire were to have any chance of continuing, that could only happen without their manager. "I remember thinking: regardless of the problems we have here, the only important thing is whether there is Wire or not Wire – and Smith has to have nothing to do with it. The only thing I could think of was: he's got to go before we can even possibly conceive of what's to be done next." The meeting concluded, and Lewis went straight to the pub to fill Gilbert in on how the group was getting along without him.

At the time, Newman saw his prospective partnership with Smith (related to the pinkflag label and Wire's archive) as something that was in the band's best interests. "I thought the basic idea was that Smith would establish things so that we would have a catalogue that would bring income into the band, and then, when it came around to everyone wanting to do something again, we'd be in a stronger position than we were the last time we'd stopped [in 1980] – when it had all fallen apart completely." He now recognises that much of this was a misjudgement on his part. "By the end of 2004, virtually nobody was talking to anybody else, and the relations were all very bad, and Smith was just stirring it like crazy. He always played one off against the other. Smith wanted control – I was too naïve to understand what he wanted at that point. I thought he was just trying to husband the resources we had: we had a catalogue, we could release historic things. Smith seemed to think Wire was an archive project, and that was what it was going to be about."

Unsurprisingly, Wire now lapsed into another hiatus, although archival releases continued to emerge on the pinkflag label: the band's 1979 *Rockpalast* performance was issued on DVD as *Wire On The Box: 1979* in October 2004, followed in March 2005 by *The Scottish Play: 2004*, and May 2006 saw the release of *Wire 1977–1979*, another boxed-set collection of the first three albums – now with the modified songwriting credits and Newman's own, extensive liner notes. Also included with the latter were three historic live recordings: the April 1 and April 2 1977 Roxy gigs and the WPIX-FM set from their 1978 New York visit. *Pink Flag*, *Chairs Missing*, and *154* were also reissued individually at this time, and the Roxy and New York performances were made available on a standalone double CD. In the meantime, Grey kept busy on his farm, Newman launched a new band, Githead, and Lewis formed 27#11 with Thomas Öberg (of Bob Hund) in Sweden. "Everything stopped," says Lewis. "I got on with my life. I didn't shrug it off, though. It was awful. I felt really depressed about it for a couple of years. Tragic's too big a word, but it was so depressing to see all that hard work and good spirit destroyed."

349

Lewis had continued to update Gilbert on Wire-related activity. "The situation I found myself in was one of having no power, no money, without Bruce being there, and playing poker from Sweden with no cards – for about two years. I thought it was my responsibility to explain what was going on with Smith, because I knew it was going to lead to some sort of legal action, and at that point, it wasn't certain who was going to be on what side of what fence. What I knew was that I was against what Smith – and therefore Colin, by association, still working with him – was doing. Therefore, I thought I had to explain to Bruce what the situation was: Smith had the idea that he was going to control our heritage."

Newman's relationship with Smith finally ran aground in spring 2006, as he came to feel that Lewis's concerns may have been well-founded. As Newman tells it, the scales fell away from his eyes when Smith set up a deal with the US label group Runt. While the deal may have seemed from Smith's perspective to be good for Wire, to Newman it rang alarm bells. "The trigger for it was me finding out that Smith had licensed the first three albums for vinyl and put the first half of the advance in his pocket. I was: hang on, I thought this guy was on our side! I had to change everything I thought. I realised that this person was just out for themselves." This spurred Newman to action, and he got back in touch with Grey and Lewis. "Graham quite happily told me: I told you so," remembers Newman, adding, "but Graham wasn't close to it on a day-to-day basis – maybe being close to it you can over-focus on one thing."

Newman, Lewis, and Grey arranged a meeting in the foyer of the National Theatre on the South Bank in May to address the band's problems. "That was the day we took the decision we'd sack Smith," Newman recalls. "I had to say that whatever working relationship there was between me and Smith no longer exists, because I can't trust this person." In spite of the circumstances, Lewis and Grey were pleased to have this opportunity to discuss the state of affairs. Grey welcomed the restoration of direct communication with his bandmate. "There was a time when we couldn't speak to Colin – we could only get through to Smith. Even before Bruce left, there was a feeling that Colin was becoming separate from Wire. And when you don't have a means of communication, everyone gets suspicious – and it gets worse." Lewis also remembers this period when he and Grey were out of the loop: "Colin and Mr Smith became extremely important. Everything was far too important for anybody else to even understand what was going on."

For Lewis, their first priority was to retake control of Wire, whose story he felt was being written by someone else and was in danger of coming to an ignominious conclusion. "My point of view was: if I don't do something about this, I'm going to get bitter about it – and that's something I didn't want to do. You've spent half your life doing something, and someone comes along and more than helps to destroy it. I wasn't willing to let that happen. Regardless of my feelings about what I thought Colin had done, or his being implicated in it, I thought the best way back at Smith was for us to do something about it – to try to give it an ending it deserves. I just couldn't let it go, I felt awful for years about this. It was so depressing. It was embarrassing. How on earth can you let this happen?"

Understandably, the National Theatre encounter was awkward, given the implications of the erstwhile Newman–Smith alliance. Grey was aware of this. "Colin was on pretty dodgy ground," he laughs, "he realised he'd made a big mistake." Lewis confirms that Newman approached the meeting with a sense of contrition: "Colin admitted he did some things that weren't right, which was big of him. It was hard. It's not something he likes to do."

While Newman's account of the meeting doesn't address the partnership with Smith as directly, he does concede that the relationship with his bandmates had been seriously compromised. "I didn't think Wire would ever work with each other again. I didn't think we'd even speak to each other. I had to figure out how to build bridges with the band again. We knew that there was a lot of water that had gone under the bridge, and there was a lot of rebuilding to do, especially between Graham and I. Rob, I'd been in contact with, and I'd never fallen out with him. Graham and I had become very estranged, but really that was a hangover from the 80s. We'd become estranged in the 80s, and it hadn't stopped really. In the end, everybody took a fairly pragmatic view."

Although the band had now agreed to dismiss Smith, the story didn't end there. The postscript was an acrimonious dispute that dragged on for almost four years. The simplest summary of the situation is that, apparently, both parties felt the other owed them money. Lawyers were enlisted, and the disagreement limped slowly toward the courts, in the process draining the band's limited funds. The matter wouldn't be settled until January 2010. By that time, Grey had grown convinced that the saga had to be ended out of court – and as soon as possible. As he recalls, this was a course of action that his bandmates did not initially seem keen to take. It was Grey's brainwave to seek the help of an old associate. "I had the idea that we had to get a second opinion from Bryan [Grant]. He was really the only person who had our confidence and knew something about how the band worked, and he was experienced in business. Until I came up with that idea, we were on a headlong course for bankruptcy and spending thousands on lawyers. It's all right if you're Elton John: it's free publicity. But I don't think we were quite in that position. I can laugh at it now because we lived to tell the tale, but it gave me sleepless nights at the time – and it went on so long and there didn't seem to be a way out. Bryan agreed with me. He was the first person who agreed with me. He thought it was always better to talk directly with someone than deal with lawyers."

True to his parting offer almost two decades earlier when he had resigned in frustration at Wire's perversity, Grant was happy to help out his old friends. "I negotiated their divorce from Paul," he says. "I got them all in a room together. It was a full-and-final settlement." This consisted of Wire paying Smith off. All the band-members now accept that this was the most sensible thing to do and, moreover, they recognise that without Grant's intervention Wire might have ceased to exist. "Thank God for Bryan," says Grey. "I mean, *really*. That's how I feel about it. He completely saved the day. In the end, it turned out to be an educational experience rather than what could have been a disastrous experience."

Of the four original band-members, Lewis gives the impression of having been the most affected by this experience, his anger still evident. "The awful thing was that I wasn't surprised by the ending. I knew what the ending was going to be as soon as I knew Smith was going to be the manager. I knew it was going to take something terrible to finish it, to get rid of him. With people like Smith, you've got to be a bit vain to think it's not going to happen to you, because it will. How on earth could Bruce have thought that it wouldn't happen to him? I think in the end that's why he quit. He understood. I think his pride took a moshing from that."

Notwithstanding this near-catastrophic episode, Gilbert, Grey, and Newman are, to varying degrees, appreciative of Smith's work. "Although we've fallen out, I still respect him in many ways," says Gilbert. He acknowledges Smith's importance both for Wire's career and his own. "He was very, very resourceful and incredibly helpful from time to time. He opened a few doors and was very helpful in setting up a couple of ideas I'd had. There were more ideas that we were going to work on together than actually got executed." Newman is typically measured in his appraisal. "He was more than helpful in getting the thing going again, after the 80s, when there wasn't a great deal of enthusiasm to do it again. But his view was that we would be going out and playing the old numbers." Grey, meanwhile, is clear about the value of Smith's management. "We wouldn't be here now without him," he maintains. "That's absolutely true," agrees Newman, "but his vision for the band was entirely different from ours. We asserted our vision, and that's a way to sum it up." Bryan Grant also feels that Wire benefited from Smith's stewardship. "I love the little devils – and they'll hate me for saying it – but I think Paul Smith helped them get more recognition."

## Escape from *Send*-world

After the May 2006 meeting, the future did start to look brighter for the band, despite the ongoing dispute with Smith. "I had thought Wire was kind of finished," Newman says, "but the conclusion we came to was that it shouldn't stop. The line that came out of that meeting was: just because Bruce has taken his ball home, we don't have to stop the game." Grey felt the same way: "It wasn't the original four people, but the other option was no Wire at all, which was the worst option. Should one person be able to say there's no more Wire or should we see if it still works between three? It's not in its pure, original form, but that doesn't mean that it can't work." However, it wasn't simply a question of establishing that Wire was artistically valid as a trio – the remaining band-members also had qualms about whether they could even work together.

As Grey points out, the foundations for any new partnership were shaky. "The doubt and suspicion were still very much in the air, and I think the bond that holds Wire together was probably at its thinnest at the time." It was a tentative process, therefore; a case of finding out if the three could be in the same room and, if so, whether they could still produce something worthy of Wire. "It wasn't as definite as saying: now we're going to continue," explains Grey. "It was more that we should see if it was workable. If it wasn't, we wouldn't continue for the sake of it. If we didn't feel it was going to produce things we'd be proud of, we'd know. If the creative dynamic was no longer there, then it wouldn't be worth pursuing. But if what had always motivated Wire was still there, then we'd be justified in carrying on."

The first steps were basic ones. "We had to rethink everything from the ground up," Grey recalls. "We established a new deal between us," says Newman, "and we designed a new setup." Having taken care of the business side of things, they didn't start playing together straight away, but took stock of their resources: the primary task was to evaluate the work they had stored up since the *Send* period, material that had been discussed for possible inclusion on *Read & Burn 03*. "Colin sent me a CD based on a lot of the basslines that had got into circulation via Rob," says Lewis, "and I remember thinking: this is very promising. It was obvious that *Send* was a bit of a cul-de-sac – an extremely good one, but it needed to go somewhere else, away from it being as shouty and inarticulate as it had been. I wanted to let some light into *Send*-world, to make things less claustrophobic."

Lewis visited Newman in November 2006, and they reviewed all the existing recordings at Swim Studio, further shaping the rudimentary tracks. "We went through everything that was on the shelf. We listened to it, reacted to it, deciding: that's the verse, this the chorus – and I put down about nine more basslines. At the end of the day, we said: there's definitely something to do here." Lewis also brought some new ideas along, among them a bass loop that would develop into the song 'Mekon Headman'.

As they began to move forward, they focused on work from 2003 with which Gilbert had had some involvement, however marginal. This enabled them to establish a demarcation line between tracks for the third *Read & Burn* EP and work for a potential album. Lewis outlines the criteria: "We grouped together anything Bruce had had a hand in, or just waved at, and that was *Read & Burn 03*; then everything else went onto *Object 47*."

Having set aside the tracks for the EP, which bore traces of Gilbert, they dealt with another issue. "With Smith out of the picture," says Newman, "we then had to see if Bruce was going to re-engage. I'm not sure if anyone thought he'd quit forever." Lewis remembers being ambivalent about the prospect: "The easiest way to find out was to send him the work, and if he wanted to be on it, he'd be on it; if he didn't, he wasn't. I certainly didn't feel like going round to persuade him, particularly after the manner in which he'd resigned. I didn't want to go there: I was sick and tired of all of that." Gilbert recalls some contact around this time, in the form of a phone call from Grey, who had apparently been volunteered to make the enquiry on behalf of the band. "I think Rob was sent on a mission. He phoned me out of the blue and said: we're doing something – are you sure you don't want to join in?"

One of my earliest interviews with Gilbert took place in May 2007, as the band were preparing *Read & Burn 03*. By then, he'd opted not to participate, but he had given the matter serious thought, as he explained: "There are vestiges of my guitar on the work-in-progress, and it seemed, at one point, an intriguing idea to contribute, to add bits onto what's been done, but I've come to the conclusion that to do it properly, to make it work properly, I'd have to re-engage – and I don't want to do that."

Having arrived at that decision, Gilbert still had to decide what, if anything, to do about his extant parts on the tracks. He appeared to make up his mind: "I'm in the strange position of having the choice of saying:

well, do what you want or just take my stuff off, and let's have a clean break. For a while, I thought, as I was involved in *Read and Burn 03*, it could be a sort of swan song, but the more I thought about it, the less attractive the proposition became. I'd like the break to be as clean as possible." He commented that he was leaning toward the latter option (having his parts removed) because he hadn't found the new material sufficiently compelling. "There is that swan-song aspect, but although Graham insists it sounds like Wire, I just can't hear anything that I'm excited by or curious about. It's good stuff, generally – but very generally. So by actually making a totally clean break, that means if the three of them want to carry on, if they get another bloke in, they've got to do it properly and actually have a clean start. They should take responsibility for it." In the end, however, he let his residual contributions stand.

### Going Dutch

While Newman and Lewis's review of the work on the shelf at Swim had uncovered plenty of prospective material for the new incarnation of Wire, they took a significant leap forward in late January 2007. The previous October, Newman had been at Frank Lievaart's Metropolis 22 Studio in Rotterdam, recording with Githead, and it occurred to him that this would be an ideal place for Wire to continue mending personal and creative fences.

"It turned out to be a magic formula," says Newman. "Rob recorded drums on the various tracks-in-progress, as well as some general drums, and we did some vocals and a bit of jamming that ended up being a couple of songs. But the being-together aspect of it was the most important. Being together, being creative, and having a laugh and enjoying doing it: enjoying being Wire. That hadn't happened since the 70s. I thought we could have fun. Good stuff comes out of it when we have a laugh. We'd been miserable for too long. I thought it would be a healing thing, because it was edgy when we started together again. It was difficult." Although Wire's need for a group hug came out of the immediate context of the previous few years, Newman also sees it as part of a familiar pattern for the band: "It's cyclical. Wire goes through these healing processes."

At first, Lewis had been doubtful about the venture. "I was still feeling pretty sceptical, and I didn't have high hopes. Things were still really fragile." And the location itself didn't seem promising, either: this was Newman's terrain – a studio he had already worked in, run by an old friend. "There was no sense of it being neutral ground," Lewis continues. "It was a difficult situation. I just thought: if we just get the drums, that'll be great – because that was considered instrumental in achieving the change of tone in the work."

In spite of these reservations, Lewis was pleasantly surprised. "We socialised a bit. That was part of the healing process. Everybody was trying to be civil and speaking to each other." Newman emphasises this side of things, especially the need to re-establish trust. "It was about team-building. We needed to start operating in a way that everything is highly visible to everyone, and everybody understands what's going on and can be involved to the level they want to be involved." This accent on visibility and involvement would be an important factor for Lewis above all, given his sensitivity to the lack of transparency during the last phase of Wire and his sense that he'd been locked out of his own band.

In this environment, with a renewed spirit of collegiality, the work came easily, and they completed all they had set out to do with time to spare. "Rob got his parts down very quickly," recalls Lewis, "but then it was: what the hell are we going to do now? So we worked a full day at the end. I'd been up most nights writing – I rewrote eight texts – and it was a great opportunity for Colin to get some of his vocals down." That final day proved valuable, according to Lewis. "It sounds so obvious, but there we were doing what we were supposed to bloody do, which was *work*. That's what we've always wanted to do, and that's what we've been best at. And the momentum built, so by the time we got to the last day, we just messed about – and, out of that messing about, we got the basis of four new pieces. So we came away from Rotterdam in good shape work-wise and in terms of esprit de corps."

Grey was also encouraged by the positive atmosphere and by what the band had accomplished in those few days. "It was quite a big step – in addition to all the other things we had to sort out – but I think it was when we were recording in Rotterdam that it started to seem like it was workable, that good things could come out of it. I think the work we did there was probably the turning point." Newman agrees: "That was the foundation of *Object 47*."

The Rotterdam session would be the only time the band worked together, in the same space, during the preparation of the tracks for *Read & Burn 03* and *Object 47*. As he had done with *Send*, Newman assembled and mixed everything at Swim Studio. Although this might not have been Grey's preferred way of making a record – after all, this was the start of a new era for Wire, one that stressed involvement and participation – he was more content with the setup than he had been during the band's previous cycle of work. "The album was still mostly put together in Colin's studio, rather than playing as a group, and in Rotterdam, we spent more time doing drum parts than we did playing together. But I was happy with the drum tracks being recorded on their own – I couldn't complain that there wasn't any played drums on it. That made it feel worthwhile for me."

*Read & Burn 03* was released in November 2007, in a David Coppenhall-designed turquoise Digipak consistent with its predecessors. The songs were Jurassic in terms of their age – in Wire Time at least. "Some had started life in 2003 and 2004," says Newman. "They were so multi-layered and worked on over such a long period of time." He places particular emphasis on *Read and Burn 03*, feeling that the tracks were more fully realised than much of the material that would appear on *Object 47*. "It's important as a stepping stone – more important than *Object 47*. The pieces on *Read & Burn 03* were more finished. It's midway between *Send* and *Red Barked Tree*, really."

While the origins of the *Read & Burn 03* tracks 'Our Time' and 'No Warning Given' can be traced to some of the bass loops that had been gathering dust at Swim since 2003, 'Desert Diving' has roots in a 2000 live recording of a classic 1978 Wire track, as Newman explains: "It came out of a version of 'Heartbeat' that we played at the Garage in London in 2000. The only thing that survived is my guitar riff." The monumental '23 Years Too Late' has a similar genealogy, reworking 2002's 'Dip Flash', itself of course derived from Wire's third single. "The basis of '23 Years Too Late' is a sample from 'Dot Dash'," says Newman. "It's hidden in plain sight. The idea was to be self-referential but referencing something that wasn't from *Pink Flag*." It's a very binary piece with its slow-fast, stop-start structure switching back and forth between Lewis's rambling, spoken verses – recorded in the very small toilet at Swim Studio – and the urgency of Newman's sung choruses. (Newman's vocals weren't recorded in the toilet. "I do all my vocals in the studio on my own," he notes. "I've got my system – as opposed to cistern.") The text is another Lewis travelogue, inspired by the band's 2002 European tour. The title deserves some explanation. "We arrived in Groningen," Lewis remembers, "which was one of the shows we'd cancelled on the 1979 tour that didn't happen [due to the unpaid deposits], and so we were playing there '23 years too late'. There were grey-haired men waiting – still expecting us to be playing the same stuff we were playing in 1979."

**Tunes with zoom**

*Object 47* (the 47th entry in Wire's discography) was the antithesis of *Send*

357

– an antidote to that record and to the period in Wire's history that produced it.

This purging of the previous era begins with the sleeve. Even before you hear a note of *Object 47*, the album's cool minimalist cover (designed by Jon Wozencroft) encapsulates Lewis's desire for the new material to let some light into "*Send*-world": the azure sky alongside the sunlit white concrete surface of an unidentified structure (the Boländerna water tower outside Uppsala) contrasts strikingly with the oppressive, dark scanner image of the *Send* sleeve. The presence of a tall object set against a blue sky evokes the band's very first album cover, but it's not quite as successful due to a minor difference: something that had contributed to the unique effect of the *Pink Flag* cover was the absence of the album title, keeping the focus on the image, which of course articulated the title. Here, the image isn't allowed to speak for itself: while it's an arresting, inscrutable object – made more curious and intriguing by the way it's framed – its clean simplicity is spoiled by the prominent placement of the album title.

Wire have never shied away from unconventional, un-rock album titles, and *Object 47* is no less obscure than *Chairs Missing*, *154*, or *A Bell Is A Cup ... Until It Is Struck*. However, given the context of this record, it could be argued that the title doesn't send a very enticing message about the band's new phase of work: if Wire were excited to be back from the brink and forging forward, then the generic, production-line tenor of 'Object 47' neither oozes enthusiasm nor affirms a sense of commitment to new, original work. To give it a positive spin, though, while it suggests 'more of the same', that's not actually a bad thing: this functional, business-as-usual title also suggests continuity with Wire's previous work, as if to say: We've been around for a long time. We've made lots of good records – 46 of them, in fact. And here's another one.

It was no surprise that, in 2007, Gilbert found little in Wire's new direction that interested him, to the extent that he felt it didn't sound like Wire – *his* idea of Wire, that is. After all, that appears to have been his view as far back as 2003, when the post-*Send* material began to hatch, and he distanced himself from it – seemingly indifferent to songs, music, and playing (or perhaps that should be "using") the guitar. Be that as it may, it's not fair to use Gilbert's perspective to frame *Object 47*; it may have no longer sounded like Wire to him, but it sounded like Wire to Grey, Lewis, and Newman. With that in mind, it makes sense to reprise Newman's remark about the band moving ahead after the Paul Smith affair, since it applies equally to the departure of Gilbert and to the ex-guitarist's opinion of their latest work: "His vision for the band was entirely different from ours. We asserted our vision."

The sonic contrast between *Object 47* and its predecessor couldn't be more dramatic. *Send* was claustrophobic and compressed, painted in aggressive, industrial-sized brush strokes, eschewing nuance and variation, and emphasising surface over depth; *Object 47* is a breath of fresh air, trading harsh monochrome for expansive widescreen colour and a pronounced melodic sensibility.

The anthemic 'One Of Us' sets the agenda for what follows. The song evolved out of the group-playing on the last day in Rotterdam, and it's the perfect opener. In earlier days, this would have been the album's 'big single'. Propelled by what Newman calls "a classic Robert disco beat" and Lewis's surging bass, and punctuated by enormously catchy choruses, it captures the optimism and excitement that the band-members describe with regard to the Metropolis 22 session. Its irresistible drive and infectious gusto defy even the most cynical listeners not to tap a foot and smile. Despite the unequivocally upbeat sound, however, in typical Wire fashion, the lyrics set a very different tone. "One of us will live to rue the day we met each other," warns Newman, against the grain of the sing-along bounce. (A home movie-style video for the song – shot by Malka Spigel – featured Newman lip-syncing on Wimbledon Common, as well as on the New York City subway, in the company of Grey and Lewis.)

Wire unambiguously re-embrace pop on *Object 47*. Alongside 'One Of Us', 'Perspex Icon' is another prime example. Dating back to 2004, musically, and to 2002, lyrically (the words recycled from 'Dip Flash'), it combines stop-start buzz-saw guitar rhythms with Newman's bright, tuneful vocal – a refreshing change from his hectoring *Read & Burn–Send* style. Lewis's two contributions to the album ('Are You Ready?' and 'Mekon Headman') are more groove-centred. While Grey enjoys 'Mekon Headman', he wasn't convinced by what he heard when the band started to develop it in Rotterdam. "The first time we were playing around with that riff, I thought it sounded much too much like a blues for Wire to be considering it as suitable. I thought it wouldn't work, but it took on a life of its own and worked out really well." By contrast, the moderately funky 'Are You Ready?' never grew on the drummer – according to Newman anyway: "We've never played it live, because Rob hates it. He thinks it sounds like Gary Glitter. To be honest, I've never warmed to it, either."

The press release for *Object 47* touted Wire's "tunes with zoom" – presumably referring to breezy, driving numbers like 'One Of Us' and

'Perspex Icon' – but the album is far from homogeneous. It's not all musical sweetness and light. Some heavier, harder-edged tracks, for instance, make fewer concessions to melody – but as they have more than two dimensions, they don't retreat into *Send*-world. Tempo changes punctuate the Massive Attack-style rolling dread on the hefty 'Hard Currency'. It's one of the earliest pieces, originating in a Lewis bass loop, although Newman pushed it in an unlikely direction: he reports that his production on the track was in part inspired by a remix of Missy Elliott's 'Get Ur Freak On'. While the closing track, 'All Fours', undoubtedly comes closest to the early-2000s guitars-and-shouting formula, it doesn't have quite the same maniacally repetitive, circular feel as many of the *Read & Burn–Send* tracks, which ended in pretty much the same place they'd started; 'All Fours' achieves some kind of release and resolution, thanks mainly to guest Page Hamilton, who plugs in with a feedback squall that adds extra menace to the album's apocalyptic coda.

The Helmet guitarist almost came to play a larger part in the band than this guest spot. Wire intended to remain a trio for their studio recordings at this point, but they knew they'd need a guitarist for live work, and Hamilton was their first choice. Hamilton, however, recalls being sounded out about what he understood to be a more permanent position: "They emailed me and said: you're the only person we would want to replace Bruce. I had a couple of months to think about it, but it just wasn't feasible for me to join their band, because Helmet was still going, and I'd moved to LA. So then they said: we'd love you to play on something – and they sent me 'All Fours'. It was something they'd done in Rotterdam, so they called it 'Rotterjam'. It was pretty much done, apart from my shit-storm of guitar. I did six or eight guitars and arranged them and said: this is my take on the build – do whatever you want with it."

A track like 'All Fours' couldn't really go anywhere else but at the end of the record. Even so, it's slightly paradoxical that, having devoted the first eight tracks to expanding their sound in such a way as to distance themselves from the *Send* phase, they should close the album with a number that explicitly re-connects with that period. Moreover, if they were keen to assert 'their' vision of Wire and to put the past behind them, it seems odd to have enlisted a guest musician to do one of the things for which Gilbert was best known. By recruiting a relatively famous guitarist to bring the noise, they were, inevitably, drawing attention to Gilbert's absence – highlighting a part of their identity, largely missing from this album, that listeners would traditionally associate with their ex-colleague.

### It's got a nice cover

The album is by no means a misstep, but there is a tentative feel to it. It occasionally sounds a little fragile – not totally sure of itself. This comes across on 'Circumspect' and 'Four Long Years'. Although these numbers had been around for a long time, as musical works-in-progress, they appear to confirm Newman's observation that the material on *Object 47* wasn't worked on as thoroughly as the *Read & Burn 03* tracks. Along with the dirge-y, listless 'Circumspect', which had in fact been among the earliest material in the work file for *Read & Burn 03*, the very ordinary 'Four Long Years' is another less-than-compelling interlude. *Read & Burn 03* had been the cut-off point as the end of the Gilbert era, but 'Four Long Years' (initially titled 'God Spot') had, in fact, been developed by Gilbert and Newman, deconstructing one of Lewis's ideas – as they had done with 'The Agfers Of Kodack'. "It came from Graham," remembers Newman, "and we took everything away that he'd given us and made this piece. Bruce and I worked on it together, but nothing of what we did together remains. I don't think Bruce actually played on it, he just commented on what I did." That anecdote is more interesting than the song.

It's not just 'Circumspect' that has a tired, plodding quality. Rotterdam had been energising, kick-starting the album's better tracks, but it also spawned the weakest link, 'Patient Flees'. Bearing in mind what Newman says about the song's origins and patchwork construction, it's perhaps not surprising that it fails to pass muster: "It was made up of bits of jamming. We weren't actually playing anything at that point – it was almost stray notes picked out and put in rhythm. It doesn't sound like a bassline a human would have played. It's just some notes cut together."

Indeed, the production method to which Newman alludes here – assembling the songs in his studio from various parts generated by the band – may account for some of the deficiencies of *Object 47*. His cut-and-paste, or what he calls "hip-hop", production worked a treat during the *Read & Burn–Send* cycle, but on 'Patient Flees' the parts don't coalesce as convincingly – the apparent excitement of the group-playing on the last day in Rotterdam is reduced to something bordering on the polite and perfunctory. This would be remedied on the next album.

'Patient Flees' also marks a low point in terms of its lyrical content, foregrounding one of Wire's less appealing habits. In the noisier context of the *Send* work, for example, Wire's random-text-as-lyric tendency wasn't such an issue, but here, in the cleaner, clearer production environment, it becomes obtrusive and awkward. The conceit is to list words ending in '-ion'.

361

To begin with, this features only in the chorus, but eventually Newman throws in the towel, and the track peters out in lexicographical purgatory. Since modernism, artists have brought all manner of linguistic experimentation to bear on song lyrics, poetry and fiction in order to subvert conventions, and there's no reason why the lyrics to a song can't be a list of words – indeed, that approach could raise thought-provoking questions about our expectations regarding the form and content of pop music. In this case, however, it just suggests a lack of imagination.

More interestingly, *Object 47*'s lyrics sometimes take an angry tone. Although the words may well be pure performance or simply artistic exercises in evoking moods or emotions in an abstract sense – with no connection to real events – it's hard not to link them to the challenges the band were facing at the time. It may not have been the writer's intention, but for the listener who knows something about Wire's managerial problems, the lyrics do take on substance, especially when they're so prominent and audible in the mix. It's not difficult to see the following examples as thinly encrypted responses to the post-*Send* debacle: "Can I make it plainer? / I misjudged your intentions / Misread behaviour / That beggars many questions / What happened to our plan / The one that we began? / … / One of us will live to rue the day we met each other /… / We're here, we will, we can / Finish what we began!" ('One Of Us'); "You were being devious / Always dark and circumspect" ('Circumspect'); "The sound of missing matter / Advances sealed and snatched" ('Four Long Years').

Despite several strong tracks, there's a feeling that something's missing on *Object 47*. It can't be reduced to the absence of Gilbert and his noisier, dissonant tendencies; after all, Gilbert had been a part of successful previous work that didn't display such characteristics (as well as unsuccessful work that did). While *Object 47* is more multi-dimensional than, say, *Send*, it fails to establish the underlying tension present, both lyrically and sonically, in Wire's better work: a tension between the familiar and the unfamiliar, the comfortable and the unsettling, the obvious and the inscrutable. From this core ambivalence in the band's most memorable material comes a sense of things never being completely resolved, never wholly present, never fully declared – this is Wire's *otherness*. Throughout the band's history, Lewis has described this as an "inexplicable ingredient" that makes its presence felt to the listener or spectator when the band is firing on all artistic cylinders, famously dubbing it the "x-factor" (long before the term became inextricably linked with vacuous light entertainment). Unfortunately, Lewis's "x-factor" doesn't declare itself here. There's nothing *other* about

*Object 47*, and the record only offers listeners one side of the equation: the familiar, the comfortable, and the obvious.

Lewis recognises *Object 47*'s weakness. In his view, it's best to supplement it with *Read & Burn 03* to get a more comprehensive and accurate picture of this creative cycle, one that incorporates tracks like '23 Years Too Late', which he considers a particularly potent piece. "I don't think it's wise to separate *Read & Burn 03* from the album, because it's an arc of work, and we divided it for practical reasons. With *Object 47*, it was very fast. We were asking a lot of questions of ourselves as to what it was, what it was going to be, and I don't think we were as secure creatively."

From an artistic perspective, *Object 47* was a minor album for Wire. But viewed with a different set of criteria, it's no exaggeration to suggest that it may have been one of their more important records: more important in terms of the band's recovery than in terms of its songs. "It's got a nice cover, shame about the music," Grey jokes, adding: "As the first album by the three-piece, I think it's all right. It wasn't painful to make. It was definitely a turning point. We certainly had plenty of doubts about it, and we were in unknown territory – but getting through *Object 47* showed us it could work." Newman elaborates on that point. "*Object 47* isn't our strongest record," he concedes. "But it's a very good transitional record, getting us from one place to another place. We had the feeling that there was a genuine need for Wire in the world. We didn't feel like we'd done everything we could do together as a band." Lewis agrees, expressing that same idea, more graphically and succinctly: "There's no way Wire was going to be left where it was. In a ditch."

## CHAPTER 12
# 2008–11

### The Enabler

By early 2008, Wire had begun to schedule live dates for the run-up to the July release of *Object 47*, and in late January they spent a couple of days at Terminal Studios in Bermondsey (formerly Terminal 24). The objective was twofold: to play as a three-piece and to audition a touring guitarist. The first day was devoted to the former, recalls Colin Newman, "to establish that we did have a 'basis' for someone else to join". Although the band-members had jammed together on the last day of their short stay in Rotterdam, a year earlier, in Newman's view the Terminal session was the first proper group-playing since August 2004. "I don't think Rotterdam really counted. We weren't playing with great intent, and it wasn't for very long. It wasn't really playing with a purpose. In Terminal, we played a number of songs from our repertoire, with intent, and sounded convincingly like Wire. In Rotterdam, the idea of what – or whether – Wire should be was still very much a work-in-progress. By Terminal, it really couldn't be. It had to work: we had gigs booked. It was a pressure we all agreed to."

On the second day, the band auditioned London-based American musician Margaret Fiedler McGinnis. In addition to her work with Moonshake and Laika, she had experience as a touring guitarist with P.J. Harvey; Laika had also contributed a cover of 'German Shepherds' to the *Whore* compilation, which Newman and Graham Lewis rated as one of the album's best tracks. Various other guitarists had been considered before Wire contacted Fiedler McGinnis. As well as Page Hamilton, the Austrian electronic artist Christian Fennesz had also been sounded out. He was a long-standing Wire enthusiast, and Newman had co-produced one of his early singles. Despite interest on his part, other commitments made it impossible for him to get involved.

It was a similar story for Steve Chandra Savale of Asian Dub Foundation. He was excited to receive an enquiry but was unable to work around his band's schedule. "Wire have been a huge influence on me and my whole approach to music and especially my guitar-playing," he says, "so of course

I was interested. When Colin asked me, it was not an impossibility that Asian Dub Foundation might have been nearing its end; if that had been the case, I would have jumped at it. As it turned out, fate gave us a new lease of life, so I couldn't. But it was a great compliment that the only band that's ever asked me to be their guitarist was Wire." Besides Savale, there was one other even more intriguing possibility. "Another candidate was Johnny Marr," reveals Newman, "but when I asked him he was just about to start working with The Cribs."

While Fiedler McGinnis had been a Wire fan since the 80s, she had never seen them perform. She had a ticket for their 1987 New York gig at the Ritz but didn't make it owing to a car accident on the way to the show. She remembers that it was her husband, a music publisher at Mute, who initially recommended her to Newman when he learned that the band were looking for a guitarist. Of the audition itself, she says: "It was kind of nuts. They gave me a list of about 33 songs. I prepared for three weeks. Constantly." According to Lewis, she brought something special to Terminal: "Not only could she play the songs, but she was able to teach us how to disinter 'The 15th' – a song which had never been performed live, post the recording of *154*." (It would feature in the band's sets during 2008.) Fiedler McGinnis recalls treating the audition, in part, expressly as a chance to play 'The 15th' – her favourite Wire track – with Wire themselves. "I didn't know if I was going to get the job, and so I just wanted to play that song with them. So I said: 'The 15th', please. And they were like: how does it go? I would have been happy had I not got the job, just because I got to play that."

Lewis was pleased to have Fiedler McGinnis on board. "We had a drink after the audition, and she was in. Her attitude and personality were good, and she loved the band's work; she was smart, road-experienced, and willing to learn to play the Wire way." Lewis also comments that gender played a part in the decision, albeit not from an affirmative-action perspective. In his opinion, having a woman onstage helped undermine, in a superficial, visual way, any perceptions that the new guitarist was intended as a direct replacement for Bruce Gilbert. "Being female meant that, potentially, any Bruce comparisons were more 'difficult'."

Understandably, in interviews around this time, the band played down Gilbert's absence as much as possible. This was a new, hard-fought incarnation of Wire, focused squarely on the future. They simply took the line that Gilbert was no longer a member of Wire, and Fiedler McGinnis was not a member of Wire but a guitarist brought in to help them play live.

However, it was inevitable that that detail would be lost on most people: they would come to gigs and see a new guitarist replacing Gilbert in the band. And if Wire were looking to remove Gilbert from the equation and to keep the emphasis off his absence, it didn't help matters that photos of Wire as a four-piece *with* Gilbert continued to crop up in press coverage of the band's 2008 live dates, as well as in conjunction with reviews of *Object 47*.

Fiedler McGinnis herself had a clear understanding of her role, her comments suggesting that the band had thought quite hard about ensuring that she not be perceived as Gilbert's stand-in. "In no way was I ever a replacement for Bruce. Exactly the opposite. I was asked not to feed back during 'Pink Flag', for example, which was kind of weird." Newman doesn't remember giving that particular instruction, but acknowledges that there was "perhaps a general instruction not to do the obvious". Fiedler McGinnis approached her duties pragmatically, seeing herself as a facilitator in Wire's recovery. "They were very, very fragile. They'd been going for over 30 years and hadn't ever worked without Bruce, and they weren't sure whether they could keep going and how they could keep going. So everybody was happy to see them playing. I was happy to see them playing. My job was to see them playing. And now they're in a much better place as well. All I ever felt was that I was an enabler, which I was really happy to be. They were one of my favourite bands, and they were in a bad place. They didn't think they could tour ever again. I felt like I could come in and get them to play some gigs. And that happened."

Wire resumed live work with a series of dates in Belgium, Holland, Italy, France, and the UK, before opening the Seaport Music Festival in New York City on May 30, in front of 5,000 people. A week later, they played to an even larger crowd at the Serralves Museum of Contemporary Art in Porto and, at the end of June, performed at the Sled Island Music and Arts Festival in Calgary. The band kept busy through the summer with European festivals, co-headlining Offset in London with Gang Of Four.

In September, Wire returned to the BBC for the first time in six years. Marc Riley had taken a shine to 'One Of Us' and invited the band up to the Oxford Road studios in Manchester. They played live on his 6 Music show and also took the opportunity to record a session for Mark Radcliffe and Stuart Maconie's Radio 2 programme. This was followed by another string of UK and European gigs and then a full North American tour in October.

The 2008 live sets in support of *Object 47* generally featured only four tracks from the album and just as many from the *Send*-era releases. Apart from *Read & Burn 03*'s 'Our Time', the rest of the material dated back as far as *Pink Flag*. The refusal to play classic material was now a thing of the past, and this mixture of old and new songs would characterise Wire's sets moving forward. By the time of their October trip to the USA and Canada, the band had even begun to introduce a few wild cards, reviving 'He Knows' and 'Underwater Experiences'.

## Someone who does the weird shit

During Wire's North American dates, Page Hamilton joined them for encores at the Echoplex in Los Angeles. "It was amazing," he says. "All of our musical suspicions were confirmed: yes, we were indeed very compatible. I was just buzzing. It was incredible. Our energy levels matched, and it was one of those things where everything was so in sync, musically. It's what you dreamt and hoped it would be. Getting to play with them, like getting to play with Bowie, was amazing." Newman noted Hamilton's exuberance that night: "Page is the only person who's allowed to high-five Wire onstage. He was so excited."

Taking his job seriously, Hamilton sought some guidance on one of the songs they were due to perform, but the band weren't able to offer much assistance. "We were going to play 'Underwater Experiences'," remembers Lewis, "and Page asked: what are the chords? We said: You must be joking! It's a bit more about what sort of noise you're going to make, Page." According to Newman, Hamilton's superior skill led to some very un-Wire embellishment: "He's a proper musician. He knows his stuff. All he needed to know was when to start and when to stop. He did play one stray extra note, though. But we'll let him off. He's American." Politeness prevented Hamilton from giving the band a quick music lesson, when he noticed that things weren't quite right during 'Lowdown'. "I thought it was funny that they played 'Lowdown' – *their own song* – wrong! That was excellent."

In Hamilton's recollection, this brief encounter rekindled Wire's interest in working with him in a more substantive way. "Colin emailed me when they were in San Francisco shortly thereafter and said: Page, we need to talk … I kinda knew what it was about. He said it was so much fun for them, which made me feel so good because I felt the same way. We said: we have to figure out how we can do this at some point. And so we agreed on that. Hopefully, we'll eventually be able to do something together – some shows or some recording."

In February and March 2009, playing mostly the same set that they had been performing in the United States and Canada, Wire undertook short tours focused on Italy and Germany. The rest of the year was given over to one-off dates and festival appearances in Sweden, Poland, and Spain, plus a return engagement at All Tomorrow's Parties, this time at Butlin's in Minehead, curated by The Breeders.

Fiedler McGinnis is happy that she accomplished her goal of enabling Wire to play live again, but she did feel constrained in the role. "They definitely had ideas about gear, and that was kind of hard," she says. "I have some really, really nice equipment, and they said: right, we want you to use this and this and this. The main thing was this all-in-one floor-pedal thing with digital out, and a lot of the processing was done at front of house. Normally, I'm more in control of my own guitar sound, and a lot more was happening at front of house than I was comfortable with. I'm sure it sounded good, but I wasn't in control of it. That was definitely different."

Although she was fully aware of what the job entailed, she strikes an ambivalent note when discussing the experience, feeling she was unable to perform to the best of her abilities. "It was uncomfortable the whole time. It was difficult because I felt the whole time I played with them that I definitely wasn't playing as well as I could have done. But that's what happens when you play for somebody else. It's not your band, and I've done that before, and you just do what people want you to do. And that's fine."

The *Object 47* phase of work ended in October 2009 with a set at Madrid's Monkey Week Festival, Fiedler McGinnis's last show with Wire. The band then began to think about building toward the next album. The feeling – largely Newman's – was that this next stage would require a new touring guitarist. He explains why this was so: "There was a general sense that we could never 'replace' Bruce, and I felt at the time this could be best interpreted by taking extra musicians for each project cycle. So Margaret played all the shows in support of *Object 47*. By the time we got to spring 2010, we were already well into the process of making *Red Barked Tree* and planned to play as many of those songs as we could live. So I felt this was definitely the time to move on and find the guitarist for the next cycle."

This was what Fiedler McGinnis had expected, but she sounds a little disgruntled about parting ways with the band. "They said: We just want somebody to tour this record, and then with the next record we'll move on. So now they've got Matt [for the *Red Barked Tree* live work], it'll be interesting to see if they do move on. Originally, they said it would be a year but it ended up being about two. I think they didn't want to have someone on the payroll."

The "Matt" in question is of course Fiedler McGinnis's successor, Matthew Simms. He was recommended to Newman by Jason White of 4AD and Associated London Management (ALM), with whom Wire were in the process of developing a relationship. White had previously run the Too Pure label, to which he had signed Simms's band, It Hugs Back, several years earlier. Simms's familiarity with Wire's work wasn't encyclopaedic. "I had the first three records," he says. "I wasn't a super-fan. I didn't know them inside out. The first time I read about them was in *Mojo*, when the first three albums were reissued [in 2006]." However, an appreciation of Wire did run in the family. "My dad had the seven-inch of 'Outdoor Miner'," says Simms. "He bought it when it first came out."

Simms's audition took place on April 28 2010 at Ritz Studios in Putney. He'd been sent a list of seven tracks to prepare: 'Lowdown', 'Comet', 'Silk Skin Paws', 'Boiling Boy', '106 Beats That', 'He Knows', and 'The 15th'. A few tips were also included. The advice for 'Comet' was: "Main thing is knowing when to stop!" and for '106 Beats That', he was cautioned: "The chords are a bastard!" A closing instruction read: "Also surprise us with one thing you can play of ours that we've forgotten" – the idea being that he should choose a song and then 'teach' it to the band, as Fiedler McGinnis had done with 'The 15th'. "I suggested 'Map Ref.'," remembers Simms, "which I think was a surprise for them. I picked it because it was one of my favourites."

Talking about his preparation for the audition, Simms emphasises that he wasn't just concerned with knowing how to play the songs. "I made sure I knew how they worked, but I also made sure I had the right sounds." This interest in sound, as much as technique, was something he had developed early on, as he began to learn his instrument. "When I was really young, and I started playing the guitar, the first record I really got into was Sonic Youth's *Experimental Jet Set, Trash And No Star*, which my dad gave me when I was about 12. It was a big influence – showing that the guitar could be something more, that you could get all sorts of sounds out of it. That's the side of the guitar I really like." This focus on sound was something that immediately registered with the band. "Even before he started playing at the audition," Newman recalls, "he was preparing to play a song, and he already had the right sound for it. And Graham said: he's like we were when we were younger."

Simms's try-out also included one tricky element. "There was one song we weren't told we were going to play, and we had to learn it on the spot. That was 'Underwater Experiences'." As far as he was concerned, this was the key part of the audition. "By playing that with them, I knew I wanted to do it. It felt like a good combination. I've never really experienced anything like that with a band I've played in – that kind of intensity. I didn't expect it. I'm not sure it exists in many bands."

Although he was sure everything had gone fine at Ritz, Simms didn't believe he was a shoo-in. "I felt it went well, but I didn't come out of it thinking I'd got the gig. They had some pretty well-known people they could have asked. I also thought that the age thing would be an issue. [He was 23.] I could see why that could cause a problem. They didn't know me. That side of it could have been more of an issue." He needn't have worried, though. "I was in Tesco later that evening, and I got the phone call. I went back the next day, and we started working on songs."

For Newman, the distinction between Simms and Fiedler McGinnis was subtle but important. "Margaret came with her own history. She was great because she'd seen and done it all before. Laika played to pretty big audiences, and she'd done stuff with Polly Harvey. She knew how it worked and the ins and outs of it. She can play guitar pretty well, she's quite musical, and she's a Wire fan – but she doesn't come from Wire. She doesn't have that same mind-set. That was the whole thing when Matt came." The difference, in Newman's view, was all about Simms's approach to sound. "Margaret has no idea how to get a Wire guitar sound. She knows how to get a rock sound out of a guitar. She's got a nice guitar, she's got a great amp, and she knows how to do it, but she hasn't got any of that obsessive thing that Matt has. He's got so many pedals. He listens. He listens to the tone combinations. It's not just about the parts, it's about the sound as well, and that is very Wire and puts him in a different category. He's got something that Margaret never had."

Newman identifies another bonus point for Simms: "We need someone who does the weird shit. That stops Graham doing too much weird shit. Matt does it with consummate ease – with no pretension at all. If you want a bit where it goes crazy, Matt's your man. Just wind him up and point him at it."

While Robert Grey had been impressed by Simms's playing, it wasn't necessarily the newcomer's ability "to get a Wire guitar sound" that had struck him. It was more important to Grey that he clearly had his *own* sensibility. "'Comet' was one of the songs we played in the audition, and Matt had the best sound – he had a distinctive guitar sound. That suggested to me that he was able to bring something of himself to the song. He could make a distinctive noise. That made me think Matt was right."

With a short French tour imminent, the band rehearsed at Ritz from May 10 to May 14, holding a final run-through at Resident Studios, in Willesden, on May 20. Resident was chosen, according to Simms, because of the "terrible" sound. "So if it sounded good in there," he explains, "we were ready." He played his first gig the next day in Lille, with the French dates followed by an appearance at the Primavera Festival in Spain. Unsuspecting revellers in the Ray-Ban Unplugged tent at Primavera were also subjected to an impromptu performance of 'Up To The Sun' by Lewis and Newman. During the French tour, by coincidence, Olivier Assayas's new mini-series, *Carlos*, aired on Canal Plus, its soundtrack incorporating 'Dot Dash', 'The 15th', 'Drill', and 'Ahead'. This was only the second major use of Wire's work in film: in 1997, Pedro Costa's *Ossos* had featured 'Lowdown'.

July 2010 saw some archival activity from the pinkflag label with the release of *Send Ultimate* and the initiation of the subscription-based Legal Bootleg series, making available gig recordings dating back to 1978. Because of sound quality, some of these are of interest only to Wire archaeologists, but they're well chosen, catching the band during radically different phases of their career: 1978 shows from Bradford University and Berlin's SO36; a 1979 Jeannetta Cochrane set; the notorious 1985 Paradiso concert; 1987 and 1988 recordings from the Town & Country Club and the Astoria in London; 2000 gigs from Edinburgh and San Francisco; and the first full *Send*-era set, recorded in Bristol in 2002. The series also included a DVD of the 1985 Bloomsbury Theatre concert: it's definitely lo-fi, but given the scarce visual documentation of Wire performing in the 80s, it's not without value.

## Trust the band

After the cut-and-paste methodology of *Send* and *Object 47*, which put the focus not so much on the band as on Newman working independently at home, *Red Barked Tree* marked a change in strategy. Newman would now write the songs in advance, present them to the group, and, together, they would develop the arrangements in the studio. Although this may not sound revolutionary, for Wire at this point it was: this would be the first time since the 70s that they'd made an album this way, working out, playing, and recording the song-based material as a band. *Red Barked Tree* would also be the first Wire album in 31 years to feature full, live kit-playing from Grey.

Newman explains his motivation: "We had some things left over from *Object 47* that didn't get anywhere, and Graham wanted to work on those, but I thought we needed to do completely new material. I thought: What Wire needs is for me to write some songs on acoustic guitar, like I used to. We learn them, and then we record them. We haven't done that for a while

371

– that'll be good. That's what we have to do. That's the purest expression of what will make a Wire record. It also went with me getting very bored with cut-and-paste as a method. I felt I'd done enough of that. It seemed to me that this would be a good way to move forward, to just record it all as a band."

Wire's return to performance in 2008 was also a factor that led them to readopt this modus operandi. In the 70s, they had used their live work as a leaping-off point for recording – not only because it had enabled them to bring road-tested songs to the studio but, just as importantly, because the band arrived in peak condition, brimming with confidence and creativity. This had always laid a strong foundation for further exploration of the material as the recording proceeded. Prior to making *Object 47*, Wire had been inactive, disengaged from a cycle of gigging and making records together; having now completed two years of live work, they were back in that engaged mode.

Granted, they hadn't been working out new material in performance, as they had often done in the early days, but the self-assurance and renewed strength that they had built up on the road could be tapped. "We'd been playing for ages," says Newman. "We did all that touring with Margaret. The band could play: we could stand, the three of us, and play together. We'd got the confidence to do that." Lewis agrees: "You want to utilise that strength and spontaneity that you have from working together on the road, because the technique's there. You have that strength, and you want to harness it. So the quickest way of doing that was for Colin to write a bunch of things on acoustic guitar, and we learned what the chords were and spontaneously put some sort of arrangement together."

In addition to the creative rationale, the decision to revive a more traditional studio process was also influenced by the band's improving financial health. At the beginning of the *Object 47* period, Wire's funds were limited; as they moved toward *Red Barked Tree*, on the back of significant touring, they were in better shape. The first choice for a recording location was Metropolis 22, the Rotterdam studio that had proved invaluable to the band's recovery, and the plan had been to start there at the end of 2009. This fell through, and they opted to record in London, booking time at Resident Studios between February 12 and 15 2010. (A second session would take place in June at Press Play Studio in Bermondsey.)

Newman had begun writing and recording demos in December 2009, using four lyrics that Lewis had emailed him. This yielded acoustic versions of 'Adapt', 'Now Was', 'Red Barked Trees', and 'Spuds' (later renamed

'Smash'). These were dispatched to Grey and Lewis, so that they could come up with ideas for their parts before the studio sessions. Despite Newman's enthusiasm, initially working from these demos wasn't to everybody's taste. "I found it difficult to come up with a part by playing along with vocals and acoustic guitar," recalls Grey, and Lewis preferred developing songs in real-time collaboration: "Many of the most 'Wire' songs occur through the ensemble's spontaneous and united reaction to the introduction of a new piece. I understood Colin's method, though: it enabled him to knock out songs quickly. It's a Colin strength."

By late January, with the Resident sessions drawing near, Newman had received no more texts from Lewis. "I'd sent out the rough acoustic versions of the four songs, and when we got to a week before we went into Resident, I still only had four lyrics from Graham. I wanted ten or 15. I started to panic that we wouldn't have enough material, so I started writing without Graham's lyrics. I thought I'd write a song a day and have seven by the end of the week. So it was all basically at the last minute. I figured that if I put pretty ad hoc words in, then Graham could afterwards 'translate' them – we'd done something similar with *Object 47*, so there was a precedent, although to be honest, there is a special kind of magic that happens when I have the finished lyric already. The songs I started that way were 'Clay', 'Moreover', 'A Flat Tent', and 'Down To This'. At that time, I also realised we could make something of what became 'Two Minutes'. So when we went into Resident, I came with 'Now Was', 'Clay', 'Adapt', 'Moreover', 'A Flat Tent', 'Smash', 'Down To This', and 'Red Barked Trees' – as acoustic songs, which we learnt as a band."

The return to an older methodology can also be seen as another aspect of Wire's healing process. Having the band work together, building the songs from the outset, fits with the renewed emphasis on transparency and visibility that Newman talked about with regard to the 2007 Rotterdam sessions. More importantly, it was a way of placing the responsibility for the material with all the band-members, directly involving them in the creative process – whereas before, the primary creative activity had been Newman's production and mixing, carried out in the absence of the group. The idea now was for everyone to feel more connected to the work. "If everybody has got the material, and we've played it," says Newman, "we'll be more invested in it. That's the idea, believing in the material and being more invested in it. The process is called 'trust the band': the band knows what the best thing is to do with the material."

Grey welcomed the idea of reinstituting continuity between Wire's performing and recording identities. "We wanted to establish the songs with the three of us actually playing together, and I suppose that sounds like an obvious process – but the idea of the three of us playing live together and putting songs together in the studio was a huge step from when we'd been making *Object 47*." From Grey's perspective, the *Red Barked Tree* material benefitted greatly from this revised approach. "As we've become more able to build the songs through playing, one of the results has been a more equal share of input. As a result, I think the playing on the album has a dynamic feeling to it, rather than being overly considered and created in Pro Tools. It's getting away from doing things like that, from being processed by computer. It has a much more human feeling to it."

Indeed, Wire's re-emergence as a live band and the reinstatement of live performance as part of the recording methodology gave Grey a sense of vindication. "Everybody was happy with the live playing of *Object 47*, that we could play without a click-track and samples and electronic assistance. I'm not very flexible about the options, but I think everybody agrees. I think the electronic phase is well in the past, and it seems that there's a certain amount of coming full-circle. Everyone recognises that it's our best format, and that it has advantages – but I would say that, because I'm interested in things that are played. For making it work with Wire as the structure is now, it seems our best option – and it's proved its worth."

At Resident, when Newman introduced each of the tracks on his acoustic guitar, "it was a matter of listening to Colin and then doing our version of the song," says Grey. Newman stresses how promptly the band completed the arrangements and the basic recording: "It went at a real lick. I don't think we played more than three takes of anything." Grey confirms this: "We recorded about 14 tracks in two days. We didn't have a lot of spare time. It was a good pressure. It's easy to waste time in the studio, messing about getting the right sound for everything."

However, Grey wasn't 100 per cent comfortable with working so quickly, even though he recognised the advantages and also appreciated Newman's desire to capture Wire in a purer, more 'live' form than he had done on previous records. Ideally, Grey would have preferred more time to explore ideas, given that his initial response to the music tends to be conservative, focused on getting the basics right. "The plan was to have a spontaneous reaction quality to it. But for me, through repeated playing, you add and change things and give it more depth. My first reaction to playing with something I hadn't really heard before would be to keep it very simple. It's difficult to play with confidence, and you don't just want to play something that you know already. You're trying to come up with something new and play it perfectly at the same time."

Nonetheless, as Grey observes, the issue of accuracy, at least, was academic since the technology was now at such a stage that the drum tracks could be edited and corrected. "It still ends up on the computer, and individual mistakes can be rectified, so it's not like a live performance where you want things to be played as perfectly as they can be. You get the best of both worlds: you're playing live, and you get the option of removing any mistakes."

Notwithstanding Simms's comments about the sound quality at Resident, Newman believes that the studio's live room was ideal for recording drums: "It was great for getting a big drum sound. I wanted that expansive drum sound. It's a classic Wire thing – the drums in a nice room – it goes back to the 70s. That's the sound of that room in Advision."

Once the work at Resident was finished, Newman returned to Swim Studio with the recordings. "The original playing was really rough – I tightened everything back up. I worked through the spring, putting the tracks together, and got everything to a certain kind of level – and then I re-presented it to the band." They then reconvened for two days in June at Press Play, revisiting the tracks and working on them to varying degrees. Run by Stereolab's Andy Ramsay, the studio not only housed decommissioned Stereolab gear but also provided a treasure trove of instruments – some of which would find their way onto the record. "Andy's got an incredible collection of musical bits and pieces, loads of old analogue gear," recalls Lewis. "That gave things a different twist or a new harmonic."

## What the fuck did you do to my song?

Wire's development and arrangement of the material as a group, in the studio, with written songs at the heart of the process, also redefined Newman's production role. With the cut-and-paste method of *Send* and *Object 47*, 'making the record' and 'production' had been mostly synonymous. This was not so on *Red Barked Tree*. Although he was still producing and mixing the material, Newman now describes his responsibilities in different terms: "The production process on *Red Barked Tree* is only there to make all the things sound together. It's not 'making' the songs – I'm not making the songs that way. The songs are already made, and the arrangements are already made. I'm just making it sound good – which is what you're supposed to do in production. It's not 'making' the thing."

Paradoxically, de-emphasising production as the phase in which the

375

songs were made had the side-effect of reinforcing Newman's control over the process: this was evident, for example, in the way it limited the opportunities for Lewis to make additional contributions, outside of the main recording sessions. That way, as Newman puts it, "it wouldn't be stuck with the inevitable thing of Graham sending parts which don't really fit. Graham sends bits, and most of the bits he sends are really difficult to fit into anything. It's mainly more of a hindrance than a help. Graham thinks it's his duty to make it more weird now because Bruce isn't there."

One might expect Gilbert's absence to have fundamentally altered the creative dynamic, including Lewis's sense of his own role. Just as *Red Barked Tree* was Wire's first attempt in decades at making a full-band, in-studio recording, it was also the first time they had done so without Gilbert – yet Lewis downplays the effect of this change. As far as he is concerned, Wire had evolved into a different entity by the time of *Red Barked Tree*, and it was no longer a case of there even being a felt absence. "I could tell you the quality Bruce might have brought or what he might have done, but it's so hypothetical now. It doesn't matter any more. The vacuum's not there any more. Once it was done, it was done, and you've got to get on with it." He also points out that the new version of Wire simply wouldn't have worked with Gilbert: "There are things now that certainly wouldn't have been possible with Bruce, things he wouldn't have wanted to be involved in."

There is one sense, however, in which Newman seems right in suggesting that Lewis had taken on a role formerly played by Gilbert: without Gilbert, the main creative tension in Wire was now between Newman and Lewis. Although Lewis welcomed the shift in emphasis back to playing and arranging together, it remained that Newman was the producer, working on his own. Despite the increased band involvement with the material in a neutral environment, Lewis's remarks indicate ambivalence about this continued concentration of the production duties at Newman's home studio. "It's about economics. For better or for worse. It's been a great facility to let us do what we wanted. It puts Colin in a unique position, and that's the position of having the final say. And it's also the position of taking an incredible amount of responsibility. That's a criticism and not a criticism."

While there was once an uneasy balance of power between Gilbert's vision and Newman's, the tension now in the band is not played out on such equal ground. If Lewis recognises that Newman's production mantle gives him the last word, Newman's observations on this matter leave even less doubt as to who wears the trousers in the relationship. "In the end, I get to decide what gets included. And sometimes I will have the discussion with

Graham where he says: you've ruined my song!" Newman gives the example of *Red Barked Tree*'s 'Bad Worn Thing': "Originally, there was another chorus, and Graham said: what the fuck did you do to my song? I told him I'd made it work. And he said: where's the chorus? I said: the chorus was awful. I told him: Graham, it sounds like somewhere between Mick Jagger and Gilbert O'Sullivan. And then he went very quiet. In the end, I have to put my flak jacket on and say: This is not going to work. This is how it's going to be – now it sounds really good. I think it's got to the point now that everyone trusts me. I don't necessarily favour my own parts. It's about making the thing work."

As well as exercising creative control, Newman was also still taking care of much of Wire's business – continuing the 'player-manager' role he'd assumed earlier in the 2000s. By 2010, with the band operating as an independent, largely self-run unit, the need for its consistent commercial viability had become paramount. "I've been looking after the finances, realistically, since 2000," says Newman. "The role I've taken on is that it's up to me to make Wire work financially, because if it doesn't work financially, the band's not going to work." But Newman was well aware that the group's survival also depended on keeping everyone happy: while the group had successfully reinvented themselves as a trio, they could not survive any further losses of personnel. This knowledge seems to inform his holistic business model for the band. "It has to work on so many different levels: it has to work financially, and it has to work emotionally. It's a total artistic and business venture and a relationship between people. Part of what's happened to the band over the past few years is that we've become much more dependent on each other, psychologically. Everybody has to be present, because you can't leave: if one person drops out, it's finished. That's it. That's the end."

In spite of Newman's comments on maintaining a healthy band ecology and rebuilding trust between Grey, Lewis, and himself, he appears to have grown somewhat dismissive of Lewis's contributions. This is presumably a reflection of Newman's awareness of his own power within the new configuration of Wire, which would not function without him. But given what he says about the ramifications of losing another original member, it seems a risky habit to fall into.

### Wire (featuring The St Agnes Girls' School Choir)

Although most of the *Red Barked Tree* material originated in Newman's acoustic-guitar blueprints, a couple of tracks arrived by a different route: the dance-friendly 'Please Take' and 'Bad Worn Thing' – both Lewis compositions. "It's the first time ever that you have two Graham songs on a Wire album and have them both be pretty good," says Newman. "Graham has his songs, and they come as a complete package, while mine have to be worked on by the whole band. I tend to come with something more basic, because I want the band to interface with it. I've got more front than Graham – I can stand there with an acoustic guitar, suffer the ridicule, and still get a result out of it. Graham still has to figure out that he can just turn up with a bassline and a vocal, and we'll try our best to make it work."

In Newman's opinion, this creative divide is significant. He views Lewis's tracks on *Red Barked Tree* as discrete items and even suggests that, in contrast with his own songs, they're not authentically 'Wire' – at least in terms of their provenance and initial development. Perhaps mindful of the creative fragmentation that began with *154*, where individual ambitions threatened to eclipse Wire's group vision, Newman sees the need to ensure that Lewis's songs become Wire songs, appropriate for a Wire album. "In a way, Graham's songs are Graham's, and my songs are the band's. That's the way it is. But I'm not producing a Graham Lewis record with Wire making gestures on it, and I'm not producing a Colin Newman album with Wire playing on it. These considerations are very important. And the distinctions have to be made: it's got to be a Wire record, and all of it has to be playable by the band."

According to Newman, Lewis's songs for *Red Barked Tree* required considerable attention and reworking: "Graham doesn't really write in any traditional sense. He turned up at Resident with three tracks which consisted of 20 tracks of drums, basslines, some vocals, and some funny noises – but the thing is, there is a tune there." (Lewis recalls bringing "four pieces" to Resident.) For 'Please Take', Newman remembers paring everything down and concentrating on the bassline. "Graham has a tendency to have the bassline doing the same as the vocal, so I just got Rob to play along with a different bassline. It was literally stripping it right down to bass, drum and vocal – and saying: let's make the song like that." Newman is impressed with the results, although it's not entirely clear if he is, in fact, still talking about Lewis's original song: "There's a fantastic, expansive elegance between the three basic elements: the drums, bass, and rhythm guitar. If it's not the best Graham song on a Wire album, it's certainly one of the best. I hope it's not about me!"

Lewis confines himself to an appreciation of the lyrics, more specifically the first line: "'Please take your knife out of my back and, when you do, please don't twist it' – this lay in my notebook for six years awaiting the right melody. Sarcastic stoic records Pyrrhic victory, employing seductive melody in lethal 'fuck-off' song." While he doesn't reveal the identity of his knife-wielding subject, he does give a clue. "About six years ago, it could have been very useful in several cases, but let's keep it universal. Let's pass it on for everybody's use." Given the time frame that he mentions, it's once more impossible not to link this song to Paul Smith or, indeed, to Newman himself – even if this wasn't Lewis's intention. ("There's generally quite a lot of complaining in Graham's lyrics that he sings himself," says Newman.)

For Grey, who had been invited to make suggestions regarding the album's running order, 'Please Take' was a candidate for the lead-off number. "I was asked to propose a track sequence, and I found it difficult initially. Then I realised that if I thought of the tracks as a series of scenes in a play or a film, it made it easier. I like the idea of the tracks telling a story: the story was the album from beginning to end. 'Please Take' was my choice for the opening track – it has an introductory feel, a sense of trouble brewing maybe …"

'Bad Worn Thing' required even more acute intervention from Newman. "It came with a more difficult birth," he says. "I had to do a lot more hacking around with that one – 'Please Take' was pretty much there, structure-wise. I tried not to do too much on this record, but if something's generally not working, I'm not going to say I'll go with it. I'm going to make it work. 'Bad Worn Thing' just wasn't working as a piece. Graham brought some bits, which I kind of sandwiched together. I made a structure for it. In the past, I would have been more brutal. He felt annoyed about it and then probably realised that it worked. There was no aim there to do anything other than to make the best possible thing that you can out of the material. I want Graham to sound great."

Newman speculates about the lyrics: "I presume it's about Britain and Graham being superior living in Sweden." Lewis confirms only the first part of Newman's interpretation: "It was written from observations made during a couple of bloody awful days spent travelling in England or, better put, *trying* to travel in England: a dreadful train journey that laid bare the inadequacies of the British transport system. Add to that the ambient noise generated by the early morning drum'n'bass soundtrack for the fevered trade in sex and drugs in London's East End."

'Now Was' encapsulated precisely the sort of process Newman had been keen to trigger during the *Red Barked Tree* sessions – the band taking his basic composition and running with it, heading in directions he couldn't have anticipated. "It's a classic example of what happens if you throw something in front of Wire on an acoustic guitar: they don't do what you expect them to do. The way that came out was completely illogical – that's what I'm looking for. Rob plays 'punk' drums and Graham plays, like, a jazz bass – rhythmically, it's a bit like 'Brazil'. It's very harmonic and not what you'd expect. They just did it. That arrangement came as quick as the song did. The structure is already nailed down from the beginning, so we can always go very fast. It all came in five minutes. There's no messing about."

This song is another fine Lewis spleen-venter. "It's about those aristocrats of arrogance, horrible cynical middle-aged men," he volunteers, keeping the focus "universal" again. "I've got my idea of who it was about," says Newman, and Grey presumably has the same candidate in mind. "I interpreted it as referring to one very specific person ... but, of course, that particular person could also be part of the general group Graham mentions." That's as may be, but a familiar muse comes to mind, especially with lines like, "Trust once shared, is beyond repair / Pledges sound hollow, which promised tomorrows". As usual, however, the pursuit of a fixed meaning – who or what it's 'about' – is the dullest approach to the lyrics. More interesting is the way the lyrics are constructed and the pleasure they take in their own textuality – chiefly in terms of the litany of witty, inventive titles with which Lewis damns his subject (eg, "the wizard of was", "the Lear of sneer", "archduke of rebuke", "the pharaoh of fluke", and "a grandmaster crashed").

It's true that a tendency toward listing manifests itself again here, but these epithets are neither throwaway nor do they sound randomly copied and pasted. They're thought out and worked through and, more importantly, they're part of a broader lyrical structure, not left to stand on their own, unsupported and doomed to failure – as was the case on, say, *Object 47*'s 'Patient Flees', with its inventory of words ending in '-ion'. Linguistically, there's enough going on around these linked phrases to make them a playful motif, rather than the focus of the song. The lively musical arrangement and the energised vocal also contribute significantly – contrasting starkly with the melodic lethargy and the resigned, monotonous intonation of 'Patient Flees'.

In Newman's estimation, 'Adapt' was one of the album's pivotal tracks, its sound unique – as well as unlikely – for a Wire song. "I knew it was a hymn as soon as I'd written it," he says. "When we came to it in Resident, I said: this is a Christmas hit! I can just hear The St Agnes Girls' School Choir singing it as a Christmas single. Had it been in former times, Bruce probably wouldn't have played on it. Just on principle: I don't agree with that kind of music. It's one of those songs." This was another number that the band took to intuitively. "We just got in the studio and played it," says Newman. "It may have been a first take. It's fairly simple – the expression is in the vocal – it doesn't need any other grand gestures in the instruments." The track did almost end up with one 'grand gesture', but Newman took measures to tone it down. "Graham put some piano on it. It sounded like Bruce Hornsby & The Range, so I put some delay on it."

Although Newman's references to seasonal novelty Number Ones and questionable American ivory-ticklers might threaten to bring the song crashing down to earth, he is convinced of its transcendent quality. "There's something absurd about it, but at the same time it's beautiful. If there's a Wire song that goes way beyond everything – beyond Wire, beyond the band, beyond our performance – it's that one."

Grey was taken with this number. "After we'd recorded 'Adapt', I forgot about it, and when Colin sent it to me as one of the mixes, I thought: this is so good. It's my favourite track. It moves you emotionally and physically. It has a pleasantly melancholic feel – not depressing, though." Newman – who seldom allows himself much enthusiasm for his own lyric-writing or others' – agrees, noting that he found something uplifting in Lewis's words. "I liked the whole idea of passing on advice to someone younger than you, the prayer-for-peace idea. It's got other ideas in it, but I really liked that." These were among the first lyrics that Lewis composed for the record. "It was a kind of 'news song'," he says. "It's lots of impressions of lots of things. It's a kind of where-are-we, state-of-the-world address: observations about extreme climate change and disaster, the failure of financial markets, child labour, hollow politics. Even Chekhov gets a name check."

Lewis's last remark requires some elaboration. "Originally, there was some swearing in it," says Newman, "but I asked Graham to take it out. The last line was: 'Adopt "fuck off" to family crest', and I said: Don't put that – it's ridiculous. You're just cutting off your nose to spite your face. You can have swearing in a song like 'Two Minutes', but you can't have swearing in a song like this." Although the original wording was far funnier, good taste prevailed, and the final line became: "Adopt 'Chekhov' to family crest." (This mirrored the band's early instance of self-censorship, with '12XU', in which the 'X' had famously suppressed 'fuck'.)

## Less of a chorus and more of a car crash

The word 'fuck' sits well in 'Two Minutes', one of the noisier, more aggressive interludes on this occasionally lyrical album. In purely musical terms, this is the only song on the record that predates 2010. The obsessively repetitive, no-nonsense riff telegraphs the track's origins. "It's from 2001," Newman explains. "I made the basic riff for *Read & Burn 01* but never developed it. I brought it to the studio and, as soon as Rob and Graham started playing on it, it sounded absolutely awesome. Then it just needed some random shouting on it. 'Fuck' isn't appropriate in 'Adapt', but in 'Two Minutes' it's fair game."

The title sets the tone for the track, which proceeds as a countdown, of sorts, with escalating urgency and intensity, Lewis's mumbled interjections punctuating Newman's verborrhea – Lewis recalls that he was asked to "react" to the latter. This was a lyric Newman had written with the clock ticking down to the start of the Resident session, but he doesn't claim sole authorship. "I needed words quick and happened to have Twitter open, so I just gathered and mashed together various tweets and got to a 'lyric' pretty quick." This variant of the cut-and-paste aesthetic actually works well because of the way in which Newman's vocal takes ownership of the words: the purloined utterances are unrelated to one another and, on their own, they stand as obscure statements, but his theatrical performance provides a context for them – making them a wholly organic, if incoherent, product of the unhinged persona that he's projecting. Newman's very much in character, but it's not a character you'd really want to meet, investing benign and not-so benign phrases alike with a sardonic, provocative edge. He manages to deliver the line "coffee is not a replacement for food or happiness" as if he's trying to pick a fight with his interlocutor over the veracity of the statement. The song ends with the assertion: "I'll tell you who I hate on a daily basis." Judging by the tenor of this valedictory dispatch, the list could be a long one. Fodder for another song, perhaps.

'Two Minutes' definitely channels the spirit of the *Send* era, with its combined sonic assault and heckling vocal. As with the best numbers from that period, its unbalanced spiel, while inadequate as an act of communication, is totally compelling. The only weak link is Newman's unwitting inclusion of a Dead Kennedys song title ('Religious Vomit') in his assortment of harvested tweets.

Lewis isn't a big fan of 'Two Minutes', but he recognises its value. "I can't really think of it as an appealing song," he says, "but it disrupts the album nicely, and it makes things a little more multifaceted." Grey, meanwhile, was a little taken aback by the lyrics. "I did think the words were very strange until Colin told me that he'd collected them from random texts. I'm not sure where he found these, but that would explain why it didn't seem to make immediate sense. It sounds like it makes sense to the person who's speaking it, but it's a very odd construction. But although it's odd lyrically, musically it's definitely recognisable as Wire – as one of our heavy numbers."

There are a couple of moments where, besides being "recognisable as Wire", tracks also evoke specific, classic Wire songs. This is the case with 'Clay' and 'Moreover'. The driving, rhythmic insistence of the latter recalls 'A Question Of Degree'. Like 'Two Minutes', it's an exercise in intensity, but with a precise, staccato relentlessness. The lyrics are a sprawling list of brief (mainly two-to-four word) rhyming couplets, seemingly more of Newman's self-described "stream of consciousness bollocks". A facile, unimaginative approach to lyrics is again saved by the performance – in this instance stern and intimidating, with hints of hysteria as the tension rises. "I was trying to get across the idea of a mad preacher, with a moronic riff," Newman says. "It's Wire unleashed." Witnesses to the recording agreed with that assessment. "The first time we played it in the studio," Newman remembers, "the engineer said: you make a big fucking noise for three people!" Grey likes the back-to-basics aspect of the track. "It has intensity and simplicity, and the fact that the studio engineer said he liked it was a very good sign."

Referring to 'Clay', Newman concedes that "the bassline is very 'I Am The Fly'," but that's as far as he'll go with the comparison. He prefers to highlight the differences between the two tracks: "It's got that cheeky Wire sound, but it's really got very little in common with 'I Am The Fly'. It hasn't got that annoying nursery-rhyme chorus. There's a bit more of a tune to it. If you take away the bassline, it doesn't actually sound like 'I Am The Fly'. So you can blame Graham." Lewis turns this back on Newman. "Colin played the tune, Rob drummed, and I played the bass. There was very little else you could do with it. That's how it came out. Simple as that." If anything, Lewis thinks it improves on the older track. "It sounds better than 'I Am The Fly'. That's one of the songs that has suffered over time: the sound is great, but the playing's not terribly good." (Something else that differentiated 'Clay' from 'I Am The Fly' was the presence of – largely imperceptible – acoustic guitar on the former. "The main rhythm guitar on 'Clay' is acoustic," says Newman. "It's doubled with an electric, so it's not obvious. But you'd hear it if it wasn't there.")

Handclaps – a vital ingredient of 'I Am The Fly' that isn't recycled on 'Clay' – feature at the start of 'A Flat Tent', with Andy Ramsay lending his manual talents. This was one of the last tracks to come together at Press Play. "It's quite jolly," Newman says. "The handclaps were written in from the beginning – I was originally hitting my acoustic guitar." While aspects of 'Clay' and 'Moreover' have clearly identifiable antecedents in Wire's catalogue, 'A Flat Tent' captures a more generalised Wire feel. "It's quite Wire-like," says Newman, "but without sounding like any particular Wire song. Wire always manage to sound like Wire, even though there's no actual brief that says what Wire are supposed to sound like. That's a key element in how it all works." One of this song's structural devices makes it unmistakably Wire, according to Newman: "I love all the stops in it – they're ridiculous. Only Wire do songs with stops like that. It has a moronic edge to it, of which I think we're the leading protagonists in the world, really."

Lyrically, the track gave Lewis a chance to revise Newman's writing. "Colin sent me a text, and I didn't understand a thing – so I thought I'd push it off the cliff." As for the deflated title, he recalls: "Its working title was 'Ten'. A new title was necessary. There's a hold in the song on *A-flat*, so I combined 'A-flat' with the first title and manufactured 'A Flat Tent'."

The anecdote behind the title of 'Smash' is more interesting. "It was called 'Spuds' for ages," Newman says. "Graham didn't want that, and he really struggled to come up with something better. We were sitting in the tour bus one day, and he suddenly said: we can call it 'Smash'. It was a combination of road accidents and mashed potatoes." Lewis expands on the title and the lyric: "It's where road kill meets potatoes, hence 'Smash' – as in 'For mash get Smash', from the old British TV commercial. A few of the images also suggest something of a perverted Narnia." In keeping with its title and the associated imagery, it's another of the record's aggressive tracks, memorable for its shifts in tempo. The sudden changes and the incongruity of some of the song's parts appeal to Newman. He's particularly keen on the chorus. "It's less of a chorus and more of a car crash. I love the way the chorus sounds like something went seriously wrong – like Japanese pop, where it suddenly turns into something you don't expect. I like that idea. It has an absurdity to it."

### The post-moronic condition

'Down To This' is a rarity in the Wire canon because of its prominent acoustic guitar – "suggested by Graham, strangely enough," Newman notes. As for the lyrics, Newman doesn't beat about the bush. "It's about everything being shit, on every level you can possibly think of – and the only thing you've got left is death. It was one of those seven or eight songs that were written in that week. Graham thinks it's one of the best songs I've ever written, but I find it pretty depressing." Fittingly, much of the track has a funereal quality, enhanced by an organ part played on one of Stereolab's retired instruments. Lewis gives his take on the song: "It projects a creeping sense of doom: urban malfunction. What happens when *all* the lights go out?" Grey also offers his own bleak two cents: "Well, it's not cheerful, is it? We all die at some point, and you can't be cheerful all the time. It contrasts nicely with 'A Flat Tent'. You have a diverse spectrum of emotions on the album. That's a good thing, involving the listeners' full breadth of emotion."

One of the album's standout numbers, the lilting, mysterious 'Red Barked Trees', came together late in the process. The band had recorded a version at Resident in February, but the drum pattern – a four-on-the-floor beat – didn't fit. "At Resident, it didn't seem obvious straight away what I should do," says Grey. "We got something down, but it didn't really click." Things fell into place at Press Play, which was ironic since the drum sound at the studio was poor – "very dry and dead," remembers Lewis. However, they turned this to their advantage: "The room suits having drums very quiet," Newman says, "and that was the right thing for that track."

At Press Play, Newman encouraged Grey to pursue a different approach to the beat. "I asked Rob to do something that goes more with how the rhythm guitar – playing in triplets – goes. And it became magic." Grey recalls the process, commenting on how he was able to move beyond his initial response to Newman's music: "When we tried again at Press Play, I was less conservative about sticking to something that was steady and more predictable, and I did come up with something – in the sense of throwing ideas at it, rather than sticking to my first reaction. It's certainly not a rock beat. Is it a folk-rock beat?" Newman follows up on this: "It's more like Pentangle than Wire. Wire have never made a track anything like it: it's in 3/4 time, with acoustic guitars, bouzouki, and organ."

Lewis takes some of the credit for one of the song's distinctive sounds. "I picked up this bouzouki when the track was playing and went *DA-DA-DA*, and I thought: God, that fits! And Colin grabbed it off me and took it over and proceeded to put this bouzouki part on it. And we thought it was great. Then he turned round and asked me: do you have any ideas for this track?"

Grey was excited by the depth and range of this song, so much so that he thought it might herald a new era for Wire. "It's more musical than the average Wire song," he says. "When Colin sent me the mix, I commented that it was post-moronic, because Colin always says Wire songs have a moronic element in them, and what's missing here is that essential moronic element. That made it stand out." If it lacks the "moronic" flavour that Newman always stresses, it also underscores the record's lyricism, a trait that's been rare in Wire's work. "The whole album is more lyrical than anything Wire have done for a while," says Newman. "This track especially. It has the quality of a journey. It's got a calm, open-eyed beauty to it – looking at the world as a mysterious place."

With regard to the words, Newman is again surprisingly effusive. "Graham and I never talk about the meanings of the songs and, obviously, there's always more than one meaning – but I like to think of the search for the red-barked trees as a search for the philosopher's stone or maybe *soma*: maybe an artistic quest for the thing that will enable you to understand everything." Lewis gives some insight into the lyrics: "It's about dismay and hope, and the wonder of technology versus the ancient knowledge of alchemy. Will we destroy rare invaluable flora and fauna before we can research and exploit their unique properties? In the end, is it going to be the red-barked tree that's going to hold the cure for cancer?"

Grey believes this is the perfect closing track. "If 'Down To This' was like a burial scene in my overall narrative of the album, then 'Red Barked Trees' is a resurrection: it's uplifting and hopeful. It has a sort of healing theme to it. Hopefully, that'll stay with listeners – we don't want to leave them depressed at the end." To Newman, not only is this the most important song on the record but, more broadly, it's a creative milestone for the band. "It's the absolute key track. It's the most innovative. It's the most different for Wire. It's the most special because there's nothing in our catalogue that sounds anything like it, and that pleases me immensely." He also grants that there may be a hint of The Beatles here: "Yes, you're allowed to mention the B-word – now that Bruce has gone."

In November 2010, with *Red Barked Tree* nearing release, Wire played gigs in Belgium (Diksmuide and Hasselt), London, and Oxford. Their sets generally included six tracks from the new album (plus 'Up From Above', a contender for a place on the record that didn't make the final cut). Only 'Mekon Headman' and 'One Of Us' were held over from *Object 47*. For the rest of the material, they followed the familiar post-*Send* pattern, drawing on most phases of their career. Also in November, Wire returned to Resident Studios – with both Fiedler McGinnis and Simms – to record *Strays*. A limited-edition release that came with copies of *Red Barked Tree* ordered through pinkflag.com, this EP featured 'Boiling Boy', 'German Shepherds', 'He Knows', and 'Underwater Experiences'.

Just as the image on the *Object 47* sleeve presented a section of a large structure (the Boländerna water tower), a similar strategy was used for the *Red Barked Tree* artwork (again designed by Jon Wozencroft). In this case, the cover was given over to a photograph (by Wozencroft) featuring a roughly two-foot-square detail of a floor-filling, multi-material, multi-dimensional Jannis Kounellis installation. As a cover photo, this is less successful than its predecessor. There's nothing particularly engaging or creative about this appropriation; it seems like little more than a superficial cultural quotation. When asked about the image, neither Newman nor Lewis was able to say much about the source material. The lack of engagement with an important aspect of their own work is, in itself, symptomatic of the rather facile process of recycling here. This apparently minimal interest and involvement contrasts with Wire's – especially Lewis's – previously active role in the conceptualisation and production of their cover art, approaching it as part of the larger project – as a facet of Wire's living sculpture.

## Back to the future

*Red Barked Tree* was released digitally on December 20 2010 and then in CD format on January 10 2011. Wire marked the physical release with another appearance on Marc Riley's BBC 6 Music programme, playing three songs from the album. This kicked off a marathon year of promotion and touring. By the end of 2011, they would have chalked up 80 gigs in 21 countries, making this their busiest year since 1978.

Having played a warm-up gig at Rough Trade East in London on January 11, Wire travelled to New Zealand and Australia. The highlight of this trip was a performance at the Museum of Old and New Art's MONA FOMA Festival in Hobart, Tasmania. To date, this is the closest Wire have come to the South Pole. As a relative novice, Simms relished the touring experience ("That was a dream come true. It was amazing to see all those places"), and he felt completely comfortable, in spite of some unfriendly treatment in Australia. "That was the only place I've got comments about not being Bruce. People were shouting things out, stuff like: bring back Bruce! – that kind of thing." There was an isolated instance of this the following month, during the band's UK tour, but this time there was less of an edge to it. "It happened when my amp broke in Nottingham," Simms recalls, "but that was more people just being funny, rather than confrontational."

After the UK gigs and a month-long run of dates in continental Europe, in April Wire set out on a North American tour. By now, they had excised all remaining *Object 47* material from the setlist and were focusing on the new album.

Wire's stock had risen noticeably in North America since the *Object 47* tour. Ticket sales were strong, and *Red Barked Tree* was garnering substantial attention, but there was also wider media interest in the group beyond the usual realm of college and independent radio: in addition to playing live on stations such as WFMU (their New Jersey home-away-from-home) and Seattle's KEXP, they appeared in Toronto on *Q*, Jian Ghomeshi's nationally broadcast CBC show. Lewis even got fellow guest Stephen Fry's autograph. More prestigiously, when Wire were in New York City for gigs in Manhattan and Brooklyn, they performed on NBC's *Late Night With Jimmy Fallon*, a television programme with (at the time) around 1.7 million nightly viewers. Taking the stage before Keanu Reeves, they played 'Red Barked Trees' and 'Map Ref. 41°N 93°W'. In contrast with their last US chat-show adventure, there was no attempted subversion or would-be absurdist theatrics; the band played it straight, exorcising the ghost of Suzanne Somers – although, in presenting Wire, Fallon did make a passing reference to the ill-fated host of yore.

By the end of the American tour, Simms was fitting in well – much more than his hired-gun status would suggest. Lewis, Newman, and Grey were excited by his approach to their work. "He's an unassuming person, and he's very un-pushy," says Newman, "but he's got a strong musical personality. You know he's there; he's no shrinking violet when it comes to doing it." From the start of his tenure, Simms had a bigger impact than Fiedler McGinnis, indirectly prompting the band to raise their game. It wasn't that he actively tried to set a direction or make his mark, but just that he brought so much extra to his seemingly limited role. As Newman comments: "We ended up getting an awful lot more than we had planned or bargained for with Matt." It may also be true that Wire, now in a more secure and confident state, were simply ready to allow a greater contribution than they had made possible for his predecessor.

It was thanks to Simms that 'Map Ref. 41°N 93°W' had been dusted off for the North American gigs. His enthusiasm for the song had been obvious at his audition a year earlier, and it was reintroduced on the eve of the tour, as the band discussed changing the set from the preceding European dates. "Matt not only knew how to play 'Map Ref.'," Newman remembers, "but had all the right sounds, so we started talking about doing it. I said: I think it's too hard – but it became a live staple. It's tougher to do, but the expectation of what the band can achieve has really gone up now." Newman sees a big difference between Wire in 2008 and Wire in 2011. "Even when we were touring with Margaret, we had to keep the material pretty easy to play so everyone could keep up – and that's pretty much going back to *Send*, where everything was one chord, and no one really had to play anything. Now, something's changed within the band in that we're capable of doing things we weren't able to do before."

Simms's unique sonic sensibility impressed Grey even more in the context of the band's live work over the course of the year than it had when he first noticed it during the guitarist's audition. "Playing live, he has an affinity for what we're doing, but he brings his own style to the playing. The solo on 'Red Barked Trees', which isn't on the record – I don't know if he'd want me to say 'solo', but his 'bit', anyway – is really good in the song. He fits in very well. The playing, obviously, but the sound is the most important thing." Lewis agrees: "Bruce had such a great ear, a great ear for sound and tone, and although I'm not initiating a comparison with Bruce, it is something Matt does have. He's got opinions about things, and he knows when to place things." Early evidence of this can be heard on *The Black Session*, a live album recorded on May 10 2011 in Paris for a radio broadcast at the start of a brief French tour (released in February 2012). Throughout this set of old and new Wire material, Simms's guitar unlocks and opens up new spaces in the songs.

Shortly after the dates in France, Wire returned to the scene of their early-2000 triumph, the Royal Festival Hall, as guests of Ray Davies, curator of the 2011 Meltdown Festival. (It hadn't actually been Davies who'd chosen them for this event but one of his management team, Chris Metzler, a former Mute employee.) While the band were pleased to have been invited, they weren't as happy that their particular night of the festival had them sharing a bill with mid-20th-century garage legends The Sonics. At this point, Wire were involved in the promotion of what was turning out to be their most successful record in some time; The Sonics, meanwhile, had released their only significant work in the 60s. "I don't think many people are fans of both bands," says Newman. "We're contemporary, pushing the envelope, doing all new stuff, and we're not relying on our past. It just felt wrong. Obviously, you don't turn it down, but it was the wrong bill in the wrong venue. Chris's original idea was to do us and The Pop Group at the Queen Elizabeth Hall – that would have been two classic older bands, but something more people would want to see."

Despite their slight disappointment about being paired with The Sonics, Wire had still risen to the occasion. "There was a sense that we needed to do something special for the Festival Hall," recalls Newman. And with that in mind, they revived two *154*-era tracks that hadn't ever received a studio recording: 'Ally In Exile' (last heard in Edinburgh in 2000) and 'The Spare One' (unplayed since the 1979 Jeannetta Cochrane shows, with a version included on the 1996 *Turns And Strokes* compilation). Lewis explains the rationale: "We thought: what can we do to surprise ourselves? And also, you've got to play with people's expectations. So we played those couple of things after rehearsing them just the day before." The restoration of these two pieces would form part of a much grander plot that the band were hatching.

Wire visited Tokyo in early July for a one-off gig. "It was nuts," laughs Simms. "There was even 'pop screaming' in the middle of songs – screaming in the quiet bits. It was like being in a pop band." The group finished off the summer with concerts in Germany in August and September. Among these was a Berlin appearance at Trafo, a cavernous decommissioned power station, with Einstürzende Neubauten and Caspar Brötzmann Massaker. Broadcast on German TV by ZDF, Wire's set culminated in a 'Drill'–'Vox Populi' hybrid performed with Neubauten, who were playing on a separate stage in the cathedral-like space.

Before embarking on another British tour in November, the band overhauled their set. After the better part of a year, the *Red Barked Tree* cycle was winding down and, as Lewis notes, it was time to shake things up. "You get to a point with material that you feel it's been explored, had its day – and it's a good idea to let it rest. Bringing in new material makes it more interesting for us, work-wise. It's awful if material stays too long, because then it tends to get trashed. People get frustrated with it and start taking liberties as soon as they start to feel it's not fun anymore. That's where we'd got to at the end of the US tour. Playing things which are fresh avoids that."

For most bands, "fresh" material means brand new songs; for Wire, it meant something different. While they retained five tracks from *Red Barked Tree*, the majority of the other numbers in the revised set were now, strictly speaking, neither 'new' nor 'old'. They were drawn from the corpus of songs that the band had begun developing in 1979 and 1980 with a view to a fourth album, but which had never been fully realised or recorded in the studio. As Lewis reports, the reinstatement of 'Ally In Exile' and 'The Spare One' had been an important step toward incorporating these vintage tracks: "They went so well that we thought we'd do more for this tour. We said: let's see what works. And after a few days we had seven of these things – and they were alive."

This material was rehearsed in two two-day sessions at Ritz Studios, either side of a one-off gig in Lorient, France, on November 11. The day after the final rehearsal, they began their tour in Birmingham. This would be Wire's most extensive run of UK dates since the 70s. (Whilst on the road, they fitted in another BBC 6 Music session for Marc Riley, as well as an appearance on Radcliffe & Maconie's Radio 2 show.) Besides 'Underwater Experiences', 'Ally In Exile', and 'The Spare One', the set now featured some seriously mythical songs from the 1979–80 period: 'Witness To The Fact', '5/10', 'Part Of Our History', and 'B/W Silence'. 'Witness To The Fact' had been on the Notre Dame Hall 12-inch that accompanied *Document And Eyewitness*. '5/10' and 'Part Of Our History' were played at the Electric Ballroom, although only the former made it onto *Document And Eyewitness*; the latter had cropped up on *Turns And Strokes*. (As Newman is keen to point out, the musical roots of the new 'Part Of Our History' lie not in that 1980 draft but in a subsequent home recording that he made once Wire had gone on hiatus.) 'B/W Silence' was a revision of 'Lorries', which had last been performed at the Jeannetta Cochrane residency and was later recorded by Newman on *Not To*, as was '5/10'. (A version of 'Lorries' from the July 1979 Notre Dame Hall gig appeared on *Turns And Strokes*.)

On the November tour, the band also played a radically rearranged version of 'Underwater Experiences', titled 'Deeper', which was in fact closer to the 1977 Riverside demo. All of this was a Wire trainspotter's treat, and the gigs were enthusiastically received. The tour finished in Sheffield, with the last concert of an extremely busy year.

## Joined-up thinking

At the end of 2011, Wire found themselves in a very different place from the precarious one they'd been in five years earlier, when they met in the National Theatre foyer. Although the strength of the band's work (old and new) was a core factor in their recovery – without that foundation nothing would have been possible – something else had fallen into place during the *Red Barked Tree* phase. Crucially, in 2010, Wire had started to delegate some business-related responsibilities to an external figure, Associated London Management's Jason White.

Newman is quick to emphasise that Wire do not have a traditional band-manager relationship with White or ALM. "Obviously, because of Wire's troubled management history and the fact that we are by now quite grown up, the idea of us having a 'manager' or even of a management company handling us doesn't really work." Instead, he describes White as a "consultant" whose company "provides management services to us". As

Newman explains it, White's working relationship with Wire is unlike anything they've experienced before. "Jason's everything Paul Smith wasn't – and he's not even the manager. He works more or less only with me, and if he doesn't have anything to say, he doesn't say anything. Once you get offstage, he's gone home. He's not in the dressing room hanging around – with Smith, it was hard to keep him off the stage. The way we pay him is fascinating. You pay a fixed amount of money per month, but when we're not working, we don't pay them anything. It's so different from the endless percentage on everything."

The arrangement with ALM has worked wonders as far as Newman is concerned. "What Jason brings is the joined-up thinking that comes from someone who knows how things are done in other organisations. Jason's ideas are worth their weight in gold – for example, the way we did *Red Barked Tree*. I've never done a release as joined-up in my life. I know how to put a record out, I've been doing it for years, but I don't know how a big label does it – the whole thing of the timing, how critical the timing is, and all the things being joined-up together. That's so key. That was a first for Wire." The results were immediately apparent to Newman around the release of *Red Barked Tree*. "The weekend before the album came out was unbelievable. The press we were getting was just unbelievable: we were even in the *Sunday* fucking *Mail*! That was mad. And Britain more than America, for the first time in God knows how long. And it carried over into radio, like 6 Music."

Lewis, too, believes that Wire have moved into an exciting new phase, now finding themselves in a position of strength, which he attributes to the organisational changes around the band: "After the first London show with Matt at the Garage in June 2010, I had the feeling that this was the first time we were in charge of what we were doing for a very long time, and part of that process is by getting other people involved, rather than having a Svengali manager." While he had recognised and valued Newman's role in maintaining Wire's creative and financial health through the 2000s, he also felt it had become necessary to try something different in order to move the band to a new level. "The last few years, by doing it ourselves, we'd lost a lot of momentum and hadn't capitalised on situations that we should have capitalised on. It's the proverbial Wire problem: it's all well and good getting good reviews, but that's got to be converted into something else, so you can push on."

As a result, Lewis had grown convinced that it would be to Wire's benefit if Newman were relieved of some business-and-management-related responsibilities. He recalls broaching the idea of looking outside the band for assistance: "I had a conversation with Colin and said I thought it would be important to get someone in so that he didn't need to do certain things. I thought it was necessary for his sanity – and my sanity – that he was distanced from things in some way, and I hoped that someone else would bring a different perspective. It's happened intermittently for us over the years and something good always happens, because then you can concentrate on what you should be concentrating on – rather than being involved in second-guessing what other peoples' perceptions are, or peddling your own reputation, which had diminishing returns and is not very elegant."

# CHAPTER 13
# 2012
# (What's Past Is Prologue)

## Better 32 years too late than never

Early 2012 was a quiet time for Wire. In February, they played the *Ox* 100 Festival in Solingen, Germany (a celebration of *Ox* fanzine's 100th issue), where the crowd was expecting a different Wire from the one it got. "It was a weird event," says Matthew Simms, "definitely a punk-rock line-up." Indeed, the first band on the bill went by the name of Sniffing Glue, and the audience was even treated to something called a "trash stunt performance". Robert Grey was unimpressed. "The audience just thought Wire represented the 70s. There wasn't a great deal of applause when we came offstage at the end of our set, so we just did 'Pink Flag' and called it a day." (To add insult to injury, everyone but Simms came home with food poisoning, courtesy of the festival caterers.)

In April, Wire paid their first visit to Russia, appearing at Avantfest in Moscow with Tim Hecker and Xiu Xiu, but more importantly, later in the month, they started work on a new record at Rockfield Studios in Wales. It would eventually be given the title *Change Becomes Us*. Taking as its foundation the archival tracks that had begun to populate the band's live sets in November 2011 (plus others, also from the 1979–80 period), this promised to be a highly original enterprise.

The germ of the concept underlying *Change Becomes Us* can be traced to Wire's December 2000 Edinburgh concert, at which they had played 'Ally In Exile' – which begat 'I Don't Understand', which begat the *Read & Burn–Send* era. After the gig, a fan suggested to Colin Newman that Wire should now make the album that they had never made in 1980. At the time, this didn't seem especially alluring. "In 2000," Newman recalls, "that wasn't what anybody wanted to hear. There was no real interest: we'd just done the retro set, so the looking-back thing was done." Nevertheless, he adds: "But the idea didn't go out of my head."

It came up once more, in a different guise, when Wire reassembled in

2006. "When we were talking about getting back together," says Newman, "one of the ideas I had – as a typical Wire version of a Don't Look Back show – was to do the fourth album live: an album no one had ever heard. It was so classically Wire, so classically ridiculous." Graham Lewis was also enthusiastic about this possibility. "We thought it would be very Wire to do a show that was all material that was never on real records – from a record we'd never made, even."

Although nothing came of it during Wire's *Object 47*-era reactivation, the idea of performing the 'lost' 1979–80 work had continued to percolate, resurfacing and gaining momentum after the June 2011 Meltdown gig, when the success of 'Ally In Exile' and 'The Spare One' had encouraged the band to revive more unrecorded tracks for the November tour. (By then, according to Newman, the plan actually to record the fourth-album material had become a very real proposition, something he had presented to the band.) Because these songs had not been fully realised in their original context, the late-2011 and early-2012 live work was another stage in their protracted gestation. This is a crucial detail: it wasn't a matter of just deciding to bring classic tracks out of retirement and relearning them – recreating decades-old versions. "It's not as simple as playing old stuff," says Lewis. "Very little of it, although written, had acquired a final arrangement by 1980."

Wire's relationship with these pieces was therefore unusual: they were both familiar and alien, as the band had created them but had in fact barely performed them. This made for a unique experience. "It was amazing how alive the ideas were," Lewis remarks. "It's incredible to step into a harmonic world of your own making but that you didn't experience for very long because we only played a lot of the stuff once or twice. It's very strange." Consequently, what took place in the live playing was another cycle of in-performance arranging and shaping, a return to the spirit and procedures of the 70s.

During the November dates, if Wire themselves were conscious of beginning a new phase, their audiences appeared to be in sync: there was a strong sense that, like the band, they were looking ahead and responding more to this new-old material, which was benefitting from the strength and confidence built up over many months of intensive live work devoted to *Red Barked Tree*. "When we were playing the old stuff," says Lewis, "it seemed to have more of a 'now' thing to it than *Red Barked Tree*. We were coming at it with the harmonic development that had come through the year's work, and audiences were connecting with it more. You could tell everyone had such enthusiasm for these new things." Newman enjoyed the way these songs changed the dynamic of the set. "It feels so exciting because it doesn't have that sense of expectation of performing classic material that everyone knows, because no one really knows it – all the early recordings of it are a bit rubbish."

Given the success of the material's live (re)incarnation, the band were more eager than ever to make it the focus of a studio recording. To Newman, the concept was very attractive. "No one else is in the position of having that amount of material – a whole album's worth of material – unrecorded. No band is stupid enough not to have recorded a potentially great album – or is stupid enough to do it over 30 years later." This was Wire to a tee, and an instance of vintage Wire perversity to boot. "It's just so classically arse-about-face Wire-ish," says Newman. "Why the fuck would you do it? You'd have to be slightly certifiable. Why would anybody go back 30 years to an album that was never released – material that everybody's forgotten and nobody's interested in – start performing it live, and *THEN* spend a bunch of money to go to Wales and record it? For what reason? Because it's fantastic fun and the material's really, really good."

Lewis takes a more lyrical view of the songs' curious ontological status – as part of an album that never was, as tracks that the fans knew but that never made it into the studio. "The story is about something that's 32 years old – but, in actual fact, it never really had a life. It was like a mayfly: it only lasted for a day, then it went away." Like Newman, though, he's also well aware of the singular and somewhat absurd nature of the venture. "Not many people have managed to lose two records before they recorded them. I don't think it's ever been done. It's not exactly the way you're supposed to go about it." Picking up on Lewis's reference to the project's unconventionality, Newman stresses that part of the appeal is rooted precisely in the idea that it's 'wrong': "It feels very transgressive – because it's the most absurd thing to do."

Alongside the unhinged conceptual charm, the perversity, and the transgressiveness, Newman also identifies a pragmatic motivation. Because the songs' blueprints were already in existence – with several arrangements more or less in place, thanks to the proving ground of the November tour – the band were spared the task of composing a totally new record on the heels of the *Red Barked Tree* album-tour cycle. "After last year, it would have been very hard to go straight into a new album," he says. Lewis agrees: "We're buying ourselves time, so we don't have to write a new record."

For Newman, this is a critical issue. "I think Graham feels very heavily the pressure of songwriting. It's something I've noticed. I don't know why it's got that way with him. It seems to take a long time for him to write any lyrics these days. One of the slight frustrations going into *Red Barked Tree* was that Graham writes so slow and there were very few lyrics – so doing a new album would mean that Graham has no lyrics. So it's a way to avoid that. It's a way of keeping Wire busy without getting into the album-tour syndrome and without getting into this massive discussion of: where's the words?"

Newman feels that a lack of lyrics hampers his creativity. "I need to have some lyrics in front of me that I can just pounce on. I think the songs are better if I have lyrics. I don't write text. I just don't do it, and I also think that's not what I should be doing in Wire. Graham thinks that because I write songs very fast that somehow it's less than his art that takes him months to do. My piecemeal work is done in making the final result. That's where I spend my weeks and weeks of knitting – but the initial idea, the initial song, comes very fast. It's always been like that. I can't write slow. I don't know how to do it any other way. It's either there in the first 30 seconds or it isn't."

## Four people in a van

Another reason for undertaking the 'missing-album' project at this juncture was that it had become, organically, a key part of the current phase of Wire's life as a *four-piece* again – now significantly influenced by Simms, who had played a vital role in the material's live development. "The point at which it was obvious that Matt had stepped into the next cycle was when we were preparing for the gig in Lorient in November," recalls Newman, "when we rehearsed-up the songs that we were putting into the set. We spent two days in Putney and put this bunch of new songs into the set, and it really felt like we'd done that *together*: we'd dredged up that stuff, and we'd learned how to play it as a band, as a four-piece – it was Matt being in sympathy with everybody else and working the stuff out together." The retention of Simms after *Red Barked Tree* and his involvement in the new album was logical to Lewis, too: "Matt's integrated into the band, and he's been playing this stuff as long as anybody else."

Beyond the creative bond with Simms around this body of work, Newman also believed that the band had started to coalesce in broader terms and that there was a definite new feel to things, one that reminded him, paradoxically, of the halcyon days of Wire. The 2011 Lorient trip was pivotal in that regard: Wire's soundman, the fifth member of the travelling party, had forgotten his passport, so the band went alone in Simms's van, with Simms at the wheel. To Newman, it highlighted the group's newfound sense of themselves as a tight, autonomous four-man unit, on a mission – engaged in something exciting and, importantly, fun. "We've got a joint endeavour going on, and it's the first time I've felt that in Wire for a really long time. Matt is very much part of the way the band feels now. It has a certain rightness to it. I knew that when we got to record, there would be a real sense of adventure and fun to it. That's what's happening with this band. This band has adventures now. It used to have adventures in the 70s. It was all an adventure. I don't think we had experiences like that in the 80s. It feels like we're being a band in a fun way again. I feel very positive about this because it's such a laugh."

Simms obviously doesn't have that same historical frame of reference, but he shares Newman's enthusiasm. From Simms's perspective, playing with Wire is a one-of-a-kind musical experience. "I don't think I've ever met a group of people so different – but on the same wavelength at the same time. It's crazy. When they're onstage, there's total commitment – and I could feel it in the rehearsal room, the first time we were playing. The power in it. I'd never been in a situation or a band that has that sort of total commitment. It might mean different things to each of them, but they really mean it."

Newman's praise of Simms sometimes borders on a man-crush, but there's no mistaking his conviction that the guitarist is a perfect fit for Wire. Revealingly, while Newman frequently plays down Bruce Gilbert's importance now – rightly maintaining that it no longer makes sense to think of him as absent, as he left long ago and Wire are now a different group – he does compare Simms with his ex-bandmate. Despite his efforts to put space between new Wire and old Wire, Newman comments on the ways in which Simms reminds him of Gilbert, in terms of his musical sensibility and, crucially, humour. "Matt's like Bruce was, but without the difficult psychological stuff. Bruce is actually very musical. It's something he loves to bury. The moment of understanding how to play 'Eels Sang Lino' at Rockfield with Matt was a moment when I remembered how Bruce and I had done it – and how it had been very funny. It's not enough to know how to do it; you've got to know why it's funny as well. It's one of the things Matt is good at. He just gets it without being told."

Newman clearly values those aspects of working with Simms that echo his partnership with Gilbert – especially the camaraderie he had with the latter because of their roles in the band. "Bruce and I have a very peculiar relationship. We always had 'being the guitarists' in common, and sometimes we would just do things together because we were the guitarists, and we knew how to do it, and that was it. It was like: sorry guys – just live with us, because we know what we're doing, and you'll have to tag along and figure it out. There's something of that with Matt. Matt is just there. He knows absolutely where it is and where it's supposed to be."

Although Newman rarely admits the influence of others, Lewis is adamant that Simms has had an impact on his bandmate's approach to his work and, by extension, on Wire as a whole. "Because of Matt's love of guitars and guitar sounds, he's completely reactivated Colin's interest in guitars and effects. That's the biggest thing Matt's done. Colin's completely changed his guitar and his guitar setup now from what it was up until the end of 2011. He changed his gear. It's a really, really positive thing – and it's made the whole thing sound different." (Unsurprisingly, Simms was promoted from touring member to a more permanent position in September 2012.)

### As I said to Freddie

As the in-studio, band-based recording of *Red Barked Tree* had proved so successful, the same modus operandi was followed for the initial work on *Change Becomes Us*. This seemed even more appropriate now: not only were Wire stronger and more cohesive as a performing unit than they had been at any point since restarting without Gilbert, but they had also just completed more than a year of live work that had, in its latter stages, involved a sizeable chunk of the material slated for the new project. This confluence of factors meant that studio sessions centring on group-playing offered the ideal opportunity to harness the songs for the album. "It's like what we did for the first three records," says Lewis.

Rather than return to one of the recording venues they had used in 2010, Wire looked outside London, and outside England, booking a week at the storied Rockfield, located on a farm near Monmouth. However, they did bring Sean Douglas, who had engineered the *Red Barked Tree* sessions at Resident. Newman had been pleased with Douglas's contribution, feeling he was attuned to the band and their working processes. "He gives me what I need," says Newman simply. (The engineer had been so taken with Wire when he encountered them at Resident in February 2010 that he'd later auditioned for the guitarist slot that went to Simms.)

Like Advision and Hansa, Rockfield is rich in music history, having hosted everyone from Queen to New Order. Lewis was thrilled to discover that Monmouth local Dave Edmunds had recorded there with Love

Sculpture, while Simms was understandably excited that Black Sabbath and Hawkwind had worked at the studios. The genial owner, Kingsley Ward, was on hand to regale the band with anecdotes about his clients over the years, beginning more than one sentence with the words, "As I said to Freddie …".

It was the first time since the grim sessions for *The Ideal Copy* that the band had opted for a residential studio, and the experience at Rockfield in spring 2012 would be vastly different from that of Hansa in winter 1986. Stark, claustrophobic pre-unification Berlin and the rolling, verdant Wye Valley were worlds apart – even if it did rain every day. Before heading to Wales, Lewis – quoting the old rock cliché – eagerly told me: "We're going to get it together in the country."

Perhaps remembering his time at Hansa, Grey was at first cautious about the residential aspect. "When we were discussing it, it seemed a bit daunting: seven days of recording and everybody living in the same place." Nonetheless, he was pleasantly surprised: "When we got there, it didn't seem to be a problem. We're possibly getting on better now than when we were recording for *Red Barked Tree*, and the lack of distractions was a big bonus."

Newman corroborates Grey's last point: "'Isolation' is the key word. Monmouth doesn't offer a lot in terms of the high life – although there was quite a good Waitrose. There's not much to do but make records. It was deliberate to choose somewhere isolated and separate so that, for a concentrated period of time, we could just work on this and this only." The constant rain only intensified the focus on the task at hand. (Accompanied by Douglas, Lewis did go into town in search of entertainment. He paints a vivid picture of the happening scene: "Robert Plant was seen shopping in Monmouth, and we missed meeting Dave Edmunds at his local by 30 minutes.")

The band spent their first full day setting up, with Tim Lewis (aka Thighpaulsandra) helping everyone get accustomed to the studio. They then settled into a pattern, emerging from their apartments, located on the same farm courtyard as the studio, and assembling for work by 11am. "We'd usually be making a noise in anger by 12-ish," says Lewis. After stopping for dinner at about 8pm, they would work until around midnight, unwinding and debriefing over a few drinks. Some meals were prepared on-site by Grey (a lentil curry – "really good", according to Simms) and Lewis (a pasta and vegetable dish); the group also soon exhausted the supply of local restaurants. Newman tried to persuade his bandmates to go back to a fish-and-chip shop they'd found in Monmouth, since he was responsible for keeping a thrifty eye on the budget, but they were unconvinced.

400

## No sax please, we're Wire

As for the contents of the album, the group had begun to think about a pool of potential tracks a few months earlier, the catchment area encompassing mainly the sets performed at the Jeannetta Cochrane and Electric Ballroom concerts. The band-members had started listening to the available recordings from this period to reacquaint themselves with the source material and, a week before commencing work at Rockfield, Newman initiated an email conversation in order to establish a roster – beyond the tracks from the live set ('5/10', 'Part Of Our History', 'The Spare One', 'Deeper', 'B/W Silence', 'Ally In Exile', and 'Witness To The Fact'). Lewis recalls certain criteria for inclusion and exclusion: "There were things that we thought were pointless pursuing, things that had appeared on Dome records or Colin's records." In the end, that didn't prove to be a hard-and-fast rule since '5/10' and 'B/W Silence', which had both featured in some version on Newman's *Not To*, would make the shortlist – the rationale being that those recorded incarnations had been radically different from their tentative Wire renderings.

The infamous 'Crazy About Love' was proposed, but the consensus was that there was already an iconic version in existence (from the Peel session). Newman was happy to proceed without this track. "I was glad because I thought it could be a total mess because it doesn't have any formal structure. Who decides how it goes? Am I going to compose a formal structure for how it goes and then be complained at? There's a version out there that is as realised as it's going to get."

While it was, strictly speaking, not part of the fourth-album corpus, as it dated from before *Chairs Missing*, 'Underwater Experiences' was also a candidate, but it was vetoed as it had been recorded for the *Strays* EP. The rearranged version, 'Deeper', was fair game, though. "It's been accepted as part of that set of material," says Newman.

Grey notes that some other, less scientific criteria came into play: "'Everything's Going To Be Nice' [from *Document And Eyewitness*] was dismissed because Colin thought it was too silly. We do have a limit, you know. Thankfully. That's the benefit of hindsight." Lewis was amused and mildly disappointed that the track should be rejected on the basis of its lack of seriousness. "I thought: it's taken Colin an awfully long time to come to that conclusion. Actually, it's a bit of a shame because that's all it ever really had going for it."

Predictably, Newman seems to have been the most exacting, and the most vocal, enforcer of quality control. "There was one track where

Graham appeared to be singing a tune but nobody else appeared to be playing anything even related to it. [This was the version of what would become Dome's 'Ritual View', performed at the Electric Ballroom but absent from *Document And Eyewitness*.] The group was quite fractious at that point. Some things had been worked out quite well, but others hadn't been worked out at all. Some things didn't even have a scheme to them. Nothing. There was also a random instrumental ['Instrumental' from *Document And Eyewitness*] that sounded like a stoned jam, and I thought: do we really need to be doing that?"

As it turned out, a 14-song shortlist was ratified swiftly and painlessly. "I thought there was going to be a big scrap," says Newman, "but it was fairly uncontentious." In addition to the material from the band's current live set, the provisional track list included 'Over My Head' (last played at the Cochrane gigs and collected on *Turns And Strokes*), 'Eastern Standard' (from *Document And Eyewitness*), 'Relationship' (which had featured on the Notre Dame Hall 12-inch), and 'Stepping Off Too Quick' (one of the December 1978 *154* demos). Also pencilled in were the *Document And Eyewitness* tracks 'Piano Tuner (Keep Strumming Those Guitars)', 'Zegk Hoqp', and 'Eels Sang Lino' – with the proviso that they needed more organisation.

For Grey, revisiting some of the archival recordings of songs that the band hadn't already been performing was neither edifying nor pleasurable. "I don't find *Document And Eyewitness* very easy to listen to. It's rather depressing. The stuff was very much in its early stages. We rehearsed it then played it. We weren't very familiar with the songs we were doing. I wanted to familiarise myself with the material, but you can't help feeling that the audience were suffering. I don't think you should treat your audience like that."

One more detail was ironed out in advance of the sessions. "Graham declared that his saxophone-playing career was long over," says Newman, adding, "which I think is probably a good thing."

### Excavating the future

Instead of beginning with the tracks from their live set, the band turned first to the untried numbers. "The strategy was to start with the things we had no idea how to play," Lewis says. "We did two new ones on the Friday, three on the Saturday, and two on the Sunday." Simms continues: "It was a bit of a weird way of tackling it, but it seemed to work. It felt that there was more of a mountain to overcome there, so it was good to get it done. Once we got to the stuff we did know, we did most of that in a day."

This was as much an archaeological dig as it was a recording session, and it was occasionally demanding, but as Lewis explains, a solid working process quickly established itself: "Some tracks were harder to disinter than others, but as soon as everybody got into it, we were taking the essence of the pieces and everybody was finding something they enjoyed playing, and we were getting this transformation of the material – which was what we wanted."

Newman remembers that, notwithstanding some initial recalcitrance, 'Relationship' was coaxed out of the past. "It was illogical, but we made it work. We sat with acoustic guitars in the control room and worked it out so that everybody had it." Retitled 'Keep Exhaling', the track is described by Newman as "a triple album in one and a half minutes".

Only one of the proposed songs failed to achieve lift-off. "'Stepping Off Too Quick' didn't make it," says Lewis. "It was stubborn. We couldn't bring it forward. It just refused. It just stayed in 1979, no matter what we did. What we were looking for was ways to make the things interesting, but it just didn't move." Grey was frustrated by this song. "It was too difficult. If there'd have been more preparation, I think I could have played it – but just picking it up from the recording is too complicated. It's too fast. It was asking for the impossible." Lewis isn't so sure. He believes it could have worked, but only if subjected to an entirely different methodology. "When we tried to play it rhythmically, it was just stuck. I think the only way to do it is to slow it right down to a ballad – something quite radical."

By contrast, Lewis says that 'Piano Tuner' (now called 'Love Bends') was an unqualified success, having morphed, improbably, into the album's strongest pop song. "It had to be turned into something else because it only really had one bit, but it developed quite easily." Newman provides more detail: "Basically, all it had in the original version was the 'octave-hopping' – that early synth-pop sound – and some mad Rob drums. That was the basis of it." Explaining how the new version has changed, Newman dusts off an old term from the Wire lexicon: *swerve*. "It's completely recognisable as 'Piano Tuner' – but swerved very much like what could have happened in the studio in 1979. This is a swerved version of 'Piano Tuner' that's become something else – unlike 'Zegk Hoqp', which is a completely new piece of music."

'Zegk Hoqp' was one of the tracks on which Lewis had been concentrating prior to the Rockfield sessions. "My particular concern was what could be done with 'Zegk Hoqp' and 'Eels Sang Lino'. They were more problematic. They'd been written for performance, not with music in mind. They'd been written around people with newspaper headdresses and an illuminated goose." Put that way, they didn't sound too promising, but as Lewis says: "Like all these things, once there was a will, there was a way." He outlines how he approached the first of these tracks: "With 'Zegk Hoqp', I came up with a rhythmic scheme, and I brought a rather grand loop that I thought might give everybody else something to lean on – for Rob to play along to, just to see where that might take us, just to give a foundation for a place to start from." Grey's appraisal doesn't directly address the musical nature of the track, but he reports some difference between the 1980 version and its revised counterpart. "It was a bit more comprehensible. It wasn't just shouting. I think Graham might have added some more lyrics." Lewis confirms this: "It's not just the alphabet any more."

Simms had doubts about 'Zegk Hoqp'. "When we recorded it, I didn't think the version worked all that well, whereas with all the others I felt we'd bettered what there already was. But with that track we weren't managing it. I suspect that it won't make the cut." In spite of these misgivings, it was marked for inclusion on the album, renamed 'Re-invent Your Second Wheel' – having been reincarnated as something utterly different.

"It's a bit of a cheat, really," says Newman. "Apart from a bit of a lyric quote, it has nothing to do with 'Zegk Hoqp'. Graham had a vocal melody and a bit of a drum loop, as well as some other bits – none of which got used. Graham did a guide vocal with those parts, and then we set about replacing everything. I suggested the descending bassline in the chorus, which made the chorus work. The verses were not so comfortable – I just thought it sounded too much like Elvis. That day, Graham was cooking, so he went off, and we started pulling the track apart by basically moving the notes in the bassline around. We had to change the vocal melody a bit by moving around lines that were singing the right melody. Graham, on returning, was a bit dubious but went with it, and we then replaced all the vocal with the right words singing the right melody to fit with the new backing. I'm getting into this weird world of making Graham sound great! He comes with really good vocal melodies but has no idea how to frame them. Of course, in the end it's a completely new track which has much more to do with 'Please Take' than anything off *Document And Eyewitness*. That's the reason why we were a bit unsure about it."

Although 'Re-invent Your Second Wheel' hadn't at first convinced everyone, 'Eels Sang Lino' (now abbreviated to 'Eels Sang') fared much better. Newman talks about the track's beginnings in 1980: "It was originally done by Bruce and I off a scheme. The scheme is mad and very funny. We worked it out to annoy Graham. Just the idea that it went to a different chord every time it had to go to the chorus – that would have been off-putting for anyone, and we laughed our arses off when we were doing it." Despite his positive memories of the song's genesis, Newman did have reservations about its viability as a candidate for the new record. "The bassline was like 'Another One Bites The Dust', and the drum rhythm was really good – it's really pumping – but it's impossible to sing. That's why Graham was screaming. I thought: if we could figure out a version which doesn't involve him just screaming at full throttle all the way through, then we could make it work."

They did precisely that, as Simms observes: "'Eels Sang Lino' was so much fun. That was a really memorable experience. We had dinner, and we came into the studio and didn't really talk about what we were going to do. We knew we were going to do that track. We figured it out quickly and did a couple of takes. And it sounded great. There was no aspect of just trying to recreate the original performance in the studio. It has the same sort of energy – which is the most important thing about why those *Document And Eyewitness* tracks work the way they do – particularly that one. The whole band are manic on it, in a good way." Newman agrees: "It was one of the things that really worked well. It's got all of that completely mad energy without the screaminess. It's more or less a rap. It's not random. It's quite heavy."

'Eastern Standard' has also undergone a startling change. Now known as '& Much Besides', it makes a six-minute oneiric-melodic mountain out of what, at the Electric Ballroom in 1980, had been a dreary, obtuse, three-minute mole hill, presided over by the unfortunate Mick Collins and a globe. (The last of the previously untested batch of tracks, 'Over My Head', experienced an equally fruitful studio rebirth, its title switched to 'Magic Bullet'.)

### Further developments

The recording of the songs the band had been playing at gigs "was really very straightforward", according to Lewis. "It was just a case of being a bit more demanding of ourselves, getting the best performances." The dirge-y '5/10', however, required a little more consideration than the other numbers. In performance, Newman had found it hard to sing comfortably, but just before the Rockfield sessions, he had an epiphany. "I realised it was in the wrong key. I tried playing it in *A* instead of *E*, using my baritone guitar. In many ways, it shouldn't be on the list, because it's on my third solo album, but in recording, it sounded pretty magical."

Newman's excitement about this track – rechristened 'Time Lock Fog' – is shared by Grey. Surprisingly, the drummer's enthusiasm centres on the simple percussive elements that he conceived for the piece. "It only has a single beat going all the way through: in the early days, I used the cymbal stand as the percussion instrument, but that progressed to a bottle because glass has a nicer sound than the cymbal stand. I put something in to fill the background space, to suggest a different atmosphere. I used some 'found' things from the surroundings, not musical things. I also brought a set of claves and an African cowbell, and I brought a thumb piano, but that was probably too melodic for percussion."

Grey justifies abandoning his traditional animus toward extra percussion since the percussion in this case had its own distinct, non-supplementary role. "This was abstract percussion, for atmosphere, rather than for playing a rhythm. Rockfield has an echo chamber, and percussion sounded very nice when it had gone through that. It seemed to go against everything you normally try to do when you're playing drums – keeping time and playing together. The percussion on '5/10' is rather mysterious and playful. The sounds aren't understandable in a normal musical sense – it's more about atmosphere than music. I hope it's improved from *Document And Eyewitness*."

'Deeper' (now 'Attractive Space') is another track that has evolved significantly, completing the process begun at Advision in 1978, when the band had failed to capture 'Underwater Experiences' in its desired format. "We thought we could get 'Deeper' nearer to what the original conception of 'Underwater Experiences' was," Newman explains. "Instead, it turned into something glorious. Originally, nobody figured out it was in 3/4 – that's why no one could play it. Mike [Thorne] should have figured out why we couldn't play it. The December 1977 demo sounds like the blind leading the blind: Rob's trying to play in 4/4, and I'm playing in 3/4, and it can't possibly work, because there's always an extra beat going on. So I realised it was in 3/4, and that's why no one could play it. It's really easy. It's only got three chords in it. It's a piece of piss. It's such an absurdly dramatic piece. And it's got a mad energy about it."

Newman's closing observation on 'Deeper' also seems to apply to 'The Spare One' (retitled 'Adore Your Island'), which he characterises as an unlikely reconciliation of archenemies. "It's the maddest bit of music: it's prog-rock meets unhinged punk – all in one song." While 'Adore Your Island' is structured around a series of slow-quick, soft-hard contrasts, 'Witness To The Fact' (now called 'Stealth Of A Stork') is the album's only consistently fast-and-loud number. "It's *Send* speed," says Newman, "but with a lightness and humour not generally found on *Send.*"

Other highlights of the session were 'Part Of Our History' (renamed 'As We Go') and 'Ally In Exile'. In Newman's view, the latter track (now 'Doubles & Trebles') was at last receiving the treatment it had warranted for so long. "'Ally' had a very loud voice," he says. "It's one of those songs that stay within the consciousness of the band. It's a really, really big song – it always has been. I remember Mike saying he thought it was better than anything on *154*. It has a certain drama to it. It's going to be absolutely colossal."

The priority at Rockfield was to get a basic draft of the music, with most of the vocals to be recorded later. This would also allow time for further work on the lyrics. Making the fourth album was, as Newman had hoped, largely avoiding the problem of Lewis not having the words ready for him to compose the songs, but several of the texts needed to be revised or replaced. After Rockfield, with work still in progress, Newman reframed the issue thus: "Few of the original texts actually survive in physical form so there have been guestimates and rewrites to varying degrees, even when we've played them live. We didn't put a lot of attention on that process in rehearsals for live shows, but now some are being completely rewritten, and some are being reappraised as part of the work on the album." As far as he is concerned, this is very much in line with the band's overall approach to this record. "It's basically all part of the same process of 'reclaiming' the material and making it relevant to us in 2012 – but also making a record rather than doing a performance."

### Closing the loop

Wire came away from Rockfield in May 2012 confident that they'd laid a solid foundation for the album, on which Newman would build by continuing to develop the material at Swim. This first phase had been enjoyable and enormously productive, and there was a great sense of anticipation surrounding the project. In Lewis's opinion, the sessions were "happy and contented, very creative, with surprising and exciting transformations". For Simms, it was especially memorable, revealing a side of Wire that he hadn't yet encountered, given his hitherto limited role as a touring member. "It was really different working within the band, seeing how it works in the studio. There's not a lot of discussion – in a good way. It seems to happen really quickly. I'm sure that comes out of them working together for so long. It all seems to fall into place very easily."

Newman offers a different explanation for the apparent ease with which the preliminary work had been executed, implicitly attributing it to his creative control of Wire. "I remember Graham making a sly comment to someone during the recording. He said: you can play what you like, but if he doesn't like it, he won't include it. He knows very well that if I think something's rubbish, then I'm not going to include it, and it makes him, and everybody else, think more about what they do. Don't just fill the tracks up with a load of crap that I have to sort out! I won't bother listening to it, let alone using it. It's a very different attitude to how we used to work." Inevitably, this leads him back to what he considers the lowest point of Wire's recording life. "Going back to *The Ideal Copy*, people would just put on any old stuff because they thought that's what should be there – regardless of what else was there."

Individual agendas aside, the bigger picture of what Wire are attempting with *Change Becomes Us* is fascinating. And it's not without its risks. Wire have obviously had an awkward relationship with their own history, as they've sought with each cycle to present themselves as modern and of the moment. In the 80s, part of their strategy for accomplishing this led them, mistakenly, to erase, or at least ignore, their older work altogether. Since 2000, however, they've repeatedly found ways to embrace and celebrate their progressively larger past without surrendering to punk-rock cabaret, without compromising their identity as a contemporary band.

*Change Becomes Us* is Wire's most inventive accommodation of the ageing process thus far. It's difficult to overstate the originality of this project, with the band reimagining previous material, albeit material that never really existed in a fully formed state – having enjoyed only Lewis's "mayfly"-like lifespan. This has nothing to do with nostalgia. They're not trying to recreate how these songs sounded in their rudimentary, unresolved versions or how they might have sounded had they reached maturity in 1980: the blueprints may be old, but the final realisation of these pre-existing ideas is wholly 'now', an enactment of Wire's current sonic identity.

Newman stresses this: "None of this material ever got the chance to be developed beyond what it takes to get from one end of the piece to the other in a live context. A big part of this work has been to resolve these pieces, which under the microscope of the recording process has taken some very far from their roots. What we're doing is a merging of the more rounded sensibility of how to make music that the band has now, with that material which was flying off the back end of *154* at full speed. Which makes for what will be a very special record." Interestingly, at this point, his thoughts turn, again, to his ex-bandmate: "I'd absolutely love to know what Bruce thinks of it. Because he'd remember those things. Working on some of these tracks reminded me of how we'd worked them out originally."

Ultimately, as Newman's reference to *154* suggests, *Change Becomes Us* is best appreciated in terms of a larger narrative: as the culmination of a journey that started with the third album, the point at which things began to go awry for Wire, continuing to do so – it could be argued – until the mid 2000s. Newman believes the work at the core of this record was squandered in 1980. "The album that was going to come after *154* was going to be as good. The material was there, and it was strong. The band wasn't there. The band was falling apart. Those songs have been waiting all that time for their chance to be made manifest." In essence, this material has been waiting for Wire to enter a stable phase with a common purpose. Wire in 2012 appear to be that iteration of the band: the very tracks that prefaced their fragmentation and dissolution in 1980 have now become – after a process of change and transformation – the shared focus and the creative glue of their current incarnation.

Lewis's comments immediately after the Rockfield sessions chime with Newman's: "I think we might have the recordings to successfully follow *154*." Nevertheless, it would be a mistake to dismiss any of the intervening stages of Wire's creative journey. Fraught and flawed as they often were, the band's 80s and (shortlived) 90s ventures produced some enduring work. Most important of all, those projects were a necessary part of the greater trajectory that Wire had to complete in order to give a proper life to the 'lost' fourth-album material. Lewis seems to be in agreement:

"It feels that there's some logic to the steps we've taken. It's something which has come about because of our history, really – I'm tempted to say because of our *failure*. In a strange way, it's because of integrity that we got ourselves into that horrible situation, and we didn't know what to do, and there was no one there to help us find a way out of it. So it feels rather good. In some ways, it completes one of those loops that one likes to close. Some things take a very long time to get a satisfactory outcome. It solves a lot of those unresolved problems that accompanied us for so long."

## CHAPTER 14
# Famous Last Words

At the end of a final group interview with the three remaining original members of Wire at Swim Studio, I asked Robert Grey, Graham Lewis, and Colin Newman what they considered to be the major missteps taken during the band's history. I invited them to suggest, with the meaningless luxury of hindsight, specific situations or decisions that they now feel could have been approached differently.

Lewis was the first to jump in, with perfect comic timing: "I've got to be in Berlin on Friday!" – the interview took place on a Wednesday. After this promising start, however, no one except Newman actually volunteered any answers. Grey and Lewis commented, but only on the topics raised by Newman.

Such a pattern was fairly representative of my conversations with the band. They were generally dominated by Newman, who tended to collapse the distinction between his own opinions and Wire's opinions. This is perhaps symptomatic of the central position that he has come to occupy in the group. A large part of Wire's story, especially since 2006, has been the story of Newman benignly consolidating that position in terms of his role as primary songwriter, main creative force, producer, mixing engineer, principal media spokesperson, label chief, and, to an extent, manager.

Under Newman's direction, Wire have gone from strength to strength, musically and commercially. Grey is happy enough with the balance of power, but that wasn't always the impression that Lewis gave during interviews for this book. He was sometimes reluctant to comment directly on creative issues or personal dynamics within the band, instead preferring to offer opaque non-answers or to hint at dissatisfaction. The tensions and divergent visions that have strained the Wire project since the outset have not been resolved, although the current settled and productive period may indicate that the band have found a successful long-term compromise.

Newman's response to the question about the band's mistakes was decisive and unhesitating. "Me, personally, being seduced by Paul Smith.

My first instinct was that I immediately hated him. I wish I'd just stuck to my instincts – but then we wouldn't be where we are now." Neither Grey nor Lewis followed up on this mea culpa – which was surprising, since Wire's involvement with Smith, and their perception of Newman's relationship with him, had significant repercussions for the band, almost resulting in its demise. On this occasion, though, nothing was said.

Newman also brought up the post-*154* period and the folly of allowing the band to disintegrate: "The way it finished at the end of the 70s was just wrong." He again linked this to early Wire's inability to think beyond the artistic side of their identity. "We didn't take seriously enough the idea of the band as a business. Robert was the only person who had any notion of the seriousness of that. We didn't engage with that at all. We didn't have a long view. We didn't have someone to say: hang on, let's not all drive the car off the cliff right now, let's take a little bit of a break. That was a big mistake."

Lewis seconded this, talking more directly about the inadequacy of the group's management at the time, regretting that they hadn't forced Mick Collins to accept a partnership with Bryan Grant. "I still don't know how we were so stupid and weak not to have insisted and said to Mick: you might as well just fuck off, then – because he wouldn't have done. We should have given him no choice. That would have made a lot of difference. The end of the 70s was a huge mistake."

Newman recalls another wrong turn, this time during the 80s, just after Wire had left EMI. "There was that strange meeting with Tony Wilson. He wanted us to come to Factory, and we were very enthusiastic. We asked: how big is the advance? And he said: independent labels don't give advances. So we said: well, we're not doing it then. It was a massive misunderstanding. If only he'd understood that he could have probably given us quite a small advance – that would have been fine because we were broke."

Lewis is now convinced that not signing to Factory may have been a blessing in disguise. "At least we're all still alive – and I mean that seriously. There were so many people involved with that label who no longer are. It might have been terrific. We might have been hugely successful. And dead."

Also a misjudgement, in Newman's opinion, was "not playing anything from the 70s in the 80s". Had they found some kind of compromise between their past and present identities in the context of the live performances during that period, he believes things could have turned out quite differently. "Maybe," says Lewis, "but, then again, we wouldn't be where we are now. That's the truth of it – you can only do what you think is right at the time. Then, it was about trying to preserve whatever idea of integrity you thought the project had. Otherwise, it's pointless. All you've got in the end is your name."

Another issue from Wire's *decadus horribilis* that Newman regrets is the increasing alienation and eventual departure of Grey. "Rob leaving at the end of the 80s was wrong. We should have figured a better way to deal with that situation and not let it get to that point." He again distances himself from the work that he, Gilbert, and Lewis subsequently did in the absence of Grey. "And Wir was wrong. We're three now, and it doesn't feel wrong; when Rob wasn't there, it did feel wrong." (Newman made this point about the 'wrongness' of the Grey-less Wir period even more forcefully in an earlier interview: "You know what? It doesn't feel like that without Bruce. That's the weird thing. When Bruce left and we started working together again, it was very fragile, but I never had that same feeling that there was someone missing, that there was someone important missing.")

Newman's closing observation gestures broadly at the intra-band problems over the years. "As much as there have been moments of high drama and appalling tension between us, I don't think anyone behaved in a truly evil way. People were only doing what they thought was the right thing to do." Lewis adds: "Even if they were completely misguided."

So much for the past. I also asked the band-members, in individual interviews, about Wire's future.

Lewis is still deeply committed to the Wire project after three and a half decades and gives no indication that he's planning to knock it on the head any time soon. Far from it. "I'm in Wire, and Wire's in me. Wire does things which no other activity or collaboration I engage with does." As far as he can see, the only thing that will put a stop to his involvement with the band is "something catastrophic or an attack of profound irrelevance".

When asked how much longer he intends to pursue his work with Wire, Grey answers: "I don't really think of it in those terms." He does add, laughing: "We've gone way past the time beyond which it's logical or sensible to be in a band, but the meaning for us is still there. When we did the Royal Festival Hall in 2000, Colin said in an interview that we were 'four old men making fools of themselves', which at the time I took slightly to heart. We've gone way past that now, but you never know if you look ridiculous, do you? I used to worry about that much more in the early days."

Pressed on whether he can see Wire stopping at some point, Grey ventures a morbid observation. "It's not very cheerful, but it's a bit like dying, really – you're never sure when it's going to happen. So it's the same with Wire dying. Anything could happen, if you want to be really gloomy.

Could it be something unplanned? Who knows?" For now, though, Grey thinks Wire are in a relatively healthy state, thanks, in part, to the group's decision to operate without a traditional manager figure. This, he feels, has improved relations between the remaining band-members. "Post-Smith, it's forced us to communicate, which you wouldn't think was difficult, but it does get difficult at times. Having that forced on us is only a good thing – in every way. You have to be more reasonable, just so that things can function."

That said, he's quick to point out that Wire has not suddenly become idyllic. "It's not as if there aren't any crises now, because there certainly are. You have to deal with them as they happen. If you can't, you end up in another cycle of non-communication and things getting worse. I think that can still tend to happen." In his view, a lack of communication and open discussion has been a perennial problem for the band, and for him the 80s, unsurprisingly, was the most challenging period in that regard. "It was pretty awful, really. There were good bits, but the low bits got longer than the good bits."

As Grey sees it, this tendency not to engage with each other was, predictably, a major factor in the band-members' loss of a shared vision. "We're fairly different as people, which can be a strength and a weakness. For myself, you sometimes reach a point of thinking, if saying something is going to cause a big disagreement, then it's probably easier not to say anything. And so where nothing's said, those things start to accumulate. I don't know what happens in other groups. Any sort of collapse of your common ground is a breakdown in communication. It must be a sign of general discontent and unhappiness. We're founded on unhappiness!"

Nonetheless, Grey remains optimistic. "There's still a future in it. I hope we're a bit better dealing with personal issues than we were in the past. Having had the experience that we've had, we should be – or we haven't learned very much."

Newman feels that the band have indeed learned from past communication lapses, and that since the mid 2000s, communication has become a priority in both artistic and business terms. "When we started again, we made a point of discussing things, saying: what do you want to do in this situation? Now I always ask the band: what do you want to do? We can make choices; we don't have to do whatever is laid out in front of us."

However, Newman also believes that there is one area in which the band's historical lack of communication indicated a unique strength: an unspoken, intuitive commonality in the creative act itself. "How can a band be so conceptual and never discuss anything? It was such a peculiar thing. We just

413

didn't have a common thing of: this is what we're doing, this is what the plan is. It seems absurd when you say it, but with Wire it always worked, and there was never any talking." It's odd that he should now say that Wire has "always worked", as the band's recordings during the 80s – and particularly his own comments on that phase – suggest otherwise. And in broader terms, this book includes instances of Newman registering his dissatisfaction with aspects of almost every Wire album. But to him, this is all part of being a creative individual. "If, as an artist, you're satisfied with everything you've ever done," he laughs, "you must be a really boring person."

Asked why he continues with Wire, Newman replies: "If it wasn't any good, I wouldn't. That's it." Despite that flip response, his connection and commitment to the band are as a deep-rooted as Grey's and Lewis's. To Newman, the real beauty of Wire is the idiosyncratic nature of the group's creative process: "What I love about Wire is that purely organic way of coming up with stuff that has its own logic that has nothing to do with anything and just does it. I'm fascinated with it to the point of obsession. It's the best thing about Wire. The great thing is we don't have to work at it. We do it without having to think about it. It's best if nobody thinks too much. You can do all the thinking afterwards. When it's done and dusted we can do all the thinking we want, but actually in the process, we just do it. It comes naturally. There's thinking before and there's thinking afterwards, but there's not much thinking in the doing."

Considering Wire now, Newman admits some surprise at how things have turned out. "After Bruce left, I thought Wire would become a museum piece and just release old records." He's surprised not only at their continued existence as a band, releasing new material, but also at the identities of the three remaining original members. "I always said Wire might end up with just three, but this is the least likely three that anyone would have imagined – and the least likely combination anyone thought would work. Anyone who knew the band in the first part of this century would have said that the person to go would be Graham. And me and Bruce and Rob could never work."

He explains succinctly why a Gilbert–Grey–Newman configuration would have been doomed: "It would be destroyed by Bruce. Bruce is destructive of himself and destructive of everything around him." Newman thinks there's still a strain of destructiveness among his bandmates, but according to him, they rein in such impulses rather than drive Wire off the proverbial cliff. "Graham is a pain in the butt, Robert is annoying – and I'm annoying as well. But they believe in it. They don't want to destroy it, and they'll step back from the edge if they're getting annoying to the point of destroying it."

Ultimately, Newman embraces Wire as a core part of his being. "Whatever I say, whatever else I've done, it'll say on my grave: here lies that bloke from Wire. You have to face that reality. That's what I said when we had that meeting in 2006: you have to think of that, and it has to govern every attitude that you take about it."

Tellingly, Newman returns once more to Gilbert, and how he imagines Gilbert thinks, when he frames his reflections on the greatness of Wire. "Bruce thinks he's escaped. But Bruce is still 'that bloke from Wire'. And he's going to be 'that bloke from Wire', whatever he does, whatever he says. So what are you going to do? Embrace it? Be part of it? Have fun with it? Or are you just going to be resenting it? I feel so lucky that we can do Wire. That we can stand on a stage and play. We're not always good, but we can be really, really fucking good. Who wouldn't want to be part of that?"

# Selected Discography

## Studio Albums

*Pink Flag* (Harvest 1977)
*Chairs Missing* (Harvest 1978)
*154* (Harvest 1979)
*The Ideal Copy* (Mute 1987)
*A Bell Is A Cup ... Until It Is Struck* (Mute 1988)
*It's Beginning To And Back Again* (Mute 1989)
*Manscape* (Mute 1990)
*The Drill* (Mute 1991)
*The First Letter* (Mute 1991) [Wir]
*Send* (pinkflag 2003)
*Object 47* (pinkflag 2008)
*Red Barked Tree* (pinkflag 2011)
*Change Becomes Us* (pinkflag 2013)

## Singles and EPs

'Mannequin' / 'Feeling Called Love', '12XU' (Harvest 1977)
'I Am The Fly' / 'Ex-Lion Tamer' (Harvest 1978)
'Dot Dash' / 'Options R' (Harvest 1978)
'Outdoor Miner' / 'Practice Makes Perfect' (Harvest 1979)
'A Question Of Degree' / 'Former Airline' (Harvest 1979)
'Map Ref. 41°N 93°W' / 'Go Ahead' (Harvest 1979)
'Our Swimmer' / 'Midnight Bahnhof Cafe' (Rough Trade 1981)
'Crazy About Love' / 'Second Length (Our Swimmer)', 'Catapult 30' (Rough Trade 1983)
*Snakedrill* (Mute 1986)
'Ahead' / 'Feed Me' (Mute 1987)
*The Peel Sessions* (Strange Fruit 1987)
'Kidney Bingos' / 'Pieta' (Mute 1988)
'Silk Skin Paws' / 'German Shepherds' (Mute 1988)
'Eardrum Buzz' / 'The Offer' (Mute 1989)
'In Vivo' / 'Illuminated' (Mute 1989)
'Life In The Manscape' / 'Gravity Worship', 'Who Has Nine?' (Enigma 1990)
'So And Slow It Grows' / 'Nice From Here' (Mute 1991) [Wir]
'Vien' (Touch 1997) [Wir]
*Third Day* (pinkflag 2000)
'Twelve Times You' (pinkflag 2000)
*Read & Burn 01* (pinkflag 2002)
*Read & Burn 02* (pinkflag 2002)
*Read & Burn 03* (pinkflag 2007)
*Strays* (pinkflag 2011)

## Live Albums

*Document And Eyewitness* (Rough Trade 1981)
*It's All In The Brochure* (pinkflag 2000)
*Live At The Roxy, London – April 1st & 2nd 1977/Live At CBGB Theatre, New York – July 18th 1978* (pinkflag 2006)
*14 Sept 2002 Metro, Chicago* (pinkflag 2010)
*The Black Session: Paris, 10 May 2011* (pinkflag 2012)

## Compilations and Reissues

*On Returning (1977–1979)* (EMI 1989)

*The Peel Sessions Album* (Strange Fruit 1989)

*Wire 1985–1990: The A List* (Mute 1993)

*Behind The Curtain: Early Versions 1977 & 78* (EMI 1995)

*Turns And Strokes* (WMO 1996)

*Coatings* (WMO 1997)

*Pink Flag / Chairs Missing / 154* (EMI 2000)

*Wire 1977–1979 (pinkflag 2006)*

*Send Ultimate* (pinkflag 2010)

## Legal Bootleg Series

25 Oct 1978 Bradford University

21 Jul 1988 Astoria, London

08 Dec 2000 Queen's Hall, Edinburgh

10 Nov 1979 Jeannetta Cochrane Theatre, London

01 Dec 1987 The Town & Country, London

19 Apr 2002 Fleece & Firkin, Bristol

12 Nov 1978 SO36, Berlin

17 Dec 1985 Paradiso, Amsterdam

02 May 2000 Great American, San Francisco

21 Jul 1985 Bloomsbury Theatre, London (DVD)

## DVDs

*Wire On The Box: 1979* (pinkflag 2004)

*The Scottish Play: 2004* (pinkflag 2005)

# Index

# Acknowledgements

*Read & Burn* wouldn't have been possible without the cooperation of Bruce Gilbert, Robert Grey, Graham Lewis, and Colin Newman. I hope it's always been apparent to them how highly I regard their work as Wire.

Colin, in particular, was enormously helpful, giving me access to numerous archival recordings, demos, and works-in-progress that played a vital part in enabling me to tell this version of Wire's story.

The following provided valuable insight, perspective, and the occasional fact-check: Steve Albini; David Buckland; Cally Callomon; Steve Chandra Savale; Rico Conning; David Coppenhall; Graham Coxon; Andy Czezowski; Jim DeRogatis; Es Devlin; David Dragon; Adrian Garston; Nick Garvey; George Gill; Bryan Grant; Page Hamilton; Richard Jobson; Barry Jones; Gareth Jones; Paul Kendall; Michael Lang; Ian MacKaye; Richard Mackness; Glen Matlock; Margaret Fiedler McGinnis; Daniel Miller; Roger Miller; Russell Mills; Nick Mobbs; John Mockett; Pamla Motown; Robert Poss; Peter Prescott; Malcolm Russell; Jon Savage; Rat Scabies; David Sefton; Captain Sensible; Peter Silverton; Desmond Simmons; Matthew Simms; Slim Smith; Ken Thomas; Mike Thorne; Geoff Travis; Ron West; Jon Wozencroft.

At Jawbone, Tom Seabrook, Nigel Osborne, and Mark Brend deserve a big round of applause for having faith in this project and making it fly. I'm especially grateful to Tom for his thoughtful editing; for his patience, flexibility, and expertise; and for his deep understanding of the much underappreciated semi-colon.

Paul Cooper has my gratitude for creating a jacket design that resonates perfectly with Wire's aesthetic sense. I'll be fortunate if readers judge this book by its cover.

I'm indebted to Watt who, during a 41-date US tour (in a van and with only three days off), came aboard and chimped such a righteous spiel.

Thanks, again, to Peter Fydler and Alison Burton for their hospitality in London.

The gold medal goes to Es Devlin for chasing down the cover image of her magnificent *flag:burning* stage set when she was in the middle of a certain rather important project.

This book is for Nicola, for everything and more. And for Rupert, for keeping it brown.

# Picture Credits

The pictures in this book came from the following sources, and we are grateful for their help. Jacket front Es Devlin jacket rear Annette Green **2** Annette Green **133** Annette Green **134** Robert Grey (diary), Annette Green **135–9** Annette Green (all images) **140** Graham Lewis (setlist), Annette Green (live shots) **277** Wire (Kings Cross), Malka Spigel (Vienna) **278** John Baumgartner (Ex-Lion Tamers), Adrian Boot (Rose Bowl) **279** Stefan de Batselier, The Douglas Brothers **280** Wire (Chicago), Es Devlin (Barbican) **281** Wire (postcard), Wilson Neate (Angel) **282** Wilson Neate (both images) **283** Matias Corral **284** Wire.

MILLION DOLLAR
BASH: BOB DYLAN,
THE BAND, AND THE
BASEMENT TAPES
by Sid Griffin

ISBN 978-1-906002-05-3

HOT BURRITOS:
THH TRUE STORY OF
THE FLYING BURRITO
BROTHERS
by John Einarson with
Chris Hillman

ISBN 978-1-906002-16-9

BOWIE IN BERLIN:
A NEW CAREER IN A
NEW TOWN
by Thomas Jerome
Seabrook

ISBN 978-1-906002-08-4

TO LIVE IS TO DIE:
THE LIFE AND DEATH
OF METALLICA'S
CLIFF BURTON
by Joel McIver

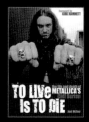

ISBN 978-1-906002-24-4

MILLION DOLLAR
LES PAUL: IN SEARCH
OF THE MOST
VALUABLE GUITAR IN
THE WORLD
by Tony Bacon

ISBN 978-1-906002-14-5

THE IMPOSSIBLE
DREAM: THE STORY
OF SCOTT WALKER
AND THE WALKER
BROTHERS
by Anthony Reynolds

ISBN 978-1-906002-25-1

JACK BRUCE:
COMPOSING
HIMSELF: THE
AUTHORISED
BIOGRAPHY
by Harry Shapiro

ISBN 978-1-906002-26-8

FOREVER CHANGES:
ARTHUR LEE AND THE
BOOK OF LOVE
by John Einarson

ISBN 978-1-906002-31-2

RETURN OF THE
KING: ELVIS PRESLEY'S
GREAT COMEBACK
by Gillian G. Gaar

ISBN 978-1-906002-28-2

A WIZARD, A TRUE
STAR: TODD
RUNDGREN IN THE
STUDIO
by Paul Myers

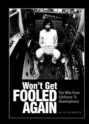

ISBN 978-1-906002-33-6

SEASONS THEY
CHANGE: THE STORY
OF ACID AND
PSYCHEDELIC FOLK
by Jeanette Leech

ISBN 978-1-906002-32-9

WON'T GET FOOLED
AGAIN: THE WHO
FROM LIFEHOUSE TO
QUADROPHENIA
by Richie Unterberger

ISBN 978-1-906002-35-0

THE
RESURRECTION OF
JOHNNY CASH:
HURT, REDEMPTION,
AND AMERICAN
RECORDINGS
by Graeme Thomson

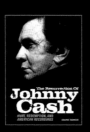

ISBN 978-1-906002-36-7

CRAZY TRAIN: THE
HIGH LIFE AND
TRAGIC DEATH OF
RANDY RHOADS
by Joel McIver

ISBN 978-1-906002-37-4

JUST CAN'T GET
ENOUGH:
THE MAKING OF
DEPECHE MODE
by Simon Spence

ISBN 978-1-906002-56-5

GLENN HUGHES:
FROM DEEP PURPLE
TO BLACK COUNTRY
COMMUNION
by Glenn Hughes

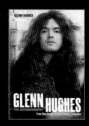

ISBN 978-1-906002-92-3

ENTERTAIN US:
THE RISE OF NIRVANA
by Gillian G. Gaar

ISBN 978-1-906002-89-3

MIKE SCOTT:
ADVENTURES OF A
WATERBOY
by Mike Scott

ISBN 978-1-908279-24-8

SHE BOP: THE
DEFINITIVE HISTORY
OF WOMEN IN
POPULAR MUSIC
by Lucy O'Brien
Revised Third Edition

ISBN 978-1-908279-27-9

SOLID
FOUNDATION: AN
ORAL HISTORY OF
REGGAE
by David Katz
Revised and Expanded
Edition

ISBN 978-1-908279-30-9

BIG STAR: THE STORY
OF ROCK'S
FORGOTTEN BAND
by Rob Jovanovic
Revised & Updated
Edition

ISBN 978-1-908279-36-1

RECOMBO DNA: THE
STORY OF DEVO: OR
HOW THE 60's BECAME
THE 80's
by Kevin C. Smith

ISBN 978-1-908279-39-2